AF470400

GEORGE WIGG

Mark Ger[...]

The Author

GEORGE WIGG

by

LORD WIGG

London

MICHAEL JOSEPH

Contents

Illustrations

Introduction

It is not the easiest of tasks to write an Introduction to this book but even so I do it with pleasure.

I have known George Wigg since we met in the Army. At that stage we were both heroically involved; I was a Major at Southern Command headquarters, conducting an intermittent battle with the War Office, which left me with no time even to remember that there was a more remote though less potent enemy across the Channel. George Wigg was (when I first met him) a Lieutenant-Colonel, but unlike myself was very soon promoted to loftier ranks. He was, as I remember, in the Army Educational Corps and conducted an intermittent but wholly friendly campaign against me and the rest of the Command in quest of the supplies, finance and other aid he needed to discharge his duties. He demonstrated then what has been his prevailing quality at all times, a wholehearted determination to attain his objective in the most complete and rapid fashion with the least possible regard to intervening obstacles. The only living creature bearing the remotest resemblance to George Wigg at full pelt is a wild bull. But a wild bull does not—before charging—plan his campaign with the meticulous skill and care of George Wigg.

I do not know anyone in the whole wide world—from Field Marshals to private soldiers—who is more impregnated with the military traditions and more admiring of military procedure. Notwithstanding that he has not been near an Army mess for twenty-five years the whole of his life, waking, eating, working and sleeping, are regulated by the Army pattern and the Army idiom. Whatever disparagements of the Army may appear in this book it is and remains George Wigg's life-long love. It trained him to plot his course with a careful assessment of the factors; to weigh up the opposition both in physical and moral strength, and even more important to weigh up the strength and reliability of his allies. It trained him also in the belief that there is no such thing as a hopeless cause. He believes, and has time and time again established, that with a stout heart and a stout sword the most recalcitrant of objectives can be achieved. But for all the importance of the Army in Lord Wigg's pattern of life it has succeeded only in concealing but not in changing the essential qualities of a most remarkable man.

His delight in controversy and his exceptional dialectical skills—to which full justice is not done by this book—conceal a human being of rare quality and kindness. The public image of a highly abrasive and somewhat quarrelsome person has some justification in relation to his public postures, but as a private person any number of people will attest that there can be no better friend and certainly no kinder heart.

It has been a source of immense gratification to me that up till now I have not needed to enlist his aid in any personal dilemma, for it would be total. My own feeble will would be over-powered and my problem dealt with by an infinite expenditure of time and trouble (and even substantial subsidy from his very modest resources). I have seen this happen times without number. Often—provoked by foolishly hostile comments about him—I have told one or two stories about his generosity and kindliness that have staggered his critics. It will embarrass him if I recount any of them so I will tell of one or two instances that are merely typical of hundreds.

I remember the appeal to him made by me for a young man born in Aden who, residing in England with his aged mother, was claiming British nationality and was arrested by the Police, under Home Office instructions, with a view to deportation because they resisted the claim, with the appalling consequences that the elderly mother, whose claim to British nationality was conceded, would have been left alone and unsupported. Although I heard of the matter with only a few hours to spare and George Wigg with even fewer hours, so determined was his onslaught on the citadels of power that a reprieve was obtained at the cost of his night's sleep and the matter ended happily with the Home Office acknowledging the British nationality of the individual in question.

I remember how George Wigg pursued a claim tirelessly for a crippled man and even spent hours of his own time keeping the man company.

I remember how he aided a news vendor who was being removed from a news stand in Central London because a property company needed the area, and the splendid terms that George Wigg made with the agents concerned.

for ever—but upon a partnership between government and people which will demonstrate in action the qualities of a fully developed, dynamic democracy.

My closest collaborator in the arduous and lengthy task of writing this book has been Sydney Elliott, an old friend whose journalistic expertise and knowledge of the Labour Movement have been invaluable. I am grateful for the help given by Mrs Elizabeth Coy, another old friend, and by Miss Dorothy Golding, my able secretary from my earliest days in the House of Commons. I appreciate deeply the advice of many friends who read sections of the manuscript, and would thank those who have permitted me to quote from conversations and private letters. I am, of course, responsible for the opinions expressed and for any errors which the devoted efforts of my friends may have failed to erase.

I have sought throughout the text to acknowledge direct quotations, books, letters and public records, and I have included a bibliography of those books to which I owe refreshment of memory and stimulation of ideas. On behalf of Sydney Elliott and myself I acknowledge the unfailing courtesy and co-operation of the staff of the House of Commons Library, the Librarian of Odham's Press Library, the officers of the British Museum Newspaper Library, the Ministry of Defence (War Office) Library, Camden Public Libraries, and the London Borough of Southwark Public Libraries. The quotations from Hansard have been made with the kind permission of the Controller of H.M. Stationery Office.

Chapter One: Boyhood

I was born on November 28, 1900, the first child of Edward William
Wigg and Cecilia Comber. I was named George Edward Cecil, and
the birth-place registered by my mother was 139 Uxbridge Road,
Ealing. My parents were married at Romsey Abbey in February
1900, my mother's age being twenty-three and my father's thirty.
Their marriage was a failure, mainly I think because my father's
family disapproved and because he himself lacked strength of
character. He was the youngest of thirteen and in the not distant
past both his parents had been moderately prosperous. In the agricultural depressions of the 1880s and 1890s, however, my grandfather's resources gradually dwindled and the family became increasingly dependent upon my grandmother.

My father was tall and well-built. He was kind and deeply devoted
to his children. The fatal flaw in his character was his inability to
face the problems of an increasingly hard life. His parents sent him
to a boarding school at Bath where, at Christmas, 1884, he sat for
a College of Preceptors' examination. He did well at some subjects
but failed at arithmetic and Latin. After a pre-marriage spell as a
shop assistant at Newbury he went to America, doing a variety of
jobs which widened his experience of life but contributed nothing to
his fortune.

As a boy he had dreamed of becoming a doctor. He may have felt
the failure to finance his medical education the more keenly because,
while a minor, he had been persuaded to make over to his father a
legacy which he expected to inherit at twenty-one. The sense of
failure persisted throughout his life and was worsened by his family
who insisted he had 'married beneath him'. The truth was that
neither his family upbringing nor his education had fitted him to
earn a living.

My grandmother and aunts and uncle, however, did buy him a
dairy business at Uxbridge Road, Ealing, maybe as a pay-off for
the lost legacy, perhaps in the hope that he might settle down to the

task of earning a living. Whatever the reason, my father, easy-going, indolent, disgruntled and lacking ambition, failed at everything to which he turned his hand. My mother, intelligent, hard-working and enterprising, did all the household chores, delivered the milk, served in the shop, kept the books and tried to inspire my father with the will to work. She went to live on and off with my grandmother at The Villa, Ramsdale, near Basingstoke, and the process of to-ing and fro-ing between Ramsdale and Ealing continued until I was born. Hence I have a hunch that, although the birth was registered at Ealing, I was born at Ramsdale.

My earliest memories are associated with our next door neighbour's shop at Uxbridge Road. This was a sports outfitters, which is still flourishing, then owned by Mrs Hearne, a relative of the famous Middlesex cricketers, J. T. and J. W. Hearne. Mrs Hearne's housekeeper, Miss Jane Branch, became great friends with my mother and, eventually, to me, almost a foster-mother. Long after we left Ealing, Miss Branch made frequent visits to Basingstoke, usually meeting me unexpectedly from school. Her visits were peak points of delight for me as, I believe, they were for her.

In all the circumstances the dairy business was bound to fail and it was sold after the birth of my eldest sister Lilian. My parents lived for a while at Ramsdale, then tried to make a fresh start as owners of a sub-post office and small general shop at Fairfields Road, Basingstoke. My father's appointment as Sub-Postmaster on September 30, 1903, required the deposit of a surety bond for £200. The salary was £12 14s. 0d. per annum, raised to £17 4s. 0d. on January 1, 1904, and to £20 7s. 0d. on July 1, 1908. The surety bond was reduced to £100 in March 1907. These facts suggest that, while the postal side of the business was run reasonably well, prosperity for the family required a vigorous development of the non-postal trade. My mother's immense vitality and drive—she bore six children at two-yearly intervals and slaved from early morning until late at night creating a home and keeping the business going— deserved success. My father's drinking habits frustrated all her toil and her hopes of saving her marriage. He resigned his Post Office appointment early in 1909 and we moved to a house in Beaconsfield Road—two rooms and kitchen downstairs and three bedrooms upstairs, minus gas, electricity and bath—where my mother eked out the family resources by taking in lodgers. My father worked for his brother Herbert at the Ewhurst dairy, a flourishing business which my father's indolence and petty peculations did nothing to expand. Eventually my mother was abandoned for a time and the marriage went on the rocks.

In modern times, I suppose, I would be dubbed the product of a broken home and the psychologists would find in that fact an explanation of my mental make-up and character. I think they would be wrong. Certainly, my father treated my mother badly. He shirked work. His contribution to the family income was negligible. Yet I cannot describe him as an utterly unsatisfactory father. His natural kindness, even his weaknesses, generated affection and gave me warning signs of some of the pitfalls in life I should try to avoid. When, at the age of ten, I accompanied him on the milk-round, sometimes cold as well as hungry and often feeling very sorry for myself, I vowed that when I grew up my children would not undergo such hardships. Years later I realized I could not seek the things I wanted for my children unless I sought and fought for them as the right of all children. That thought became an essential part of my Socialist faith.

There was another side to my father's weakness. His shortcomings highlighted my mother's qualities. No home over which she presided —and she presided all right!—could be described as 'broken'. Her personality inspired love and unity and the joy of living. She had dark brown eyes, framed in raven black hair. Her young beauty still haunts all my recollection of our wonderful life together. Yet her beauty was the least powerful quality of a compelling personality. She could dance and sing and pray, and she led the family in all these activities; and, when occasion demanded, she could swear. That a woman of such slight build could summon up so much vitality was, and remains, a source of amazement and inspiration to me.

My mother's father was born in 1845. He joined the Rifle Brigade in 1859 and was discharged in 1882 from the 3rd Battalion. Looking at his parchments and Certificate of Discharge I became curious as to whether it was correct to describe the Regiment as The Rifle Brigade or the Rifle Brigade. I had the good fortune to read *The Rifle Brigade Chronicle for 1921** which records the considerable controversy that existed on the subject.

In 1816 the Regiment was named The Rifle Brigade in order to

---

* *The Rifle Brigade Chronicle for 1921*, compiled and edited by Major H. G. Parkyn, O.B.E. (John Bale, Sons & Danielsson, Ltd.).

distinguish it from the many Rifle Brigades composed of Volunteers formed during the Napoleonic wars. In the official Army List for the years 1817 to 1819 the Regiment was described as The Rifle Brigade but from 1820 to 1861 the prefix 'The' was omitted. Queen Victoria conferred the title of The Prince Consort's Own Rifle Brigade on the Regiment in memory of her husband, the Prince Consort. In 1881 the title was altered to Rifle Brigade (The Prince Consort's Own) and in 1921 it became The Rifle Brigade (Prince Consort's Own).

Incidentally, my grandfather's discharge papers spelt his surname Coomber, although my mother always spelt the name with one 'o'. My mother was born on August 30, 1876, on the strength of the 3rd Battalion Rifle Brigade. She often told us stories of her grandfather and great-grandfather who had also served in The Rifle Brigade, providing an unbroken link, in point of time at least, with Sir John Moore's Light Division. She had memories of the Army in India, where her father and mother contracted tuberculosis; both were dead by the time she was fourteen. Often, as I reflected on her early life, I found myself paraphrasing in my mind Kipling's lines on Admiralty:

> If blood be the price of Empire
> Lord God, we ha' paid in full.

For my mother the price of Empire was a childhood of bitter poverty and struggle. Her experiences contrasted sharply with those of my father's family who did nothing for her except remind her how fortunate she was to marry their son. Of course, I was on my mother's side; I still am. Yet I have never ceased to feel a sad affection for my father whose many appealing qualities were wasted in his weakness. He lived until 1934. In unexplained circumstances he was reported missing and, some days later, his body was found in Ewhurst Lake, within a short distance of his birthplace. Why he was at the lake and how he got into it remains a mystery. The coroner returned a verdict of death by misadventure.

My mother remarried and her second marriage brought her real happiness. She was in love with her husband for, I think, the same reason that she once loved my father. Both men needed and rejoiced in the help of a strong-minded, dominant personality.

My mother was the maturing influence in my life. As long as I draw breath I shall cherish her memory and my love for her will never fade. She possessed, and communicated to her children, both deep respect for sincerely-held religious conviction and a withering contempt for sanctimonious cant and humbug. She was the head of the family, and its heart and soul. She strove to keep all of us well fed, well clothed, and healthy in mind and body. Right through her long life she shared with me her affection for horses and her interest in horse-racing. I used to tell her she was the best backer of horses after they had won I had ever known.

When I entered Parliament and came to lodge in London I often took her racing. We had a formula all our own. As we neared her home in New Malden I used to say, 'Well, Darling, you have had a nice day, haven't you?' The answer was always 'Yes'. Then I would comment, 'You mustn't be out of pocket. How much did you lose?' The answer was always the same; she had lost a pound. I enjoyed handing over the note in the knowledge that she was putting it across me and found great pleasure in so doing. She was anything but a 'mug' punter. Not caring tuppence about form, she chose a jockey and followed his mounts with shrewd discretion. The 'system' gave her many long-priced winners. Among her favourite jockeys were Frank Wootton, Danny Maher, George Hulme, Brownie Carslake and, towards the end of her life, Duggie Smith. During her last few days she was frequently unconscious, but when I called to see her on the Saturday before she died her mind was quite clear. I was going to Sandown and she wanted a bet. She scanned the newspaper, saw that Duggie Smith was riding *Final Score* and handed me a note which read: '2s. 6d. each way *Final Score*'. The horse won at 100-to-8, and I took the winnings round to her that evening. It was her last bet and it was a winner!

She was my closest companion for over half a century and, from the time I started spare-time work, she shared with me all her troubles and her joys. There was much, much more joy than sorrow in our long companionship. I wish I could live it all over again with her. She slipped away on Bastille Day, 1955.

During my public career the name of Wigg—like my long ears and rather morose nose—has been a fruitful subject of comment for political journalists, cartoonists, and even comedians. Yet there are fifteen names spelt 'Wigg' and eleven 'Wiggs' listed in the London Telephone Directory of 1969, and the name appears in Basingstoke's historical records often enough to suggest that, if it was not very common, it must have been distinguished.* In these records it takes three forms: Wigg, Wigge and Wygge. Wiggs from all over the world have written to me and visited me at the Palace of Westminster when seeking to trace their ancestors. My own favourite point of departure relates to a bequest of 'Four score pounds' made to the Fraternity and School at the Holy Ghost Chapel, Basingstoke, by William Wigge in 1608 or 1609 with this instruction: 'The use thereof is to be paid unto the Schoolmaster of the same school for the teaching of a Child brought from Bramley in the County of Southampton'. Twice during the next hundred years rascally school-masters sued Church and School claiming personal possession of the gift which enabled the Aldermen and Warden to declare the school free. In the first action the claim made was that the interest on the gift of William Wigg (the 'e' in the original document had been dropped) had been misappropriated. In the second action the school-master petitioned the Lord High Chancellor that the Town and Corporation, while admitting receipt of £100 given to the Chapel by one, Wigg, tried to claim that 'part of the money is lost'. Happily, Church and Town won both actions.

Ancient rent rolls—the earliest is a strip of parchment five and a half inches wide and twenty inches long and is believed to date from 1428—name several Wigges among the owners and managers of land. I readily assume, however, that references to my own near kin are more likely to be found in Basingstoke's police court records. John Wigg, for example, was fined 3s. 4d. on August 30, 1539, 'for breaking into the pinfold of the proved men' of the town. I think kindly of Widow Johanna Wigge, fined 12d. on January 30, 1551, because she 'received and housed common vagabonds and other poor persons who misbehaved themselves'. And I would be proud to trace my lineage to the Quaker Wiggs, John of Preston Candover and Richard. They were active dissenters before the Civil War and, in 1657, went to prison rather than pay tithes. Thomas Wigg, Sergeant-at-Mace, also arouses my curiosity. He was appointed in 1761 to apply the Corporation's regulations controlling the Wednes-day market. On October 2, 1769, the Corporation, 'having taken into consideration the ill-behaviour of Thomas Wigg', agreed to expel him from his office. What was his offence after eight years'

* *A History of the Ancient Town and Manor of Basingstoke*, F. J. Baigent and J. E. Millard, (Simpkin, Marshall & Co. 1889).

service? Did he celebrate a winning bet unwisely, or tweak some local dignitary's nose?

I have enjoyed occasional researches into my family roots. They suggest that the Norfolk Wiggs might be senior to the Hampshire Wiggs. I was not surprised when I entered the House of Lords to learn that a record for 1634 grants arms, apparently of Elizabethan origin, to the Wiggs of Burlington, and the name occurs in the Norfolk records of Witchingham from 1433 and South Elham from 1647. What did excite me was the discovery that I was not the first Wigg to enter Parliament. Ricardus Wigge or Wygge represented Winchester City, of which he was also Mayor, in the Parliaments of 1353, 1362, 1368 and 1379—even longer than I represented the people of Dudley and Stourbridge—and a Willielmus Wigge sat in the 1388 Parliament.* I like to think that both these gentlemen may have earned the accolade of 'Wiggery Pokery' which, six centuries later, the Press and political opponents accorded me.

Basingstoke at the turn of the century had a world reputation for its steam rollers, the product of Wallis and Stevens, one of the oldest iron foundries in England. Thomas Burberry, who opened his workshop each morning with a prayer meeting for his work-people, was already winning markets overseas for his gaberdine waterproofs. John I. Thorneycroft's brought modern industry and more work-people to the town. The coach-builder's craft flourished in an area whose population still depended mainly on the horse for transport. There was a declining saw-milling industry and, of course, there was May's brewery. No trace of industrial smoke seriously smudged the face of a quiet, attractive countryside. The tiny red brick houses, typical of the growth of an industrial proletariat, were not yet defacing the character of a market town which had remained almost unchanged for centuries and whose deepest communal memories were of the Civil War. The speed of life was slow, determined by the pace of herds of cows, flocks of sheep, and carts carrying farm produce to market through the narrow streets. Congestion in the town centre was relieved by even narrower alleyways called twittens, gloomy to aged adults but, to children, places of hidden doorways and spine-chilling adventures, as stimulating to the imagination as the excitement offered by woods and lake, the River Lodden, and what remained of the disappearing Basingstoke Canal.

* *Members of Parliament 1231–1702*, Published by Order of the House of Commons, 1878.

I must have been one of the town's most precocious and aggressive children. I resented authority, defying even an adored mother's effort to dress me in finery and crown me with curls in our early years of comparative prosperity. The only orders I remember obeying promptly were when my mother called the family indoors on the news that a prisoner had escaped from jail, and when crowds of louts, fortified by the religious fervour of local publicans, were attacking the teetotal Salvation Army. Non-conformity, whether of religion or politics or ideas, was never popular in the Basingstoke of my boyhood. John Wesley, after a visit to the town, is said to have written: 'I have fought with beasts at Ephesus'. The Salvation Army's first appearance in 1890 provoked the formation of an opposing army of 'Massagainians', whose activities on a quiet Sunday morning in 1891 caused the Riot Act to be read and the calling out of the Artillery then stationed in the town.

The snake hiss of religious intolerance echoed through the streets in the Basingstoke of my boyhood, for the Vicar was still a real boss. I recall my mother's indignation when he ordained hell-fire for any members of the community who dared to attend a meeting on birth control to be addressed by Marie Stopes. My mother's indignation was expressed even more vehemently when the Vicar of a nearby village rebuked a relative's young daughter for approaching the altar-rail before the Squire!

I was a faithful attender at Sunday Schools of all denominations because my mother's Bible tuition enabled me to answer many of the questions and carry off some of the prizes. I was an inquisitive scholar and I had an exceptional memory. From an early age I tried hard to win. While still very young I learned one could not win without effort. I usually did well at examinations and sports. Outside school, the world was a place of wonderment where I went swimming in lake and river, raided hen-roosts, mastered the art and practice of ferreting, and rejoiced in presenting my mother with the trophies of the chase—stolen fruit and flowers, watercress and radishes, and an occasional rabbit.

These boyhood escapades were not interrupted when, around the age of ten, I joined my father to work at Ewhurst Dairy, owned by my Uncle Herbert. I was paid one shilling a week for cleaning the stables, filling the milk-cans with brick-grit and scrubbing them out, and doing odd jobs round the dairy. Early each morning, before school, I accompanied my father on the milk round. The pubs opened early in those days and I discovered he had become a heavy drinker. This gave me a dread of alcoholism which has remained with me ever since. My father's weakness meant I often had to take charge. Sometimes in my childhood world of romance I climbed on the nag's back and, with legs dangling over the shafts, I would career along country lanes and quiet, deserted streets. I began, slowly, to understand that my fun and games as poacher and aspiring jockey had a raw economic edge. They provided an urgently needed addition to the family larder and my weekly shilling was important.

On the death of Uncle Herbert's first wife he had set up house with a Miss Hooker, who looked after my cousins. Like Miss Branch of Ealing, this lady interested herself in my educational welfare. She taught me to tell the time, read to me and, even more important, made me read to her. Thus at school I was always well ahead of other children in reading ability. Miss Hooker also reinforced vigorously my mother's desire that I should attend Sunday School and learn The Bible. Perhaps to help eke out our family budget, or because Uncle Herbert's son Maurice did not fit in at his own home, Maurice lived with us; to me he was more an elder brother than a cousin. Inspired by my mother's stories of the Army and its promise of foreign travel, Maurice joined The Royal Inniskilling Fusiliers, finished his term of Colour Service in 1913, and was called up at the outbreak of war in 1914. He was reported missing, believed killed, in the spring of 1915. The name of Sergeant Wigg is inscribed on the Roll of Missing at the Menin Gate.

The influence of my mother, Miss Hooker and Miss Branch stimulated an insatiable desire to read everything I could lay my hands on. Those were the days before the cinema, the travelling theatre and the public library. My mother found coppers for the cheap reprints of morally uplifting stories published by religious organizations. She enjoyed family reading and I read with her books like *The Swiss Family Robinson, Uncle Tom's Cabin, Robinson Crusoe* and, of course, The Bible. A memorable present from her on my fifteenth birthday was a year's subscription to the Mechanics' Institute which had a library. The Institute's rules were strict and I risked expulsion one day by joining a school playing ha'penny nap. I was sorry to get caught, but the experience stood me in good stead when I joined the Army. There, almost the only relief from boredom was card playing.

Market day in Basingstoke was always exciting. In her beautifully illustrated book *Within Living Memory*—a prized gift to me from Basingstoke Round Table—Miss Diana Stanley re-awakens much of my own nostalgia. I remember well the itinerant dentist who administered 'painless' extraction while assistants with drums drowned the yells of his victims. The snake charmer who, incidentally, sold cures for boils and warts and pimples, was a source of amazed delight. So was the karate expert breaking flints with bandaged fists. 'Watch his hands, never mind his talk!' my father warned as a conjuror performed another trick. I recall, too, the politically-minded radical butcher who, when he failed to sell a piece of meat, announced sarcastically, 'I'll send it to the soup-kitchen'. That soup-kitchen provided many a free meal for the local poor—a constant reminder that, to the orchestra of Basingstoke life, the few contributed hiccoughs from overfull bellies and the many groans from empty stomachs.

'High society' was dominated by Hackwood House, home of the mighty Lord Curzon. His Lordship's interest in ordinary folk was confined to permitting them to scavenge for firewood and broken branches on his estate once a week. I was a frequent visitor to Hackwood House for a different reason. I acquired a taste for the eggs of those of His Lordship's hens foolish enough or wise enough to lay in places adjacent to a public footpath running through the park. My one, very remote, family connection with the Big House derived from my father-in-law to be, the late Harry Veal. He was a real gentleman, honest, hard-working and kind. A product of the racing stable in the days when horses were treated far better than the 'boys' who 'did' them, he loved horses as deeply as he loved people and with a profound understanding. Apprenticed with the late Joe Childs, he became Stud Groom to the Dowager Lady Curzon after experience in several stables. It broke his heart when, after years of devoted, ill-paid service, he received, one memorable Monday morning, a note which read, 'Veal, I shall not require you after next Friday'. I never inquired, but I imagine that dear Dad Veal voted Tory all his life. Then, I could never understand why. Now I do!

Following the Vine Hunt was another of my activities, and a quite profitable one. I was attracted at first by the spectacle of the Meet, which I attempted to follow on foot. Then I realized that, for most of its members, the Hunt was just another social occasion. Beautifully dressed and superbly mounted, they jogged along lanes and through open gates. I used to obtain advance information by reading in the *Hants and Berks Gazette* where and when the Hunt would meet. Then I explored by talking to the locals and memorized the short cuts from gate to gate. On the day, I went round and closed as many gates as I could. When the 'quality' jogged along I was on hand to re-open the first gate and collect a copper or two as my reward. Taking the short cut to the next gate and, if my luck was in and I had chosen the right lane, I would repeat the performance. I often earned a shilling for my day's work—good pay at a time when a farm labourer was fortunate if he earned fifteen shillings for a week of honest toil. And, of course, great fun.

A regular attender at the Hunt was Basingstoke's best-known character, Georgie Ayres. He was a lovable man and a great friend of my mother, who always gave him a meal when he came round our way. Georgie was no tramp, although that was how the locals described him. His sister, Betsy, was the local Queen of the Gypsies, notorious for smoking a pipe and chewing tobacco. Georgie appeared at the Hunt in a discarded outsize pink coat and breeches, and wearing in his hat coloured ribbons and empty flower seed packets. For him my mother was a warm-hearted soft touch. She saw in Georgie the vital human spark that marks the man of personality. Both were ebullient, each rejoicing in and responding to the other's capacity to communicate their gaiety to people around them; they created an atmosphere of sympathy which made our whole world kin. This coming together and sharing the quirks of personality is something almost lost in our battery-hen society, but in my boyhood we were all together at Christmas and Easter, at the Vicar's Garden Party and the Flower Show and sporting events and, above all, at the Michaelmas Fair, where labouring folk attended in the hope of being hired. The shepherds wore wool in button-holes or in their caps, the ploughmen whipcord, and the cowmen straw. The cooks sported red ribbons and basting spoons, and the housemaids blue ribbons and brooms. Roundabouts, hurdy-gurdies and side-shows were erected in the market place, in Thornton's meadow, and at what was called the 'Top Fair'. Shopkeepers seeking their share of fairing money encouraged trade by offering free meals to customers who bought goods beyond a certain sum. All this has gone. Much of the simple enjoyment of community life has gone with it.

Between the ages of eleven and twelve, there came for me a turning point and an awakening to a new, exciting experience. I was a pupil at Fairfields Council School and had reached Standard Six in the class of the late H. G. Lewis. He was an inspired teacher who identified himself with the individual interests of every boy in his care. 'Buck', as we called him, conducted us on rambles, bringing local history alive and arousing in us a feeling for literature and poetry and the life of the mind. He took us in small groups to his home, providing tea out of his paltry salary, and he made himself familiar with our characters and ambitions. Under his guidance I developed as a keen and critical reader and a real devotee of Dickens. Years later, when I took up the study of economics, I was surprised and delighted to discover that, thanks to 'Buck', I already had a grasp of the Ricardian theory of rent to which Marx and the Fabians owed much of their inspiration. I understood, to paraphrase George Bernard Shaw and G. K. Chesterton, that on the rolling English road the Englishman had become a vagrant and, off it, a trespasser. Dear 'Buck' gave me the most precious of all the possessions of boyhood—faith in my own ability as a person and a pupil.

In homes where shillings mattered in balancing the family budget a boy's proper ambition was to enter the Labour Examination and, by proving his competence in the Three Rs, obtain permission to leave school at the age of twelve and start work. My name was entered for the 'Labour Exam'. 'Buck' Lewis went to see my mother to plead that I should be allowed to stay at school. Despite the need for my earnings, he had no difficulty in persuading her to share his confidence in me. She placed me in his hands. For the first time in my life I came under a grinding discipline I was willing to accept. He took the view that, although I could win an envied Aldsworth scholarship, the fact that the Vicar set and marked the religious papers raised a hurdle I was not likely to jump. So my name was submitted for a Hampshire County Scholarship. Sometimes in his home, sometimes in mine, and often wearing overcoats because of lack of heat, 'Buck' Lewis and I worked in a comradeship of learning. When I came out at break on the morning of the examination, 'Buck' was there awaiting me. He looked over the questions, asked about my answers, and remarked with grim pride, 'If you do as well in the afternoon session you will win'. Weeks passed until, almost unexpectedly, and with all prospects of the scholarship nearly forgotten, the Headmaster, Mr S. Rossitter, walked into class and announced, 'I have here the results of the Hampshire County

Scholarships'. After an eternity of time he reached the letter 'W' and read, 'Wigg, George Edward Cecil'. I didn't wait for more. I ran out of school and rushed home to tell my mother. I feared a 'tanning' when I returned in the afternoon. Happily, everything was all right. Mr Rossitter called me by my Christian name for the first time and told me, 'From now until you leave at the end of the term to go to the Grammar School you will have to work on your own. We will start you off on French.'

I felt ten feet tall, but my real thrill was in my mother's pleasure. From somewhere or other, probably from a little nest-egg put by against emergency, she raised a few bob and announced she was taking me to London on the following Saturday. To London we went. I still remember it. I still smell it. And I still taste it. She took me to the London Opera House, later the Stoll Theatre and now a cinema, to see what I believe was one of London's earliest revues. *Come Over Here* was a lively mixture of individual variety turns and exciting scenic features. I can recall a Minstrel singer, a spider dance, and—wonder of wonders—a railway engine on the stage. We had a meal at the 'Popular Café' in Piccadilly, until then the most splendiferous place I had ever entered. My day was made, finally, by a visit to Ealing to see Miss Branch.

Never did boy go more willingly to school than young Wigg to Queen Mary's Grammar School. Never was boy brought down to earth with a more sickening thud. The Headmaster was a clergyman. Nowadays he would be called a snob, but the epithet would be un-fair and inadequate. He described me and other scholarship students at the school as 'boys for whose education your [the other boys'] parents are paying'. He was a drinker who used the cane to cover up his own weaknesses of character. He blamed scholarship boys for every misdemeanour and belted them—and especially me— mercilessly. I handed the beltings on; my victims told their parents; the parents told the Head; and he belted me in what became a never-ending process. I hated him and I hated the school, but I got quite a lot out of it. I acquired a smattering of languages and science, subjects not taught at Fairfields Council School. I shone in geography and history, my star subjects under 'Buck' Lewis. I was wounded by the continual reference to the fact that my mother took in lodgers and that my books and fees were paid for by the parents of other boys. I learned the true meaning of the 'glorious' Church of England hymn, so popular in my childhood:

> The rich man in his castle,
> The poor man at his gate,
> God made them, high or lowly
> And order'd their estate.

What satisfaction would have been mine if I had known then what I discovered long afterwards, that my scholarship flowed from the benefactions of my forbear, William Wigg, who endowed the school three centuries before. The knowledge might have helped to erase my worst memories of a twentieth-century version of Charles Dickens's Dotheboys Hall. A lasting lesson of a nightmare experience was hidden from me until I grew old enough to understand upon what the good life in democratic society really depends: the realization by teachers and parents that all educational opportunity should be based upon the principle of universality. At thirteen, I could not have understood what this means. What I did understand was that there was one standard of values for the rich and another for the poor. Although my short period at Queen Mary's was hard-won and horrible while it lasted, it left me convinced that the soundest feature of the English school system is the Grammar School, and I have always opposed any proposal that might impair its value. Often, when looking round my Parliamentary constituency, I have asked myself what Dudley would have been like without Dudley Grammar School. And I am willing to believe that what is true of Dudley is true of every town in Great Britain. My school days ended for economic reasons. World War I had started. The family was growing up and pressures on its budget were increasing. Moved also, I think, by my misery, my mother sought permission from the Hampshire County Council for my withdrawal.

My working life began at Thorneycroft's, which I soon left to join a firm of timber merchants. There I found, as foreman, an old friend, Billy Drew, a Christian Socialist and self-taught naturalist, whose qualities of mind and character were to win him the honour of Mayorality. I first met him years before when out on the edge of Hackwood Park with another boy on a marauding expedition. We came upon Billy conducting a nature study ramble with a group of youngsters, and we tagged along. Nearing the cottage where the group was to have tea one boy pointed to us and said, 'Mr Drew, these two are not with *us*'. 'They are all with us,' replied Billy with whom, subsequently, I went on many trips. He was one of

God's good men. While I worked under his guidance he instructed me in the principles of Socialism and explained the social value of the Co-operative and Trade Union Movements. He and 'Buck' Lewis nurtured my young imagination and inspired in me the faith expressed in Elizabeth Barrett Browning's words that 'earth's crammed with heaven'.

I began to attend meetings under the Reformers' Tree, a hornbeam once standing beyond the last lamp in Brook Street, and a traditional place of assembly for dissenters, radicals and preachers of new and unpopular creeds. The late Russ Howard, who had shared the ha'penny nap adventure at the Mechanics' Institute, was a regular speaker, and a very good speaker too. He had left a job on the railway to become an organizer for the Transport and General Workers' Union. In the 'thirties he called a strike of stable boys at Lambourn, backed by his boss, Ernie Bevin. The Lambourn trainers broke the strike by borrowing boys from Newmarket and, so tradition says, inflicted upon Ernie the only defeat in his great Trade Union career. Russ Howard was to emerge a fine local Labour leader and, like Billy Drew, a loved and respected Mayor. Harry Round was another powerful pioneer who tried to organize the workpeople at Thorneycroft's and lost his job there for his trouble. He was, in turn, travelling handyman, street pedlar, a much shipwrecked seaman, and motor mechanic. A vigorous, attractive personality, he re-entered my life when, as a young soldier undergoing treatment at the Royal Herbert Hospital, Woolwich in 1923, I met him in Charlton and visited his home. Through him I first met Herbert Morrison. Round took me along to a meeting to be addressed by Herbert outside the fire station at the Charlton end of the Blackwall Tunnel, giving me the role of 'fall guy'. I was rather too aggressive. Morrison decided I was not on his side after all, and we got involved in a lively argument. But we quickly attracted a big crowd and that, as Herbert agreed over a glass of ale afterwards, was the object of the exercise. Round was elected Mayor of Camberwell in 1938. He was a well-beloved local hero during the blitz years, yet was expelled from the Labour Party on an issue which, today, would be regarded as trivial. He died in 1954. I count myself fortunate in having known him.

Starting work put some hard-earned coppers in my pocket each week and I began to expand my social interests. The 'penny gaffs' visited Basingstoke. Groups of itinerant players would set up a marquee, present a different performance each night and move on when their audiences began to decline. They were a counterpart of the travelling circuses, and were the successors of the travelling theatre companies who came to places like Basingstoke before the First World War for one or two nights only. They were sources of amusement and, on occasion, of education. They were followed by the repertory theatre companies. The economic basis of the peripatetic entertainers was eroded by the visiting bioscope, and then finally destroyed by the cinema, which was permanently established in Basingstoke in a derelict long-closed swimming-bath. Films were changed twice weekly and its success was immediate. My first and only cinematograph enthusiasm was for Charlie Chaplin. It was he who attracted me to the cinema and, in ways I did not fully understand, his genius caught me in a web of laughter and tears with my fellow men and women.

I enjoyed the anonymous contact with people provided by rare visits to the nearby 'big' town of Reading. When these became frequent the First World War was in progress, and over all hung the heavy atmosphere of casualties, call-ups and shortages. By this time my stepfather-to-be was serving; my cousin Maurice had been killed. My father had tried to join the Army but had been rejected for medical reasons, although he was accepted later. Many of the friends who had influenced my adolescence were now engaged in war factories or were in the Forces; many had become casualties. In 1914 and 1915 Basingstoke became a military camp. A quiet-mannered, likeable young Argyll and Sutherland Highlander from the Shetland Isles, John Thompson, was billeted in our home. He won the affection of us all, maintained correspondence with my mother, sisters and me and, having no kin of his own, came to us when on leave. He was killed on November 19, 1917, and was buried in a little cemetery, which I have visited, by the level-crossing at Fampoux, four miles to the east of Arras.

A few weeks before my seventeenth birthday, I joined the Hampshire Volunteers, and volunteered for Colour Service in 1918—a baby soldier if ever there was one. I left behind a very reluctant mother.

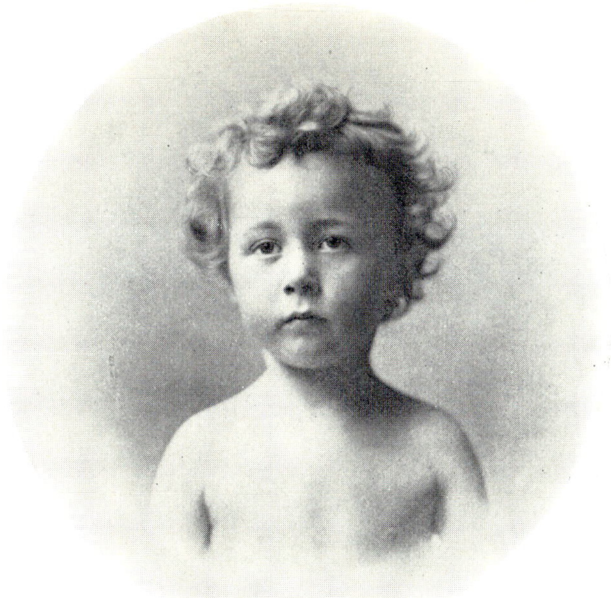

The earliest photograph of the author

The author (left) with his parents and sisters

The school football team, 1915: the author
is seated, left

An army football team Turkey, 1922:
Corporal Wigg is second from the right

Chapter Two: The Army

My mother did not object to my joining the 'Week-end Cavaliers', the nickname of the Territorial Cyclist Battalion, to which I was posted. Her disquiet arose when, encouraged by my father, then serving in the Army Service Corps, I began to talk about enlisting on a regular engagement.

I joined the 2/9th Battalion Hampshire Regiment at Hadiscoe near Yarmouth. It remained thereabouts throughout the War and some of its officers and senior N.C.O's acquired the pleasant habit of spending their week-ends at home—hence the nickname. Its role seemed to have been inspired by the widely-held belief that Zeppelins and, subsequently, other German military aircraft, were guided to London by motor-cars with powerful headlights! Every evening at dusk, patrols from Cyclist Battalions stationed in East Anglia put barbed wire gates across the main roads then, just before dawn, went out to clear the roads for normal traffic. The Battalion was also a holding unit for men who had been wounded and were still not fit for posting overseas.

The Commanding Officer was said to have been a clergyman in civil life. Certainly, on my first Church parade we had a second sermon from him. The lesson I learned came not from the Colonel, but from experienced old soldiers. They taught me the significance of the word 'old' in the title of the immortal song of World War I, *Old Soldiers Never Die*. It meant, among other things, knowledge of the arts and crafts of dodging boredom imposed upon other ranks by pompous officers who inflicted second sermons upon them! My advisers urged me to change my religion—and quickly. I went to the tent serving as an Orderly Room—we were under canvas—and announced that a mistake had been made: I was not Church of England; I was Unitarian. I had no idea what this meant. What mattered was that on Sunday mornings I avoided inspection and paraded with the United Board who marched off to a Non-Conformist

Chapel while I fell out and went down to the rifle range to play Crown and Anchor.

My conversion, although premature, became lasting. In later years curiosity induced a study which led to acceptance of my adopted religion, and the change was regularized by the correct entries being made in my documents.

My adolescent thoughts on the relationship of man to God and on the value of Sunday observance were influenced by another funda-mental urge—hunger. Army rations, minus deductions by thieving cooks, kept us in a state of near starvation which could be appeased only by those with enough money to buy back their purloined rations over the canteen counter. In fairness to the N.A.A.F.I., I may be referring to a time when canteen services were provided by private enterprise and when the scandals which led to the creation of the N.A.A.F.I. had not broken surface. Whatever happened to our rations we certainly did not get them, and those of us without money went hungry. Sunday was our most eagerly anticipated day. If we were lucky enough to get a pass we could seek an endorsement permitting us to use our Army cycles, and off we would go to Yarmouth. There, at the Y.M.C.A., we could eat bread and butter and jam and, some-times, watercress and radishes *ad lib*, washed down with mugs of tea—and all for sixpence! We set out for Camp with bellies as tight as our bicycle tyres, and dreamt of next Sunday's blow-out on the cheap. Although often hungry, I liked soldiering. But I did not like the 2/9th Battalion Hampshire Regiment. The officers were a poor lot. I remember a cycle patrol in pouring rain when we halted half-a-mile from a pub while the officers went inside for a meal.

The old hands tried to entice me into a Regular engagement. I would be sent, they told me, to the Depot which was the 3rd Battalion stationed at Victoria Barracks, Gosport. They fired my imagination with the wonderful time one could have in Portsmouth and I, having been to Gosport on a course for a few days, listened eagerly to tales about the wonders of 'Pompey'. Alas, Nemesis, in the form of my mother and my birth certificate, was hot upon my trail. My mother would not listen to my pleadings to become a Regular soldier; they served only to stir up memories of partings and agonizing loss. She supplied the authorities with a copy of my birth certificate and, after being threatened with a charge for having falsified my age, I was sent back to Civvy Street. I found life in Basingstoke dull and a job in a London bank even duller. Soon,

World War I was over, but the call of the Army persisted. My mother's fears receded. My father still favoured a Regular engagement on condition that I joined the Machine Gun Corps. If I got down in a field, he argued, I should be perfectly safe; with ears like mine I would be 'mistaken for a bloody rabbit!'

Thus I joined the Tank Corps on September 3, 1919. I was sent to the 1st Battalion at Wareham in Dorsetshire and, in little over a month, received a brisk reminder that I was in the Army now. I was posted as a 'volunteer' to form a pool of men available for use during the big railway strike of October 1919, and despatched to Aldershot. I had not volunteered and, if I had been given the choice, I would not have chosen any such service. I sympathized with the railwaymen's protest against wage reductions proposed by the Coalition Government. I did not share the official view that the strike was an anarchist conspiracy. I did not want to be associated with any Government-sponsored strike-breakers disguised as 'volunteers' for the job.

The strike over, I returned to the Tank Corps Depot Battalion at Wareham and was granted seven days' leave given to all who had 'volunteered' for service as strike-breakers. In fact, I never left Blenheim Barracks, Aldershot. There we hung about for days on end with nothing to do and, needless to say, we began to gamble and played pontoon. There was a sequel. I was holding the bank and doing well when in stalked the Sergeant-Major. 'Leave it down!' he ordered, picked up the cards and money, and walked out. Although, according to all form, we should have been put on a charge, nothing happened. Discreet enquiries revealed that no statement had been made at the Orderly Room and no money handed in; the Sergeant-Major had pocketed the lot. I was the big loser, all my money having been in front of me, and now I was broke. That cruel fact gave me courage to knock at his door and, when he bellowed, 'What do you want?' I answered meekly, 'I want my money back.' Then the dialogue went as follows:

S.M.: 'You are lucky not to be on a charge.'
Wigg: 'I want to be charged, and I want my money back.'
S.M.: 'Go to the Orderly Room for it.'
Wigg: 'I am going, Sir.'
S.M.: 'How much did you have?'
Wigg: '£3, Sir.'

S.M.: 'You bloody liar! There was only thirty bob.'

Realizing that I was winning, I made my final bid and commented, 'All right, I'll go to the Orderly Room and find it, Sir.'

S.M.: 'I'll give you £2.'
Wigg: 'No, Sir, I want £3.'
S.M.: 'I'll give you £2 10s. od.'
Wigg: 'No, Sir, I want my £3.'
S.M.: 'Here's £3, and if ever I get the chance you'll find yourself inside.'
Wigg: 'I know, Sir, and thank you, Sir.'

Returning from leave, I was posted to the Tank Corps Central School at Bovington and so took fond farewell of the Sergeant-Major. I was put in charge of Messing Returns and appointed an Acting Unpaid Lance-Corporal. I can never express in words my joy in the magic moment when someone said 'Yes, Corporal' to me. Those who have never experienced such a moment have missed something.

My early impressions, as I recall them now, were that the Army reflected many of the harsh, stupid class distinctions with which civil life had made me all too familiar. There were neither social nor human contacts between officers and men. Yet my days were filled with interest and excitement. We went on cross-country runs as part of our training and I became interested enough to want to improve my performance. The Dorsetshire country still possessed the unspoiled charm described in Hardy's novels. I ran across it and enjoyed every minute of every run. I walked through it and enjoyed it even more. My growing knowledge of the contours of the countryside and experience gained in following the Vine Hunt came in useful. Together with my turn of foot they won me prized coupons for food in the canteen. I was proud to represent the Unit in the 1920 South of the Thames Cross Country Championship. I did not do very well, but my name was printed in the *Sporting Life* as coming in fifty-second or thereabout, and my mother's pride was unbounded; she kept the newspaper cutting until it wore out. As a gangling youth growing into welter-weight I got good marks and some good hidings at boxing—and more food coupons. I began to feel confirmed in my taste for Army life.

Army discipline never worried me. I soon learned the hackneyed truth about its meaning in those far-off days: doing what you don't want to do when you don't want to do it. This form of discipline became integrated with my every interest and activity, outside as well as inside the Army. I am convinced it helped me to make even my leisure reading more concentrated and purposeful. Not less important in building character was the discipline of the barrack-room. That, I am certain, contributed as much to my philosophy and way of life as the increasing understanding given me by reading and discussion. In the barrack-room a man was accepted for what he was. If he did not wash, somebody would scrub him. If he borrowed and failed to pay back, nobody would lend to him. If he stole, sooner rather than later, somebody would clout him. There was, of course, a distinction between stealing and scrounging. Stealing deprived your friends and those with whom you lived. Scrounging was the art of 'capturing' the next hut's coal ration for the benefit of your friends. The moral difference is beyond the ken of all who have never had the privilege of serving in the Army; only we who have enjoyed that privilege can understand and applaud the scrounger.

In the fundamental human experience shared in the barrack-room a man learns the basic principles of human association. Certainly my comrades revealed to me the value of social discipline and of honouring shared decisions which, I often thought during my political life, is the first duty any Parliamentary Party owes to British democracy. The test I applied frequently to leaders of all Parties was whether they would have been accepted in a barrack-room. Many of them would have failed that test. Perhaps my greatest shock in politics was to find how corrosive of human decency the search for place and power can be. Never in my life before 1945 had I found men hating other men to the point where they hoped the wounds would fester. We exchanged blows in the barrack-room, often violent blows; but in the end hating had no place. Although human nature is the same everywhere, political ambitions can become limitless and can outrun a man's abilities and moral worth. Then the overdraft is on integrity. The difference between my experience in the Army, eighteen years of it spent in the ranks, and my experience of political life was that in the Army, despite its ups and downs, I never had to worry about the stab in the back. Hence my deep attachment to and affection for those politicians I was able to trust through and through, first among them being Emanuel Shinwell.

The capacity of the Army to find 'volunteers' is unlimited. In May 1920, I found myself selected as a volunteer to work in the Army Pay Office at Woking. While there I continued to run whenever I could. One day, suffering from a violent stitch in the side, I was taken to the Military prison and transferred to the Connaught Hospital, Aldershot, to be operated on immediately for appendicitis. Who operated or how, I do not know, but every medical man who examined me thereafter has looked at the broad track of the incision with amazement. The result of the emergency operation with out-of-date techniques was a frequent return to medical care and years of worry about stomach trouble. Leave followed my discharge from hospital and I returned, as instructed, to Wareham where after some days, they told me they had never heard of me! So back I travelled to Woking. From there I was transferred to Aldershot. I learned that, by 'volunteering' for clerical duties, I would now be promoted Corporal with a rise in pay from four shillings and sixpence to six shillings and ninepence per day, the increase being pre-dated for quite a while. Thus was broken my resistance to leaving the Tank Corps.

I was attached to the Details, 2nd Battalion Royal Scots. I enjoyed the new life in Aldershot. The pay rise enabled me to increase the allotment to my mother and went a long way towards justifying my choice of career. Having gained a Second Class Certificate of Education while at Bovington, I was now studying for my First and, in addition, I joined English, history and science evening classes held at Aldershot Grammar School.

Perhaps the most important lesson I learned was taught me by a wise man, Lieutenant Broad, Officer Commanding, Royal Scots Detail. At the height of a 'flu scare I went to the dining-room to find the Orderly serving tea from a bucket with a basin from which he himself was drinking. I ordered him to stop drinking from the basin. He gave me a 'mouthful' and I, then a full Corporal, with Lance-Corporal Witley of the Royal Scots, put him on a charge. Getting another 'mouthful', we fetched the Sergeant in charge of the Detail, and the Orderly was put in the Guard Room. Next day, he was brought before Lieutenant Broad, who listened to the evidence of Witley and myself and asked the prisoner for his side of the story. His reply was, 'Sir, you never know when you have got Corporal

Wigg and Lance Corporal Witley and when you haven't.' He was remanded until next day when the Lieutenant told the prisoner, 'I have been making enquiries and, in the ordinary way, I would remand you for a summary of evidence.' (This is the first preliminary to a District Court Martial.) 'I am not doing that. I award you fourteen days C.B. March the prisoner out. The two N.C.O's stand fast.' The Lieutenant turned to Witley and me. 'My enquiries,' he said, 'show that both of you have been calling this man by his Christian name. You expect a man with practically no education to accustom himself to being addressed in friendly terms one minute and then given an order the next. You are as much to blame as he is. I have given him fourteen days C.B. and both of you can enjoy it with him.' I hope Mr Broad is still alive to read this acknowledgment of a never-forgotten lesson.

Then came a dramatic change, promising the thrill of travel and thrusting me into the centre of world politics. I was posted to the British Forces of Occupation in Turkey. I sailed from Liverpool on the S.S. *Eboe* with Nos. 25 and 207 Squadrons, R.A.F., and some Army units, bound for San Stefano, near Constantinople. Officer Commanding troops was Squadron Leader Tedder, later Lord Tedder. He had the reputation of being austere as well as able. Bawdy songs were banned at concerts. When, on the long sea journey, the 'old sweats' sang:

> 'We won the War—
> Whatever for?
> You can ask Lloyd George
> Or Bonar Law.'

Tedder gave orders for the song to be stopped and anyone singing it to be put on a charge.

The verse, of course, defies any definition of doggerel. Ill-constructed and 'mean' it certainly was, but it was also a shrewd comment on the current political situation. Many of the men on the *Eboe* had fought through the 'War to end War'. They knew that the promises of peace and 'homes fit for heroes' and work with good wages were a mockery of their dead and maimed comrades. Some of them had served recently in Ireland where Black and Tans had been recruited, at ten shillings a day for rankers and twenty shillings for officers, as an extra-military force whose conduct had brought undeserved disgrace upon the British Army. Others had been engaged between 1918 and 1920 at Archangel, at Vladivostock and at Baku in the Caucasus in a futile attempt to thwart the Russian Revolution. Moreover, the Genoa Economic Conference of all the European Powers had recently flopped, marking the end of the Triple Entente and underlining the historic differences between Great Britain and France still, as I write, manifesting themselves in the politics of the European Economic Community.

On the day of my arrival in Constantinople the state of military and diplomatic play was far from clear. Britain and France were two of the three Powers—the third being Italy—in occupation of the city. The Turks were fighting the Greeks, who had invaded Asia Minor and occupied the Turkish town of Smyrna with the support of Britain. The Turks, led by Mustapha Kemal, using French and Russian arms, were licking the Greeks! Moreover, Italian influence was supporting France in backing the Turks; a quarrel threatening to develop into open war with Britain. The capture and attachment of parts of Asia Minor had become a Greek war aim encouraged by Lloyd George and the British Government. Pressure against Britain was being applied by Indians sympathetic to their Moslem brothers, the Turks. Before long, my modest efforts to unravel the frightening and ridiculous tangle would sharply increase my interest in the question:

> 'We won the War—
> Whatever for?'

I was posted to the old Turkish École Militaire, one of the dirtiest places I have ever entered. The interior had been partitioned with sacking, long since dirt- and disease-ridden. Bugs were everywhere. Men slept on sacks of straw on bed boards and often wakened in the morning to find their arms made raw by bug bites. Diarrhoea and dysentery were endemic. The sanitary arrangements were a disgrace. I remember, as Orderly Sergeant, finding a lad named Jones lying on a bed unattended for two or three days. Much to the annoyance of the Medical Officer, I insisted on a doctor being called and narrowly escaped being put on a charge for making a nuisance of myself.

Years later, while I was Manny Shinwell's Parliamentary Private Secretary at the War Office, Sir Jocelyn Lucas, M.P. for Portsmouth

South, told me of a constituent who had been discharged from the Army as medically unfit in the 1920s, was unable to earn a living, and had been refused a pension. The man involved was Corporal Jones. Sir Jocelyn was determined, rightly, to press the case and together we succeeded in getting a meeting at the War Office under the chairmanship of Michael Stewart, then Under-Secretary. I could not comment on the medical factors involved, but I could testify that Jones had been left for days without proper attention. Sir Jocelyn's devoted efforts to secure justice for Jones were successful.

The job at the École Militaire, Headquarters of the British Forces in Turkey, did not last long. While soldiers were being piled into Turkey to meet Kemal's threat to Chanak, I was sent with two comrades to Adrianople. We were given no specific orders before our journey; what we went for and what we were supposed to do, God alone knows. Even at our journey's end we could receive no specific orders because our officer spoke neither Turkish nor Greek and did not begin to understand what was going on. Worse still, we had no food. We were wedged in between Greek soldiers who would shoot anybody for fourpence and Turks ready to shoot at anything or anybody for nothing.

I fell victim to dysentery and was taken back to hospital in Constantinople where I discovered that the only treatment then known for the ailment was starvation. When you were reduced to a bag of bones you were put on a chicken and egg diet—if you had not already died from diarrhoea. During my water and starvation period I lay in the next bed to a soldier who had passed the crisis and who, at every meal, smacked his lips loudly over hard-boiled eggs or chicken. Unable to bear this symphonic succulence, I hid my head under the blankets. One day I came up prematurely for air. My neighbour was looking round the ward in triumph at the prospect of eating his chicken and there it lay, unguarded. In a flash my skinny paw had grabbed the prize and I was down under the bedclothes, munching ravenously. The deprived neighbour made a hullaballoo and an orderly appeared. Because the chicken aggravated the dysentery, I was evacuated to Malta instead of facing a charge. On the way somebody gave me a bottle of chlorodyne and, having recovered before the ship reached Malta, I was packed back to Constantinople and the École Militaire. But not for long. I was told to take charge of two Officers' Messes at Nichantache. As an additional job I was concerned with Intelligence Officers, mostly Greek and Armenian, who wore officers' uniforms and were engaged to read vernacular newspapers and comment thereon. Some of them were suspected of being Kemalists in disguise. They probably were. Kemal's army was in force in the city. According to rumour there were no fewer than 20,000 Turkish troops in civilian clothes, plentifully supplied with arms by our French allies for use against us, the occupying troops. Certainly, the local telephone exchanges were tapped by Kemal's intelligence officers and there was no doubt in my mind that, if we got involved in active operations, we would have had a difficult job on hand.

I found the sparkle and bustle of the Golden Horn and the Bosphorus as beguiling and imaginative as the architecture of the mosques and minarets. I was a constant visitor to the St Sofia and the Sultan Ahmed Mosques. I knew nothing about architecture and I do not know much more now, but I was lost in wonderment at what I saw. Those buildings inspired me to read all I could find about Constantinople and its history. Being all on my own at Nichantache except for the mess servants, I had plenty of time for reading and a not too successful effort to improve my French and learn Turkish. I also enjoyed blissful hours of swimming, being ignorant about the powerful currents and polluted waters of the Bosphorus.

Constantinople was crowded with refugees. What we now call 'the permissive society' was in full, foul blast. The one ingredient missing was the modern debilitating drool of 'pop' music. To the thousands of men in uniform from many nations there were added thousands of White Russians, arrogant in the memory of their riches, expressing contempt for their country of origin by speaking only French and, as far as I could see, living largely on the earnings of their good-looking wives and daughters. Their contempt for people like me did not hurt; it was mutual. Night club patrons turned the streets into rivers of vice and alcohol. Robbery and assault were commonplace in a city where, even in daylight, it was dangerous to move away from the main thoroughfares. Black markets flourished everywhere. Drawing between eight and ten lira to the pound, the troops found drink and tobacco cheap. They also offered a mass market to the houris and harpies. Soon, everybody expected, the top would blow off this hell's-broth of a cauldron from which I found refuge in writing letters to my mother. Her replies begged me to remember the beliefs she had tried to teach me, to cling to them and to fortify my faith by regular attendance at Church. I took her advice and attended services at the British Embassy Chapel, but my church-going did not last. My Unitarianism had taken root.

Soon after I arrived in Constantinople the physically-enervating and morally-numbing city was gripped by a new mass hysteria. The Turks were marching on Chanak, the neutral zone on the southern shore of the Dardanelles held by British troops under the Treaty of Sèvres.

The story of Chanak has been told in many books and with many interpretations. For me the crisis marked the beginning of a life-long interest in the Middle East, its people and its problems. It impelled me to study the relationship between diplomacy and defence. It provided my first insight into the appalling—and, alas, continuing —ignorance of politicians and their advisers about the realities of defence and diplomacy in overseas areas about which they assert a claim to special knowledge.

The Committee of Union and Progress—the Young Turks—won world-wide sympathy in July 1908, when they proclaimed the Constitution of 1876, providing for Parliamentary government, an end to the theocratic state, freedom of the Press and the abolition of the Sultan's private Army. Abdul Hamid capitulated, and immediately set about organizing a counter *coup d'état*. In May 1909, Enver Pasha, leader of the Young Turks, sent his troops into the capital and replaced the Sultan by his brother Mohammed V. The new movement promised a political solution to problems involving Turkey and Europe's Eastern States, hitherto engaged in constant warfare, of which the most fearsome feature was the mass massacres of Christians. Within Turkey, the grant of equal rights to all religions gave promise of progress towards a more democratic way of life. Soon, however, Enver revealed himself as a self-indulgent, self-seeking adventurer. He proposed an alliance with Britain which our government rejected although, being eager to win Turkish contracts for warships, it maintained a British Naval Mission in Constantinople. Enver was also in negotiation with Germany, which had established considerable commercial influence in Turkey and, for a decade, had been developing the Berlin-to-Baghdad railway as an instrument of German domination of the East. For even longer—since 1881—the Germans had been 'advisers' to the Turkish Army. Now they supported, in Constantinople, a mighty Military Mission which ran the local munitions industry. On the eve of World War I, Germany was training the Turkish Army and Britain, with two Turkish keels laid down in British shipyards, was training the Turkish Navy! The British, French and Russian Embassies were headed by diplomats of the old school, living in regal state and almost completely unaware of life and affairs outside their palaces. Arraigned against them was a vigorous German whose Embassy was a 'cell' of Imperial German influence inside the Young Turk administration. The German Ambassador convinced Enver that, although Britain might command the seas, the coming war would be decided on land. France would be overrun quickly. If the Turks closed the Dardanelles and the Bosphorus to Russian trade and contact with her Western allies, revolution against the Tsar was likely, and an historic enemy of Turkey would be humiliated. There would be restored to Turkey from Britain control of Egypt and Cyprus, from Greece, Salonika and Crete, and from Italy, Tripoli. Other Turkish possessions in Europe would be protected against the claims of Bulgaria and Serbia. Indeed, a dazzling prospect to the ambitious Enver.

On August 2, 1914, Turkey and Germany signed a secret pact. On August 3, the First Lord of the Admiralty, Winston Churchill, announced that the first of two Turkish warships expected to sail from the Tyne in a matter of days, and her almost completed companion, had been requisitioned for the British Navy. The announcement dealt a shattering blow to the confidence in British power of hundreds of thousands of ordinary Turks who had made collections in every town and village to buy these ships. And what a gift to German propaganda—proof that British promises were worthless! Worse was to follow.

Two German ships, the *Goeben* and the *Breslau*, sailed for Turkish waters. The British ultimatum to Germany was due to expire at midnight on August 4. Up till 5 p.m. on that day the shadowing British ships could have out-gunned and sunk the German vessels although they could not out-speed them. Darkness fell. The *Goeben* and the *Breslau* slipped away to Messina, coaled there, then headed for Constantinople; the Admiralty expected them to sail, not southeast, but west or north. Meanwhile, on August 8, Enver, certain that the British Fleet must have sunk his German reinforcements, offered to sign a Russian-Turkish agreement and abandon the Treaty with Germany he had signed a few days before. Next evening, the *Goeben* and the *Breslau* sailed through the Dardanelles.

The diplomatic fiddle-faddle following these events included an

Anglo-French-Russian proposal to guarantee the Ottoman Empire from attack in return for Turkish neutrality. That proposal, had it been made a fortnight earlier, might have kept Turkey out of the war; according to some commentators, it might even have prevented war. Now, in the light of Churchill's blunder, it was an empty gesture; the Turks were under the Kaiser's thumb. On September 9, the British Naval Mission was withdrawn and the Germans were left in control of the Turkish Navy as well as the Turkish Army. When, on September 26, the British stopped a Turkish torpedo boat at the mouth of the Dardanelles, the Germans commanding the fortifications replied by closing the Straits, free passage through which was guaranteed by international convention.

The strange, almost farcical, situation came to a climax a month later. On October 29, the *Goeben* and the *Breslau* led a Turkish squadron through the Black Sea and, without warning, opened fire on Odessa harbour. They renewed the attack next day, when the Allied Ambassadors delivered a twelve-hour ultimatum to the Enver Government. Enver, no doubt, was anticipating the rewards of treachery. French resistance at the Battle of the Marne and Russian victories in Austria, however, frustrated the Kaiser's hopes of a short war and, soon, Mustapha Kemal (Ataturk) was to emerge as the saviour of his country. Kemal believed in the Young Turks as a national movement of liberation and regeneration. He opposed German control of his country. He was thought to be on the point of deserting his diplomatic post at Sofia when he was transferred to Rodosto at the head of the Gallipoli peninsula. The appointment proved to be fateful for Enver, and for the Allies. Kemal, given a roving role in the defence of the Dardanelles in March 1915, became for the Turks the hero of the campaign.

History has not dealt kindly with British commanders at the Dardanelles. Kemal's activities, however, have to be judged in relation to the fact that, two months earlier, the Turkish Army had lost an estimated seventy-five thousand men in a 'mystery' battle, led by Enver, against the Russians in the Caucasus. Kemal rallied his depleted, disease-ridden forces, devised and conducted a shrewd policy of defence against the Allies, and proved himself to possess qualities of leadership which the world was later to acclaim.

The Allies took control of Constantinople following the Armistice of Mudros in October 1918, and, when it became evident that America wanted no part of any mandate for the area, occupied the city in

March 1920. Meanwhile, Kemal had organized a congress at Sivas which, in September 1919, formed the 'National Pact' and insisted upon the Sultan calling an election to a Grand National Assembly. This Assembly superseded the puppet government at Constantinople and established its own seat at Angora (Ankara) in 1920. From this base Kemal launched guerrilla operations against the Allies on several fronts. It was to meet the Kemal threat that Lloyd George encouraged Greek claims to share in the spoils of the 'dying' Turkish Empire. The British Premier was on terms of personal friendship with Venizelos, Prime Minister of Greece, and the British Cabinet was led to believe that Greece could become a Middle East power friendly to Britain. So Greek armies, already in possession of Smyrna, which previously had been promised to Italy, moved far into the interior of Anatolia and also occupied Adrianople and Eastern Thrace.

This Greek advance convinced the Allies that they could now impose peace terms on the Turks. The Treaty of Sèvres, signed by the Sultan on August 10, 1920, gave to France a mandate over Syria, to Britain mandates over Palestine and Mesopotamia, and to Greece possession of Eastern Thrace within twelve miles of Constantinople, Gallipoli and the Aegean Islands. Smyrna was to be administered by Greece for five years and, thereafter, to decide its own future by plebiscite; the population of Greek colonists in the area, it was hoped, would grow sufficiently to enable Greek control to continue. Because the Soviets had repudiated the Allied war aims of giving the Straits and Constantinople to Russia, the Straits and the Dardanelles were to be de-militarised and delivered over to international supervision. Three months later, however, British friendship for Venizelos was rendered meaningless. King Alexander of Greece had died from the bite of a pet monkey. His father, the pro-German Constantine, had returned to the throne from which Allied influence had deposed him and had sacked his Prime Minister. When the *Entente* fell into disarray, Kemal seized his chance. He built up his army, imported weapons from France and Russia, and ruthlessly routed the Greeks at Smyrna on August 22, 1922. Soon he was advancing on Chanak.

In London, Lloyd George, whose Government had lost twenty-one by-elections between 1918 and 1922, decided that Chanak raised an issue—war against 'the unspeakable Turk'—which might enable him to go to a country stirred up into a new, patriotic war frenzy. A mistake by Churchill, as ridiculous as his 1914 decision to requisition the Turkish warships, reduced this political plot to a futile farce. On September 15, as Secretary of State for the Colonies, he prepared a message to the Dominions asking for military support. He released the message next day, too late for publication by the Sunday newspapers on September 17, but forgot the difference in time between London and the Dominions. Thus the Prime Ministers of Canada and Australia read the secret statement in *their* Sunday papers before it could be decoded in their own offices on Monday morning! Mr Mackenzie King and Mr 'Billy' Hughes objected to what looked like a communiqué committing them to war without prior consultation. Canada said 'No'; Australia's reply was unsympathetic. When the clarion call reached Capetown the imperturbable Smuts was in Zululand, and stayed there. Only New Zealand, reluctantly, and Newfoundland offered support.

The long-term consequences of Churchill's ineptitude revealed themselves over the years. The Dominions became distrustful of Whitehall and intent upon conducting their own diplomacy. The first sign was their exemption from the military obligations in Europe accepted by Great Britain in the Locarno Pact of 1925. They insisted upon equal status with the Mother-country at the Imperial Conference of 1926. In 1927, Canada asserted her independence of London by appointing her own Ambassador to Washington. Following the Imperial Conference of 1930, Parliament passed the Statute of Westminster in 1931, making the foreign policy of each Dominion independent of the Mother-country. The Dominions had come of age, as was right and inevitable, but under circumstances presaging a weakening of the bonds of Empire and Commonwealth.

With British public opinion rallying against a new war, and Conservatives in the Coalition becoming fearful for their prospects as an independent political party, the Government instructed General Sir Charles Harrington to deliver an ultimatum to the Turks.

Harrington was a wise man as well as an able soldier. He did not fear Kemal. British naval power could still guarantee that, although Harrington faced big odds, a long-drawn-out conflict could have no place in the plans of his intelligent opponent. Harrington also knew that, whatever the result of battle, the peace must cede reasonable conditions to Kemal who, alone, could represent Turkey at the Peace Table, and that the sack of Constantinople was the most probable result of hostilities. And he knew that Kemal knew all this. Harrington did not issue the London politicians' ultimatum. Although the French and Italian governments had deserted the British—both, in fact, had made peace with Kemal and abandoned the punitive provisions of the Treaty of Sèvres—Harrington had kept the military commanders of these Powers in line. While preparing to meet every contingency, he turned blind eyes and deaf ears to the soldierly exchanges of tea and sugar across the barbed wire and challenges to 'come on over and fight'. Harrington, in fact, was creating contact with Kemal, confident that the Allies must offer to parley with the Turk leader before the ultimatum deadline date of September 30. The decision came on September 23—a joint Allied invitation to Kemal to confer aboard H.M.S. *Iron Duke* at Mudania on the Sea of Marmora. The greater part of Eastern Thrace, including Adrianople, was to be restored to Turkey. Allied troops were to be withdrawn from Constantinople as soon as the conditions of a secure peace had been obtained. Throughout all the alarums and excursions of the next eighteen days a wise, brave General kept his head. The Pact of Mudania was signed on October 11, 1922. Peace was saved and the era of sporadic warfare in the Balkans drew to a close.

During these crisis-ridden days in Constantinople, I made my own reconnaissance and decided upon a course of action if the worse came to the worst. I would swim the Bosphorus and join the Navy!

Meantime, in London, with Bonar Law re-entering politics to denounce the policy that led to the Chanak crisis, powerful elements in the Tory Party decided to ditch the Coalition. On October 19, a Carlton Club meeting of Tory M.P.s determined, by 187 votes to 87, to fight the next General Election as an Independent Party. Lloyd George, their hero while he was destroying the Liberal Party, but now their prisoner, resigned. Before the election, in which the Tories and their former National Liberal collaborators won 407 seats, Mussolini had seized power in Italy and Fascism had begun its march through Europe. Outside Europe, Kemal was making Nationalism a force to which Imperialism and Colonialism had no answer, although it took another World War to convince Western statesmen of the need for change in India and Africa. And control in the Middle East was seen to mean more than access to India and the perpetuation of Imperial glory. It meant, also, access to a rich new source of physical power—oil. The smell of oil, indeed, seems to have been pervasive even in the Cabinet Room at 10, Downing Street. A libel circulated by a Paris newspaper charged Lord Beaverbrook with seeking peace with Turkey because he controlled the Mesopotamia oil-field. The canard, Lord Beaverbrook claimed, came from Ministerial circles in London.

A Peace Treaty between Britain and Turkey was signed finally in 1923. It by-passed the Treaty of Sèvres which Kemal, now head of the Turkish Republic, had ignored anyway. It dropped all Allied claims to Smyrna, Armenia and Kurdistan. Curzon's great triumph in negotiating this Treaty of Lausanne was to make 'legitimate' the military capture of the Mosul oil wells. Thus Britain's betrayal of Arab hopes for self-government and freedom was anointed with the oiliest of oily water.

The background to this dirty deal was the Sykes-Picot 'arrangement'—so-called after its British and French negotiators—of May 1916. Syria was ceded to France and Mesopotamia to Britain on condition that Russia agreed. Tsarist Russia gave consent in return for Armenia, a concession repudiated by the Bolsheviks in 1917. Italy, bribed into the War by the promised possession of the Tyrol, Istria and part of Dalmatia, advanced claims to land in Asia Minor which were not conceded until August 1917, again subject to Russian consent. In the pre-revolution turmoil the Russians forgot to reply. On November 8, 1917, the Balfour Declaration recognized Palestine as a National Home for the Jews. The French, traditionally sympathetic to Jewish aspirations, interpreted the move as an attempt to reduce their influence in Syria and create a buffer-state between Palestine and the Suez Canal, a traditional battle-ground of French and British commercial interests.

British troops occupied Syria after the defeat of the Turks. A small French force remained on the coast, but the interior was controlled by the British from Palestine, where General Allenby, as wise a politician as Harrington proved himself to be, had rejected out of hand the demand of Picot, his French adviser, to set up a French provisional government. In Aleppo, Homs, Hama, Damascus and east of Jordan the Arabs were operating as a government under Emir Faisal. Bright prospects of Arab progress flowed from the Peace Conference of January 1919. The Arab provinces of the Ottoman Empire were to be detached from Turkey. Some of them were to be placed under trusteeship as a preliminary to independence after ascertaining the wishes of the local inhabitants. The process of ascertainment was frustrated by the French. An unofficial inquiry, undertaken by two American investigators and presented to their President, opposed a French mandate for Syria and expressed doubts about the wisdom of the Balfour Declaration. Its contents were not made public until December 1922. Meantime, in September 1919, Britain and France re-affirmed the basis of the Sykes-Picot programme and in April 1920, one month after Emir Faisal had been nominated as King, the Great Powers finalised the carve-up of Syria. Palestine and Mesopotamia were placed under British mandatory rule, Syria and the Lebanon under French mandatory rule. The work of great British civil servants, then seeking to create, with Arab Ministers, a democratic form of government in Baghdad, was reduced to ashes.

The foregoing account of events is the picture I have gained over the years, going back to 1922. My slowly developing grasp of events acquired fresh meaning from the life around me at that time, by what I read, and from conversations with anyone who would talk to me about current problems affecting Turkey during war-time and in the pre-war period.

Unfortunately, the complications following on my operation at Aldershot persisted, and I was again admitted to hospital. Hernia was diagnosed, but as the evacuation of the British forces was pending the operation was postponed. When I did return to England I was transported immediately to the Royal Herbert Hospital at Woolwich. There a kindly doctor, Captain H. H. Munro, did more than operate efficiently. He convinced me that the only way to make my physical disability tolerable was 'to get it out of my mind'. Thirty-six years later I met Dr Munro again, by this time a General. He was a fellow patient in the Queen Alexandra Hospital, Millbank, London. Among many interesting reminiscences was his story of sailing up the English Channel on August 4, 1914. He was on his way from his native New Zealand to Edinburgh to continue his medical studies. On disembarking he joined the R.A.M.C. and was posted to Millbank. One of his first assignments was to take two horse-drawn ambulances to Waterloo Station to meet the first hospital train bringing home the wounded from Mons. They numbered two thousand. General Munro learned his first lesson in military medical logistics: great Army doctors must be masters of administration.

After leaving the Royal Herbert Hospital, although still far from fit, I was stationed at Woolwich, and reading occupied much of my time. Henry Noel Brailsford's *The War of Steel and Gold* had illuminated for me the influence of vested economic interests on politics and policies. Now he was editing, for the Independent

Labour Party, the *New Leader*, which gave expression to the Socialist faith in art and literature and through which I became familiar with the writings on the cause and cure of unemployment by J. A. Hobson and E. F. Wise. *New Leader* contributors introduced me also to novels like Mark Rutherford's *The Revolution in Tanner's Lane* and to moving short stories like R. B. Cunninghame-Graham's *How Capitalism Came to the Village*. My emotional response to the poetry I used to read with my mother—Kipling's *If*, Tennyson's *Charge of the Light Brigade* and Charles Kingsley's *The Sands of Dee* were among our favourites—found new depth in reading and re-reading A. E. Housman. *A Shropshire Lad* holds a place of honour on my bedside book-shelf. H. G. Wells was still a power in the land and George Bernard Shaw an exciting entrepreneur in ideas. Chesterton and Belloc were preaching their proposals for distributing wealth more fairly without disturbing City interests. Professor Frederick Soddy had published his *Cartesian Economics*, soon to be followed by his attack on the money system as an *Inversion of Science*. The most persuasive tract for the times, I found, was Professor R. H. Tawney's *The Acquisitive Society*.

In the world beyond my hospital room I saw mass unrest injecting into all reform movements a vitality born of hope that the next General Election could return a Labour Government. All England seemed to be a vast public meeting in constant session. People everywhere were alive with what Robert Lynd, the radical journalist, described as 'the passion of labour . . . to make the world a better place for the people who inhabit it'. There was gaiety and a spice of adventure in changing occasionally into mufti and joining a Brixton group of canvassers to recruit members for the Labour Party.

I heard much talk about Lord Haldane at Workers' Educational Association classes held in a Working Man's Club at Woolwich. A friend of the Workers' Educational Association he was now building up the British Institute of Adult Education as part of his plan to extend the extra-mural activities of the Universities to a wider audience. From my general reading of political history I knew that Haldane had supported the 1902 Education Act against the views of his own Party. He thought the Act would help to unify the educational system and, since Germany's growing commercial power in the world was a product of the 'thoroughness' of its educational policies, he feared that unless the British emulated the Germans in esteem for learning, German competition would endanger our economic survival. Here was an expression of patriotism in one of its truest senses. Yet Haldane's view was distorted and exploited during the War especially by the *Daily Mail* to suggest that Haldane, pioneer of the Imperial College of Science and Technology, was pro-German! The campaign drove Haldane from office and out of public life when the country's need for his talents was most urgent. His resignation as Lord Chancellor was the base and basic condition upon which, in 1915, the Tories agreed to serve in the Asquith Coalition, and Asquith, weeping, threw his closest friend to the wolves of Fleet Street.

An announcement that Haldane was to speak, probably under the auspices of the British Institute of Adult Education, aroused my interest. I do not remember the place of the meeting; only that the experience was traumatic. The man himself—his tubby appearance and rather pontifical oratory—was unremarkable. What was remarkable was his simplicity, and the sincerity and urgency of his plea that education must be organized as a continuing process throughout adult life if democracy and British influence in the world were to survive. Here spoke a man who had looked deep into the heart of things and who, like Tennyson's *Ulysses*, had enjoyed greatly and suffered greatly and, although then aged sixty-six, still believed 'some noble work may yet be done'.

Most impressive to my youthful mind was the expression of his faith that the more experience is spiritual the more it is real. I identified this testimony with my mother's respect for religious conviction and her belief that the individual's conduct in relation to the family and the community lives on from generation to generation and for ever. I decided that newspapers capable of calumniating such a man were anti-social and evil. I became an avid reader of works by and about Haldane. I agreed with the verdict of history that this man, who created and equipped the British Expeditionary Force and sustained our home defence by developing the Territorial Army (or, as he described it, the Second Line), did more to save Europe in 1914 than any of his contemporaries.

I felt confirmed in my view of Haldane as a result of a pleasant association with Sir James Grigg, Permanent Under-Secretary of State for War from 1934 until 1939 and from 1942 Secretary of State in the Churchill War Cabinet. Grigg had been asked by Duncan Sandys to head an inquiry into Army recruiting and called me into consultation. At the end of one meeting we discussed Secretaries of

State for War. Grigg was a forthright man, holding and expressing strong opinions. He owed much to Churchill. I expected vigorous opposition to my statement that Haldane was pre-eminent in the office and, moreover, was the man to whom Britain owed most in this century. Grigg's reply was succinct and, to me, final: 'I would not dissent.'

To record the debt owed by my generation and the country to so great a man and public servant, I proposed in the House of Commons on July 31, 1956, that the House should celebrate the centenary of Haldane's birth by erecting a statue to his memory. It is usual in proposing such a Motion to seek the support and set down the names of sponsors, and in a matter relating to public monuments, to inform the Home Secretary of one's intentions. Mr (now Lord) Butler, then Home Secretary, gave me a bland brush-off. He understood and shared my admiration for Haldane but did not think it would be right to erect a monument to him at public expense. Courteously, he added an interesting piece of information. Only about ten such monuments had been erected in London during the last hundred years and, he felt, it was arguable whether public opinion would agree that Haldane should be the eleventh.

My letter to Sir Winston Churchill inviting him to be a sponsor evoked this reply: 'I had and have a high opinion of Haldane, but even so I do not feel that I could add my name to your Motion. There are, I think, far too many statues in London—not all of them very good—and the trend has been to add to them increasingly in recent years. This does not mean of course that I oppose your suggestion in any way, but I do not think that I can actively support it. Pray, nevertheless accept my thanks for thinking of me in this connection.'

Of course I had moments of levity during those great days at Woolwich. Perhaps one of the most startling was my attendance at a whist drive where, at the seventeenth hand, if you had a score of one hundred and thirty tricks or more, the eighteenth to twentieth hands were watched by a scrutineer. Came the eighteenth hand. My partner and I had good cards. One of our opponents, having more than one hundred and thirty tricks, was being watched. Although we won trick after trick, our opponents picked up twelve tricks and so won the first prize of fifty pounds. I was dumbfounded and at a loss to know what to do. Leaving the hall I told a friend what had happened. He advised me, 'Keep your mouth shut or you'll get done'.

Going downstairs to the street I was bundled into a lavatory and a bunch of notes was thrust into my hands. Outside, I picked up my friend again and continued my story. 'Keep your mouth shut if you don't want to get cut up,' he insisted. On this, my last big-money whist drive, I did as I was told and was eight pounds the richer.

Chapter Three: Middle East

While I was at Woolwich, for the first and only time during my Army service, an officer showed interest in my welfare as a human being with hopes and ambitions. A Colonel Hanson inquired about my health and, after discussing my spare-time activities, suggested I should aim at something better than a low-grade clerical job. He advised me to go for a 'Y' cadetship, something about which I had never even dreamed. I had taken Army First Class and Second Class Certificate of Education in my stride. I had attended evening classes in the hope of improving my general education. The idea of a commission from the ranks, however, was flying high indeed. Alas, these dreams were short-lived. My patron was ticked off, so he told me, for interesting himself in the affairs of other ranks. 'I have landed you in trouble as well as myself,' he explained, 'but it is worse for you. The best advice I can give you is to get out of here.' I had three more years to serve on my current engagement. Finances at home were not easy and the special Colonial allowances in Baghdad seemed attractive, so I volunteered for service in Mesopotamia, or Iraq, as it came to be called. By so doing I hoped to escape from a difficult situation and, at the same time, to increase the allotment to my mother from my pay. I attained both objectives.

Life in Baghdad, apart from the climate, was pleasant enough. As always, I enjoyed swimming, and there was horse-racing. I was stationed at Brigade Headquarters, on the old road to Hinaidi, a few yards away from the racecourse. I was out there at dawn every morning and often got a chance to ride work. The Arabs would let me trot and canter, but that was all. Fast work was left to their own jockeys, always against the stop-watch.

Soon after arriving I had the good fortune to meet Miss Gertrude Bell. Miss Bell's maid was friendly with a friend of mine, an ex-Royal Army Veterinary Corps Staff Sergeant who, on leaving the Army, had settled in Baghdad, and this lady often passed on to me books and magazines with which Miss Bell had finished. Thus Miss

Bell became quite interested in my reading and, although a little too conscious of our difference in social class, she gave direction to my eager study of Arab affairs. Her book, *Amurath to Amurath*, introduced me to Arab history and archaeology. From Miss Bell herself I was to receive some insight into the significance of the Young Turks' revolutionary movement and to grasp how the Sykes-Picot plot and all that derived from it had destroyed her dream of Arab freedom at the moment of its realisation. As a member of the British Intelligence Service and Secretary and adviser to Sir Percy Cox, our first High Commissioner who, as early as October 1920, had ended military rule and created an Arab Council of State which, after a referendum, proclaimed Emir Faisal king in August 1921, Miss Bell had won the confidence of the Arabs. Her idea of a Museum of Antiquities, which she promoted in 1918, found expression in a permanent building with Miss Bell as its first Director. She died in her sleep during the night of 11–12 July 1926, and was buried in the British Cemetery. I attended her funeral.

Miss Bell did much to clarify my mind about Britain's Imperial policy. The Allies had not broken up the Ottoman Empire in order to bring unity and democracy to the Arabs although their war-time propaganda had endorsed those Arab aspirations. The Allied policy was to ensure commercial conquest by promoting division among the Arabs and this could be achieved by playing off the Shia and Bedouin tribes against the millions of Sunni Moslems. For the British, too, Basra was an invaluable prize. It was a vital stores base for the troops stationed in Iraq. Equally important, it was a vital link in any plan to send reinforcements from Iraq to India, and it provided essential re-equipment and maintenance facilities for troops coming from India, and even from Egypt and the United Kingdom, in the event of serious trouble in Iraq and neighbouring areas.

Against this cynical background the moral appeal of declaring Palestine a National Home for the Jews was degraded into a pawn in the diplomatic power game. Obviously this cruelly-tortured people would look forward passionately to the end of their long dark night of sorrowful dispersal. Obviously the commercial and political influence so talented, public-spirited and generous a people had gained in the councils of the West would be exercised in favour of this solution. What too few politicians asked was the simple question: is the Balfour Declaration, as it came to be called, the right solution for both today and, more important, tomorrow? The question remains unanswered after half a century, a second World War, and the flooding of the Middle East with rivers of uncleansing blood.

Fundamental to Miss Bell's political philosophy, as I understood it, was that rule on the old Indian-Imperialist model was dying everywhere and could not be restored anywhere. Apart from passing the time of day she avoided small talk. Thus I took note of her laconic description of the members of the Alwiyah Club—they included civil servants and officials of the Iraq Petroleum Company—as 'the Alwiyah trash'. Whether she was referring to their social habits or their conduct generally I was still too shy and unsophisticated to ask. About T. E. Lawrence she made only one comment I remember: 'A bit of a publicity seeker.'

Heat, persistent and pervasive, tormented us. We called Mesopotamia 'the land of two rivers and Sweet Fanny Adams in between'. We lost man after man from heatstroke. I remember being lined up at dawn for a funeral ceremony during which two men dropped to the ground; by sundown both were dead. Christmas brought bitter cold and even frost. By March temperatures would rise to 80 degrees in the day time. With April we experienced another 10 degree increase, sandfly fever, and often a rise of many feet in the river level, resulting in a flooding of the surrounding desert. June, with the temperature at 100 degrees, brought a threat of bubonic plague. By July and August the whole area was sweltering at near 120 degrees in the shade. Only the desert responded gratefully to the heat and moisture of April. Then, as swiftly as bird-song at sunrise, it burst into flower and, for too short a while, we glimpsed a new, rare beauty, making tolerable for the imaginative among us the grim harshness of a dead, flat, alluvial desert. Standing on the banks of the Tigris at Baghdad it was difficult to believe that Basra lay five hundred miles away to the South; there was not even a hillock in between for we were only fifteen feet above sea level.

The huts in which we lived were made from muttee, a mixture of straw and water, and the alluvial deposits spread down the centuries by the floods of the Tigris. They had high roofs made from rushes with layers of muttee on top. We had electric fans, and our living conditions were, comparatively speaking, luxurious. I often wondered what it was like on the Mesopotamian Plain for the prisoners of the Turks captured at Kut-al-Imara, and among the troops of General Maude's relieving Army. It must have been hell. Even for us, with our ice and electric fans, life was difficult enough.

The morale of the troops fell so low that during periods of extreme heat men feared to be left alone.

By accident I discovered a prescription for our climatic ills. I ate what I could, drank lots of tea and took plenty of exercise. Against the ravages of sandfly I rubbed my wrists and ankles with bamber oil, and slept in the open air in pyjamas which were never washed once they had become impregnated with the oil. These pyjamas were a most effective repellent. I escaped sandfly fever, but my friends declared they could tell from a distance of fifty yards down-wind whether I was in bed or not.

What never ceased to amaze me was the lack of research into the basic problems arising from the fact that the health of British troops, on active service or in fulfilling garrison duties, either in the Middle East or in India, was always seriously at risk. The problems arising from excessive heat, inadequate diet and water supply were never sufficiently researched and, consequently, the provision of protection in both war and peace was invariably far short of what was possible. That was true at Gallipoli. It was true in the Palestine and Mesopotamia campaigns. It was certainly always true in India. It was true, once again, at Kuwait in 1961.

At one time we were attached to R.A.F. Headquarters in which the officers were old Army types and men who had opted for flying from a sense of adventure or because they saw no prospect of advancement in any other field of service. Their one idea for dealing with heat was to order the wearing of a topee and the carrying of a cap until sundown, then you donned the cap and carried the topee! I was once placed under open arrest for wearing my topee after sunset. When I pointed out that I was not an airman no charge was made. Inoculation against bubonic plague was almost as bad as the disease. It knocked men out for a fortnight. I discovered some senior officers had decided not to be inoculated, so when I was summoned for inoculation I refused on the ground that rats and bugs were not respecters of rank. My A.B.64—the soldier's personal record—was endorsed in large letters written in red ink: 'Refused inoculation'.

Another brush with authority taught me that respect for other human beings could even pay a dividend. During a cold spell when I slept inside I had gone for a walk leaving alight the oil stove in my hut. This was, of course, against orders. I returned to learn that a Flight Sergeant had entered, seen the walls covered with the residue from oil-black smoke and had forthwith put me on a charge. My 'boy', an Arab aged thirty, said smilingly, 'Master, you go sleep in another bunk; tomorrow morning you see.' I spent the night on top of a table in a near-by office and went back at first light to see what I would see. My hut was spotless. During the morning I paraded at the Camp Commandant's office and was marched in. To the charge that I had not extinguished the stove and that my oil-lamp had blazed and blackened the walls of my bunk I replied that I did not understand. Back to the scene of the crime marched the three of us, the Camp Commandant leading the way. The place was in perfect order and the charge was dropped. My Arab 'boy' had worked all night to rescue me. I never struck him. I always paid him exactly what I promised. I never sought to have his miserable pay docked as punishment—which really fell on wife and family—for minor misdemeanours. I had sub-consciously followed the code of conduct the Army had taught me: mean what you say, try like hell to be fair, and give the other man the simple respect as a human being that you expect him to show you. Once again, the formula had worked. To some this will seem to be self-righteous. To me it is just plain sense.

The Army's legacy of muddle and the atmosphere of lethargy encouraged rumours of maladministration and dishonesty. Basically, the causes of the trouble stemmed from the way the Mesopotamian campaign had been fought. The seizure of the cable station at Fao in 1914 had been followed by a campaign conducted from Indian bases and run on Indian Government lines. It led to General Townsend's surrender at Kut-al-Imara. He had launched an advance using the Rivers Tigris and Euphrates as lines of communication and, in October 1915, was almost within sight of Baghdad. Then he was driven back to Kut where he was besieged by Turkish forces led by German officers and, in April 1916, he surrendered. The run of disaster continued until the harsh, austere General Maude took command and brought the Expeditionary Force under the tighter, more efficient control of the War Office.

Many old Indian traditions survived. One officer who ran horses successfully in Baghdad, Basra and Bombay actually drew pay, stores and equipment for a non-existent Arab battalion. This episode ended in a Court Martial, but many instances of dishonesty went un-punished. According to rumour the mobilization stores in Basra were run down in exchange for a few lakhs of rupees and those responsible got away with it because there was no extradition treaty between the

newly-formed Iraq Government and Great Britain! The story first
blew up when civilians attached to the R.A.F. were sent home because, it was alleged, they had objected to peculation in the handling
of the stores. By this time, some of the guilty men had left the
Services and gone into business and were safe as long as they stayed
out of Iraq. I remember reading the old Command Orders before
the R.A.F. took over; the accounts of the numerous Courts Martial
findings read like pages from the *Police Gazette*.

I spent three years in Iraq. Most of my comrades hated it. So did
I in the early days. Miss Bell, however, opened up one avenue of
exciting interest; racing provided another; a third attraction was my
pay as a Sergeant of nine shillings a day plus three shillings and
ninepence Colonial Allowance—and twelve shillings and ninepence
a day in the 1920s was quite a lot of money. I supplemented my
income by moderately successful punting. With Shoey Austin, my
ex-R.A.V.C. friend, I went to a sale of the assets of the Diyalah
Cotton Plantation Company, formed by the late Lord Chelmsford,
which had gone 'bust'. There, tied up, a nice little Arab pony, just
short of fourteen hands, excited my interest. Austin teased me, 'Why
don't you buy it?' I bid a hundred rupees and the pony was mine.
The question was what to do with it. Austin was Superintendent of
the Iraq Government Veterinary Hospital and he agreed to keep it
there, so we hired an Arabana—a horse drawn carriage—and the
pony trotted alongside to its new home. The miracle of good food
and slow work made us wonder whether or no it would race. One
glad morning we worked it with an Arab boy up; it ran well, and
we decided to enter it in a maiden race. I went to the Racecourse
Office to register the pony and my colours. The idea of an N.C.O.
owning a horse brought about a state of near collapse. I announced
my pony's name, Saiyarah. Colonel St John Bell, the Club Secretary,
ex-Indian Army, grunted, 'Do you know what it means?' 'Yes, Sir. It
is Arabic for motor-car.' 'That will cost you two rupees.' I paid, and
announced my colours as Khaki shirt and a sky-blue cap, having
bought the cap from an Indian syce, or groom, for eight annas
(ninepence). Colonel Bell, by now recovering his form, bellowed:
'There's no such colour as Khaki. It was invented by the War Office
during the South African War.' Thus Colonel Bell decided that my
racing colours should be olive green and a sky-blue cap. They still
are.

I had great fun with Saiyarah, running him in several races with tremendous élan and no success. Occasionally I rode other people's horses, although I was much too heavy and I did not ride very well. I once rode a whaler owned by the Brigade Commander in a four-furlong scurry and was going well until I was pushed into the rails. My stirrup was torn off and I went to hospital. At Whitsuntide, 1926, I got involved in a ridiculous escapade. An Arab asked me to ride his horse in an amateur race on condition that I, weighing over eleven stone, should get down to ten stone two pounds. In a temperature of well over 100 degrees I swallowed countless laxative pills, put on numerous shirts, and ran round the track in an Army greatcoat. I rode at ten stone four pounds, finished fourth, and was cursed for failing to reach the first three.

I had my first real 'tickle' when an Arab jockey, Hamid Jassim, offered me a half share in a pony named Ghatruf. He said his uncle owned it. Nobody really knew who owned it, but I 'grub-staked' the horse and, probably for the first time in its life, it got plenty of food over a sustained period. In a mile race in a large field Ghatruf 'popped up' and paid one hundred and sixty rupees to five for the win. I had three five rupee tickets, and drew four hundred and eighty rupees—for me a small fortune. Wins like this were not frequent, but I also 'grub-staked' a pony called Gratia, which won a couple of races at good prices. The Arabs never sold their mares; they came mainly from the marsh Arabs and were the property of the tribe. They were brought into Baghdad to race by an individual who had to depend upon credit and what he won to provide the needs of himself and the horses. Thus the 'grub-staking' formula was one that suited all parties, and was satisfactory so long as the pony you 'grub-staked' won a race or two.

I was sorry to leave Baghdad. The last Army Unit, the King's Regiment (Liverpool), marched out on March 17, 1927, ten years from the day when General Maude led his victorious Army into the city. I stayed on with one other N.C.O. before travelling overland to Cairo. When I was first posted to Iraq the journey, *via* India, took the better part of a month. Our letters from home came in about ten days. They were either flown from Cairo *via* Amman to Baghdad or they were brought by overland transport owned by the Nairn brothers, two enterprising New Zealanders who used Buick cars to cover the route from Beirut to Damascus and on to Baghdad. This was the way I moved out.

We motored from Baghdad to Ramadi on the Euphrates, then

struck westward through the Wadi Haurun into the desert and so to Rutba. Swinging north we followed the caravan track to Palmyra, then on to Damascus where we headed for the coast and Beirut. This was a journey I shall never forget. I was saying 'au revoir' to the desert. Its effect on me was always electric. What a man who had lived only in London might feel if transported to a remote island could not compare with my reactions to the way of Arab desert life. All the aids and assets of industrial and social organization as I knew them were absent from this fierce, unrelenting struggle for survival. Here only religious faith and spiritual values nourished the quality of the family and the social group.

Beirut brought me back to the Western World and the bustle and barter of any seaport anywhere. Then, as now, its most highly developed commerce was in banking and as a centre for gold, diamond and drug smuggling. We made the trip from Damascus to Beirut at night. Climbing above the snow line, we crossed the magnificent mountain ranges of the Anti-Lebanon and I saw the Mediterranean glittering far below—my first sight of the sea for nearly three years. With the dawn, sunshine and shadow gave exciting colour to the glory of the Beeka Valley. But, oh, the aching misery of the Armenians living, many of them, in holes in the ground; that was a source of sad wonder. The bidonville was, and is, a monument of lasting shame to British and French failure to clean up the mess which half a century of incompetent, and often un-scrupulous, diplomacy had created.

Haifa gave me my first glimpse of Palestine. The port was already acquiring the characteristics of a university town. In after years I found myself comparing it with Cape Coast, in Ghana, which I grew to love. From Haifa we moved to the quiet and peace of Nazareth and then to Jerusalem. Jerusalem was anything but quiet. It was Eastertide. The hotels were crowded with tourists. Arabs were restless and were expected to demonstrate in force. In control were the Palestine Police, many of them recruited from the Black and Tans. They wore khaki drill, dark green puttees and topees with dark green puggarees. I have never seen civilians treated with such senseless brutality. On Easter morning, near the First Station of the Cross at the Convent of Notre Dame de Sion, I saw a group of Arabs being moved on roughly by the Palestine Police. One Arab resisted. A policeman reversed his rifle and hit the Arab in the mouth with the butt. Teeth and blood spat all over the place. I protested and was told to ——— off or I would get a dose of the same medicine. Soon I was traversing Kantara's 'shuffling sands' on my way to Cairo. Looking back from Kantara across the desert there came to mind a thought I have pondered often since, very often in these grim days of Israeli-Arab conflict. The corruption of the Ottoman Empire was not liquidated by Jewish hands nor by American nor Russian hands, but by the valour and sacrifice of the men of our race. It was they who bled and suffered at the Dardanelles, on the plains of Mesopotamia and in the thrust from Kantara which finally overthrew Turkish military might. And all without Jewish help. Indeed, when British troops first crossed the Canal and began their push to Gaza there were not six Jewish settlements in the whole of Palestine. I am persuaded, and profoundly, that Great Britain's influence as a World Power required and was sustained by her ability to maintain a dialogue with Islam. This ability has vanished and the world is the poorer. Yet we might have stayed, and at little cost, if in the early 'fifties, when Mohamed Neguib assumed power after the overthrow of Farouk, we had tried to understand what Egypt's revolution was all about and had refused to be obsessed by either the Balfour Declaration or the McMahon promises of 1915 and 1916.

I left Jerusalem with another N.C.O. on our way to Cairo. We had ridden the winding railway down to Lud to catch the main-line train from Haifa to Kantara. Arriving at Kantara North late in the evening, we had to clear the Egyptian Customs across the Canal and join another train running between Port Said and Cairo. Our train was crowded with American tourists bearing mountains of luggage and the Egyptian Customs officials demonstrated their feelings of loving-kindness towards the British Army by holding us until the last.

We had been told that on arrival in Cairo we should report to the Military Police post at the station while transport was arranged to take us to Abbassia because movements of soldiers in uniform were strictly controlled. Troops in uniform were allowed out of barracks only in pairs, and parties had to travel armed and by military transport. Once, in the House of Commons, I found myself involved in an exchange with an ex-Guards officer who, having served in Cairo at that time, seemed to find my account of life there much mistaken and, I think, misleading. He, of course, could wear civilian clothes when off duty, and found life was delightful; he was able to frequent fashionable areas without the surveillance of the Military

Police or the risk of being beaten up. For Tommy Atkins, however, condemned always to walk out in uniform, it was a life hemmed in by restrictions of all sorts. Whole areas were out of bounds and could not be entered at all. Other areas could be traversed only if we were travelling by tram and were accompanied by another soldier. Military Police were everywhere. The tensions were a hangover following the murder of the Sirdar in November, 1924.

During my stay in Cairo I tried hard to understand Egypt and Egyptian problems. My first shock was to discover my own massive ignorance about Egypt's enormous contribution to our victory in the 1914–18 war. I do not believe that if the British public had been aware of Egypt's sacrifice in men and money it would have acquiesced, against the advice of a great soldier, General Sir Reginald Wingate, in Curzon's refusal to consider independence for a faithful ally. The history of Britain's occupation of Egypt is a bad business. Every attempt by an Egyptian patriot to serve his people was frustrated by successive British Foreign Secretaries. Zaghlul Pasha, for example, had taken part in the Arabi Pasha revolt of 1882, which was suppressed at the battle of Tel-el-Kebir; in 1906 he became Minister of Education under Lord Cromer. Zaghlul expected in 1918 that Egypt would share in the fruits of victory since, in 1914, Britain had unilaterally declared Egypt to be a British Protectorate, and Zaghlul had won for Britain the support of the Egyptian masses. That was vital to us, Egypt being our main base in our struggle to defeat the Turks. Then, in 1918, the war over and won, Britain the Imperial Power committed to freedom for all Arabs turned its back on our war-time loyal supporters and wondered why Egypt's incipient nationalism became violently anti-British. When Zaghlul and two other leaders of the Wafd telegraphed the Peace Conference, opening in Paris, protesting against Curzon's decision, they were arrested and, on March 8, 1919, deported to Malta. Thus Britain took the first blundering, foolish steps towards driving Egypt into the arms of Soviet Russia. The Middle East of 1970 is the logical outcome of 1920 and after—from Curzon and Lloyd, Bevin and Eden, even to Michael Stewart.

My study of all this belonged to the future, but I formed strongly held opinions. One was that newspaper reports should never be regarded as prime evidence, especially in relation to foreign affairs. Most Foreign Correspondents live by the grace of the Press Officers of the Foreign Ministries, and their so-called objective reports are

Riding in Turkey, 1922

With Turkish
children, 1922

Baghdad, 1924

often little more than re-written hand-outs, frequently not even wholly re-written. Even more important is the tragic fact that the record of every British Foreign Secretary of modern times reveals the same fundamental lack of understanding of Middle Eastern affairs, often even about the geography of the area.

Only three Britons, in my judgment, have shown wisdom and courage in their handling of Middle East affairs: Wingate in the Sudan and as High Commissioner in Egypt, Allenby in Palestine and Harrington in Turkey. I think I would acclaim Allenby as the first among equals. He took a realistic look at the three conflicting and mutually destructive policies he inherited when he captured Jerusalem on December 9, 1917. Britain pledged herself to restore to the Arabs the integrity of their lands and to foster democratic governments therein. Britain committed herself to ceding Syria to France and, in the month before Allenby's great victory to which the Arabs had contributed mightily, Balfour promised Palestine to the Jews. Allenby gave a soldier's answer. He discharged his responsibilities by maintaining law and order and administering the territory on the basis of international law. This required as little change as possible in its existing form of government. He prohibited publication of the Balfour Declaration and insisted that only one flag should fly in Palestine, the Union Jack. He gave the politicians time to consult the wishes of local populations and to learn and reflect upon the facts of Middle East life. The politicians made waste of his victory. I often think in fancy of my three noble heroes in the Shade, and I hear them singing:

> 'We won the War—
> Whatever for?'

Chapter Four: Political Awareness

My years in Iraq and Egypt were lonely. Loneliness, certainly, was a factor in developing what I regard as significant facets of my personality. The soldiering side of me compelled mastery of my job and the need to give loyal service to the limit of my capacity, even to those superiors I did not respect. A different George Wigg, enthusiastic about racing and riding and swimming, came easily to terms with varying climatic conditions and enjoyed the friendship and life of a Sergeants' Mess. And there was yet another Wigg, valuing beyond price the privacy of his own bunk, where he could be alone with his books and his thoughts, and to whom this inner life was the most precious of all heaven-sent gifts.

The soldier required of me, the student, that I should read *The Official History of the Great War* and everything else I could lay my hands on about the organization of the Armed Forces. What fascinated me then, and still does, was the nuts and bolts side of Army life. My studies quickly brought me to grips with the problems which faced Haldane when he became Secretary of State for War in 1906. I came to understand the conditions leading to his creation of the Territorial Army. I appreciated the genius behind his 1914 mobilization plan, which enabled the British Expeditionary Force to land in France on August 9 and make contact with the enemy on August 22, to the intense surprise of the Kaiser's Generals. Maybe it was the potential politician in me who rejoiced in Haldane's success, despite the significant fact that the Government delayed mobilization because they did not want to interfere with the 1914 August Bank Holiday festivities!

Choosing a short reading list for those who would wish to appreciate the Haldane mobilization plan, I recommend the first chapters of three books: *The Official History of the Great War—Military Operations in France and Belgium;* General J. F. C. Fuller's *Memoirs of an Unconventional Soldier;* and Private Frank Richards's *Old Soldiers Never Die*—incomparably the best book I have read (and again and again!) about World War I. Organization, administration, quartering and supply were my basic interests in military affairs and the core of many of my speeches in the House of Commons. Neglect of these problems brought us near to defeat in both World Wars. In my view the cause of neglect was the ossified class structure of British society. The study of supply and quartering problems were not subjects which could be expected to interest gentlemen! I cite our ablest living military analyst, Correlli Barnett, in *The Desert Generals*:

> It is generally true that an army is an extension of society; military disaster is often national decline exposed by the violence of a battle. Examples are Imperial Russia and Austria-Hungary in the First World War, France in the Second. Any army thus reflects in sharp focus the social structure, the state of technological progress and the creative vigour of a society. The opposing armies at Crecy illustrate this general rule. However, the British Army in the Second World War is an exception, perhaps the only one in history. Although the army of a twentieth-century social democracy and a first-class industrial power, it was nevertheless spiritually a peasant levy led by the gentry and aristocracy. Its habits of mind and work, its mental and emotional life were those of the social order based on birth and lands that had passed from supremacy in the national life by the end of the nineteenth century.*

Study of the class structure of the Army by an N.C.O. was unheard of in my time. Had it become known it would have been regarded as subversive. My study evoked admiration for the courage and integrity of the Regular Officer class and wonder at its stupidity. By the early 'twenties I was convinced that, in the event of a Second World War, the gap between the peasantry and their equipment would be exposed as an out-dated, self-defeating sham. That truth loomed fearsomely over the horizon in 1940.

My 'dangerous' reading was not confined to military matters. I discovered R. C. K. Ensor's *Modern Socialism* which enlarged my political thinking, especially in its analysis of the programmes of European Socialists, always more theoretically minded than their British counterparts. Leaders like Karl Kautsky and Wilhelm

* Correlli Barnett, *The Desert Generals* (William Kimber 1960).

Leibnecht in Germany, and Jean Jaurès and Alexandre Millerand in France, as I understood them, were all intent upon maintaining the social solidarity of their countries despite the destructive class divisions created by the rise of Capitalism. All argued, too, that in the Europe of their day social solidarity was an essential element in national defence.

Equally provocative, although not so new to me, was Ensor's selection of comments on Marxism, the economic and social ideas of which have been betrayed, and savagely, by Communist dictatorships. Division of labour, the basis of modern production, is a social, co-operative process resulting in an ever-increasing output of goods and services. The social process, however, stops dead at the point of distribution; there, output becomes the subject of private capitalist appropriation. The application of science and technology to industry does not replace division of labour. On the contrary, it magnifies the social act of production and intensifies the economic inequity and social iniquity of maldistribution. The incompatibility between social production and capitalistic appropriation, in the words of Marx's most intimate collaborator, Engels, completes the now historic cleavage 'between the means of production concentrated in the hands of capitalists on the one side and the producers reduced to possessing nothing but their labour power on the other. The contradiction between social production and capitalistic appropriation appeared as *an opposition between proletariat and bourgeoisie.*' The late Lord Baldwin, although not the first Tory Prime Minister to recognize the conflict between the Two Nations as the basic problem of modern politics, endorsed the Marxian view of its origins in his oft-quoted comment: 'The Conservatives cannot talk of class war. They started it.'

For me, recognition of the existence of class war aroused no desire to wage it. My aim was, and is, to abolish it; and central to this aim is the preservation and political expression of Britain's social solidarity. Social solidarity enabled England to challenge the dictatorship of kings. Down the centuries it secured the physical and political integrity of our island home. It is the basis of our democracy which, alone, can secure to every man the right and responsibility to live his own life in his own way subject to respect for the law of the group. The legal reformer in Britain, irrespective of the political label he has worn, has always held an honoured place because he has enhanced the quality and equity of the democratic heritage we are all entitled to share. This principle of sharing should seek to extend to every citizen, especially in education where the social life of every citizen begins, the equal opportunity to develop his capacity to the full. The concern that the individual shall have freedom to develop his special individual talents to the full, to his own and to the ultimate advantage of society, is the responsibility of us all. This is my socialist faith.

I am persuaded also about two principles of political action. It is a denigration, even a denial, of Marxism—as Engels averred—to confuse economic facts and theories with ethical values and to found lasting spiritual conceptions upon any economic system which, by its very nature, must be under constant pressure of change. I believe, also, that freedom of thought and human dignity cannot flourish in the withering atmosphere of dictatorship, whether Communist, Fascist or Capitalist. This is my democratic faith.

My reading of Ensor led to rejection of the idea of Soldiers' and Workers' Councils, then a subject of Communist propaganda. At best, the conception was a delusion. At worst, it was a political plot to deliver the State into the hands of a dictatorship. The obvious purpose was to convert dissatisfaction with the Army into disaffection within the Army. This policy, had it succeeded, might have led to the abolition of Parliamentary democracy and brought into being the exercise of autocratic powers such as those used by despotic Monarchs three hundred or more years ago.

The British Army developed through the centuries, and especially during the seventeenth century, as a servant of our unfolding democracy, an instrument, like the police, of the democratically-elected civil power. The soldier's tradition is to put his duty to those he serves before himself. Queen's Regulations provide for the enlistment and training of the soldier as a soldier. The Army Act, as revised by the 1952 Select Committee, gave modern expression to a basic fact too often overlooked: when a man becomes a soldier enlistment does not diminish his status as a citizen. He retains that, and adds an additional duty—that of a soldier. My studies led me to identify the Army with the community as a whole, and to think in terms of integrating the individual soldier fully with the community to which, some day, he must return. Such a policy would close the gap between officers and other ranks. It would make the education of the soldier as a soldier and as a man one piece, and would result in making the Army a career of talent and a stepping stone to a worthwhile job in civilian life. I was fascinated to discover that Army reformers were trainers and educationalists, from Sir John Moore, who established the Light Division and a system of training which eventually defeated Napoleon, to Field Marshal Montgomery who, above all, was a great trainer of men and armies. The basic idea, common to all Army reformers was that to train men you must treat them like soldiers and like men—you must, in short, find the common touch and develop it, and combine it with respect for discipline and for the man himself.

This idea of the Army assuming the responsibility for the nation's manhood entrusted to its care seems only to emerge in time of war. At the end of the 1914–18 War, Lord Gorell in his *Education in the Army* gave an account of the responsibilities imposed upon the military authorities by the sheer pressure of events. The concept of a man being able to find himself within the ranks of a discipline which he respects, and which respects him, inspired men like William Cobbett, Robert Blatchford and Edgar Wallace, all of whom served in the ranks of the Regular Army with great advantage to themselves. It became fundamental to my own thinking about defence, and led me to the belief that some form of national service is an essential part of our democracy.

National Service as a principle of Socialist action has a respectable place in Socialist literature, notably in the works of G. D. H. Cole, and the Irish poet 'A.E.' (George W. Russell). I believe, even more strongly today than when I first began to think along these lines, that our society would be the better if all our young people, girls as well as boys, were required to undergo some form of full-time national service. I do not argue that such service should necessarily be military in character. But it would be the means whereby our young people would live for a time during their most formative years in obedience to rules that civilized life in a community requires. I also now believe that such a concept has become specially important for present day society, and that politicians, aided by their military advisers, have broken the matrix which might have made it possible. Today, another aspect of the problem arises. Advocates of our entry into the Common Market forget that all the countries of N.A.T.O. except Canada and ourselves have some form of compulsory military service. Do we really expect the French, the Germans or the Dutch to welcome us into a defence system where their young men undergo full-time service and ours do none? Will the

Americans continue to draft their young men to defend Europe while our young men throw ball-bearings under the hooves of police horses in Grosvenor Square in protest against American policy?

Another important influence on my thinking at this time was the Report of the Ministry of Reconstruction Committee on Education in the Army, (Cmd 321) published in 1919. The Committee noted the German declaration that it was their schoolmasters who had won the wars of 1864, 1866 and 1870, and commented: 'They certainly showed in this war what formidable strength can be produced by a universal scientific systematic instruction resulting in an extraordinary unanimity of national aim and an undeniable capacity of service for an ideal.' This confirmed my growing belief that the education of the soldier as a man was as vitally important as his training as a soldier. Indeed, the general education of the man and his training as a soldier are inseparable, and I cast my mind back in an endeavour to understand what happened.

The early days of World War I had disclosed grave weaknesses because the Armed Forces were not responsive enough to the ever-changing organization and logistics of defence. The business of having the right force with the right supplies and equipment at the right place at the right time was not looked at as a whole problem until the arrival of Haldane. With the outstanding exception of Haldane, few Ministers concerned with defence have shown more than the vaguest understanding of the relation between economic organization, technology and military operations. Few soldiers, and fewer politicians were, or are, capable of exercising the foresight which an intelligent study of defence organization and logistics might be expected to stimulate. In times of crisis politicians call for courage and condemn cowardice both, in this context, drug words obscuring political failure to provide for the country's defence needs. And always, the 'Poor Bloody Infantry' pay in blood for political folly and neglect.

In 1914, the horse, long since superseded by mechanized transport, was still held in reverence by class-conscious Army leaders who dreamed, right up till the Armistice, of the break-through and the use of Cavalry to finish the job. From 1914 onwards, the obvious need was for lorries and drivers. When this need was recognized, there were some lorries but few drivers. A bid to get drivers of mechanised vehicles to join the Army Service Corps at six shillings a day caused bitterness. The A.S.C. driver living in moderately comfortable conditions with three meals a day, was drawing his six shillings whereas the Infantry received one shilling a day. General Monash, an outstanding General of World War I, when asked what was the difference between his Australians and the British soldier, replied 'Five bob a day'. That put the problem in its starkest form.

When the War ended, and before efforts to kill off the Tank Corps had gathered momentum, a reorganization of pay was undertaken. Army Order 325, of 1919, introduced rates of pay in two categories: normal and tradesmen's rates of pay. To the normal rate was added proficiency pay to qualify for which a soldier had to have at least one year's service and possess a Second Class Certificate of Education. N.C.O.s could be promoted to Warrant Officers only if they possessed a First Class Certificate of Education. Thus the anomalies of the wartime pay structure and the weaknesses in the Army's efforts to handle the training-cum-education programme were joined in a rationalized system of rates of pay, and the Army Educational Corps came into being. The Old Guard, now freed from the discipline of defeats in the field with their appalling casualty lists, were thinking of reorganizing the Regular Army in terms that would bring the serviceman back under the control of barrack discipline and, once again, teach him only to be a soldier. In the result, the education of the soldier, which should have been made the responsibility of the Adjutant General, became a General Staff matter. Successive Directors of Military Training squeezed the life out of Army education, and military training was confined more and more in a strait-jacket prescribed by 'duly constituted military authority'.

My cogitations and reflections on Army organization and the place of the soldier in society came to an abrupt halt when I arrived in Egypt. There it was barrack-room soldiering with a vengeance. I hated it. I was stationed at Abbassia on the outskirts of Cairo. It was a large cantonment surrounded by a barbed-wire fence to keep out Egyptian loose-wallahs. The fence kept out strays but not those on the steal. Outside Abbassia we could walk-out only in uniform and in pairs. Walking-out in civilian clothes was a privilege for Warrant Officers. One exception to this rule was that we could go by tram to Heliopolis, which included the Heliopolis racecourse. That was where my luck held. An ex-R.A.F. friend with whom I served in Baghdad was working for Imperial Airways and had a flat near Heliopolis. I left my civilian clothes with him and on my way to Heliopolis or Gezirah racecourses I would call at his flat and complete the journey in 'civvies'. Happily, a Command Order was published permitted Sergeants and above to wear civilian clothes when off duty, so my subterfuge became unnecessary. Once again I could indulge my three-fold existence. In barracks I did my duty; off duty I was a regular member of the large Sergeants' Mess where life was pleasant but not very intellectual. And I could read and browse alone, go to the museums and old places, and speculate on what might have been achieved if there had been real British-Egyptian friendship.

Alas, Britain's contribution to that friendship was a theatrical High Commissioner, Sir George (later Lord) Lloyd. The story was told that the Prince of Wales had enjoyed himself greatly when visiting Cairo because, as he was said to have remarked to Lloyd, 'You gave me an inkling of how royalty really lives'. I shall never forget a Searchlight Tattoo staged at Gezirah during the Lloyd régime. It ended with a set piece in which British troops attacked Egyptians and, of course, made mincemeat of them. This performance was seen by thousands of Egyptians of all sections of society. Anything more likely to inflame hostility against the British could not have been imagined. The entire show was a vulgar expression of jingoistic insensitivity.

Lloyd was no hero to the British Army in Egypt. His conduct created an atmosphere of tension with its under-tow of possible civilian disturbance. Many threw their hats in the air when the Labour Foreign Secretary, Arthur Henderson, sacked him and I still find pleasure in reading how 'Uncle Arthur' knocked out Lloyd's fire-eating friend, Winston Churchill, in the House of Commons debate on July 26, 1929. Churchill opened his case for Lloyd by warning Henderson that he 'must begin by learning that he is not going to intimidate me'. Churchill then went on to assert that the Foreign Secretary told Lloyd he knew the latter had seen Churchill because 'he [Henderson] took steps to find out who it was that he [Lloyd] went to see'. This suggestion of shadowing Lloyd and spying on a high official of the Crown raised a bogey which Churchill pursued with ardour. Henderson denied he had made any such statement and to Churchill's thundering demand, 'Perhaps the Rt. Hon. Gentleman will say how it was that he knew,' answered mildly: 'If the Rt. Hon. Gentleman has got himself into a difficulty I am not going to get him out.' The enraged Churchill, now shifting his ground, went in, as he thought, for the kill. 'The Foreign Secretary', he thundered, 'chose to bring up in his great position as Secretary of State for Foreign Affairs, an interview which had taken place between two private persons and he used that for the purpose of influencing the debate. Therefore, in view of that, may I not ask him on what he based that statement? It was quite true, but on what did he base that statement?' 'Uncle Arthur' eyed the frothing Churchill calmly and applied the stiletto. 'I based it', he informed the House, 'on the statement of Lord Lloyd, who told me that he had "seen Mr Churchill".'

On my first night in Abbassia an old friend, 'Smudger' Smith, a Regular of pre-war days who had gone through the retirement from Mons in 1914 back to Le Cateau in 1918, warned me: 'Wiggy, this ain't the Army we used to know. Most of the officers are war-time promotions with no feeling for Army tradition. The place is run on King's Regulations interpreted to suit them. We have no privileges. We are treated like dirt. The bastards can do anything they want with you except put you in the family way.' 'Only if you let them, Smudger,' I replied, and it was not long before I had to prove my point by action.

I soon found myself up against authority. On routine inoculation I produced my A.B.64 showing I had refused a bubonic plague inoculation in Baghdad. I was preparing to have the T.A.B. inoculation, had taken off my tunic and bared my arm when the medical officer cursed me roundly, adding: 'You refused inoculation in Baghdad; don't try that game here.' I said: 'No, Sir,' pulled down my sleeve and donned my tunic. 'What are you doing?' he asked. 'I am refusing the T.A.B. inoculation, Sir.' The poor man almost had a heart attack. 'This is insubordination. You are on a charge.' In due course I was marched in front of a Major with a Scottish name, I think MacCrindle. The troops called him Hackney Mac. He wore field boots and could just about see over the top of them. After being wheeled in, stormed at and bullied, I said quietly, but firmly, 'I will not be inoculated'. I was forbidden to sleep in the barrack room as it was said that I might contaminate decent people. For months I slept on the verandah; it was very pleasant.

Another clash came a few days later. A Command Order announced that returning troopships, having delivered reinforcements to Shanghai, had passages available for troops stationed in Egypt to go on leave to the United Kingdom. The condition was that men granted leave must deposit the cost of their return fare. My financial state was modest but sound. I was in credit at banks in Basingstoke and Abbassia, and I had the Egyptian equivalent of thirty pounds in my pocket. So I made a written application for leave. Hackney Mac summoned me. He expressed amazement that I should dare to apply for leave when I had only just arrived in Egypt. He suggested I was trying to attract attention to myself and advised me to withdraw my application. 'No, sir,' I answered. 'The Command Order invites applications. With respect I have been overseas since 1922.' I went on to explain that I had served in Turkey and Iraq and troops serving in Iraq usually returned home after two years. For a reason I did not appreciate I had been sent to Egypt. Hackney Mac refused to listen. 'You are making a fool of yourself,' he bawled. 'I shall, of course, forward your application, but I shan't recommend it. That means you won't get leave. This is the second time you have rejected my advice. Watch out!'

The application was forwarded to Headquarters for decision by a Colonel whose Sergeant-Major had served with me in Aldershot, and to whom I told my story. Two days later Hackney Mac announced my leave had been approved and asked for my ten pounds passage money. He then questioned me about how and where I got it, and ordered me to be medically examined at the Citadel. His hope, no doubt, was that at the Citadel Military Hospital my A.B.64 would be inspected and in revenge for my refusal to be inoculated it would be found I had contracted some disease which would prevent my embarkation. With a Sergeant Gold as escort I set off for the Citadel. We called at British Military Headquarters at the Eden Palace Hotel in the centre of Cairo. There we encountered a Captain Holmes who said, 'I understand you are going on leave, what are you doing here?' I answered that Sergeant Gold had been ordered to call at H.Q. on our way to the Citadel. The Medical Officer who saw me expressed surprise that I should have been sent to the Citadel for a formal medical embarkation examination. Nobody asked to see my A.B.64. I was passed fit.

Immediately we returned to Abbassia I was ordered to appear before Hackney Mac—and the plot uncovered itself. 'You won't be going to England,' he crowed. 'You are under arrest for making a false statement to an officer. You told Captain Holmes you had been sent to the Eden Palace Hotel when you had been sent to the Citadel. You will be brought before me on Monday, and I shall remand you to the Commanding Officer.' My blood boiled at the trick to keep me from sailing on the *Derbyshire* next morning, a Sunday—and my wits sharpened. I asked to be excused and said: 'I want to go to Barclay's Dominion Bank to withdraw the balance of money necessary to purchase my discharge and pay my passage. When my case has been disposed of I shall purchase my discharge. Whatever happens I am going to England.'

A few minutes after leaving him I was joined by the Sergeant-Major who chuckled, 'You have a bloody nerve. Give me your ten pounds return passage money and watch out when you return from leave.' I handed over the money with a request to see Hackney Mac again. He thought he had finished with me but I had a rod in pickle for him. I thanked him for approving my leave, told him I had deposited the passage money and wanted a receipt, and requested an advance of sixty-one days pay and ration money. The pompous midget said he didn't know what I was talking about. I invited him to read the Article to the Royal Warrant on Pay Advances to N.C.O.s. It entitled an N.C.O. going on leave to the U.K. to an advance of sixty-one days pay and ration allowance. Now almost demented, Hackney Mac yelled, 'I haven't got the money and the banks are closed. It will be sent on to you.' 'With respect, Sir,' I countered, 'the regulations say the payment should be made in advance. If I cannot have it before I go, you won't object if I make it a cause of complaint on my return?' I was paid in full and given a receipt for my passage money. And I walked aboard the *Derbyshire* at Port Said on a beautiful Sunday morning.

Three months in England included backing the winner of the Stewards' Cup, *Priory Park,* which followed a nice tickle for me in the first race at Goodwood. Johnny Dines rode the winner, *Gallopade,* owned by Sir Walter Gilbey. On the way to the course I met Johnny, whom I knew slightly, and he told me he had a chance so I had ten shillings each way at twenty to one. Very sweet!

Returning to Egypt in the autumn, I soon discovered I was in for a warm time. I was sent to Khartoum, then to El Obeid, an unpleasant place. Liking Khartoum, I applied to be seconded to the Sudan Defence Force. The application was rejected, presumably as a rebuff, and I was ordered to the Canal and Cyprus. I enjoyed my trips. They enabled me to escape from Abbassia.

Back there in December, lists were passed round the Mess to ascertain those wishing to attend the Families' Christmas Party. All wanted to attend except two—Dawes, an ex-Royal Garrison Artillery man, and myself. Dawes was not interested in women and children and hated the clatter of it all; I just did not want to go. Hackney Mac accused us of engaging in an Act of Mutiny! It was all of a piece with my behaviour over inoculations and leave to England. My offer, that if my presence would give pleasure to anyone I would go, was regarded as a final piece of insubordination. I was told I would get no meals in the Mess on Christmas Day nor on Boxing Day, the day of the party. On those two days I went to the Y.M.C.A., fed on bacon and eggs and large mugs of tea and—to the surprise of the manager—asked for a receipt. When the pay accounts came round for signature I was charged a full month's messing, and refused to sign. I pointed out to Hackney Mac that I had had no rations on either Christmas Day or on Boxing Day and produced bills for my meals at the Y.M.C.A. I claimed two days ration allowance and exemption from messing deduction for those days. He stormed and raved and chased me away, but in the end I won. I was granted two days leave with ration allowance; the messing charges were withdrawn.

Hackney Mac's treatment of me was not typical. He, no doubt, thought I was a bit odd. Many soldiers were treated by the Hackney Macs as I was, but there were not many of his type about. I regarded his conduct, and his kind, as an affront to the Army, and I thought I was doing the right thing by standing up to him. The trouble was I got to like being the odd man out and it was as well that I returned to the United Kingdom to make a fresh start at the end of 1928.

I was posted to London and married a girl I had known most of my life. We experienced many of the miseries of living in badly-equipped lodgings as weekly tenants who could be evicted when somebody able to offer a higher rent turned up. I was in a safe job, and luckier than most tenants; my wife could have gone home to her relatives and I could have slept in barracks. First-hand experience of 'rooming' conditions made me sympathetic to house hunters who, in after years, sought my help as an M.P. It also filled me with contempt for well-breeched politicians who think the housing problem can be solved by leaving everything to the pricing system. How cruelly that system operated, I often thought, for the poor devil on the dole. My form of protest was to work harder for the Labour Party. I canvassed for the then new *Daily Herald* which enshrined our Socialist faith. We enlisted readers by canvassing with offers of free gifts and insurance rights, and Odhams Press paid a fee to the local Labour Party for every new reader. We had a Labour

Government. My friends and I gloried in the hope that the *Daily Herald* would hold the Capitalist Press at bay. What mugs we were! When I looked at the *Daily Herald* and its successor the *Sun* I often asked myself, 'Did I really spend time, energy and enthusiasm to protect that?'—a printing job to reduce Odhams' overheads and increase the profit on its Sunday publication, the *People*.

We left London for Canterbury in the middle of 1930. I regretted the posting. Although we could now live in married quarters, I missed the excitement and opportunities of life in London. Having no friends I made a bee-line for the local library housed in the Beaney Institute, so called in memory of a doctor who emigrated to Australia and left ten thousand pounds as a contribution towards the cost of the library building. The librarian, Henry Thomas Mead, was an erudite, kindly man; nothing was too much trouble for him. His deputy, Leonard Butcher, cast in the same mould, aided my efforts in what was to become a very constructive period in my life. I studied the Luddite Movement by reading about it in the files of old newspapers and thus became knowledgeable about the history of Canterbury and East Kent. What a joy that was! I discovered the glories of the Cathedral and began the enjoyment of some great friendships.

There was Charlie Scriven, who had served in the 16th Lancers. Scriven, married, unemployed and a member of the Labour Party, was seeking to come to grips with the forces that prevented him from earning a living. I met Miss Amy Carter, who had been mathematics mistress at the Simon Langton School, one of the most widely read persons I have ever known. She had been an enthusiastic, non-militant supporter of the Suffragette Movement and although her earlier political loyalties had been to the Liberal Party she was now enthusiastic in her belief in Socialism. Miss Carter knew the Cathedral like the back of her hand and she could make that knowledge live. Scriven introduced me to Frank Harbottle, a Northumberland miner who sought employment in the Kent coal-fields only to find that nobody wanted a North Country militant. So Harbottle was on the dole and subject to the Means Test. In those days a man on the Means Test had to do test work. Harbottle made a practice of presenting himself to perform his menial task wearing spats and armed with a profound knowledge of the law, ready to pounce on any official who sought to infringe his legal rights. He was a barrack-room lawyer fighting the cause of the Army of the Damned—our millions of unemployed. I shared with these fine people the conviction that our society was unjust and inefficient and was heading for economic depression and war.

A group I joined met weekly at the Beaney Institute. In the absence of a tutor each person in turn read an extract from one of G. D. H. Cole's many books and then opened a discussion on the subject of his reading. These discussions were always exciting. The group had a link, which we all wanted to strengthen, with the Workers' Educational Association. We approached the Oxford University Delegacy for Extra-Mural Studies and, in the absence of a volunteer, I was press-ganged in association with Miss Eva Blunson, a local school teacher, into becoming Group Secretary of a University Extension Course. Our chairman was Sir Anton Bertram, former Chief Justice of Ceylon. Another member was the then Bishop of Dover who had a reputation as a powerful preacher. We asked the Oxford Delegacy for a lecturer on modern international and economic problems and they sent us Mr A. T. D'Eye, a Delegacy Staff Tutor. The course started in the Autumn of 1931 at the height of the economic blizzard and attracted many students. D'Eye became my hero and great friend. A former Post Office worker who had served in World War I, he gained an Extra-Mural Scholarship to Balliol, obtained a degree in Philosophy, Politics and Economics, and returned to his beloved Kent where he now enjoys retirement but still lectures and conducts tutorials. No man has done more to widen the horizons and enrich the lives of his fellow men than D'Eye. He and I were estranged for a time when the War separated us and neither quite understood the changes the years had wrought in the other; today we are close friends again.

D'Eye's lectures produced a profound change in my outlook on life. I had never thought of myself as being intellectually equal with those regarded as my 'betters'. I had never even tried to assess my intellectual qualities against those of my officers in the Army. D'Eye's teaching altered all that. Each lecture was followed by questions and discussion. Thereafter a smaller group stayed on and, for them, D'Eye set an essay subject and suggested books for more intensive study. At the end of the course an examination was held for which the Oxford Delegacy required at least a dozen entrants. As a member of this inner group I wrote essays, read avidly, but did not enter the examination until it was found we were short of the requisite dozen. So I made up the number. To my astonishment I won the prize—an edition of Bernard Shaw's works. The entrants included intellectuals whom I admired greatly and persons of academic attainment, including the Bishop! Thus I awoke to the possibility that, if I studied hard enough, my mind could be made capable of doing battle with my class superiors and not always losing. Harbottle helped me over the immediate hurdles. He was positive that working-class men and women could take on the possessing class. I differed from him on only one fundamental political issue. He advocated the violent overthrow of the capitalistic system. I believed the social solidarity of the British people would enable us to achieve a peaceful, democratic revolution.

The Labour College, run by the National Council of Labour Colleges, of which Harbottle was a product—he was a student with Nye Bevan—captured some of the best minds in the Labour Movement and split the Trade Union Movement—tragically and disastrously in my view—on whether or not education should be purposive and biassed. For our dogma-dominated upper-class teaching it sought to substitute a dogma of social change. The Master of Balliol, A. D. Lindsay, exposed this fundamental heresy in his study of the German Social Democrats. That mighty Movement swallowed the Marxian Materialistic Conception of History, which implied that the forces of history were on the side of the revolutionary masses, as a principle beyond challenge of thought and argument. It forgot the teachings of its modern leaders on the importance of social solidarity; and it collapsed pitifully when faced with the brutal, materialistic onslaught of Hitlerism.

In a lesser degree Labour College teaching led many a British trade unionist into the same *cul de sac*. All the N.C.L.C. students I met during my political life, sustained by faith in the 'forces of history', tended to put the power of words above the need for understanding and organization. The brighter they were the more they were beguiled by the 'bitch goddess' of oratory. Nye Bevan became their star performer. A superb public speaker, Nye was master of any audience. His real test came in his bid for leadership of the Parliamentary Labour Party, the peak of his personal battle for power. He was an 'also ran'. How I wish men like Harbottle and Bevan had gone to Oxford. There, revolutionary zeal based upon the Marxian critique might have been harnessed to intellectual discipline and an acceptance of responsibility. The result might well have been the realization of my dreams of the rise of an effective reforming Movement during the 1930s when Tory politicians by and large had lost their nerve, their confidence in Capitalism, and—some of them—their sense of patriotism.

Meantime, tutors like A. T. D'Eye and public figures like Archbishop Temple, Professor Tawney, James Mallon of Toynbee Hall, A. D. Lindsay and many others fought the more fundamental battle for objective thinking and working class opportunity *inside* the Universities. Readers and tutors drew strength and direction from the Tutorial Classes Committee, part of the Oxford Delegacy for Extra-Mural Studies, and its stalwart, saintly secretary, Edward Stewart Cartwright. 'E.S.', diffident and dedicated, lived for the ideal of an England made homogeneous and great by, to quote him, 'the seeping through of responsibility based on knowledge.' One of my ambitions, which this self-effacing man would have deplored, was to have his work recognized by the inclusion of his name in an Honours List. A democracy as mature as 'E.S.' wished for England would insist upon honouring men of his stature.

Realization of all we owed to these great men came in 1940 on a Sunday following the fall of France. My Army experience made me aware of the dangers the country faced under its inept political and military leadership and I was full of foreboding. Over the radio a quiet, familiar voice began to speak. Sandy Lindsay, in a series of talks entitled *I Believe in Democracy*, was expressing the faith which lifts men nearer to the angels and raises democracy from a political expression to a spiritual experience. Like many others, I was refreshed and strengthened in my faith and determination that the British people would survive.

My mental turmoil in the early 'thirties made me politically active. Although still serving, I joined the local Labour Party. I enjoyed the Dr Jekyll and Mr Hyde role of professional soldier and part-time political organizer, and I worked hard for Canterbury's Labour candidate in the 1931 election. We failed, but the dedication of the Kent people and Paul Winterton's fine campaign as candidate enabled us to increase the Labour vote. That, in 1931, was quite something. This experience widened my horizons. George Dexter, District Secretary of the South East District of the W.E.A., suggested I should become an honorary Area Organizer for Kent. The post carried an allowance of ten pounds a year which was anything but expense account living; I travelled all over East Kent, often with Charlie Scriven, by train, by bus, and on my two feet, to open up classes and discussion groups. Well-known personalities were attracted to the area to lecture at weekend schools. In 1932, in Canterbury, R. H. S. Crossman gave what I believe was his first W.E.A. weekend school lecture. Hugh Gaitskell, Parliamentary Labour candidate for Chatham, was another visitor. On one journey together he and I discussed the approaches to Socialism then being debated vigorously within the Labour Movement. Gaitskell was as passionately reformist as he was anti-Marxist. My impression was that he looked to the State to provide the dynamic of social change whereas my own inspiration came from Sandy Lindsay's *The Essentials of Democracy*, in which he argued that Hobbes and Locke marked the great divide in politics from the seventeenth century down to the present day. Like Lindsay I was, and am a disciple of Locke, who bequeathed to the English people a philosophy of democracy and unity which has become characteristic of the English way of life.

In those days Alfred Leslie Rowse, another visitor to East Kent, seemed to possess the qualities we looked for in a Labour leader. He was a Labour Candidate at the 1931 General Election, during which he repudiated Ramsay McDonald and avowed himself a follower of Herbert Morrison. Rowse revealed attractive gifts of personality spiced with an intellectual arrogance which, we hoped, time would temper. Unfortunately, he was dogged by ill health and retreated from politics into the rarefied atmosphere of All Souls'. He has drifted politically from 1931, a process which seems to have become permanent.

These were, indeed, wonderful years in Canterbury. Our three daughters, Cecilia, Audrey and Maureen were born there. To the happiness of home life there was added experience that deepened my political thought and purpose. I learned anew the value of the discipline of well-directed study and the equally important power of discussion and debate in developing the democratic idea. *There* is the real beginning of political community life, the inspiration that translates ideas into action, the dynamic of social progress. Party politics are either a continuing voluntary educative process or an exercise in pursuit of personal and, often, anti-social interests. Here and now, what is called 'the generation gap' threatens the homogeneity of our society because, as I see it, although all three Parties accept democracy as their ideal none is adequately fulfilling the educational function which the early Labour pioneers accepted as their essential task. Among modern political leaders only Lord Butler trod the path blazed by the early Socialists. His vision of a Conservative Party educating itself in order to educate the nation into understanding and acceptance of Conservative aims rejuvenated his Party after its crushing defeat in 1945. The true task of political leadership today is to induce the adult population to become amenable to, because it is capable of understanding, the impact upon society of new thought flowing from our ever-growing resources of knowledge. The education of the adult population is the British way to change.

Among the fringe benefits of my job was contact with outstanding personalities interested in the W.E.A. The Rev. R. H. L. Sheppard, whose pioneering religious broadcasts from St Martin's-in-the-Fields had made him famous, was Dean of Canterbury. Sheppard's hatred of war, expressed in his 'We say No' campaign out of which the Peace Pledge Union grew, was so deeply personal that it seemed sometimes he had lost all hope for human happiness. Yet his expression of faith was always compelling in its clarity. I still find myself reading R. Ellis Roberts's *Life of Dick Sheppard* in order to renew my own belief in the cleansing, uplifting power of human love.

Sheppard's successor as Dean was the Rev. Hewlett Johnson. Tall, handsome, extrovert and utterly simple, the 'Red Dean' was a trained engineer induced to study Social Credit by Major C. H. Douglas who, in World War I, developed the port of Richborough. The Dean had been chairman of the Monetary Reform League in Manchester. When he came to Canterbury he talked eagerly, in public and in private, about Social Credit. By 1938 his faith in the Douglas theory had all but vanished. He brought to his clerical duties a love of humanity and simplicity of mind and he subscribed with absolute conviction to the idea that Social Credit was the be-all and end-all of political reform. He embraced the Communist philosophy by inadvertence.

Lindsay was visiting Canterbury in 1933 and, as W.E.A. Area Organizer, I asked the Dean whether a W.E.A. lecture could be held in his garden. The Dean was delighted and offered to provide tea if the students would help his man, Fred, with the washing up. Lindsay talked as only he could to students who afterwards listened to the Dean's enthralling account of life as an engineer, his conversion to Social Credit, and his belief in Christianity and life hereafter. At such student rallies the Dean met D'Eye and a friendship grew between two good men who saw in Communist Russia a great liberative Movement. They saw no ill because to both of them evil things were incomprehensible. I remember the Dean saying to me: 'It does not matter whether you call yourself a Christian or not, or whether Russia calls herself Christian. Judgments are formed not on what men or nations say, but on what they do. If a man or nation seeks to help the poor and weak he, the individual, or the nation, is doing Christ's work.' This may have been bad theology; I don't know. Certainly, to my unlettered mind there were dangers in the Dean's next words: 'If they are doing Christ's work they are Christians.' That, at any rate, was not a sound basis for political judgment; but the Dean was not a politician. He was, I repeat, a simple man, and simple men often get pretty rough handling from their fellow Christians.

Once, when a fire broke out in old property and rendered some people homeless, the Dean housed all he could in the Precincts of the Cathedral. This kindly action only added venom to the vicious personal criticism invariably meted out to him in all his works. He had the imagination of a poet and, when preaching or talking, he built word pictures. He was not a Communist. Had he himself been asked to sum up in a sentence his controversial books on Russia and China, I think he would have paraphrased Julius Caesar's announcement after the Pontic campaign: 'I came, I saw, I *was* conquered,' and for reasons which he saw as absolute truth. Nothing can chill my heart-warming memories of Hewlett Johnson's generosity of spirit. If the Church of England today possessed a thousand or even a hundred Hewlett Johnsons it would not be what it is now, almost leaderless and largely ignored.

My voluntary work did not deflect me from my interests as a student. D'Eye encouraged me to apply for an Oxford Extra-Mural Scholarship. Of course, the prospect of going to Oxford and reading for a degree was exciting. My responsibilities to wife and family, however, had a prior claim, and I felt I might find myself out of my depth. In the event, the prospect went cold. It was renewed on my posting to York in 1935. By then I had decided that Oxford was not for me and I was seeking an opportunity to satisfy my own unfulfilled hopes in another way. A young soldier, Noel Fish, son of a Yorkshire miner, who had joined the Army as an alternative to going into the pit, was an eager, able W.E.A. student. When the war was over I urged him to apply for an Extra-Mural Scholarship on the basis of a paper he had written about the Nigerian Development Plan. He went to Balliol, obtained a Second Class Honours degree in

Modern Greats and, subsequently, entered the Civil Service. When I became a Minister I asked that he be appointed my Private Secretary, but Civil Service rules did not permit his transference from the job he was doing.

Fish's success indicated that the pre-war Regular Army contained men who, given the chance, would have made first class officers. I felt too that Britain possessed tremendous resources of human skill which, because of the class nature of society, we had never begun to tap: and this is still true, although to a lesser extent. As a nation we are drawing off talent earlier in life, and forgetting that education is a process starting in the cradle and ending only in the grave. Failure to recognize this fact is depriving the community of the benefits of vast human talent. Thus we are very short, everywhere, of that essential element, good non-commissioned officers. Those who have ability, irrespective of birth, have no excuse—as there was excuse in my day—for not developing their abilities to the full. The wastage lies with the remainder. They are left to chance. The ambitious and self-seeking will find what they want. The not-so-ambitious, the vast majority, will start to climb the ladder only if they are pushed. The facilities are there. What is lacking is the organization to do the seeking out and the driving of the adult student to the place where he can fulfil his educational potential.

As is only to be expected, the role of the W.E.A. has changed. Folk who once attended tutorial classes in search of the 'Holy Grail' now go on under their own steam to gain their Honours degrees and their Ph.D.s. The social urge stemming from denial of opportunity has been weakened and the W.E.A.'s missionary role has, therefore, changed.

Scriven and I, urged on by D'Eye, tramped the roads of East Kent because we believed in education as a key unlocking the door to social advance. That door is now wide open, but the need for new missionaries, more sophisticated, more professional, certainly less brash than we were, is greater than ever before. The W.E.A. has become more concerned with providing cultural activities for those who seek them than in helping those who want to change our society. Local Education Authorities, however, offer similar facilities over a wider field and in a more professional way. What is sadly lacking is the missionary zeal. I have always thought that the Labour Movement should interest itself in adult education; its claims to govern are based on its capacity to inspire desire for the good life. The Wilson

Government may have found a key in its attitude to the Arts Council. There, Lord Goodman has succeeded brilliantly in devising a formula that has enabled the Arts to flourish to an extent few would have believed possible. He and his colleagues, backed by Lady Lee, nourished the Arts with State aid while freeing them from any threat of bureaucratic control. The Arts Council is not a voluntary organization as that term is usually understood, but it does its job in a spirit of adventure that is so often the prerogative of voluntary organizations. A similar type of organization might fertilize the field of adult education. Concern will doubtless be felt by some people that with the Arts Council doing what it is doing and with an adult education movement operating on similar lines we should then be moving towards a Ministry for Culture. That thought does not worry me. The conception of a Minister for Sport has worked well in practice. I see no reason, after all the initial shudders and letters to *The Times* have worked through the body politic, why a Minister for Culture should not fulfil a role where he could be pump priming, guiding and advising, although never himself controlling.

I was posted to York, but I yearned for Canterbury. Soon after this posting I decided to leave the Army with a small pension, a gratuity of two pounds and a plain clothes allowance of about the same amount. E. S. Cartwright had written to enquire if I would consider going to North Staffordshire, with Stoke as headquarters, as District Secretary of the W.E.A. This was an envied prospect. North Staffordshire was the home of many heroes of adult education. Tawney had taught the first tutorial class at Longton. Men like Lindsay and Archbishop Temple held the Potteries in high regard, and Jimmy Mallon and Harry Tawney were still remembered with affection. There was never any real doubt that I would apply for the job. My wife and I talked over every detail. Could my pension eke out the salary of £2 18s. 9d. a week until the District's affairs improved and the W.E.A. could offer more than half pay for a very full time job? Minnie's attitude always represented the simple commonsense of our domestic problems. 'Your heart's in that job and you should go for it,' she said. 'My job is to keep the home going and keep the children well fed and healthy. I think we can just get by.' I could give up smoking, which was a bit of a hardship, and my occasional half-pint of bitter. We worked through our accounts and decided we could make do. So I left the Army, commuting part of my pension to buy a house and furniture, and started work. In our careful calculations we had overlooked the danger of my becoming ill. I contracted pneumonia and was on my back for six weeks with another six weeks, of which a month had to be spent at the seaside, to recuperate. With Minnie's help I came through. My reward came when I rejoined the Army in 1940 and Cartwright, at heart always a Potteries man, wrote: 'I always believed that North Staffordshire with the right leadership was the ideal ground for the Workers' Educational Association, a belief which you have abundantly justified.'

Chapter Five: Back to the Army

The Munich crisis precipitated a new ambivalence among my friends. Many of them wanted to stand up to Hitler, defend Czechoslovakia and Poland, and support Russian resistance to German Hitlerism. When I suggested we needed conscription and the re-equipment of the armed forces with modern weapons, I was denounced as a 'blimp'. Passing resolutions demanding action by the League of Nations met with enthusiastic support. Action to prepare for armed resistance to Hitler and Mussolini was considered reprehensible. I developed a contempt for political pacifists and fence-sitters which I still feel. I have profound respect for the true pacifist and pray that in the long run he may prove to be right. Among those I esteemed highly was the late Emrys Hughes who became a valued friend. Emrys was immensely more knowledgeable about defence matters than many who derided his pacifist beliefs.

History holds the Men of Munich in derision. They were so determined to maintain the class structure of British society, which war must shake to its foundations, that they watched with equanimity the rise of Fascism in Spain, the re-armament of Germany in defiance of the Peace Treaties, Mussolini's assault on British Empire communications in his aggression against Abyssinia, and Germany's re-entry into the Rhineland. Yet they were class war realists. Chamberlain's National Government put the lion's tail well and truly between its legs and convinced themselves, if and when the crunch came, that a people thus impoverished in spirit would slink away from battle. And the Labour and Trade Union Movements were not blameless. Too few leaders faced the facts of the kind of world in which we lived. They under-estimated the limitations imposed on British power by our losses in World War I. The sacrifices aggravated by the incompetence and cowardice of politicians, through the years of uneasy peace, had destroyed national unity and divided Britain between 'us' and 'them'. Fortunately, when the crunch did come, our people stood true to the British tradition of solidarity. This quality of mind and spirit ensured the survival of our country, and of democracy in the Western World.

I regarded the introduction of conscription as inevitable since war was certain, given the Chamberlain policies. Thus I pondered on the problems the Army would face and must solve when planning for rapid expansion to meet the needs of war. The demands on technical education facilities would be enormous because the Army's needs were bound to conflict with those of the Royal Air Force and the Navy. My mind turned to what happened in World War I. Then the problem of providing educational facilities, particularly in liberal studies, was not even contemplated until hostilities were all but over. Surely, I thought, we should at least learn some of the lessons of the 1914–18 War and treat our precious young manhood with care and imagination.

Military necessity forced Army reform and consequent reorganization during the Napoleonic Wars. The new military pattern demanded an understanding of the role of the individual soldier and recognition of his increased importance as the change from mass movement to the tactics of the Light Divisions grew apace. Much higher educational standards particularly among the Officers and N.C.O.s were required. Improved education, reflected especially in training techniques, was an essential part of Sir John Moore's methods. The Royal Military College was established in 1802 and Moore issued a circular defining the work of regimental schools formally established by Royal Warrant in July 1812. The Duke of York's Royal Military School opened in 1803 and the Royal Hibernian School, founded by the Church of Ireland in 1765, was taken over by the War Office in 1806. It is easy to over-estimate the development of military schools at this period and the acceptance by the Army of responsibility for educating the soldier and his child. True, action was taken only under pressure of events. It must be remembered, however, that the first Education Act was not passed until 1870. Yet as early as 1846 the special rank of Schoolmaster Sergeant was established by Royal Warrant and a department was opened in the Duke of York's School for training Army schoolmasters. In 1849 an Order required recruits to attend school for two hours daily. In 1857 an educational standard for promotion to non-commissioned rank was defined. Thus the progress of education in the Army was well ahead of progress in civil life.

How odd, then, that the battle for Army education had to be

fought again in 1918! Even more extraordinary, in the light of World War I experience, that the battle had to be re-fought and won yet again in 1939 and 1940. The first shot was fired in February 1939. I raised with Ernest Green, General Secretary of the W.E.A., the proposition that, with the certain coming of conscription, the War Office and the other Service Departments should be required by Statute to make provision for education in the Armed Forces.

My conviction about the trend of events was endorsed in a conversation with Edouard Benes whom, with Dr (later Sir) Barnett Stross, I met in London in August 1939, to discuss our work in aid of Czech refugees. That heroic man was certain that the Second World War was inevitable; it would continue the turmoil of the First World War; and, the struggle being ideological, conflict would continue throughout this century. He forecast that countries would change sides in the course of the struggle and that morale and the formation of opinion would be vital factors in the fight to preserve Western values. My own interpretation of this analysis was that the Regular Army as then recruited and organized was not fitted for the task ahead.

Talks with Green bore fruit. The central Executive of the W.E.A. set up an Emergency Committee to which I was co-opted. A group of M.P.s was harnessed to the task of securing in the Military Service Bill a clause making education in the Army a statutory function of the War Office. Its leading figure, the late Arthur Greenwood, was probably the best-loved man in the Labour Movement at that time, and represented the pioneering spirit of the W.E.A. With E. S. Cartwright he had been Joint Secretary of the Adult Education Committee appointed by the Ministry of Reconstruction which had produced the famous Report recommending that the educational experiments launched during the First World War should be unified and extended as a permanent feature of Army Education. I expected that Leslie Hore-Belisha, Secretary of State for War, or his advisers, would have read the Report prepared by, among others, R. H. Tawney and Dr Albert Mansbridge, founder of the W.E.A.; certainly I hoped that, faced with piloting the conscription legislation through Parliament, Hore-Belisha would include some of its recommendations in his Military Service Bill and thus give it an attractive social content. I was, however, disappointed by his attitude and I was far from pleased with that of many of my Labour Party friends who showed little interest.

My constituency Member, the late Ellis Smith, and several other Labour M.P.s stayed at the Bonnington Hotel when in London. Ellis Smith arranged meetings there between individual M.P.s and myself. All were convinced that (a) we must stand up to Hitler and Mussolini; (b) war must be avoided; and (c) conscription was a capitalist device to control the working classes. My view was that the Military Service Bill was necessary and that we would be failing in our duty if we handed our young men over to the care of Brass Hats who were courageous and honourable but oh! so stupid. Recommendations in the Report of 1919 had been applied by the late Lord Gorell who, appointed Deputy Director of Staff Duties (Education), sought 'to bring educational facilities within the reach of every officer and every man . . . and to view them educationally from the moment of enlistment to the moment of discharge'.

One M.P. with a mind attuned to the challenge of the times was the late Arthur Creech Jones. A Vice-President of the W.E.A., he became a convener of our new Parliamentary Group. The others, all familiar with my work in North Staffordshire, were Josiah Wedgwood, Ellis Smith and Arthur Hollins, President of the North Staffordshire W.E.A. and General Secretary of the National Society of Pottery Workers. On May 18, 1939, Creech Jones and Ellis Smith moved this amendment to the Military Service Bill: 'It shall be the duty of the Army Council, in consultation with the Board of Education, and through national organizations interested in adult education, to provide educational and social facilities for persons called up under the Act.' Hore-Belisha gave the fullest assurances. He spoke with understanding of the human problems involved in withdrawing young men from civilian life. He promised that the Army Council would define a curriculum of educational training in co operation with the Board of Education which would do even more than the amendment asked. Most people were delighted and the amendment was withdrawn. I did not throw my hat in the air. I knew the Army better than my friends did. I had no confidence in the advisory role of the Board of Education which invariably regarded any new idea as unworkable. My fears were not appeased when R. H. S. Crossman, then Assistant Editor of the *New Statesman*, and I toured Militia camps in the Aldershot area for young men called up under the Militia Act. It was obvious that the Director of Military Training exercised complete control of the training programme and the assurances about educational facilities given by Hore-

Belisha were not worth the pages of Hansard on which they were printed.

Meantime, representatives of the W.E.A. Emergency Committee met the Parliamentary Secretary to the Board of Education for preliminary discussions. This also looked suspicious; the talks should have taken place at the War Office where the new ideas would either be given a fair run or strangled. The Minister's scheme was presented on June 6, 1939. It proposed that the character of the work to be undertaken should accord with the wishes of the soldier students and, in the early stages, would be regarded as experimental and informal in the sense that courses of long duration could not be provided. Lectures and courses would be conducted in the camps where soldiers were stationed. The work would be undertaken by tutor-organizers who understood the techniques of adult education and could adapt them to local needs in the light of experience. Finally, control would be exercised by a Central Advisory Committee of Organizations recognized by the Board of Education and including Education Authorities and Services representatives.

The W.E.A. Emergency Committee, having approved the scheme, invited the co-operation of the Young Men's Christian Association and the Universities through their central Joint Advisory Committee for Tutorial Classes. The voluntary organizations' plans developed smoothly and amicably and, on July 1, the Board of Education was asked to receive a representative deputation. This request was rebuffed. The Parliamentary Secretary did not think the situation had developed sufficiently to make a meeting worth while! So I initiated a demand to meet the President of the Board of Education. He was seen on July 28. It was then agreed that educational facilities should be provided in the camps, and that camps within the areas of the respective University Joint Committees should be supervised by local Sub-Committees of representatives of the University Joint Committee, voluntary organizations and the Local Education Authorities. We had penetrated officialdom's petrified forest, but I still feared that the Board of Education's equivalent of barbed wire had not been cut. On August 16 the Board issued a circular to all Extra-Mural bodies inviting them to appoint representative committees to take action in co-operation with the Board and Educational Officers of Army units to provide facilities for education in Army camps. Within five weeks of this call to action the fruits of co-operation with the Board, never large, turned sour. On the outbreak of war the

conscripted Militia was merged under the Armed Forces (Conditions
of Service) Act with the Regular Forces of the Crown; and on
September 22 the Board of Education announced that, in view of
the merging provisions of this Act, the War Office had informed the
Board it would be impossible to proceed with the arrangements
contemplated for providing educational facilities for the Militia!

The Board and the War Office were incapable of understanding that
the Armed Forces had a major problem on their hands because,
quite apart from its size and nature, the social life of Britain had
undergone revolutionary changes in the years between the two wars.
The soldiers of 1914 were the products of a working-class taught to
pull its forelock and to remember its place in a society which was
thought of in static terms. The way the 1914 War was fought, the
impact of the Russian Revolution, the years of mass unemployment,
the mockery of the slogans of the 'War to end War' and 'the land fit
for heroes to live in', had produced men who echoed the words of the
old song:

'We won the war . . .
Whatever for?'

What was certain, although the Army high-ups did not realize it, was
that the recruits in 1939, the sons of these men, were completely
disillusioned with the Establishment and all it stood for. They certainly lacked the innocence, or the enthusiasm, of the recruits of
1914. They were going into the war because it could not be avoided.
They had no illusions that it meant fun and games, or that there was
glory at the end of the road. And that was not all the story.

Before 1918, the working classes relied upon themselves in organizing their leisure time. Cinemas were not then widespread. Dog racing,
dirt-track racing and wireless were unknown. Horse-racing was for
the few. Between the wars, however, the use of leisure had been
revolutionized by cheap travel and mass educational facilities. Men
called to the Colours in 1939 were accustomed to having their
leisure occupied fully by diversions they took as a matter of course;
their morale could be shaken severely by the absence of such pursuits
and by the boredom of hours of doing nothing and having nothing
to do. Moreover, the Board of Education and the War Office ignored
the fact that, whereas during World War I, troops were concentrated
in Britain and in France in large groups, the tendency in 1939 was

for troops to be stationed, particularly in Anti-Aircraft Command, in penny packets. Indeed, many Belisha camps, built to receive the Militia men, were situated in remote places, and the inherent problems of morale were accentuated by the circumstances in which the 1939 War began and developed until the end of the 'phoney War' in 1940.

Among my papers is a letter written to Sandy Lindsay early in 1940 by the then Chancellor of the Exchequer, Sir John Simon:

> I was much interested in what you said last night about bringing some intellectual life to these pockets of men in uniform stranded in outlying places and gazing into the sky for the raider who does not arrive. I had some further talk with Salter about it this morning and I also spoke to Oliver Stanley about it when we met at the Cabinet. He would, I am sure, welcome a personal talk with you if you felt this would be useful. As you said last night, reform in these things (and, indeed, in most things) involves a further claim on the Exchequer, and I must not make rash promises. But I told Stanley that I was much impressed by the need for getting something done to improve the morale and outlook of these people and thereby also to improve the tone of the countryside which must tend to become dejected when it sees them without occupation in their lonely duty. (It certainly would be a remarkable result of the Anti-Aircraft Defence of Great Britain if it turned our fellow countrymen into a race of profound astronomers!)

Fortunately, the resources of our democratic system were not exhausted. We sought to meet the situation created by the Board of Education's rebuff by setting up a Central Advisory Committee for Adult Education in H.M. Forces (Home Services), and held two conferences under Y.M.C.A. auspices. The new Council was presided over by Sir Walter Moberley, Chairman of the University Grants Committee; Sandy Lindsay was Vice-Chairman; Dr Basil Yeaxlee, who had been a member of the 1918 inquiry, was Secretary. I attended as a representative of the W.E.A.

This Council created Regional Committees, many of them under the chairmanship of Vice-Chancellors of Universities and Principals of University Colleges. Some Committees were already surveying Army educational needs and supplying lecturers and tutors to the troops. Service Ministers supported our work by appointing observer-members to the Council of the Central Advisory Committee. The Board of Education, no doubt reluctantly, agreed to be the medium of contact between the Council and the Service Ministers, its Divisional Inspectors performing similar duties for the Regional Committees. And Sandy Lindsay, already active in his own regional area of Oxford, harnessed his arts of advocacy and his mastery of democratic procedure to the good cause. He began by tapping sources of voluntary financial aid. An appeal for a modest £200 to the formidable Tom Jones, former Deputy Secretary to the Cabinet and Chairman of the York Trust, elicited a reply indicating the bewilderment caused by inertia at Government level. Jones wrote on December 26 from his home at Harlech: 'A grant of £200 will go nowhere ... and would only delay action by Whitehall. ... When I get back to Town I will talk to Sir James Grigg and discover where the block is and if it is at the War Office will he remove it.' He concluded with the question in every informed mind: 'Presumably the Board of Education is doing its duty?' The answer was still in the negative.

Lord Lindsay of Birker, as Sandy subsequently became, had long since won my allegiance, both as a man and as a leader of the Adult Education Movement. He had served on Haig's staff in World War I and had been mentioned in despatches. He had gained academic distinction in England, America and Europe. He had spent a lifetime expounding democracy as a philosophy men could carry into fields, factories and workshops. He lived his democratic faith. To him every individual was a unique personality capable of enriching society if given the opportunity to live a full, free individual life. Lindsay devoted rare talents of exposition and administrative ability to the achievement of that social ideal. Within minutes of meeting him— an unforgettable experience, not of date or place, but of emotional release—I became aware that here, for the first time, apart from my mother, was a human being seeking to treat me as a mature adult person. He gave me self-confidence and clarity of purpose by presuming I possessed them. I became an eager student of all his writings which influenced my political beliefs and my personal philosophy. We were comrades and partners in many adventures, and so we remained until his death in 1952.

The growing influence of our cause aroused interest in the Press and was reinforced by Lord Gorell, especially in an article in the *Spectator* of January 26, 1940. Hore-Belisha, in a resignation speech —he had been sacked by Chamberlain for complaining about the inadequacies of the Maginot line!—had described the Army as 'part of the nation', adding that, in a nation that is a democracy, it is impossible to think of either nation or Army without education as its basis. What the retiring Minister had *not* told the House of Commons, wrote Lord Gorell, was that 'the education of the Army is now largely at a standstill. On the outbreak of war in September last the Army Educational Corps was broken up and most of its personnel transferred to other duties, such as cipher work ... for which they had no special training.' Gorell's article was a devastating argument against the view that an Army exists solely for fighting and, in time of war, cannot afford to have any of its energies devoted to education. 'The answer to that simple saying,' the article ran, 'is this: it was said and acted upon in 1914, it was regretted in 1915–16, it was rejected in 1917, its opposite came actively into being in 1918 with feverish extensions as the Armistice loomed near in November, all through 1919 it was exposed on a huge scale as a fallacy, and in 1920 a permanent Corps was established as absolutely essential to the Regular Army of the future.' What was then demonstrated, urged Lord Gorell, was that 'a modern Army, especially an Army which is part of the nation as our great civilian Army must be, is made up of men who have minds as well as bodies, and neither can be neglected with impunity'.

The *Guardian*, on January 30, picked up Gorell's theme in a leader entitled 'A Strange Blunder', commenting acidly that 'the military authorities had all the prejudices against education which is so strong a tradition of the old governing class,' and concluded: 'the first thing to do now is to repair this blunder.' Early in February the *Times Educational Supplement* wrote: 'It seems almost incredible that in these days, when the mental qualities of an Army are as important as its military equipment, the Army Educational Corps should have been disorganized and many of its personnel transferred to other duties.' Sandy Lindsay wrote a letter to *The Times* on February 9, expressing the hope that 'righteous indignation about past folly will make the repentance of the authorities complete and active'. He recounted what was being done by voluntary organizations and described the demand already arising within the Army for lectures and short courses by authoritative speakers on many subjects. He urged the desperate need of the isolated detachments of Ack-Ack and Searchlight Units scattered all over the country. Pointing out that it took the authority and drive of Lord Gorell to make the most of opportunities in the 1914 War, the letter concluded with an appeal that a man of similar stature should be selected by the Army now.

Meantime, Sandy Lindsay's considerable private correspondence was producing results. A letter to Brigadier Bromley-Davenport brought an invitation to meet General Sir Robert Haining, then G.O.C., Western Command, who, from his Headquarters at Chester, had encouraged our efforts to get things moving in the area. By February 19, General Haining had increased the tempo of local action and raised the broad problems involved with the Adjutant General. Soon Sir Walter Moberley, Lindsay and Yeaxlee were engaged in high level talks at the War Office. On March 8, Lindsay told General Haining that his approaches to Lord Halifax and Sir John Simon had secured promises of support at Cabinet level. My personal knowledge of these facts was derived from a close-up of the Master's superb management of democratic procedures. He kept copies of his own letters and of most replies, recorded significant conversations and comments, and circulated them to his intimate colleagues. Thus all of us were in a constant process of absorbing and generating fresh ideas and suggestions. Sandy Lindsay was a *supremo* among political public relations officers.

Before March was out, The Army Council set up a small committee under the chairmanship of General Haining, now Vice-Chief of the Imperial General Staff 'to draw up a scheme of further education for the Army in War-time, in subjects other than military, and also to consider provision required for the welfare and recreational needs of the Army'. We entered a springtime of hope confident that, soon, success would follow.

Lindsay, giving all of himself to the task, expected no less from his associates. He kept me frantically happy. I organized lectures and classes in my own area and moved into others when invited. A growing team of voluntary helpers was ironing out difficulties, mostly related to lack of co-ordination between civilian organizations and the Army. We recruited an able band of lecturers and tutors, assessing their abilities and teaching some of them the techniques of the job. We brought the aid of public and private libraries to Army units, especially in remote places. Colleagues like the late Stephen Swingler, R. H. S. Crossman, T. L. Hodgkin, Gladys Malbon (now Mrs Fred Harris) and many others, raised the quality of our field work. In July 1940, for example, Crossman, reporting on a tour I organized of the North-Western area under the direction of General Waddington, found the men, mostly intakes of the twenty-seven age group, in high spirits, delighting their C.O.s with their independence of mind and their desire to understand what the war was about and how it was going. What emerged clearly was that the modern soldier, while enjoying E.N.S.A., did not regard education as an alternative to E.N.S.A. but as a keenly anticipated part of military training.

General Haining invited me to meet his Committee. The Committee did not impress me, but I did urge one important point which General Haining himself had obviously hoisted aboard. We discussed at length whether education in the Army should be—as I urged—under the control of the Adjutant General, Sir Ronald Adam, whose Department was concerned with the soldier as a man, his physical, mental and spiritual well-being, or under the control of the Director of Military Training, whose interest was in the soldier only as a soldier. Ultimately, Army Education was transferred to the Adjutant General. Sir Ronald Adam was an enthusiast for Army education in the widest sense. He stimulated the process of ridding the Army of class snobbery and promoting men according to their ability. He exercised foresight in relation to the problems of demobilization. I regard him as one of the chief architects of our victory over Hitler. His work left a permanent mark for the better on the Army.

Before that triumph was achieved, however, the Haining Report had to be exposed and repudiated as a heart-chilling frost. Although not prepared with a view to publication—what was issued was a short pamphlet entitled *Education in the Army*, published in September 1940—we expected its purposes to compare favourably with the objectives described in the Army Order of September 24, 1918, when Gorell began his great adventure: '(a) to raise morale, both indirectly by providing mental stimulus and change and directly by means of lectures on German methods, aims, etc.; (b) to broaden and quicken intelligence, both by stimulating a desire for study and by giving men a wider realization of their duties as citizens of the British Empire; (c) to help men in their work after the War by practical instruction, as far as may be possible in their professions or trades.' Alas, the theme of the Haining Report, twenty-two years later, was that 'education and welfare stand on the same footing and education may be regarded as one among many aspects of welfare provision—a natural element in the general make-up of Army welfare'. The sweet little thought that 'mental contentment as well as physical comfort' was necessary to maintain morale was a paltry pep-pill for people standing alone against the fury of the Nazis. Its acceptability was not made easier after another visit to the War Office. I decided that the gentlemen charged with implementing the Haining proposals knew little about Army organization, less about Army education, and nothing at all about the ferment within the Army.

General Haining was also concerned in an odd business in which I became involved in June 1940. I was a member of the North Staffordshire Committee of the Ministry of Information. In that capacity I was asked to arrange for the Chief Regional Officer of the Ministry, who was visiting Stoke on Sunday, June 23, to speak, mainly at Working Men's Clubs, on the importance of stopping idle chatter and the spread of rumours.

Towards the end of his visit we met two French soldiers from a contingent of several hundred French troops who, following the collapse of France, had arrived at Trentham Park on the outskirts of Stoke. Later, when I took these men to my home, it became apparent that they were bewildered by the events in France and fearful that by staying in England they might be regarded as deserters. Contact with these and other French soldiers roaming the streets convinced me that a serious situation was developing out of the widely divergent and strongly-held opinions among the Frenchmen, many of whom carried arms. A visit by General de Gaulle to Trentham did nothing to ease the situation. The French soldiers asked: 'Who is de Gaulle?' and gave him the 'bird'. His visit lasted a brief twenty minutes.

A telephone call from the Ministry of Information's Chief Regional Officer informed me that a man once attached to the British Embassy in Paris would be sent to weigh up the situation. I was asked to help him make contact with the British Liaison Officer at Trentham Park, whom I went to see on June 24. I then gathered that the idea of sending any official to put the British point of view was unwelcome. However, as the Ministry of Information had so decided, he gave me a pass valid for one day only in order that I might bring the Ministry official to Trentham. I made my own position clear, produced my National Registration Card and expressed my view that a dangerous situation was threatening, the French troops being restless, armed, and far from friendly. The Liaison Officer did not agree.

The situation, he felt, was well in hand and the morale of the French troops was high.

My account of the strange happenings at Trentham Park is contained in a report I was asked to send to the War Office. Now, thirty years later, it reads like fiction. It seemed to me that the greatest chaos and confusion existed. The British Liaison Officer had been given a task which, even on the organizational side, was beyond his ability. If he thought morale was high he was either blind or lacked an elementary grasp of the situation. Talks with soldiers at Trentham Park and in Stoke disclosed a clear division between officers and men. There were two Battalions of Chasseurs Alpins and two Battalions of the Foreign Legion. All the units had fought in Norway and on the eve of the Armistice were returning to France. Following the Armistice they were diverted to Britain and stationed at Trentham. The French regulars, bewildered by events were concerned chiefly about their status, pay and promotion prospects; they felt bound to the constitutional government of France. Only a small group of officers and men grasped the real significance of the situation and gave signs of being willing to fight on. The two Battalions of the Legion, made up mostly of Spaniards, Poles, and Italians, were bitterly anti-French. In Norway, it was said, some officers and N.C.O.s had let the men down badly. The Legionnaires were willing to fight under British Officers and N.C.O.s but were determined to finish with France and the French. As I suggested in my report, the Legionnaire's dislike of the French had become tinged with contempt. Another group at the Camp had reached this country individually or in small units from the depots of Northern France. Like the majority of the Chasseurs Alpins, they lacked fundamental understanding of the situation, knew nothing of the terms of the Armistice, and thought that the war was over and they could return to France and take up life where they had left it before hostilities began.

The troops' outlook could be divided into four categories: the professional officers who looked to the constitutional government of France and who were a definite obstacle to any effective presentation of the British point of view; those officers and men who were prepared to serve under British officers; that part of the Foreign Legion which would fight under British officers and N.C.O.s but would have nothing to do with the French; and the very large group who simply wished to return to France.

In my report I stressed the vital importance of the British case being presented speedily and with vigour even though the bulk of the men would be disinclined to believe it. It also seemed elementary that a check should be made on the large number of men and some women in civilian clothes.

On June 26 ten thousand copies of a Ministry of Information pamphlet arrived, incorporating a statement in French and English by General de Gaulle. These the French officers, in agreement with the British Liaison officer, refused to distribute. On that same day one hundred and seventy Legionnaires refused to obey their French officers; this incident was described as a 'Communist plot'.

On June 30, a Legionnaire visited my home, sent by a member of the family of the late Colonel Josiah Wedgwood. A Jew of Rumanian extraction, he had volunteered for service at the outbreak of war and, against his will, had been forced into the Foreign Legion. He appeared to have had a rough time. He complained of anti-Semitism and of anti-British feeling among the officers, and asserted that some of them were pro-Hitler. He had met Colonel Wedgwood in Rumania in 1938. This contact prompted him to seek out the Wedgwood family and to let them know that there were over a hundred Jews in the Legion at Trentham Park who would give loyal service under British officers and N.C.O.s but would rather be shot than have anything more to do with the French.

On July 1, the War Office informed me they were sending a man down to Stoke and requested me to give him assistance. I was, in fact, met by two men who handed me a letter on War Office paper introducing themselves. We went to Trentham Park where we were asked to wait at Headquarters for the arrival of the British Liaison Officer. The senior War Office man was called. He did not reappear. The second man was summoned. He, too, failed to return. After a lapse of about ten minutes I was called to see the Liaison Officer, who attitude was truculent in the extreme. I was searched and put into a room with a private soldier who kept pointing a loaded revolver at me while explaining that he did not have the least idea how to use it! A tremendous commotion arose outside, and a call for rifles and live ammunition. Then a Sergeant and two Privates arrived, proceeded to 'shove one up the spout' and kept the loaded rifles pointed in my direction.

My detention lasted for approximately half an hour. Thereafter my papers were returned and I was taken to the Officers' Mess and given tea. These goings-on were only part of the story. Events justified a question put down by Colonel Wedgwood on the Parliamentary Order Paper:

> To ask the Secretary of State for War whether he has yet taken any action in connection with the French Legion and other troops; whether such members of the Legion as decide to continue to fight for us under British Officers will be given the option of taking up British citizenship. . . . ?

This question was followed by an exchange between Colonel Wedgwood and the Secretary of State for War, Anthony Eden, during which one of Colonel Wedgwood's supplementary questions was:

> Is the Rt. Hon. Gentleman not aware that after trying to see him, I was asked to see the Under-Secretary, that I gave the whole facts to the Under-Secretary, that he promised that an inquiry would be held, and that nothing further has been done about it?

Everyone who had done anything to make life more comfortable for the French troops or to assist the Ministry of Information in making known the British case was subjected to assiduous police scrutiny, much of it of the clumsiest character. Having made my detailed report to the War Office I kept silent and was eventually vindicated by a letter from General Haining in which he wrote, 'I am taking steps to see that Wigg is not troubled further. I agree that he has done much good work.'

My reward came when the two Battalions of the Foreign Legion were taken to Avonmouth to return to France. Many of them, although encircled by armed British troops, refused to embark. In June 1942 these troops stood at Bir Hacheim fighting with their backs to the wall alongside their British comrades. Our faith in their desire to fight Hitler was justified.

Filled with a sense of tedium and frustration, I decided to rejoin the Army. My own assessment of my military prowess suggested I should apply for an Army Emergency Commission in the Pioneer Corps. Lindsay argued that the machinery we had created and the enthusiasm aroused must be sustained and urged me to stay where I was. There was sense in this. I was nearing forty and since leaving the Army I had had an illness from which I had not recovered fully. In November 1940, however, I was invited to join the Army Educational Corps with the rank of Captain, and informed that I would be given a Grade III Staff Appointment. I was sent to the 11th Anti-Aircraft Division then being formed at Wightwick Hall, near Wolverhampton.

The third officer to join the new Division, I was soon engaged in a variety of tasks besides Army Education. The role of odd-job man sprang naturally from the fact that I had more than a nodding acquaintance with Army organization. I recall a circular from Western Command Headquarters announcing that money was available for entertainment. Not knowing what to do with it, the Command Entertainment Officer called a meeting of representatives of Formations in the Command area, outlined the War Office proposals, and explained that, if he did not spend the allocation before March 31, 1941, the unexpended sum would lapse and the grant for the following year would be cut accordingly. He wanted suggestions. Unit representatives made bids for fifty and a hundred pounds. One bold character bid for two hundred pounds. I enquired how much money was available. On being told twenty thousand pounds I asked for ten thousand pounds, pointing out that I represented an Anti-Aircraft Division scattered from the outskirts of Liverpool and Manchester to the Oxfordshire borders and including a large chunk of Wales. I undertook to see that the money would be spent properly and to supply the necessary receipts.

I returned to Divisional Headquarters with a cheque for ten thousand pounds, and asked that an N.C.O. be attached to me with knowledge of entertainments and, if possible, journalistic experience since my many jobs included that of Divisional Public Relations Officer! I came up with a real find. Sergeant Dick Richards, in civilian life on the *Sunday Pictorial* staff, joined me. We bought every musical instrument we could lay hands on. We formed four-piece bands throughout the Division as well as a Divisional Orchestra. Richards, as organizer and impresario, put on a first-class show at Wolverhampton Hippodrome, raising several hundred pounds for the C.O.C.'s Welfare Fund. Another of my jobs arose from Anti-Aircraft Command's public relations effort, the *Ack-Ack Beer-Beer* programme. The producers, including Howard Thomas, currently a T.V. tycoon, approached Anti-Aircraft Command to get authentic material from the sites. With Richards' skills backed by my Army 'know-how' we were able to produce two Divisional shows in this celebrated radio programme, one broadcast from Birmingham and

the other from Bristol. Besides being good entertainment these enterprises helped to ease a major problem of Anti-Aircraft formations—
boredom.

Meantime, the campaign for Army education continued. In August
1941 Mr (now Sir) William Emrys Williams, secretary of the British
Institute of Adult Education and a distinguished pioneer in the
field, initiated with the authority of the Chief of the Imperial General
Staff the exciting proposal that discussion in the Forces should be
sustained through the Army Bureau of Current Affairs. The idea
was a success, the Bureau's fortnightly issue of expertly written,
attractively produced pamphlets touching off an astonishing demand
for non-vocational adult education. Soldiers everywhere took the
opportunity to develop their knowledge through what is the real
secret of adult education, learning from one another. A.B.C.A.
pamphlets were supplemented by publications entitled *British Way
and Purpose*. Each scholarly production included a bibliography.
They became prized possessions of many men who had never before
engaged in serious reading.

In the *Times Educational Supplement* of November 29, 1941,
Lindsay recorded developments in Kent and related them to larger
issues. 'The remarkable progress of English education in the years
between the wars, especially of adult education, has borne fruit,' he
wrote. 'These men wanted to argue and discuss and they were being
encouraged to do it. There was almost universal testimony that
discussion was free and felt to be free, that men, N.C.O.s and officers
discussed together. I got the impression that there had not been an
Army in England which discussed like this one since the famous
Puritan Army which produced the Putney Debates and laid the
foundation of modern democracy.' Pointing out that the Extra-
Mural departments of Universities were reporting a growing demand
for classes on current affairs and that the Army was a cross-section
of the adult population with the same interests, Lindsay concluded:
'The outstanding fact is the Army's collective interest in affairs which
vitally concern a citizen Army. The new venture known as A.B.C.A.
is rightly seizing the opportunity which these facts have disclosed.
It has now started a scheme which should ensure that this wide
potential demand for discussion of our common concern is made
real on a scale of which we have hardly dreamt.'

There followed for me two years of strenuous effort. I left 11th
Anti-Aircraft Division early in 1942 but returned to 4th Anti-

Aircraft Group, which included the 11th Division, some months later and stayed there until, in 1943, I was promoted Lieutenant-Colonel on taking up a Grade I Staff appointment in Southern Command. I was posted to the Eighth Army. This was cancelled, however, and I found myself working in the Midlands and Southern England with the Americans. In Southern Command I met Arnold Goodman, now Lord Goodman, who was an officer there. Then, as now, to work with him was a great pleasure. Together we have managed to get done many things which might have remained undone.

Spurred on by Lindsay, I was beginning to think about a political career. In his Balliol Lodgings one day he enquired what I proposed doing after the War. That seemed a long way off and I answered: 'I shall go abroad. Two wars are enough: I think we shall try our luck in Canada.' Lindsay replied: 'You should think again about that. The disastrous years following 1918 were decided as much as anything by the mood of the demobilized soldiers. They thought in terms of a land fit for heroes, and when they found that the promises were not being fulfilled they went sour. This time we must have a first-class demobilization plan which will work smoothly. The War is going to last more than four years, and making up for lost time won't be easy. But the returning soldiers must be given an opportunity to understand the difficulties confronting the country. Without their understanding we shall find, once again, that the sacrifices will have been for nothing.' To my question, 'What can I do?' he answered, 'You can stand for Parliament.'

Reflecting now on these conversations I think my life's experiences had given me some insight into the tricks of the politician's trade, some understanding, too, of 'participation' as a vital factor in a democratic system. I grasped its open secret: the collective interest of citizens in matters in which they are expected to participate. In my view, too many politicians just do not know what participation is about. They think of it as an exercise in public relations long since vulgarized into a form of market research to be exploited for commercial purposes. Instead of seeking to understand and identify themselves with the collective will by stimulating its free expression, many politicians first formulate their own policies then harness their publicity resources to put these policies over to the people. They fail to realize that participation must invoke the voluntary spirit, always an enriching element in the communal life of the British people, and they try to 'sell' what cannot be the subject of any sale—ideas about policies affecting people deeply in their everyday lives. Hence, the ever-widening chasm between the people and Whitehall, between the citizen and Town Hall, and the increasingly exasperated vigour of public protest. Adult education for politicians might be the beginning of wisdom in British democracy.

In the Autumn of 1942, the late Tom Wintringham suggested I should become organizer of Common Wealth, the new party led by Sir Richard Acland. Tom had contributed much to the development of Commando combat and Civil Defence training and he and I shared a common interest in military weapons and methods. He won distinction in the Spanish Civil War. By repudiating the Communist Party of which he had been a functionary, he demonstrated his strength of character. I respected the promoters of the Common Wealth Party although I doubted the wisdom of their approach. I held Sir Richard Acland in affection and admired his honesty of purpose. The late R. W. G. (Kim) Mackay, an Australian, was another Common Wealth leader whose drive impressed me. Aside from the personalities involved I felt there was a genuine need for a Party like Common Wealth to widen the Socialist appeal and bring to Labour's aid the intellectual qualities, panache and practical experience of affairs of Common Wealth's middle-class supporters. My doubts sprang from my working-class upbringing and ingrained loyalty to the Labour Movement. These misgivings increased when J. B. Priestley resigned the Chairmanship of Common Wealth. Priestley's superb qualities as a writer flow from a love for and a belief in ordinary folk and, in the context of Common Wealth, a down-to-earth attitude to social and economic problems. Pressure on me increased and I sought advice from E. S. Cartwright. He, too, had interpreted Priestley's withdrawal as a sign that Common Wealth was failing to define clearly its purpose which, Cartwright thought, should be to create 'a new Movement that would voice and genuinely attempt with all its strength to realize the aspirations of the great mass of workers in a way that conventional political Labour and the trade unions seem incapable of doing.' Common Wealth, he feared, was too formless to satisfy my aspirations, but if I thought I could make Common Wealth an effective instrument of social change I should go right in. I decided to stick to the Labour Movement although I valued the work of Common Wealth in preparing the nation for social change.

Decision about a political future was determined finally after a visit to Bishopthorpe with T. L. Hodgkin. Hodgkin and his family were life-long friends of Archbishop Temple, the man who, in the opinion of many, was the most significant figure in the religious life of our country this century. He was shortly to leave York for Canterbury, and Hodgkin and myself arranged to visit him and urge him to use his very considerable influence to get someone outstanding, with drive and democratic dedication to be put in charge of the civilian side of the Forces' education. I learned subsequently that the Archbishop did discuss the matter with Sir James Grigg.

Temple reinforced Lindsay's view that I should enter politics. The way this was put suggested that Lindsay, who knew of our visit, had spoken to Temple about me. When I returned to Nottingham in the evening Temple telephoned and reiterated his view that my post-war place was in Parliament. That clinched the matter. Within weeks I appeared at a selection conference as a runner against the late Albert Davies in the Burslem constituency. The experience taught me a lot. I did not canvass as I had been asked to let my name go forward; I was rightly taken for a 'sucker'. The 'opposition' canvassed even those who nominated me! Then came the chance of nomination for Dudley. Three rivals greeted me. One of them, the late Stanley Evans, asked where I came from. When I said Salisbury, he commented: 'It's a shame bringing you all this way. It's cut and dried.' Remembering my Burslem experience I was not pleased when Stanley, waving a cheque book, continued: 'This is what the local boys want to know. How much can you put up? I can write a cheque for six hundred pounds.' At that moment I was called for interview. Almost the first question was: 'If you are adopted how much money can you find?' My reply was, 'None. I haven't got any and, even if I had, I would not help you financially. If you adopt me I shall work with you and, together, we shall win the seat. But, as regards money, not a stiver.' I left convinced I had 'had it'. Later I was called to a final conference at which, to my delight, I was adopted. So began a twenty-two year association which brought much hard work and increasingly heart-lifting pride and pleasure in service to Dudley and Stourbridge. When I resigned from the Commons I turned my back on the House very regretfully; the severance of ties with hundreds, indeed thousands, of constituents I had come to know well was a hard blow. The absence of those personal contacts has left a gap which time has not filled.

Soon after being adopted for Dudley I was sent to Africa. My Staff appointment was to the War Overseas Pool and I was attached in turn to East and West Africa Commands. I flew in civilian clothes to Portugal, thence to Rabat where I changed into uniform, and on to The Gambia. My job was reconnaissance to learn how to establish an educational scheme for British and African troops.

Educational provision for Africans, apart from correspondence courses, had been confined to teaching spoken English as a part of military training. Responsibility for organization at West Africa Headquarters in Accra rested on one over-worked Staff Officer burdened with several other jobs. A decision had been taken early in the War to substitute English for Hausa as a *lingua franca* but, as far as I could ascertain, nothing much had been done about it. There was no trace of instructional methods; nothing beyond a directive that the teaching of English to soldiers should be regarded as part of military training.

Until the outbreak of war, responsibility for West African Forces, including seconded officers and non-commissioned officers from the British Army, was vested in the Colonial Office, liaison with the War Office being maintained through an Inspector-General, General Giffard. A wise Christian gentleman, Giffard realized that as the West African Forces had been recruited from the Hausa speaking peoples an urgent problem would arise if war came and West African Forces were rapidly enlarged. The officers and non-commissioned officers seconded from the British Army before the War were highly trained volunteers whose first job was to learn Hausa. The quality of the men so seconded was lowered under the pressure of events while recruiting was taking place in The Gambia, Sierra Leone, the Gold Coast and all over Nigeria. Finding a *lingua franca* as the basis of instruction had become a military necessity. An additional complication was that in Nigeria there were upwards of a hundred different vernaculars, most of them without an alphabet. English had to be the medium to teach West Africans even the rudiments of simple mechanical operations.

The Army Commander, General Nosworthy, had been ordered to improve English teaching but by 1943 little had been done beyond appointing a Staff Officer to what was still a part-time job. By August, 1944, it was apparent that unsatisfactory language teaching was causing operational problems. An order was issued in these terms: 'The General Officer Commanding in Chief considers that the present low standard of English among African other ranks is most disquieting. However excellent other forms of training might be they are largely nullified in battle if a man cannot understand his orders.' Some failures in the Arakan fighting were thought to have been due to this cause. In October, 1944, instruction was standardized and teacher training was introduced. To stimulate interest a badge was awarded to African other ranks passing proficiency tests. The elementary methods never really advanced beyond teaching 'pidgin'. But the results were effective although far from polished. I recall an example on a visit to an Anti-Aircraft site in Sierra Leone. The Battery Commander pointed to a light anti-aircraft gun—a Bofors—and said to a West African soldier: 'What be that?' 'That, Master,' came the reply, 'be humbug for steam-chicken'. 'Steam-chicken' in the vernacular meant an aeroplane!

I visited every major formation and most small units in West Africa. British Officers and men and West Africans were all enthusiastic about the value of education in war and about the importance of education in encouraging social discipline and purpose among African troops. I was persuaded that if enough young Africans adopted English as a *lingua franca* and acquired some understanding of British history and political tradition, we might begin to find one answer to the problems of the future. Obviously the mobilization of thousands of African troops must influence political changes following the war they were helping us to win.

West Africa's war was primarily against Japan. The only African troops engaged in the European theatre were a limited number of Nigerian pioneers, nursing orderlies and West African Army Service Corps personnel serving in the Middle East. In 1940 the task facing East African Forces was to capture the Italians in Eritrea. This was done successfully by using native troops. Then General Jan Smuts insisted on the withdrawal of East African troops from Eritrea; defeat of white troops by Askaris was not to the liking of South Africans. This same emotional reaction explained the reluctance to teach English to African troops. In West Africa the problem was clear cut. If Forces were recruited outside the Hausa speaking peoples the *lingua franca* had to be English. The reaction elsewhere was not entirely racial and political. It stemmed also from an atavistic paternalism that sought to preserve tribal customs because they were so picturesque!

By the time of my arrival General Nosworthy had been replaced by the late General Brocas Burrows. A Balliol man, Burrows became a Regular Officer before World War I, was captured in August 1914, and spent his war in a prison camp with some Russian officers. He learned Russian and, on his release, went off to Archangel and won a D.S.O. fighting for the White Russians. When the Soviets entered World War II, Burrows was sent to Moscow as Head of the British Military Mission. He regarded this as a first class blunder. The Russians raised no objection to his appointment; they just showed him nothing! I got on with him like a house on fire. An intelligent, die-hard Tory, he had a first class mind. He came to firm decisions and spoke plainly. Towards the end of our Service association he told me he might stand for Parliament, probably for Dudley. 'Don't waste your time, you old rascal,' I told him, 'because if you do I will beat you.' General Burrows and I discussed the provisions of educational training for British personnel and the more urgent problem of an effective programme for Africans. He agreed that I should prepare and present to his staff a scheme which he would remit to the War Office. When it came to fights with his staff I would carry on my own struggles, leaving him free to come down on my side at the appropriate moment. General Burrows was the most intelligent and straightest G.O.C. under whom any man could wish to serve.

East Africa presented a different problem. Any African who spoke English to a white man was qualifying for a belting. This fact produced a ludicrous situation. African troops were drawn from tribes speaking many languages. The policy had been to use Kiswahili and Chinyanja, and British personnel were required to have a working knowledge of one of these languages. To assist them they attended courses in Kiswahili only. The parallel use of Kiswahili and Chinyanja imposed such limitations on cross-posting that by 1944 language policy was reviewed. Since it was impracticable to teach Chinyanja to British personnel they had to do the best they could when posted to Chinyanja-speaking units. This often meant that key personnel were ineffective. As a result of the policy review Chinyanja was retained, facilities for learning Kiswahili were made available in Chinyanja speaking units, and Kiswahili remained the official language even for those serving in Chinyanja speaking units! This nonsense arose from settler influence in East Africa Command. They would not give up their opposition to

Africans learning English even to aid the war effort. They thought English speaking Africans might give themselves airs and threaten white supremacy. They insisted on maintaining what they regarded as a God-given right to be called Bwana every time an African addressed them. I argued the case for teaching English with senior officers on military grounds. I stressed the importance of East Africa Command in the Japanese War. Thinking I had won them over I travelled to Khartoum to inform a War Office Inspecting Officer that the G.O.C., East Africa Command, had agreed on English as a *lingua franca*, and for strictly military reasons. The Inspector went to Nairobi, secured the G.O.C.s agreement to this policy and, back in Lagos, told me that in both East and West Africa *lingua franca* policy was all 'buttoned up'. We journeyed together to London. By the time we reached London, the Colonial Office, that incredible institution, had gone back on the decision. Thus little was done about teaching English and less about teaching Africans how democratic institutions worked. East African development might well have been different if the Army had taken over from the Colonial Office and stimulated among the Askaris the educational policy set out in a White Paper published during the War, entitled *Mass Education in Africa.*

My own heart and mind responded to what I thought of as the beginning of a unifying sense of social responsibility in Africa and my personal hope for sustaining British influence in the post-War world. I made this a point in my maiden speech in the House of Commons on March 4, 1946, and of other early speeches, arguing that Colonial Forces could help to solve our defence manpower problems while the Army developed the Africans as citizens and members of their own community. On the diversity of tribes and religions I feared that moves towards self-government before we had laid a permanent educational foundation were fraught with menace. Thus I pleaded for mass education based on English. My contribution after leaving the Army was to discuss with Sandy Lindsay the problems of adult education in West Africa. The Oxford Delegacy for Extra-Mural Studies had pioneered adult education on the University side in Great Britain; here was a chance to extend this influence to the Colonies. Lindsay was the driving force in arranging for T. L. Hodgkin, Secretary of the Oxford Delegacy, to make a survey of the possibilities. As a result, adult education in West Africa in the early post-War period benefited from the work of

Hodgkin who, himself, became a recognized authority on the growth and development of African Nationalism.

I initiated action in another field. The late Harry Guy Bartholomew, maker of the successful *Daily Mirror*, had acquired an interest in Nigeria and sent a thrusting young executive, R. T. Suffren, to Lagos to re-invigorate a daily newspaper there. Included in the deal were two London based journals, the weekly *West Africa* and the monthly *West African Review*. 'Bart' had placed the direction of these journals in the hands of the *Daily Mirror*'s Political Adviser and leader writer, Sydney Elliott, who had devised and conducted the 'Vote for Him' campaign which contributed powerfully to Labour's Election victory in 1945. Already a friend of several years standing, Elliott engaged me as an occasional contributor to *West Africa* and with his colleague, Sydney Tremayne, literally bullied me into becoming a reasonably competent journalist. He backed my Extra-Mural idea enthusiastically and induced 'Bart' to help get the project going. This support continued when, having broadened the interests covered in *West Africa*, Elliott recruited David Williams from the Central Office of Information to be Editor of what is now the most important journal in its specialised field. The contribution made by Williams towards good relations between British and West African interests is incalculable. He had commanded a Company of the King's African Rifles in the Abyssinian campaign. He exemplifies what our countrymen can do in building a bridge between our culture and the African way of life, a bridge resting on the twin pillars of respect and understanding.

The tragedy of this story is that the Colonial Office failed to change with the times. To make English a *lingua franca*, the traditionalists argued, would be destructive of tribal cultures. In the immediate post-war era, Nigerians, irrespective of ethnic origin, responded magnificently to our adult education enterprise in a dozen urban centres in all three regions of Nigeria. Classes were crowded out. A movement was initiated which, given a modicum of Government support, might have promoted some unity among peoples whose differences instead burst loose from 1967 to 1969 into a civil war that nearly sundered the Continent.

Chapter Six: Parliament

I imagine that to every candidate in an election, win or lose, the result comes as a shock; the declaration of the poll produces the final tremor after a long period of suspense and nervous tension. I was as sure as every member of the magnificent team supporting me that I would win Dudley. Yet when victory came it was awesome and almost frightening.

Dudley was included in the itinerary of Clement Attlee's General Election Tour. Labour's quiet-mannered leader, in a broadcast, had blown the larger-than-life Churchill and his assertion that Labour meant Gestapo rule right off the air. Dudley's reception of Attlee revealed how deeply the ordinary folk of Britain resented Churchill's impudent slanders. My other vote-compelling stars included J. B. Priestley, Harold Laski and Hugh Dalton. We had crowded halls and overflow meetings. The whole nation, like the Army under the impact of A.B.C.A., was listening, questioning and debating. The longer the Election lasted, the more certain, I felt, would be a Labour victory. Attlee shared my hope but not my view. The mood I caught in my talk with him was the possibility of stalemate. Certainly he, and Dalton too, thought another Election following the end of the Japanese War could be on the cards. The polling at Dudley was: George Wigg 15,439, Major E. Brinton, Con. 9,156; Labour majority 6,283.

I shared two emotions common, I suppose, to every new Member of Parliament: exhilaration at being elected one of the 'chosen few' and a sense of dedication to a new life within the shrine of an historical tradition. Almost at once the new boy learns that battles within a party can be as bitter and more personal than battles between parties. After all, the chaps in the other party don't know any better; too much should not be expected from them! The men and women in your own party, however, do know; or, at least, should know; only perversity prevents them seeing the truth as clearly as you do yourself!

This sense of shock eases as one finds friends dedicated to one's own policies and discovers, quite often among political opponents, men and women who share some of one's own ideas and ideals. Co-operation and conflict within and between parties give drama to the Westminster scene. They are also vital elements in the continuing tradition of a House where policies and principles expounded in free and open debate are put to the decision of a popularly elected assembly.

On August 10, 1945, the Rt. Hon. Emanuel Shinwell, Minister of Fuel and Power, and a member of the Cabinet, invited me to become his Parliamentary Private Secretary. I had met Shinwell once before during a York by-election and knew him by repute. His letter was challenging. 'I am conscious.' he wrote, 'that there is a big and difficult task ahead and that the next few years will be both important and interesting.' He had offered the job to Harold Wilson, who already had accepted a post in the new Government. My own problem appeared to raise difficulties. Before the Election I had been selected for promotion to Brigadier with a posting to the British Army of the Rhine, the condition being one I could not accept—I must resign my candidature at Dudley. Immediately after the Election I was ordered by telegram to report to the War Office and told I had been appointed Command Education Officer, Eastern Command, with special responsibility for getting No. 5 Formation College started—the first of its kind and a stepping stone back to civilian life for thousands of young men and women. Moreover, my personal political ambition was to make such contribution as I could towards developing an effective defence policy and its essential concomitant, the cohesion of the Commonwealth through mass education, especially in Africa. Thus Service responsibilities and half-formed political objectives pointed away from the 'strait-jacket' job of P.P.S.

A personal meeting with Shinwell resolved my doubts. I found him a man's man, straightforward and excitingly realistic about the magnitude of the problems facing a Labour Government. He wanted me at once, but would make no exacting calls upon my time prior to the Second Reading of the Bill to nationalize the coal mines. So began an enduring and endearing comradeship with one of the truly great men in British public life.

There remained one obstacle to closing with Shinwell's offer. The G.O.C., Eastern Command, Sir Alan Cunningham, although not enthusiastic about having a newly elected M.P. on his staff, was eager to get No. 5 Formation College started. Luton Hoo, owned by Sir Harold Wernher, was Eastern Command Headquarters and the arrangements were that Headquarters should move to Hounslow and No. 5 Formation College would take over Luton Hoo. The need to establish No. 5 Formation College and support the Commandant-elect, the late Colonel George Fillingham, convinced me I must see the job through, which meant remaining in the Army for two or three months. In the event, No. 5 Formation College was opened by the Rt. Hon. Jack Lawson, Secretary of State for War, on November 5, 1945, and I left the Army in January 1946 to begin my commitment to full-time service as a Member of the House of Commons.

Parliamentary service, I soon learned, required mastery of the rules of Parliamentary procedure. I studied Erskine May with the intensity I once applied to King's Regulations. I discussed puzzling points with officers of the House and, often, with the late Sir Frederic William Metcalfe, Clerk of the House from 1948 until 1954. The House of Commons Librarians guided my reading expertly and earned lasting gratitude for assistance which, throughout my membership of the Commons, was always prompt, courteous and indispensable. Among my models were Bill Brown, ex-Socialist turned Independent, and D. N. Pritt, who, I thought, should have been a Law Officer in Attlee's Government. The man to whom I owed most, however, was Lord Winterton. He knew what Parliament was about. He was outstanding as a master of procedure, particularly in the Tory Party whose 1945 influx did not include many serious students of parliamentary form.

The redoubtable trio of Brown, Pritt and Winterton taught me the basic fact that once a Member catches the eye of the Speaker he gives way to nobody as long as he keeps within the Rules of Order. This is the essence of the back-bencher's strength. Grasp this fact and a Member need never be apprehensive about Mr Speaker's control. The best Speaker in my time was Colonel Clifton Brown. He was neither an intellectual nor a lawyer, but a plain straightforward man who always tried to be fair. On one occasion Winterton described me as the rudest man in the House. That was quite a tribute from him because at the time I was not trying very hard and Winterton himself could be pretty rough. He was a great House of Commons man and I was delighted on the last day of the 1950 Parliament, October 4, 1951, to be called by Mr Speaker immediately following Winterton's farewell speech, and could thus pay tribute to the Father of the House and one of my mentors. Even more delightful was the receipt next morning of Winterton's gracefully written acknowledgement.

My interest in Parliamentary procedure notwithstanding, I approached my maiden speech with trepidation. Shinwell, as usual, provided the political aspirin. 'Don't worry too much about style —certainly don't worry about grammar,' he advised me. 'The vast majority of Members are reasonable human beings many of whom have experienced your emotions. They will always listen with respect to a Member who has mastered his facts and speaks with sincerity.'

Another influence in my developing sense of belonging to the House of Commons was the fact that Sandy Lindsay accepted a peerage soon after the 1945 election. He had been invited in 1943 by Churchill to join the small group of Labour Peers and had declined because, I think, of Mrs Lindsay's opposition. In 1945 the offer was renewed though not with any great warmth. Attlee never showed much regard for men of the intellectual calibre of Lindsay, Tawney, Laski, H. L. Beales, who introduced me into the exciting, stimulating Laski 'circle', and G. D. H. Cole. His dislike and distrust of Laski I could understand, although I did not approve, but I regretted his reluctance to recognize the service to Labour of some of its greatest men. Lindsay accepted on the understanding that not too great a claim would be made on his time. He attended the Lords once a week and we arranged to lunch together on that day. We began by arranging to have a meal in the Members' Dining Room of the House of Commons one week and in the House of Lords Dining Room the next. And thereby hangs a tale.

When lunching in the Members' Dining Room, Mr L. H. Mumford, the Superintendent told me I was out of order in bringing Lord Lindsay into the room. I apologized and said I had seen other Members of the House of Lords there. 'Yes,' Mumford explained, 'but the privilege is confined to those Peers who were formerly Members of the House of Commons.' I expressed regret and promised not to err again. A few minutes later Mumford returned to say that the complaining Member insisted that Lord Lindsay should leave the Members' Dining Room at once. I noted that Mumford had gone to the Shadow Cabinet table where Churchill was sitting. I picked up our plates and carried them to the Strangers' Dining Room. Time can revenge the wounds it heals. One day in 1952 Churchill, now

Prime Minister, had Lord Woolton as his guest for lunch in the Members' Dining Room. I called Mumford and, greatly though I regretted embarrassing him, insisted: 'Treat them as Mr Churchill treated Lord Lindsay.' Back came the answer: 'It won't happen again.' I had the final word: 'You remember Lord Lindsay was made to move. Now Mr Churchill's guest can do the same.' After lunch I called on Mr Speaker and told him what had happened. I said I was undoubtedly out of order in the first incident and perhaps I should have apologized to the House or to his predecessor. I told Mr Speaker it was my intention to bring this second incident before the House as soon as it met. Mr Speaker Morrison asked me to leave the matter with him. I agreed on the understanding that I did not forfeit any of my rights by delay. Next day, when Mr Speaker told me he had rebuked the Member concerned, I readily agreed to let the matter drop.

Life in 1945 was made the more pleasant by sharing it with two great friends, Harold Davies and the late Stephen Swingler. Our homes were in North Staffordshire. We had been good companions in the W.E.A. and in the Labour Movement. During the War Stephen's wife, Anne, had a flat in Millman Street, Bloomsbury, which we took over. I tried to organize the ménage and laid myself open to the charge of running it with the iron hand of an N.C.O. in charge of an Army hut. Swingler was a man of fine intellect and integrity and with a personality of engaging charm. His untimely death in 1969 cut short what would certainly have been a distinguished Ministerial career. Davies who became Parliamentary Secretary to the Ministry of Pensions, and subsequently Parliamentary Private Secretary to Prime Minister Wilson, is a man of compassion and humour and a loyal friend.

Our shared experience in adult education convinced us that the spearhead of Labour progress must be an informed public opinion. We set down on paper how we might help the Labour Movement and approached Morgan Phillips, General Secretary of the Labour Party, only to be told how slender were the Party's financial resources. Morgan Phillips said that if he were given additional money and had to choose between expenditure on organization or education, he would opt for organization. Morgan Phillips had a point, of course, but I recall that, on the other side of the political fence, R. A. Butler did exactly the opposite. In 1945 the Tory Party could have slipped out of the mainstream of national thought and tradition. In the aftermath of savage electoral defeat it might have splintered or taken a vicious Right Wing turn. Lord Butler, when he decided to reorganize the Tory Party, used adult education techniques in preparing the ground for 1951 and saved his party. He also made an important contribution to the well-being of Britain; Labour's electoral victory had aroused passions that could have resulted, as too many Tories desired, in an ugly political atmosphere.

Swingler, Davies and I often discussed whether British democracy could stand the strain of a Labour Government that meant business, coupled with all the hardships and difficulties involved in transforming a nation from a war to a peace-time footing. After our rebuff by Morgan Phillips we organized a question and answer team under the title *Any Questions*. We had operated this technique in North Staffordshire before the war. I think the successful B.B.C. *Brains Trust*, started in 1941, and the less successful pre-war *Town Meetings of the Air* may have been inspired by our W.E.A. experiments. We held *Any Questions* meetings all over the country. Instead of delivering speeches, we answered questions on subjects raised by members of the audience. Ian Mikardo, who became one of the most skilful practitioners in the *Any Questions* field and a pioneer of the *Tribune Any Questions* team, was taken by us to Orpington and there introduced to the technique for the first time.

The first duty of a Member of Parliament is to look after his constituents. I learned what that meant on my first day in the House as a Member. At the House of Commons Post Office I collected bundle after bundle of letters from constituents, many of them in the Forces. Back in the Millman Street flat, with help from two or three Service friends, we tackled this mass correspondence on military lines. Numerous problems simply had to be discussed personally because the letters were not informative enough or the writers had difficulty in expressing themselves clearly. So I started 'political surgeries' in my constituency where I met constituents face to face. I estimate that as an M.P. I wrote upwards of 75,000 letters covering about 25,000 constituency cases, besides dealing with the voluminous general correspondence that comes to all active M.P.s. Without the voluntary help of Mrs Elsie Welch, who exemplified in her service to her fellow-citizens the best that is in the Labour Movement, and many good comrades like her, my 'surgeries' might never have got off the ground. Equally helpful were the local officials of Dudley and Stourbridge Councils. Much of my work would have been fruitless but for the courtesy of Ministers and Parliamentary Secretaries, Tory as well as Labour. One ex-Serviceman, sick with frustration, had added to his papers the request that I should not refer them to the War Office as the Minister was a Tory. I told him that the then Secretary of State was among the most sympathetic and honourable men I knew; and I could have said the same about almost every Service Minister who held office while I was in the House of Commons.

A heart-warming experience was to meet many members of other political parties at my surgeries. They came, I felt, because of the conception of duty I expressed to constitutents on each of the seven occasions I was declared their M.P. The campaigns were always hard fought. Twice they were pretty rough. Always, however, I recited the same post-script: 'We have had a hard fight. What we now need to recall is that our democracy only works, and will only continue to work, if we never forget that the things that unite us are infinitely greater than the things that divide us. As your Member of Parliament I will always be mindful of that basic fact.' During twenty-two years as M.P. for Dudley and Stourbridge (joined to my Dudley constituency in 1950) I made friends in all parties. I recall with gratitude that of all the constituents seeking my help I can count on the fingers of one hand the number who were phoney or dishonest. Of course people tend to put on their story a gloss favourable to their case—that is human nature—and I had no means of testing the facts placed before me. Thus I acted on the basis that my job was to be an effective link between the individual citizen and the point where decisions were taken. I promised in 1945 to be a friend to every constituent in need, irrespective of political allegiance. This enabled me, in each succeeding election, to campaign on the same slogan: 'George Wigg—Your Friend in Deed'.

On the morrow of Labour's Election victory, the Japanese war ended and Lend-Lease was stopped summarily on August 21, 1945 —a crippling blow to a nation mobilized so completely for war that conversion to peace could not be easy. Many Labour Ministers in the Coalition did not want a 1945 General Election. Tom Williams, at that time Parliamentary Secretary to the Minister of Agriculture, expressed the view that the Party's decision to force an Election was disastrous, and Shinwell often related how, at the Blackpool Conference of 1945, he and Nye Bevan had forced the pace in the teeth of opposition, in particular from Ernest Bevin, who wanted the

Coalition to continue until the Japanese War had ended. A critical point was reached when Morrison joined Shinwell and Bevan. The decisive voice, however, was that of the Labour Chief Whip, Willie Whiteley, who told the National Executive—I quote his words to me—'the lads would not stand for continuing the Coalition', the 'lads' being the rank and file of the Parliamentary Labour Party.

After the General Election doubts about the Government's zeal in applying Party policy were bound to follow some of Attlee's appointments, doubts that were still potent when he gave office to Evelyn King in 1947 and Aidan Crawley in 1950. One story was that Attlee met King in a train, urged him to stand as a Labour candidate, then gave him office. The story deserves to be true; its truth would provide some logical basis for helping King into Parliament, although Attlee's reasons for giving him office still defy analysis. At least Crawley played cricket!

I was busy as Shinwell's P.P.S. and he, being a good boss, encouraged my interest in defence affairs. By 1945 the Regular Army had almost vanished. Although World War I lasted four years and three months, many N.C.O.s and men remained serving on Regular engagements and formed a nucleus around which the post-war Army could be built. World War II lasted six years and, consequently, the Regular nucleus still serving was tiny. In 1919 the Army had been reconstructed with the aid of a recruiting programme offering special terms to men signing on for special short-service engagements of from two to four years duration. They got leave and a bounty. In 1945 there was an obvious need for a policy to plan and develop resources of Regular manpower, but little forward planning was done before V.E. day. The nuts and bolts side of the Army, as usual, had been relegated to a very back room.

Remembering the plans of 1919 and 1920, recorded in two special Army Orders, I talked to the Secretary of State for War, Jack Lawson, who had served in the Royal Field Artillery in World War I. My proposals were these: efforts should be made to recruit Regular soldiers by offering one year's leave and a substantial bounty; the Territorial Army should obtain men by offering soldiers accelerated release in return for their agreement to join the Territorial Army. Lawson gave me a kindly welcome, listened intently, asked no questions, took no notes and did nothing. Later, I had a somewhat similar experience as member of a delegation to the Minister of Defence, A.V. Alexander, to impress upon him the need for reorganization of the Army Supplementary Reserve and make proposals about other aspects of our manpower problems. 'A.V.' took a lively, intelligent interest in what we had to say, but Fred Bellenger, then Secretary of State for War, gave us little encouragement. Shortly afterwards, several of our proposals were adopted by the War Office. They were already in the pipe-line when the Ministers met us, and Fred Bellenger, certainly, was completely unaware of what the War Office was doing! Another chastening experience was the rumpus created by the famous 'Clyde group' when, pleading for Army education, I pointed to the high rate of illiteracy among recruits from Scotland. The fierce refusal of Clyde M.P.s, especially the Rev. Campbell Stephen, to face the known facts astounded me. Where, I pondered bitterly, had the radical realism of the Left Wing gone?

Fortunately, it had a faithful custodian in Shinwell. A Czech friend, who came to Stoke as a refugee in 1939, was threatened with deportation during the anti-Communist passion let loose in 1948, and I gave notice to raise the matter on an Adjournment Motion. The Chief Whip summoned me. Waiting in his room were Chuter Ede and Herbert Morrison. They warned me that if I persisted the Prime Minister had ruled that I must resign as P.P.S. to Shinwell, then Secretary of State for War. I asked Morrison if Shinwell knew about Attlee's decision. On his negative reply I commented: 'Don't you think he should be told?' He agreed, so I 'phoned Shinwell. After I had described the situation he said: 'Do what you feel you should do.' I told Shinwell that I would pursue the matter on the Adjournment next day and that Morrison had asked me to announce my resignation during my speech. Very early next morning—it was still dark—my telephone rang. Shinwell asked: 'Did you tell the Press you were going to resign?' and continued: 'I ask because they have been on to me. What are you going to do?' I reiterated my intention and Shinwell told me: 'Do not announce your resignation. If they force you to resign, I shall resign too.' That story is my answer to those in the House, and there were some, who sought to doubt Shinwell's loyalty to his friends.

The flat in Millman Street was a place of lively discussion. We thrashed out the pros and cons of the American Loan; hammered away at questions of foreign policy, trying to fathom how Foreign Office officials could have captured Ernie Bevin; and we struggled to understand the philosophy of the Attlee Government.

Our discussions led to some M.P.s forming the *Keep Left* group. The famous *Keep Left* pamphlet was written by Michael Foot, R. H. S. Crossman and Ian Mikardo. They took responsibility for the detail and form of its arguments, with the whole group of concurring M.P.s sharing responsibility for its contents. We sought to define a modern philosophy for Labour and to represent, quite properly, the 'politics of expectation'. We drew heavily on the thinking of R. H. Tawney, A. D. Lindsay, William Temple and Harold Laski. Unfortunately, after the Party went into Opposition, 'expectation' became a synonym for personal ambition. Some of the twenty or so *Keep Left* groupers were close friends of Bevan. I admired him and got on well with him. I thought his success at the Ministry of Health had earned him promotion to the Chancellorship of the Exchequer that went to Gaitskell. Bevan was passed over for two reasons. Attlee distrusted him and Morrison, who had not been a success as Foreign Secretary, would not agree to be out-distanced by any rival.

Bevan, despite wide knowledge and acute intelligence, failed to appreciate the political limitations of some of his friends. His career might have been even more distinguished if he had attached the importance it deserved to some of the political advice he was offered. He had one tremendous Parliamentary triumph about which I can testify personally. Churchill, in the 1951 Defence debate, knew that Labour policy was right but tried to split the pacifist Left from the Government and encompass the Government's defeat on a major issue, thus forcing a General Election. To the last we hoped the patriotism of the Shadow Cabinet expressed, according to our information, by Butler and Eden, would prevail over Churchill's opportunism. It did not. On the second day of the debate, February 15, Churchill moved this amendment: 'That this House while supporting all measures conceived in the real interest of national security, has no confidence in the ability of His Majesty's present Ministers to carry out an effective and consistent defence policy in concert with their allies, having regard to their record of vacillation and delay.'

I can recall no proposition more clearly intended to tickle the ears of the groundlings during my time in Parliament. It sought to denigrate defence from a national issue into a vulgar Party brawl. Bevan, Minister of Labour and National Service, replied for the Government. He asked me to brief him on the defence aspects.

Throughout our long discussion and argument he took no notes. Yet he mastered the case completely and handed out devastating punishment to the Opposition. Several times he trapped Churchill into interruptions then smashed him into sullen silence. Churchill, Bevan teased, once the decoy of the Tory Party, had undergone a transformation; he had become their Jonah. Labour, Bevan went on, had brought into productive industry 1,800,000 men and women, who in 1939 had not been mobilized either for the Armed Services or for the civil economy. In the last three or four years we had made a greater contribution to defence than any country of comparable size. The Tory Party, like the Communist Party, was a century out of date; it was incapable of defending Social Democracy against dictatorship, Soviet or, indeed, any other kind. Bevan destroyed the amendment, supported by several hours of Tory oratory, in twenty triumphant minutes. I doubt if Hansard has ever reported so scintillating a success achieved in so short a space of Parliamentary time.

Bevan was a genius, but an undisciplined genius. How else could so able a man assume that no administrative change could be tolerated in the National Health Service? This, surely, was an aberration of genius in search of power. It is not practical politics to turn problems of social administration into issues of high principle, as Miss Jennie Lee was forced to agree when she discovered that the re-distributive policies of the 1966 Labour Government, and its pursuit of social justice, were more important than an increase in the price of prescriptions.

A matter of regret to me was that Bevan and Shinwell never hit it off together. Both were a credit to the working-class Movement. Neither had anything to fear from the political ambitions of the other. Shinwell was more steadfast and more reliable than Bevan and—dare I say it as his closest friend?—he chose his companions with more wisdom. Yet Bevan was a giant among men. A mighty tribune of Socialism, he also made a decisive mark on social legislation. If only he had kept clear of Lord Beaverbrook and, later, of the political pygmies who walked in his shadow, the Labour Movement might well have avoided the plight into which men of less vision led it.

Meanwhile, for Shinwell and me, 1946 had begun a long, long day of travail at the Ministry of Fuel and Power. There was a tragicomic aspect to Shinwell's introduction to the job. When instructed by Attlee to nationalize the mines, he inquired at Transport House

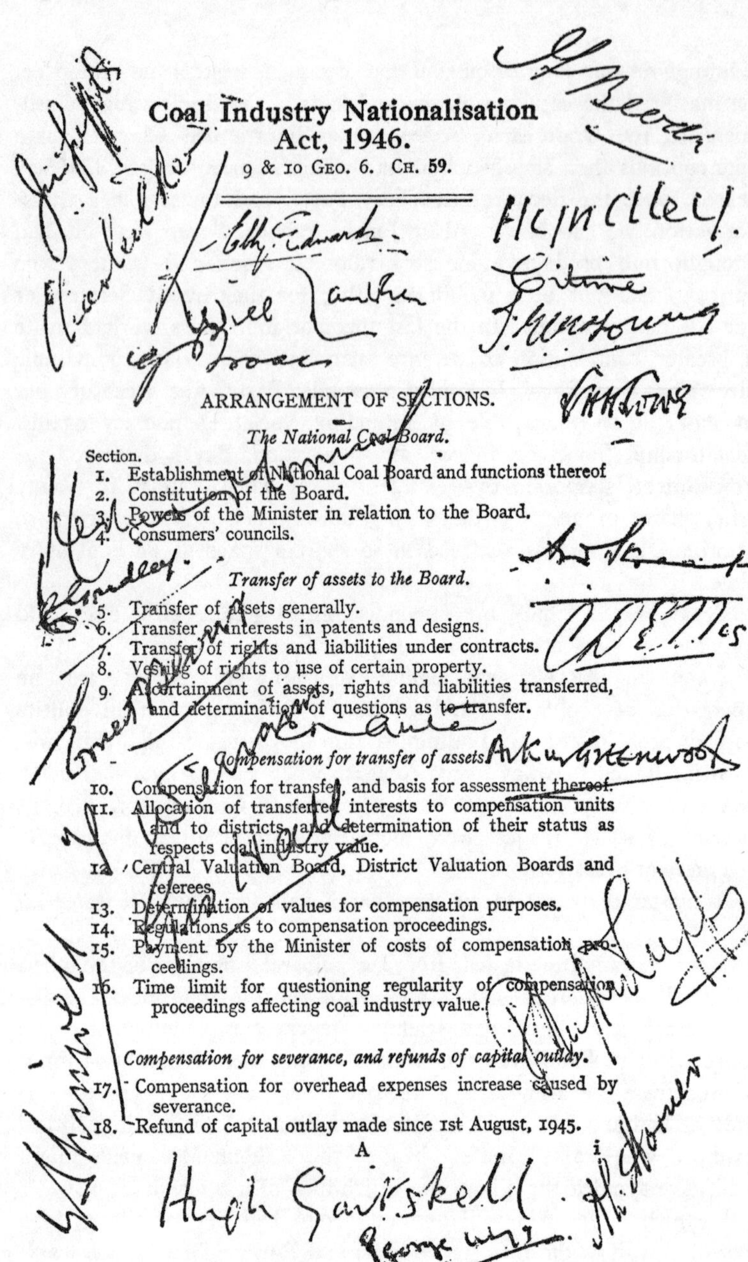

*A copy of the Coal Industry Nationalization Act
signed by all the members of the Cabinet*

124

for the products of Labour thinking over the years. After all, this was not a new subject. Coal nationalization had been on Labour's programme for a quarter of a century. Somebody must have worked out something at some time. The archives were ransacked and revealed two copies of a paper written by Jim Griffiths, one of them a translation into Welsh!

Our problem, as a nation dependent on coal, resulted from neglect and short-sightedness in dealing with the mines in the years between 1906 and 1929. During that period, while other countries reorganized their coal production, concentrating on mechanized output, British coal owners did little or nothing to ensure a prosperous future for their industry. The picture was clearly outlined in Sir Charles Reid's 1945 Report on Coal Mining:

> British mine owners usually leased small areas of land around a single pit, and often the result was an unduly small or awkwardly shaped lease. Elsewhere, both the concession and the mine were established on a much larger scale.
>
> In the British system there was heavy pressure on the mine proprietor to work his lease for immediate results. This was a short-term policy that built up problems for the future.
>
> The grouping of mines under a single ownership facilitated the closing down or merging of uneconomic mines and a more concentrated use of common hoisting and service operations.
>
> In Britain, ownership was widely dispersed and, although the Coal Production Act of 1930 had increased the machinery of carrying through amalgamations, recourse to do so was optional, and few made use of it.
>
> In European mines the basic skeletal lay-out was straight passage-ways through solid strata, from which coal seams could be reached directly and efficiently.
>
> In Britain, the underground lay-out in the main followed the inclination of the coal seam. The passage-ways were undulating and circuitous, and the task of reconstruction was thereby rendered more difficult and quite costly. . . . The British failed to change their techniques to meet the changing circumstances in their own mines.

In 1946, however, an immediate crisis faced us. Men were leaving the pits at the rate of 70,000 a year while the demand for coal, particularly from electricity generating stations, was rising rapidly.

Already in 1942 war production had been endangered by falling output although the facts were not revealed to the public. A scheme for full-scale fuel rationing was prepared by Lord Beveridge, approved by the War Cabinet and truncated by the still pervasive influence of the Tory 1922 Committee. Sir John Anderson's request for the release of 7,000 miners was turned down by Churchill for military reasons.

In the winter of 1943 coal stocks stood at twenty million tons. Fuel rationing did not stop them falling to fourteen million tons in 1944. After a War Cabinet decision to speed up the release of miners from the Forces, Churchill instructed the Minister of Fuel and Power, on April 30, 1945, to 'make sure there would be no coal shortage this winter'. This decision, alas, came too late to prevent a fall to eleven million tons, the total stock Shinwell inherited in August, 1945.

He expected a safety margin of twenty million tons; we were nine million tons short. The scheme to allow for the quick release of miners from the Forces never really got off the ground. It brought in a mere trickle while there was an increasing outflow of 'Bevin Boys' and those who had entered mining in preference to military service—all this at a time when coal production was our most urgent national need. Cripps at the Board of Trade was expanding the use of electrically-generated machinery to increase productivity while, simultaneously, denying the coal industry electrical equipment needed to raise output and assure the success of his own passionate endeavour to speed the conversion of industry from war to peace. The Government, too, was pursuing the barmy policy of filling shops with domestic electrical goods while we lacked the fuel to keep the power stations going, especially at peak hours.

Shinwell decided the problem required immediate attention at Cabinet level. In the autumn of 1946, Morrison, Lord President of the Council and co-ordinating Minister, was given figures showing the losses, because of lack of transport, of deep-mined and open-cast coal which would otherwise have been available to consumers. He was also informed that the number of miners had fallen to well below 700,000. Attlee instructed Dalton, Chancellor of the Exchequer, to examine the problem together with the Minister of Labour, George Isaacs, the Minister of Transport, Alfred Barnes, and Shinwell. I thought Attlee's move was a blunder. Dalton was preoccupied with Treasury problems besides being opposed to open-cast operations.

Although disturbed by the facts, he took no action. The amazing truth is that, apart from Shinwell, the Ministers charged with responsibility for co-ordinating action never understood the reality of the problem. Our manpower situation was grave, but there was no shortage of fuel at the pitheads. Our difficulties were rooted in transport, not in coal production. Coal de-stocking began during the first week in November to meet the large demand during the months of December, January and February. Re-stocking moved into full swing during March. Keeping stocks in balance depended upon the 'bull' weeks when miners boosted output to earn holiday money. Bad weather in February, therefore, might be disastrous. It was!

This, to my lance-corporal-trained mind, was a matter of organization and logistics. We should tackle manpower shortages by offering demobilization inducements to miners still in the Army, and we should offer other soldiers stepped-up inducements for service in the pits. To many men early, indeed immediate, release from the Services would be a great attraction; to those in distant stations with many months still to serve it would be an irresistible bait. This was our best hope and Shinwell pressed it unavailingly on the Service Ministers. Bevan's imagination cottoned on to our quick action policy and he was an enthusiastic collaborator in allocating new housing in mining areas. From mid-June onwards, many ingenious proposals were advanced to economize the use of fuel, ensure swifter repair of wagons, and improve methods of distributing coal. All tended to be overtaken by industry's growing demand and the reluctance of Cripps either to release new machinery for the mines or temporarily to restrict industrial production, especially of electrical consumer goods.

Dalton and his Cabinet Coal Committee never showed any sign of life. At a meeting in December 1946, he received a report that lorries were being sent to the Midland coalfields to shift accumulated stocks. In theory, one hundred and fifty lorries were available; in fact, eight were working! On the rail side, too, reports were disturbing. Turn-round of wagons had not speeded up; nothing much was done about it.

No man could have worked harder than Shinwell. His treatment by some of his colleagues was deplorable, Dalton being especially vindictive. Looking back, I think Shinwell should have insisted upon explaining the position to his fellow-countrymen. Dalton, then, would have had to get on or get out. Shinwell believed he could win through.

He knew and trusted the miners. They knew and trusted him. He thought they would respond to his appeals. They did. But both were beaten by the collapse of transport and bad weather.

In the critical weeks following nationalization in January 1947, a work force of comparative size produced, on average, twenty-nine thousand more tons of saleable coal per week than in the corresponding weeks of 1946. When the big freeze started over one million tons of coal were laid up at pitheads and railway sidings, unable to move because of the inaction of the Dalton Committee. The country was let down by lack of co-operation in the direction of the Government's economic strategy and, of course, by the British climate.

At the beginning of January, estimated stocks were more than double the figure for November. On January 3, Shinwell reported on stocks to his colleagues and again drew attention to lack of transport. Although figures for January were good, distribution problems had been intensified, as foreseen, by the volume of transport traffic over Christmas and a serious shortage of locomotives. Shinwell suggested transport of coal should be given over-riding rail priority for one month, as military traffic had before 'D'-Day. This proposal was put to the Dalton Committee on January 6. Hugh Gaitskell, Parliamentary Under Secretary, representing Shinwell, explained that we wanted to reduce the coal in the pipelines, but got little support. Instead he was given a gloomy report on the transport situation. Railways were not working at week-ends. Absenteeism was giving trouble. The National Union of Railwaymen had failed to inspire a co-operative attitude among its members. The Minister of Transport considered the Ministry of Fuel and Power's proposal would disrupt other traffic and create more difficulties than it would solve. Nevertheless, the Committee referred the decision to the Cabinet. Shinwell informed Attlee personally that coal stocks at gas and electricity plants were dangerously low. Neither Attlee nor the Cabinet acted. At a later meeting of the Dalton Committee Shinwell pointed out that there were nearly nine-hundred thousand tons of coal in the pipelines compared with a normal figure for a mid-winter day of six hundred and eighty thousand; two hundred and twenty thousand tons of coal were immobilised for lack of transport. Meantime electricity consumption was rising and at the end of January reached an all-time peak.

On January 30 the worst snow blizzard for fifty years hit the country. Ships could not leave North-Eastern ports, loading facilities at docks were paralysed, railway lines were blocked and points were frozen. Many collieries closed because miners could not reach them. At any time such a climatic disaster would have threatened the national life. Coming when the traffic crisis had reached its height, it was catastrophic. Shinwell, the responsible Minister, was now paying the price of his colleagues' irresponsibility.

I retain strange memories of those days. Shinwell asked the weather experts, in the interest of forward planning, if we had experienced, as somebody had surmised, the coldest winter since 1894. The answer was that no deduction could be made 'as, for the earlier period, the figure is given for the full three months, whereas the three months we are experiencing have not yet finished'! Since 1840 there had been only six winters with twenty-three or more days of snow. In 1947 up until mid-February there had been twenty days. Cabinet colleagues, Bevan, Isaacs, and Griffiths, came to offer such help as they could. When I informed the Minister of Transport, absent in Glasgow at a Co-operative meeting, that electricity supplies were threatened, Barnes kept what would now be called his 'cool'. He promised to look into the situation when he returned on the following Monday morning!

At the height of the crisis, the situation facing us was this: unless supplies of fuel got through to the power stations, organized life in Britain would come to a halt. Without electric power many areas would have no light, no water and, in some places, sewage would not be pumped. The one solution, whatever the weather, was to treat the problem for what it was—a transport problem. And that was how it was solved. A pleasant memory was that Gaitskell, Dalton's nominee in the Ministry, did his job ably and faithfully. He was in continuous session presiding over a committee, tackling problems as they arose, improvising and generally making the best of a bad job.

Before the crisis had passed into history the long-maturing plot to oust Shinwell erupted. Dalton was plotter-in-chief; he had to cover up his incompetence as Chairman of the Cabinet Coal Committee. Shinwell was harassed and worried but he was not without comrades. I suggested a talk with Sydney Elliott of the *Daily Mirror* whose parents Shinwell had known as personal friends. I met Elliott from a train after midnight. He stayed at the Ministry as 'a sympathetic ear' for several hours. This contact did a power of good. When I returned to the Ministry next day, Shinwell was his usual clear-minded, energetic self. He was chuckling over a *Daily Mirror* leader which stated the plain facts, asked what Dalton had been doing, and answered, 'Damn all'.

Those after Shinwell's scalp wanted Bevan's as well. Only the circumstance that Morrison was away ill concentrated the attack on Shinwell alone. Among his stalwart supporters was Arthur Horner. Communist he was but, during Shinwell's spell at Fuel and Power, Horner showed qualities of patriotism and integrity. A dispute arose over the length of the stint at a Yorkshire coalfield. Horner was the one miners' national leader who, with Shinwell, faced angry strikers at many meetings at which both Horner and Shinwell told the miners that the country could not spend vast sums on mechanising the mines without getting increased production.

Irritated by the sniping of his enemies Shinwell talked about resignation. We had our usual wrangle and did not reach agreement. Attlee was planning a Government reconstruction. He told Shinwell that, with the nationalization of coal and electricity completed and gas nationalization well on the way, it would no longer be necessary to have the Minister of Fuel and Power in the Cabinet. This, Shinwell thought, was Attlee's way of breaking the news. Attlee also indicated that Cripps, as well as Dalton, was determined to get him out. Shinwell was hurt as well as angry. He thought of Cripps as a friend. During the crisis Cripps had written one of his red ink notes expressing sympathy and support. Now the 'Saint' emerged as the 'Immaculate Deception'.

Shinwell eventually accepted he must leave Fuel and Power, but was uncertain about his future although, as appeared later, Attlee intended to send him to the War Office. Backed by his family, he wanted to resign. The argument raged for days. I called in Harold Laski who told Shinwell he was letting down those who believed in him and his policy. Hopeful that Shinwell would do nothing rash I went home to Stoke on Friday, October 3, planning to return on the eve of the announcement of Ministerial changes, due on Tuesday, October 7. The Saturday and Sunday newspapers were full of inspired tittle-tattle. The *Daily Telegraph* front page 'splash' on Saturday suggested that Cabinet changes might be delayed; Attlee could not find replacements for junior Ministers wanting to move; senior Ministers were resisting co-ordination; Bevan and Shinwell would resign rather than accept a reduction in status. By Monday the *Telegraph* decided that the changes might be sweeping. On Tuesday, following week-end speeches by miners' leaders in support of Shinwell

and Bevan, the newspaper declared that Attlee's prestige was at
stake. Because Griffiths was to make a speech on the fuel position a
few days later it assumed that he would become Minister of Fuel and
Power.

Meantime, on Sunday morning, Shinwell summoned me back to
London. He was more determined than ever to throw his hand in.
More wearing hours of argument stimulated a small hope that he
would make no move before Tuesday. On Tuesday morning, before
information was issued to the Press, Shinwell learned that Dalton's
nominee, Gaitskell, was to succeed him. This was denigration with a
vengeance. His anger knew no bounds. He 'phoned Attlee to say
that he was on his way to No. 10 to resign. I accompanied him.
On the short journey to Downing Street from Smith Square the
situation was transformed. Thinking aloud, Shinwell muttered: 'Who
do they think I am, asking me to be Secretary of State for War?' I
exploded, demanding who the hell *he* thought he was. Any man should
be proud to be political head of the Army. I peppered my criticism
with appropriate adjectives, emphasizing that there had not been a
good War Secretary since Haldane and that he should be honoured
to have the chance to be answerable to Parliament for the Army and,
above all, to be answerable to the Army for what Parliament required
it to do. I spoke more violently than I had ever done before.
Shinwell continued to detail reasons for refusal. With seconds to go,
and while I was still bawling him out, he put his hand on my shoulder
and said, 'Yes, there is something in what you say, George'. Then,
very quietly, he asked: 'If I become Secretary of State for War will
you be my Under-Secretary?' I told him Attlee would never accept
such a proposal and went on: 'I'll tell you what I'll do, I'll continue
to be your P.P.S.' As we reached the door of No. 10 Shinwell decided
to go to the War Office on the condition that he received all Cabinet
papers on defence. Attlee agreed, and Shinwell entered upon a new
career which earned for him, among all ranks of the Army, the
respect and affection in which politicians of all Parties and the British
public now hold him.

The truth was Attlee had to move Shinwell. The evidence of lack
of co-ordination in the Government had convinced him that he must
carry through a full-scale reconstruction. The Cabinet was reduced
from nineteen to eighteen. Five senior Ministers were sacked—Joe
Westwood (Scottish Office), Lord Inman (Lord Privy Seal), Fred
Bellenger (War), John Wilmot (Supply) and John Hynd (Pensions).

Six junior Ministers were dropped. The new intake included George Brown, James Callaghan, Michael Stewart, Arthur Bottomley and Alfred Robens. Harold Wilson became President of the Board of Trade and Cripps was made responsible for all aspects of economic affairs.

There was one more moment of concern during the personal drama within the national crisis. The public announcement of Gaitskell's succession was certain to arouse lobby gossip and comment which I wanted Shinwell to miss. I asked Elliott by telephone to help me get him away from the House. Elliott chuckled over the prospect of keeping Shinwell away from the Press by hiding him in the flat of a newspaper Boss, Harry Guy Bartholomew, and replied: 'Tell Manny Bart wants to have tea with him. I shall fix things with Bart and collect Manny in fifteen minutes.' Bart travelled to his flat by taxi, sending Elliott and Wiggs, his devoted friend and chauffeur, for Shinwell. That was my most enjoyable ploy for many months past.

Shinwell has a gift for so organizing his time that, despite pre-occupation with departmental problems, he could promote policies on other big issues. While at Fuel and Power he tried to convert the Government to the need for a National Wages Policy, first mooted in the *Daily Mirror*. The two-fold nature of the problem, as Shinwell saw it, was that, with full employment and a general labour shortage, wages might rise at a rate that would impair price stabilization policy and increase the difficulty of securing wage differentials for high priority, under-manned industries. The core of the case was this: *relative* wages influence the flow of labour into one industry or another; *thus the desired relative wage structure cannot be arrived at by any method of fixing wages in one industry alone.* Shinwell went on to argue that independent collective bargaining, industry by in-dustry, could not guarantee avoidance of inflation and ensure a rational distribution of manpower. A National Wages Authority should be responsible for ensuring price stabilization and distribution of labour in accordance with Government economic policy; it should guarantee reasonable living standards and give maximum in-centives to efficiency; and it should exercise controls to reduce the scope of employment in less essential industries. There, in 1946, was one possible answer to problems still plaguing politicians in the 'seventies.

Before and after the coal crisis, Shinwell revealed that courage which is his outstanding characteristic. He told the Labour Party Conference in 1946: 'In embarking on industrial experiment we must not depend exclusively on slogans, but on careful and well-thought-out preparation. . . . If, in the coming years, the Movement is to embark on a programme of industrial and economic legislation more comprehensive in character than we have designed for the present Parliament, research is a primary pre-requisite. . . . I regret to say that, apart from a re-affirmation of principle, there has been very little guidance on detail.' Addressing the Co-operative Congress in 1948, he said: 'If there were defects in Labour policy and its application it was only right that they should be exposed. When the mining industry was nationalized . . . we thought we knew all about it; the fact of the matter was, we did not.' Some people deplored this plain speaking. A young politician, James Callaghan, denounced Shinwell's plea for the exercise of foresight as being destructive of public confidence in Labour Party policy. Perhaps he knows better now. Callaghan's letter, informing Shinwell that he would raise the issue at a Parliamentary Labour Party meeting, was 'lost' as an act of kindness by the recipient of his foolish criticism.

A persistent memory of the coal crisis and its aftermath was Attlee's calmness of spirit. True, he gave a man a job and expected him to get on with it; yet there was more, much more, to Attlee than that. He had an uncanny understanding of the individual charac-teristics of all his Ministers. Since he expected them to act in character he never flustered in times of trouble. He had to appease the vindictive spirit of those who wanted to destroy Shinwell. He did appease them but he did not destroy Shinwell. His Cabinet, in my opinion, was too representative of vested interests within the Labour Party. He regarded it right to make it so. He gathered around himself Ministers of such calibre that if anyone kicked over the traces exactly nothing happened; Bevan, Wilson and John Freeman resigned together without rocking the boat overmuch. Attlee devised the Overlord system of government, made it work and be-queathed it to Churchill, who failed to keep it working. There are those who claim that Attlee betrayed the social revolution. He did not believe in social revolution. He regarded the Labour Manifesto of 1945 as a blue-print for what he himself called 'an adventure in social justice'. His duty was to implement the Manifesto in those terms. He did. Many of us argued in 1951 that if he had held on for four months Labour would have been returned again with a reasonable majority. He felt the public interest required a General Election in 1951, and so it happened.

While, as Paymaster General, I was Chairman of the Governors of the Royal Hospital, Chelsea, concern arose over Attlee's fast failing health. I consulted his family about a proposal to find him a flat in the Hospital where he could live with his faithful batman and have immediate access to the best medical advice. Attlee would not agree. When he died a private family service followed the public funeral. At this service the four guest mourners were all old friends, Arthur Moyle, Harold Wilson, Manny and myself.

Chapter Seven: Shinwell's P.P.S.

Emanuel Shinwell's return to the War Office as Secretary of State was greeted with more than official politeness. He was remembered as an efficient Financial Secretary and appreciated as a 'bonny fighter'. Field Marshal Montgomery recognized in him another man of dimension and character; they became firm friends. Shinwell started off by meeting staff at all levels, listening sympathetically to their problems and indicating his approach to the job as he saw it. These informal meetings culminated, in June 1948, in a party at the Albert Hall attended by three thousand people from the Adjutant General, Sir James Steele, down to the youngest typist—a new departure in War Office staff relationships.

Critics of Shinwell's appointment, of course, were thick on the ground. Pacifists were vociferous. The less scrupulous hinted that he had been a pacifist in World War I although, in fact, he had been exempted from service because his organizing work among seamen was of national importance. Some sections of the Press were vitriolic. The *Sunday Express*, on October 22, 1947, printed Shinwell's home address in Tooting and said of Mrs Shinwell, 'She keeps house and still washes her own doorstep'. Another snide snigger was that Shinwell borrowed twopence from Churchill explaining 'I want to telephone a friend'. 'Here's fourpence', was the alleged reply. 'Take it and you can call all of them.'

Within a month Shinwell was *en rapport* with the Army rank and file. He inspected the Wessex Training Centre at Bulford, informing himself about facilities, accommodation and married quarters. He visited the Staff College at Camberley, an Army Corrective Establishment at Colchester, and Western Command, then went down to Southampton to greet troops embarking for Port Said. He observed all the courtesies, taking his hat off on entering a Sergeants Mess and conversing informally with officers and men. The troops called him 'Manny' and the Secretary of State lost no dignity in his enjoyment of their camaraderie. This civilian Minister was a human link with home, even when speaking about closer co-operation between the Services and insisting that the Army be trained in modern methods with modern weapons. He was elated by growing public understanding—cartooned by David Low in the *Evening Standard*—that the policy he had pursued at Fuel and Power was bearing fruit. By the end of 1947 the soreness of having been ousted from the Ministry of Fuel and Power had vanished. Shinwell was operating like a man who had been in the job for years.

We made a memorable visit to Cologne, Hamburg and Berlin early in 1948. Shinwell's obvious pride in the British Army of the Rhine evoked a spontaneous, heart-warming response. Our one surprise, at a Four Power reception, was when a public relations officer prevented him from being photographed in the company of Russians. The Cold War was freezing simple courtesies. It was pleasure unalloyed to follow on with trips to Northern Command, Malta and Gibraltar.

The Shinwell success story was anathema to the Tories. They hated the idea that any civilian, especially a progressive in politics, should head a Service Department. Civilians like Haldane and Shinwell, with a capacity for mastering military problems and the courage to defend the Army in Parliament, were bound to be Army reformers; and Army reform had never featured in any Tory policy. That is less true nowadays, largely because national necessity had to triumph over political prejudice in 1940. Churchill, in *The Second World War*, tells how, in the rush of events, he promised to give King George VI a list of the first five members of his Grand Coalition, the selection of Service Ministers being vitally important. A. V. Alexander (Labour) was appointed to the Admiralty. Sir Archibald Sinclair (Liberal) became Secretary of State for Air. Anthony Eden (Tory) went to the War Office to be replaced by Captain Margesson (Tory) who, on February 12, 1942, was supplanted by a Civil Servant, the Permanent Under-Secretary of State for War, Sir James Grigg. So emerged the picture of the Tory Party which, as its leader admitted by his actions, did not possess a man fit to undertake the job of Secretary of State for War. That wound was still unhealed when I entered Parliament in 1945. It explains the often petty attacks on Labour Service Ministers by Tory M.P.s.

In April 1948, Shinwell piloted the Army and Air Force Bill through Parliament. The origins of this annual process intrigued me. The Army Act, which the Air Force Act follows closely, was based upon the Army Discipline and Regulations Act of 1829. Its provisions were incorporated in an Act of 1878, following the work of a Select Committee appointed to consider a Draft Bill consolidating and defining Military Law as it had developed down the centuries in Mutiny and Marine Mutiny Acts and in the Articles of War. Military Law, this Committee reported, had remained in the condition condemned by H.R.H. The Field Marshal and Commander-in-Chief (the late Duke of Cambridge) who told a Courts Martial Commission in 1869 that 'everything connected with Military Law should be made clear and simple so that he who runs may read and I do not think that is the case now'. A basic and continuing provision was that the Army and Air Force Annual Bill had to be passed by April 30 each year. If the Bill did not pass on the due date, the Army and Air Force Act automatically lapsed. This cumbersome procedure was born of the seventeenth-century conflict between Crown and Parliament. Its principle was established in the Bill of Rights: 'that the raising or keeping of a standing Army within the Kingdome in time of peace unlesse it be with the consent of Parlyament is against the law.' Thus, the House of Commons was required to examine the Army Estimates and approve before April 30 the number of men and the amount of money which the Army would need during the financial year. This simple procedural arrangement had far-reaching consequences; it resulted in Britain from 1689 onwards being free from the fear of political power being usurped by the Army.

Nevertheless, the 1878 Act, although preserving invaluable traditions, was fantastically out of date in its operation. I talked often with Shinwell and his officials about the threat to any Government facing an Opposition capable of exploiting the requirements of this Act. The Tories, if they had been efficient in 1950–51 when Labour's majority numbered six, could have brought us down with ease. My experience then inspired a dream I was to help make come true in 1952.

The most tantalizing aspect of Parliamentary control of defence expenditure, as I have previously indicated, arose from the exercise of arbitrary powers by the Stuart monarchs. For example money voted to feed the Army was mis-used by Charles I to pay an Army larger than Parliament desired or had decreed. Parliament's remedy was to allocate money for specified purposes and in watertight compartments and to decide the total strength of the Army from year to year. The Permanent Secretary of the War Office, the Treasury link, acted through his Local Auditors, later called Command Secretaries, to ensure that money was spent as Parliament intended. In peace-time this rigid system, the source of much sloppy administration in the Army, operated through innumerable Regulations, Army Orders, Army Council Instructions, Royal Warrants, Queen's Regulations and the like. Everything a soldier did from the moment he took the King's or Queen's shilling was and is still governed by some Regulation or other. Pay, discipline, rations, married quarters, transport, leave, hospital treatment and, when that failed, burial, were all embraced in an inflexible straitjacket. The successful soldier was, and probably still is, he who either obeys regulations implicitly or breaks them so skilfully as not to be found out! In war-time, of course, most regulations went through the window. The late Sir Charles Harris sought full-scale reform by creating the Corps of Military Accountants. Immediately after he retired in 1924, the Corps was wound up and dreams of freedom from finicky interference vanished. The problem was to make effective and acceptable Parliament's control over affairs in the detailed way required by Parliamentary procedures.

Change and reform can create as many problems as they solve. After World War II the Army Council was a collection of equals but a member of the eminence and personality of Lord Montgomery could be more equal than the sum of all his equals. Monty's conception of an Army based upon three elements – the Regular and its Reserves, National Service, and the Territorial Army – was eminently sound. Such a policy, however, required that the Adjutant-General and the Quartermaster-General should be officers of independent mind and outstanding ability. This was particularly necessary as the retirement of the Adjutant-General, General Sir Ronald Adam, a great administrative soldier, left a gap well nigh impossible to fill. He was succeeded by a distinguished officer enjoying the approval of Field Marshal Montgomery whose dominating influence meant, in practice, that unwittingly he was becoming Commander-in-Chief of the Army. This was an undesirable development since, if the Army Council were to function properly, the administrative problems of the post-war Army needed to be examined on a basis of strict objectivity. Another difficulty was the fact that the top jobs in the War Office were held for only three years, during which time officers had to learn their way around the War Office, the Ministry of Defence and Whitehall in general. The system did not encourage bold decisions, for any advocate of unorthodox policies needed to remind himself that senior posts were filled by selection. It was certainly asking a great deal of senior officers that they place their future careers in jeopardy by taking a stand on issues which ran counter to the known views of their Service and/or political masters. To my knowledge there were men who had the courage to do just that, and they paid the orthodox price. They left the Service without receiving the promotion that should rightfully have been theirs; Service orthodoxy is a totem which has cost Britain dear.

Shinwell's immediate inheritance was an Army scattered all over the world in support of policies fashioned by the Foreign Office which, for a century, had fallen into error after error of its own making. Ernest Bevin was a giant of the Labour Movement and a patriot who contributed to the war effort on a scale unsurpassed by any of his political colleagues. He devised a demobilization plan embodying the principle of fairness and ensured that it was administered with humanity and skill, in marked contrast to the chaos that followed World War I. Alas, he had become a Titan grown weary. The Foreign Office exploited his reputation and, taking advantage of his failing powers, continued unchecked its normal routine of unplanned catastrophe.

There was little challenge to Foreign Office assumptions that Service Departments existed only to do its bidding. Attlee's agreement that Shinwell should see Cabinet papers, however, had valuable results in those critical times. Hitherto, Cabinet papers had reached only Service Chiefs and Cabinet Ministers. No wonder I found that Ministers often knew little about what was going on and were thus at the mercy of their better-informed advisers. The system was as much to blame as the men too indolent to change it. Shinwell did know what was going on; he could and did voice his opinion about foreign policy. And there was never any doubt about his understanding of policy in relation to the War Office. With Churchill ever on the prowl, there was a constant interplay between politics and defence in which Defence Ministers, with the exception of Manny, were money for old rope. More important, Shinwell could discuss his problems frankly with top civil servants. They knew he shared all the information they possessed. He was the boss from whom they derived and to whom they gave strength. There was a lighter side to Shinwell's special relationship with Attlee. On an early visit to No. 10 Shinwell walked right into the Cabinet Room past Ministers waiting their turn. The disapproving glances of Dalton and Cripps put a sparkle in Shinwell's eye.

Meantime, manpower difficulties were mounting. In May 1947, the Regular Army numbered just over 100,000. Regular and National Servicemen together totalled around 800,000. There were 35,000 Territorials. Reserve Forces, outside those with a liability for recall after completion of their National Service, including men released since the end of the War, were negligible. Our aim was to build up the strength of Regulars and Territorials and to re-create the Reserves despite continuous pressure to cut down expenditure.

Among my proposals was a re-shaping of Section A of the Army Reserve. Men in this Section accepted a liability over and above any general recall of Reservists. They were Reservists who, pre-war, on the issue of individual re-call notices, immediately re-joined. They received an addition to normal Reserve pay in return for acceptance of this obligation. Liable to call-up at twenty-four hours notice and being fully trained, these men were first-class material for, say, bringing a slightly under-strength battalion speedily up to full establishment. They had provided excellent reinforcements between the wars, notably at Chanak in 1922 and in Palestine in 1936. Surprisingly, this proposal was opposed. Shinwell appointed himself Chairman of a Committee of three, the others being the officer handling such problems and myself. We thrashed the problem out and a new Reserve Act reached the Statute Book. Thus a modernized Section A came into being.

A campaign in August 1948, to raise more Territorials was less successful. Allied control of Germany had collapsed in March and the Russians decided on a *tour de force*, bribing West Berliners with guaranteed rations of food and fuel to cross the sector boundaries and register as citizens of East Berlin. This move, the Russians believed, would stop the flow of refugees from East Germany to the West which, besides politically affronting the Soviets, was threatening the defence in depth that Russia desired to build against a resurgence of Nazi militarism. The Russian strategy failed. Fewer than 100,000 of Berlin's two million people registered for Russian rations. In September, Stalin, having decided that the West could not supply Berlin by air, especially in winter weather, initiated the most brutal peace-time attack known to history on a civilian population. The Allied air lift, in which Britain played a full part, beat Stalin's blockade. With the approach of the nuclear age all conceptions of the balance of power began to give way to a balance of terror. Whether or no these events influenced our recruiting campaign is a matter for conjecture. Despite all-Party support, Territorial Army strength barely touched 60,000. Our handicaps, I felt, were lack of money, a certain residue of war-weariness, and the unending upsurge of both new and distant liabilities imposing ever-increasing strains on our resources.

Concentration on current affairs never interrupted my examination of Army organization. I sought to master, for example, the history of Command. Before 1825 the system was chaotic. The soldier was fed by the Treasury and armed by the Ordnance Board. The Home Secretary controlled his movements within Great Britain. He was paid not by right, but by grace and favour of the Crown. Discipline governing his every action was defined by Military Law so ancient that, today, it would be regarded as a music-hall joke. Although the confusion of authority surfaced tragically in the Crimean campaign of 1853–56, reform was slow. It was 1870 before Cardwell brought all the Army's business into a single department. Then the Commander-in-Chief assumed responsibility for command, discipline, promotion and intelligence; the Surveyor-General-in-Ordnance controlled commissariat, stores, ammunition, barracks and transport; and the Financial Secretary prepared the estimates. The Financial Secretary was to be in the House of Commons and the Under-Secretary of State for War in that House where his Chief was not. The Commander-in-Chief was seated in the Horse Guards and the Secretary of State for War in the War Office; these two were separate organizations.

The Boer War mess and muddle cried aloud for examination and reform. The office of Commander in Chief was abolished, its place being taken by an Army Council comprising the Secretary of State, the Under-Secretary, the Financial Secretary and four military members. To these were added the Permanent Under-Secretary of State who, in practice, was a Treasury watch-dog; thus the Horse Guards were swallowed by the War Office. In 1904 the Committee of Imperial Defence was created as a Standing Committee of the Cabinet.

Lord Esher, whose Committee reported early in 1904, was the genius behind these reforms. Esher may have been a political fence-sitter. I regard him as a true begetter of my own humble campaign to elevate defence above the cut and thrust of Party politics. He refused office, relying on the patronage of King Edward VII, who associated himself with Army re-organization just as, later, he backed Haldane. The Esher Committee Report struck hard at maladministration and provided a basis for Haldane's far-reaching changes. It led to the creation of the General Staff system which survived two World Wars. The evidence suggests that, without the efforts of Esher and Haldane, the burden laid on our Armies in 1914 and 1940 would have cost even more in British blood and might not have been borne so successfully.

Overall, 1948 was a good year for Shinwell. On November 20, the *Daily Telegraph*, not an ardent admirer, reported that, meeting members of the House of Lords to discuss the Territorial Army, he had surprised their Lordships 'by the grasp he had of his subject and by his responsible and co-operative attitude'. I expected the next story to report the surprising news that a Labour Minister knew how to use a knife and fork. However, the newspaper's succeeding piece of earth-shaking intelligence was that Shinwell was the obvious successor to A. V. Alexander as Minister of Defence. This fact was a measure of his success with the Army, the War Office, the British public, and the Labour Party. By January 1949, he felt strong enough to discuss his policy and objectives in public. The task, he said, 'is to co-operate with my colleagues in the Army Council and build up an efficient and well-equipped Army able to make its contribution to national defence, and to promote the very best conditions in the Services. These objectives are complementary. We cannot fulfil them without contented men. We must have good barrack rooms, comfortable and habitable, with proper heating and lighting and cupboards and other amenities. There must be facilities for study. All this is a long-term objective.' Shinwell, too, refused to assume that we could have majorities and minorities among men in uniform. The discipline of the man when a soldier, he realized, is the same basic element in the democratic freedom of the man when a civilian. As a soldier he adds obedience to his basic duty to society. The truly democratic Army is one in which every soldier feels he belongs to something greater than himself. That is the spirit which releases the qualities of individual personality and responsibility.

1949 was a year of much to-ing and fro-ing which I would have missed if, in January, Shinwell had not induced me to withdraw my written resignation. A young man's life and five R.A.F. planes were

lost as a result of sending them into a battle area over the Egyptian–
Israeli border with orders not to fire unless they were attacked. The
order was both an act of folly and a contravention of the Anglo-
Egyptian Treaty of 1936. The Foreign Office and the Air Ministry
gave evasive explanations. Shinwell's advice was that I make my
protest in my own way and deal with circumstances as they arose.
My way was to state my view publicly and to persuade some colleagues to abstain from supporting the Government in the division.
Bevin was furious. He and I exchanged insults in the corridor, but
nobody was disciplined.

Russia's most dangerous move in the Cold War—the abortive
blockade of Berlin—had opened the way for German adherence to
the emerging European Economic Community. Defence of Germany
and German re-armament loomed large on the agenda of World
business. The Western Powers were concerned to contain German
military ambition but not at the risk of permitting domination of
Europe by Stalin. Shinwell, addressing the European Assembly at
Strasbourg, got into hot water with Dalton, which did not worry
him at all and pleased me greatly. 'No doubt European unity is
desirable,' he announced, 'but it is just an ideal and it is far from
being a reality. . . . Commonwealth unity is a reality. It has survived
two Great Wars and is as vital to the economic and political interests
of Britain as Europe. I am not prepared to abandon the British
Commonwealth for all the tea in China.' And, he added, Lord
Beaverbrook's 'Empire Free Trade ideas are a lot of poppy-cock.
No self-contained British Empire is possible, and any incentive to
create one would be an invitation to war'.

An enormous stir was caused by Shinwell's comments on the
Lord Mayor's Banquet which he attended in November. I opposed
acceptance of the invitation, arguing that the City contained some of
the most arrogant, hide-bound, class-conscious men I had ever met,
who hated the Labour Party and invited its representatives only as a
matter of form. Shinwell's experience was that guests walked up
an aisle of City dignitaries who clapped them in or not as they
chose. Labour Ministers got the frozen mitt, Tories the glad hand.
And the food! Shinwell said publicly: 'Quite frankly if that was a
banquet—perhaps they had ladled out the austerity deliberately—
give me the good old fish and chips wrapped in paper.' He summed
up his impressions by saying: 'They are not so keen to improve the
economic situation as to get rid as rapidly as possible of the Labour

Government.' When as a Minister I was invited to the Lord Mayor's Banquet, I declined.

The meanness of City magnates was soon forgotten in a visit to the Canal Zone, although what we saw there shocked me. Our troops were a garrison holding a strategic position in the hope that somehow, at some time, the Americans would commit themselves to defence of the Zone and the Middle East. We heard talk about the likelihood of a Russian thrust through Persia into the Middle East—to me, baby talk. Pressure on Turkey and Persia, yes; infiltration and trouble-making, yes; but the idea that, with the Canal as a base, we needed large forces to meet a Russian invasion of Middle Eastern countries was a lunatic nightmare emanating from the Foreign Office. Bevin's Middle East policy was thought by some critics to be anti-Semitic. I never accepted that view even during those tragic months in 1946 and 1947 when Foreign Office policy touched a Hitlerian low by blockading the Palestine coast against Jewish refugees. I excuse Bevin; the simple truth is that he took his foreign policy from the Foreign Office. I came to believe that Foreign Office policy was related to a 'hand-to-mouth-no-policy' philosophy. That at least provided a rational explanation of Foreign Office incompetence in the Middle East. Britain paid for this ineptitude with thousands of lives and thousands of millions of pounds. In Egypt we could certainly have come to terms with Zaghlul, and later with Nahas; when Neguib took the reins another chance came our way; and to my certain knowledge we took every possible precaution to avoid even talking to Nasser. No wonder British Middle East policy was foredoomed to failure.

During the war millions of tons of stores had been poured into Canal bases and the real job of the Army in 1949 was to guard those stores against well-organized thievery. Egyptians had turned theft into large-scale business. They prepared shopping lists, knowing exactly what they wanted and where it was located, and they were excellent shoppers. In the end Nasser got the lot.

On our outward journey through Tripoli and Libya, Shinwell heard all the uninformed speculation that lack of intelligent policy and clear communications always incites. All our soldiers really knew was that they did not know why they were there at enormous cost to the British tax-payer. Homeward bound, we visited Cyprus and Athens and later, with Udine as our headquarters, watched crack Alpine troops at work in the Italian mountains. At Trieste, a real trouble spot, the border with Yugoslavia was closed. The Yugoslav troops were too trigger-happy for comfort. If anyone put a foot over the frontier he stopped one.

My absorbing War Office duties were no bar to my activity as an M.P. I have recounted earlier how I kept contact with my constituents, engaged in Labour Party propaganda, and handled an ever-growing correspondence, now involving many contacts with American military experts as interested in British administrative problems as I had become in theirs. I was a Commons critic of the Government's economic policy. I served on Colonial Office Committees and spoke on Colonial affairs. I made myself available to colleagues of all Parties seeking remedy of ex-Servicemen's grievances. I was even one of the 'victims' of Ernie Bevin's megalomania when, at the Labour Party Conference of 1946, he charged *Keep Left* with stabbing him in the back. Bevin's allegation that the *Keep Left* Group's honest criticism was an effort to do him down when he was negotiating additional food supplies for the British public, including his would-be assassins, was a piece of peevish nonsense which added to my anxiety about his general conduct and grip of foreign affairs. Bevin could hand it out all right. Told once that 'Nye Bevan is his own worst enemy,' he replied: 'Not while I'm alive, he ain't.' When Bevin had to 'take it' he wept as long and loudly as did the Persian, Dr Mohammed Mussadiq. But although Bevin was not very good at 'receiving', he was still a great man.

A fascinating focus of my attention was Churchill and his oratorical mesmerism, although that soon wore thin under Attlee's mild but always withering counter-attack. The Labour Prime Minister's easy dominance in debate was a surprise to M.P.s although not, of course, to ex-War Ministers; they knew how effectively Attlee had deflated Churchill when his verbosity was a nuisance to colleagues eager to get on with winning the war. Exchanges between the two were not always acrimonious. One story enjoyed in the Smoking Room was that Attlee pushed a note over to Churchill warning him that his fly was open. The note was returned with the consoling comment: 'Pray do not worry. Old birds never fall out of their nest.'

As a young student reading about Churchill's adventures in 'the battle of Sidney Street', mobilizing 50,000 soldiers during the railway strike of 1911, and his antics at Antwerp in October, 1914, I wondered whether he was a lunatic or just a mountebank. Examination of his record in 1919 and 1924 convinced me that he was a national menace. To reduce the R.A.F. immediately after World War I was desirable; Churchill dismantled it so effectively that when expansion became necessary in 1923 the R.A.F. had to be reinforced by officers from other Services. Later, as Chancellor of the Exchequer, he applied the Ten Year Rule to Defence Planning as an economy measure and destroyed the intricate apparatus of research, industrial organization and skilled labour necessary to efficiency in this field. He assumed that the prospect of peace for ten years absolved him from preparing against any possibility of war, and all this at a time when he was lusting to undertake military operations in Ireland and demanding armed intervention in Russia. The great man's long campaign in the 1930s to restore our defences was well founded; no politician knew more about our dangers because no politician was more responsible for the disarray into which Britain's defence was allowed to fall.

The return to the Gold Standard was Churchill's most notable achievement in the arts of statesmanship. It precipitated the General Strike of 1926, the long depression, mass unemployment and, in reply to organized Labour's protest, the campaign of Trade Union bashing which poisoned industrial relations for more than a decade. I did not find it strange that Churchill should answer Labour's 'Hands off Russia' campaign with the taunt that Labour was 'unfit to govern'. That was merely to eat dirt before the portals of Toryism from which Churchill sought favours. What amazed me was that the man given the opportunity by Labour to express the finest qualities of the British people in war should persist, after victory, in mouthing a calumny destructive of his own reputation.

I caught one personal glimpse of how small a man Churchill could be. He tried to treat Shinwell with a condescending disdain. Reporting on a Consultative Committee of the Brussels Treaty, Shinwell described the build-up of the 'infra-structure', a combination of two simple enough words recently introduced into the international vocabulary of logistics. 'What is "infra-structure"?' the out-of-date Churchill sneered. 'We shall have to consult the dictionary about the new word with which Mr Shinwell has dignified the language.' Shinwell commented quietly: 'It will do Mr Churchill no harm to add another word of international origin to his already large vocabulary.'

The undying shame of Munich came alive again when, on March 10, 1948, Jan Masaryk committed suicide. Left-wing socialists remembered the activities of the Revolutionary National Committee, formed on September 14, 1941, the anniversary of the death of Czechoslovakia's first President, Thomas Masaryk, Jan's father, to sustain the underground fight against Hitler. That combination of Social Democrats and Communists united a nation in completely boycotting Nazi-controlled radio and newspapers. It created a barrier against any Nazi thrust into Russia through Czechosolvakia. It cut in half the output of factories by turning out massive quantities of defective products. In 1943 it forced Hitler to dissolve VLAJKA, his Nazi propaganda agency. Now it appeared that another breach was being forced in the growing gap between Socialist Movements in Europe. There was even a suggestion that Jan had been murdered by the same Soviet-inspired elements who had once armed the Revolutionary National Committee. Crossman and I decided to see for ourselves. We flew to Prague, bearing a wreath from our colleagues of the Parliamentary Labour Party.

Arriving too late for the funeral we went to Lany to place our wreath on the grave. While signing the visitor's book I glanced at the opposite page. There was Jan's signature, made only a day or two before he killed himself by jumping from a window. I felt, sadly, that Jan must have been communing with the spirit of his father on the sorrows of a brave people betrayed by Chamberlain and then by Stalin, and had decided to join his father in 'the silence and the peace supreme'. We dismissed the murder theory.

No brief visitor dare assess the mood of any nation in an hour of anguish. We saw few signs of revolutionary change. No armed guards paraded the streets. Well-stocked shops were open. Essential services were normal. The basic fact was that the Communists, who had won 38 per cent of the votes in the 1946 election and had formed a National Front with the divided Social Democrats, had become unpopular. A bad harvest in 1947 was followed by a refusal, on Soviet orders, to accept Marshall Aid or participate in the European Recovery Programme. Social Democrat members of the Government announced they would seek Marshall Aid if, in the elections in June 1948, Communist influence were reduced. Klement Gottwald, the Communist leader, did not fear the people who had elected him democratically. The stooge Minister of the Interior, Vaclau Nosek, had already packed the police with Communist sympathizers. Gottwald ousted the Social Democrats and changed the country, overnight, into a Stalin-type dictatorship.

147

Talks with people in their homes offered little evidence except that fear had become all-pervading and freedom as we know it had disappeared. My most informative contact was with a young Czech who had returned home after living in Birmingham. I caught up with him at Masaryk's grave well out of the hearing of the crowd. He told me he was one of eleven hundred employees in an engineering works where a shop steward made a list of organizations invited to appoint representatives to an Action Committee. This Committee compiled a list of twenty-eight names of unreliable workers 'not genuinely behind the drive to make nationalization a success'. The twenty-eight were sent home on paid leave. After further investigation, fifteen of the men were reinstated and thirteen reported to a Regional Action Committee to determine whether they should be dismissed or transferred to other work. Similar Action Committees operated in the professions and all essential services. Following a talk with Dr Cepika, Minister of Justice, I concluded that the Action Committees, an instrument of Communist infiltration, had acted spontaneously in what was a quite brilliant piece of improvization. The Press was not free. An interview Crossman and I gave was distorted beyond the limits of honest error in reporting.

Much of the political analysis of my young contact was repeated in an interview with Rudolf Slansky, Secretary General of the Communist Party, whom I thought a clear-eyed Marxist and an honest man. In 1952, the 1936–38 Moscow-type trial based on forced confession was repeated throughout Eastern Europe, the Jew Slansky being its first and most notable victim. One of the charges against him was association with George Wigg and Richard Crossman, 'fascist imperialist agents'. In a campaign to give Communism a civilized façade after Stalin's death in March, 1953, Slansky, having been executed, was 'reinstated'.

Back home my interest was captured by the Report of the Boundary Commission and its proposals to re-draw constituency boundaries. Agreeing with Churchill's argument for 'one vote, one value', I launched a one-man campaign to shake Labour out of its lethargy towards an important issue of principle. In the 1945 Parliament, the representative of a Borough was returned for, on average, 46,746 electors whereas a County constituency averaged 60,251 electors. The Representation of the People Act simply reversed the disequilibrium; a County vote became worth 61/55ths of a Borough vote. Variation in vote value revealed itself also at national level. A seat in Scotland in 1945 included, on average, 49,443 electors, in Wales just over 51,000 and in England 58,628. The Government did not accept the first Report of the Commission. Constituency boundaries were re-drawn on the basis of a second Report which, on my calculations, gave the Tories an extra twenty seats. I turned our flat into an operations room, pasted up the Commission's maps, worked out the figures, and at a Party meeting where many Party officials and perhaps ten M.P.s turned up presented my findings. The response was a yawn. A Scottish M.P. moved that no objection be taken to the Report. Then the late Dick Windle, National Agent, advised me: 'You want to mind your own business, George. These are not matters for you. They concern only Transport House.' I gave Windle my maps, wished him the best of British luck and wondered why the hell Herbert Morrison and Maurice Webb had no second thoughts about that second Report.

The issue affected my own constituency. Dudley, a County Borough, was a small Worcestershire area surrounded by Staffordshire. Report No. 1 aligned it with the neighbouring area of Sedgley. Report No. 2 linked it with Stourbridge which was not contiguous. I consulted my Dudley friends and the leaders of the local Conservative Party and, with their agreement, put down a motion to amend the Bill. Dudley and Stourbridge Tories ran out on our bargain. Without explanation, they attacked the speech they had agreed I should deliver.

As I write, the electoral imbalance, partly because of young voters coming on the register, has reached menacing proportions. Home Office figures record eighty-three English constituencies with more than 80,000 electorate and twenty constituencies with 40,000 or fewer electors. Six top constituencies have over 100,000 electors, in which relations between people and M.P. must tend to become increasingly remote. The six smallest constituencies comprise electorates running from under 19,000 to over 30,000; there the value per vote is high enough to make the electoral system look absurd. This, surely, is an issue above Party. It requires agreement that reports of the four permanent Boundary Commissions should be implemented by legislation early in the life-time of a Parliament rather than be treated as a left-over for the dying days of any Parliament. Wilson, with 108,301 electors in Huyton, knows all about the problem; I saw to that. While Prime Minister he allowed a simple act of statesmanship on this issue to elude him.

The fifth session of Parliament ended on December 16, 1949, and although the political pundits thought a General Election was imminent—one ridiculous Press lie was that Attlee had warned Shinwell and Bevan not to make speeches offensive to middle-class and floating voters—Morrison told the Commons that the new session would be opened on January 24, 1950. Attlee, however, was persuaded by Cripps that a mid-winter poll, historically unfavourable to Labour, would give Government a new lease of life. Without consulting Party opinion, Attlee broadcast on January 11, 1950, that the King had accepted his recommendation to proclaim the dissolution of Parliament on February 3; polling day would be February 23. The Government had a fine record of achievement. It had made vast, progressive changes, never to be reversed, dearly though some Tories would still like to reverse them. Although hag-ridden with a balance of payments problem that was to persist down the years, Labour had made full employment the major aim of economic policy and thereby changed fundamentally the future of Capital-Labour relations in Britain. The Government had not fulfilled all my hopes but it had established the significance, to quote Lindsay, of the people's triumph in 1945: 'the struggle for power between the old English governing class and the new active and rising elements in English politics has at last been settled. . . . The calm assumption that the governing of England was their particular business has been shattered.'

I hoped for a May election and a Labour victory of around fifty seats and my experience in Dudley appeared to justify that view, although the Dudley Tories were cock-a-hoop. They looked to Stour-bridge to give them the balance of power. They dismissed their candidate—an unoffending solicitor from Herne Bay—in favour of a soldier whose name was well-known, Major Roy Farran. At the count a Tory ex-Mayor assured me I was out by 4,000 votes; I won by just over 13,000.

So Labour returned with a majority of six, a Prime Minister tired and disappointed, a sick man as Foreign Secretary, and Cripps in failing health. Among our leaders only Shinwell enjoyed a favourable change of fortune. He took over from Alexander as Minister of Defence and re-entered the Cabinet. His come-back in the country, as in the Party, was complete. Almost at once he was alerted to the kind of difficulties that can arise as defence problems become the subject of world politics. A story, spread by an American source and published in Britain without checking, suggested that at The Hague Conference of Atlantic Pact Defence Ministers a proposal arose to withhold military secrets from John Strachey, then War Secretary, on grounds of his pro-Communist past. Shinwell denounced the canard at once. When he obtained the full text he added: 'Now that I see the article, it is more than staggering.... How anyone could have thought it up is beyond me. Mr Strachey's name was never mentioned at The Hague.' Shortly afterwards, the American Minister of Defence, a Mr Louis Johnson, was replaced by a great American, General George C. Marshall.

Everybody soon learned what a small majority requires: well or ill, every Minister and Member must always be available to vote. A few Tories gloated publicly in the vulgar violence of Opposition which brought sick M.P.s from hospital beds in ambulances to Westminster. Once, running a temperature, I rested on a couch waiting for an important division; it was an exhausting and undignified process. Maintaining a majority during the Finance Bill was especially important. Thus alarm arose with a rumour that Shinwell had had a stroke. Shinwell himself diagnosed food poisoning. We got him into a room near the Lobby to await a division. There the truth emerged. My irrepressible friend was taking tablets to repel an attack of gout but, the gout not responding quickly enough, he had decided to get well twice as fast by doubling the dose of tablets and taking them at two-hourly instead of four-hourly intervals! The provision of a bucket and numerous glasses of water worked a miraculous recovery.

Suddenly out of the summer sunshine came the crisis of the Korean War. On June 25, 1950, North Koreans crossed the 38th Parallel. Shinwell's reaction was immediate. Our far-stretched Army boasted nothing like a strategic reserve; but in Hong Kong we had forces enough to give some help to the South Koreans and to our American allies. We told the United Nations that we would send reinforcements of infantry, armour and artillery, engineers and administrative troops. Churchill reacted as usual. The man who, in 1945, complained that we were not running down the Army fast enough now complained that we were not doing enough fast enough!

The acute problem was that intelligence did not enable us to be sure what lay behind the North Korean action. The one certainty was that Russia and China both supported the North Korean moves. The view that Russian action was pre-empted by Chinese support for

North Korea—Korea had been a vassal-state of China for five-hundred years prior to its capture by Japan in 1905—did not abate the current fear that the Russian attitude might prelude a major attack in the West. The Russians put everything into the struggle and the magnitude of their effort is still only dimly realized by democratic countries. They had learned the lesson of Hiroshima and Nagasaki. They resorted completely to Cold War tactics as a method of buying time while they sought first parity and, ultimately, superiority in atomic weapons.

Hindsight suggests that a major movement of Russian troops in Europe was never very likely. Nonetheless, N.A.T.O. forces in Europe were being weakened by the demands of Korea. So, in September 1950, Bevin, Acheson and Schumann met in New York to consider German rearmament. Europe, Acheson argued, could not be defended without German soldiers. The Foreign Ministers, agreeing in principle, called in the Defence Ministers, General Marshall, Jules Moch and Emanuel Shinwell. They, in turn, convened a Conference of the Defence Committee of the North Atlantic Treaty Organization in Washington on October 26. Before the Conference opened, France produced the Pleven Plan so called after the French Prime Minister. It was not a Plan; it was an aid to Moch's stonewalling tactics. Every N.A.T.O. country shuddered under the shadow of Russia's threat. To France, however, with memories of 1870, 1914 and 1940, the threat of a new Russian attack was less real than the danger that a new German military colossus would arise. This Conference could only define difficulties. Among its overtones was the view, said to have been conveyed through the Indian High Commissioner, that the Chinese would intervene if American troops approached the Yalu River or bombed north of that river. The American fire-eaters were General Douglas MacArthur, Commander of the U.N. and U.S.A. Forces in the Far East and General Twining, Commander of the U.S. Air Force. They were said to be hell-bent on using the atom bomb.

While Shinwell journeyed from Washington to Ottawa I obeyed the summons of the Whips to return to London. My depression was not eased by the conditions of the trip. The Treasury allowed us sixteen dollars a day and we were booked at an hotel charging twelve dollars a room. I could eat or sip an occasional soft drink only by persuading Shinwell to attend every function to which he was invited and purloining three of his spare dollars. The odd dollar bought a drug-store breakfast. I arrived in New York without enough money to pay the transport charge from the airport to B.O.A.C.s office. Fortunately, an American Colonel aboard loaned me five bucks which I still owe him. That was exchange austerity carried, I thought, to excess.

Shinwell told Parliament that nobody liked the prospect of German rearmament; even inside Germany many feared the resurgence of German militarism. Yet if the Russian threat proved to be real, Americans, Frenchmen, Scandinavians, Belgians, British and the Dutch could not be expected to act in defence of the German homeland while Germans themselves were onlookers—mere spectators at a play.

During November and December the Korean situation worsened. MacArthur, on November 24, began an offensive towards the Yalu River, lost a large portion of his Air Force, and failed to interrupt seriously Chinese supply services. Six days later a wedge fifty miles wide had been driven between the American Eighth Army in the West and the American Tenth Corps in the East. This operation ought to have been entitled, 'Asking for it and getting it'. The danger grew that MacArthur would resort to atom bombing, a danger intensified by our fears that his activities were not being controlled effectively from the White House. On the eve of Attlee's dramatic visit to President Truman, Shinwell spelled out again Labour's policy in Korea. Objectives would be strictly limited to peace-keeping; we would not enter into direct conflict with China. Attlee showed supreme courage in travelling to meet Truman on December 4. British and American differences were real. Britain had recognized the Chinese Republic; America still supported Chiang Kai-Shek. Under no circumstances would we agree that any issue between the United Nations and an aggressor State should escalate into a clash of colour. Any American President, especially one representing the Democratic Party, was subject to considerable Jewish pressure—financial as well as political—to contest British policy in the Middle East.

Despite all this Attlee, to whose ability and astuteness Dean Acheson, Secretary of State, later bore public witness,* provided Truman with the arguments enabling him to call a halt to MacArthur's designs and, soon afterwards, to dismiss him. Shinwell

* In an oft-repeated B.B.C. interview with Kenneth Harris.

made valid the British case for a limited commitment by sending troops to Korea and encouraging the build-up of an effective Commonwealth Division there. An abiding memory of those dark days was the success of Attlee on the world stage. Tories, always willing to denigrate their country in order to discredit any Labour Prime Minister, referred to Stalin, Truman and Attlee, it may be remembered, as 'The Big Two-and-a-half'. Attlee was revealed for what he was—in human terms the biggest of the Big Three.

The problem of German rearmament came to a head around Christmas time. Foreign Ministers and N.A.T.O. Defence Ministers met in Brussels to take the first decisive step towards stability in European defence. General Dwight D. Eisenhower was appointed Supreme Commander and N.A.T.O. acquired some cohesion. A sad note was the state of Bevin's health. He had a rough journey from London, too rough for a dying man. One of my voluntary duties was to rustle up cups of coffee and help him in and out of the Conference hall. Bevin knew the end was near. Nevertheless, he applied all his strength of mind to the task in hand while his colleagues did their best to help him eke out his declining physical power.

In the House of Commons the atmosphere had become pre-Election. There was row after glorious row, the House always filling up when a division seemed likely. I got into trouble, and deserved to, when I said of the Tories: 'Hon. Members can laugh, but I am used to alcoholic jeers from the Hon. Members who are sitting several yards away—and I can smell it.' Lord Winterton snapped: 'If that is not a logical imputation of alcoholic excess against those who sit on this side of the House, I do not know what is.' My reply that I had not charged anyone with being drunk, that being a matter for medical examination, only seemed to add to the commotion. Commander Pursey, a real old salt who had come up the hard way from the lower deck, made a mock-serious complaint that Tories had once accused him of being drunk and him a life-long abstainer.

For me the question was more serious than the hilarity suggested. There was too much drinking in the House. I wanted all bars closed at 10 p.m. Every good Officers' Mess, where a man likes to stand on equal terms with those whose life he shares, checks treating. That would have been a good rule in the House of Commons as I knew it. I would have been happy to see Labour M.P.s agreeing to drink only with meals. The motives prompting Tories and Liberals are varied and are their business. A Labour representative, however, wins an election through the work and sacrifice of men and women who hope he will be faithful to their ideal of a better life for ordinary folk. Sobriety is essential to pursuit of that ideal. My proposals attracted support and, of course, rough opposition. The *Sunday Express* denounced me as 'a pompous prig pursuing a political vendetta'. My view persisted. The temptation to drink was encouraged by the way Parliamentary business is organized in a place where M.P.s must spend long hours without proper facilities for study and relaxation. Doubtless, things are better now. They should be.

One odd episode in which I was involved, willy-nilly, was Nye Bevan's decision, following his resignation from the Cabinet in April 1951, not to join the *Keep Left* Group if I remained a member. Some of his ill-founded antipathy to Shinwell brushed off on me. Crossman, then a Bevan supporter, asked me to be punctual at one meeting because, he said, 'We are going to dissolve'. 'What you mean,' I retorted, 'is that you haven't got the guts to say you are going to dissolve and re-form the Group without me.' 'That's about it', Crossman admitted, adding: 'Nye won't join if you are there. He thinks you talk to Manny.' What made that remark so funny was that on Tuesday evenings Willie Whiteley, the Chief Whip, regularly gave me a detailed account of the proceedings of the *Keep Left* meetings, sometimes including those I had attended myself. His informant was one of Bevan's friends; and I can attest that this fellow was a very accurate reporter. I laughed outright during a Parliamentary Labour Party meeting when Bevan accused me of a Press leak which, in fact, had been made by Whiteley's contact and Bevan's bosom pal. The incident ultimately produced one of Bevan's wickedest wisecracks. Bevan had fallen out with the leaker, and to his invitation to have a drink, snorted, 'I suppose it is being paid for by one of those thirty pieces of silver.'

In the Spring of 1951 I became interested in the movements of an American, George McGhee, who was Assistant Secretary for Near Eastern, South Asian and African Affairs at the State Department. A former oil man, he was a millionaire. He had studied at Queen's College, Oxford. McGhee turned up in Cairo in February 1951, for talks with the Egyptian Foreign Minister. Then his presence was reported in Colombo. In March he interviewed Jawaharlal Nehru in New Delhi and Liaquat Ali Khan in Karachi. Soon he was urging the Iranian Government to accept Britain's offer of a fifty-fifty share in Anglo-Iranian oil and, back in America, advising the State Department on their non-intervention policy in Iran. Early in April, McGhee met Herbert Morrison in London. Morrison was not pleased about the gentleman's peripatetic diplomacy; McGhee was thought to have given Dr Mussadiq, Prime Minister of Iran, the impression that if we got out American technicians would go in and there would be no American objection to Iranian oil nationali-zation—the policy which precipitated the Abadan crisis and pro-vided a grave rebuff to Morrison's reputation. There was much sympathy, especially among Left Wing critics, for the nationalization of Iranian oil. Nationalization of anything, anywhere, was presumed to be a good thing. The end result, in this instance, was that the tearful Mussadiq was arrested, Iranian oil was handed over to an international consortium, and American capitalists acquired very sub-stantial new profit-making interests. Reports were current that the State Department was hectoring the British Government. Many of our troubles in the Middle East were aggravated by competing oil interests. One of Shinwell's achievements at the Ministry of Fuel and Power was to activate an oil agreement which Lord Beaverbrook, on behalf of the British Government, had concluded with Harold Ickes, acting for the United States, proposing international action to ensure that the world's oil would be used for the world's benefit. That Agreement was never ratified. United States oil interests refused to accept it at any price.

I resigned as Shinwell's P.P.S. in June 1951. I did not need to tell him that if he ever wanted me I was at his service. My position was quite simple. I was no more responsible for Government policy than any other back-bencher and I wanted to be rid of any implica-tion that I agreed with policies which, in fact, I rejected. The fire had gone out of the Government's belly. I was unhappy about the rearmament programme. I felt that Hugh Gaitskell's influence was becoming too pervasive in the Party.

One pleasure of being free was to have fun and games with a Right Wing weekly, *The Recorder*. The owner-editor, doubtful about Churchill's fitness to become Prime Minister by popular election, issued cards to Tory M.P.s inviting replies to this question: 'Would the Party's prospects be better at the next General Election without Mr Churchill as Leader?' I had the card copied and sent fake re-turns recording 45 votes 'for' Churchill and 48 'against'. I hoped to ridicule an abuse of the opinion polls. The operation succeeded beyond all expectation. The owner-editor rushed to Scotland Yard, got large scale publicity in the Press and headed his own story: 'MR CHURCHILL'S ENEMIES RESORT TO FORGERY'. I reported at once to Scotland Yard that I was available for interview, apologized for any trouble I had caused them, and there the matter ended.

Still plagued by indifferent health I welcomed an invitation in August, 1951 to pay a return visit to Israel. I joined the fast sailing *Kegmah* at Marseilles and at once was impressed by the dedication to their young country of the many youthful kibbutzim aboard. A fellow passenger, a former Left Wing Socialist member of the Knesset, gave me expert tuition in Israeli politics. A young lady Sabra—the name given to those born in Palestine—who had been a member of Haganah with her husband, an ex-Gordon Highlander, was the most aggressively patriotic of my companions. Yet her hope for Israel was that it would become a country like Britain! Most of these young people bore burdens of painful memory. They resented concessions made to the Arabs when their new State was born. They detested Bevin's Middle-Eastern policy. Nevertheless, their overriding desire was to bury the past and nourish friendships for the future. Nearing Haifa they identified for me the wrecks of refugee ships. A young ex-member of the Palmach (the striking force of Haganah) reminded me that at Tel Aviv I would see the wreck of the *Altalena,* destroyed while carrying recruits and arms to the Stern Gang— an occasion when Jews killed Jews on the orders of a Jewish Prime Minister.

Not less fascinating were the Jewish tourists abroad. An old man of German origin had opened a tailoring shop in Walthamstow on a capital of ten pounds, built up a flourishing business and now, broken in health, was taking a reluctant wife on a pilgrimage to Israel. To live in England and to die in Israel seemed to be fair summation of his pride in yesterday and his hope for tomorrow. I wondered—and still wonder—how true that is of millions of Jews living outside Israel, and how the conflict between self-interest and desire for national survival would affect the future. A different type of passenger was a prosperous English holiday-maker whose objection to Labour government in Britain was that she could no longer distinguish her husband's factory hands from her own daughters because they wore the same kind of clothes. I found it hard to envisage her fitting into a kibbutz, the basis of Israel's Socialist economy and, in its discipline and idealism, Israel's real hope for survival and growth.

Immigrants were entering Israel at the rate of a thousand a day, some of them from the Yemen and North Africa bringing problems of indiscipline, dirt and unwillingness to work. All political parties, however, were agreed that the gathering in of all Jews who wished to enter Israel should continue whatever the economic and political cost; immigration was basic to the country's defence. The nature of the defence problem could be seen at Natanya, halfway between Haifa and Tel Aviv. The distance from the sea with foothills forming the frontier with Jordan is about five miles. At Tel Aviv from sea to frontier is about ten miles. With such frontiers, offering no natural barriers, the problem of infiltration, whether for robbery, sabotage or espionage, was acute. My hosts caught fifty infiltrators a night.

At the Basic Training Centre in Sarafand my first reaction was one of shame. When the British left the area in 1948, Sarafand was the size of a small Aldershot and, in my earlier memory, the base of the only British troops in the country, a Signal Company. They seemed to have engaged in wanton destruction, blowing the roofs off those buildings they had not gutted. No British troops in my experience would have acted thus except under orders and I found it hard to believe that responsible senior officers would give such orders. Was a Secretary of State responsible? Or was the destruction a result of spite or local anti-Semitism? My second reaction was more comforting and mildly comical. The layout and the atmosphere made me feel I was back in a British camp. The Commanding Officer had served in the British Army as a Corporal. I felt certain that every senior officer had seen British service. Their moustaches were trimmed *à la* Aldershot. The R.S.M.'s stick was in evidence. Every kerbstone was white-washed. There, at the Guardroom, was a full length mirror for recruits to see they were properly dressed.

National Service identified the entire population with the State in terms of defence, the economy and, since literacy in Hebrew was a vital necessity, education. From the age of fourteen, boys and girls could enrol voluntarily in Gadna, or Youth Battalions, headed by military experts and controlled by the Ministry of Education, to be trained in sports, aviation, nursing, technical communications and afforestation. All men and all unmarried women became liable to call-up at eighteen. They served full-time for two years then enrolled as reservists until they reached the age of forty-nine. The compulsory reserve required one month's service each year, with an additional week for all soldiers of the rank of corporal and above, plus one additional day per month until the age of forty. Thereafter, reserve service consisted of two weeks per annum plus one day a month.

Spearhead of this mass civilian army was a small body of Regulars. It consisted of long-service officers and other ranks invited to engage for five years subject to notice on either side. After a qualifying period of service Regulars were given a guarantee of civilian employment on terms at least as advantageous as those gained by the individual at the end of his Colour service. This raised doubts in my mind. It was the basis of the German system which enabled the Kapitulants to obtain an iron grip on the machinery of public life and, when Hitler rose to power, meant kaput to democracy in Germany. It was a political form, not of defence, but of militarism which, I thought, Israel would have been wise to avoid.

The camp's domestic economy was impressive. Barrack rooms were clean and orderly. Discipline, maintained by promising recruits acting as unpaid lance-corporals, was excellent. Psychological tests were used for selecting drafts for the Army, Navy and Air Force and for specialized branches within them. After nine months service men and women could opt to enter a kibbutz and study agriculture while still in military training. The basic training would have done credit to the British Army. Saluting and turnout were smart. Care for the self-respect of the individual encouraged a high sense of duty. No soldier could say that the Army took all and gave nothing. I had reservations about the musketry system; men were allowed to shoot long before they had learned how to hold a rifle. Most British drill movements had been retained.

Among the kibbutz I visited was Givat Brenner, established in the late 1920s by settlers from Russia. Now consisting of over one thousand people, Givat Brenner received from neighbouring kibbutz citrus fruit for conversion into juice. The processing, canning and bottling of juice and fruit and vegetables was highly industrialized and capable of vast expansion. The kibbutz could have absorbed at once two hundred more families. Pride and hope gave purpose to life. Yet over all hung a huge question mark as obsessive to my hosts as it was to me. The nation's defence consciousness, stimulated by raids from the Lebanon, Syria, Jordan and Egypt—the Israelis thought these raids were aided and abetted by Britain—threatened to become a form of war neurosis. Moreover, uncontrolled immigration must result, some time, in Israel bulging at the seams and being tempted to become aggressive.

When the House adjourned for the summer recess speculation was rife about the date of a General Election. Attlee and Whiteley, tired after more than a decade of toil and strain, were ready to retire. They consulted only each other, and decided to go to the country in October 1951. Labour won a majority of votes, but the Tories gained a majority over all Opposition Parties of seventeen seats. That majority sustained them for four years and paved the way for Tory power which continued for a total of thirteen years.

I returned to Westminster disenchanted and depressed, and the mood and spirit of many of my colleagues did little to cheer me up. True, defeat had engendered a comradeship long since lacking. There was consoling pride in the fact that Labour was now the only alternative Government. And there was confidence that the Tories, eager to dismantle the Welfare State and beset by the difficulties of a small majority, would soon show signs of collapse. All that Labour M.P.s had to do was to lie low while the Tories sweated it out until the next General Election.

Few Labour M.P.s recognized the significant pointer that the influence of R. A. Butler rather than Winston Churchill would determine the style of the Conservative administration. The first Bill presented by the new Government in November 1951, the Pneumoconiosis and Byssinosis Benefit Bill, was the last Bill introduced by the Labour Government in July of that year, and the Tories improved on Dr (now Baroness) Summerskill's proposals. The Bill brought dust diseases within the scope of Workmen's Compensation. Miners, the largest industrial group affected, were among my constituents. Silicosis, known in Stoke as 'potter's rot', was a scourge in Dudley. Dr Summerskill had been an active, bureaucracy-ridden Minister. All representations for the benefits of her Bill to be antedated had been rejected because such action would raise administrative problems; and in my constituency there were a number of young widows bereft of the help that ought to have been accorded them.

R. H. Turton, Parliamentary Secretary to the Ministry of National Insurance, accepted my plea that his Government should ease the lot of victims of what Barnett Stross described as 'the oldest known industrial disease'. Even after this event Labour leaders, including Herbert Morrison, Chuter Ede and Willie Whiteley, were reluctant to believe that the rabid Tory Right would not be permitted to spoil their Party's electoral victory. For me, the Tory attitude was as significant as Wilson's exultant cry when President of the Board of

Trade that he had made a 'a bonfire of controls', and the Marxist Strachey's endorsement of the Capitalist pricing system when he de-rationed sweets. They were straws in the wind of change. Socialists and Conservatives alike were edging quietly from the politics of principle towards the pragmatism of 'the mixed economy'.

My post-election depression was deepened by a bout of ill health and, more seriously, by the death of Harold Laski. He and his wife, Frida, encouraged me in my work in the W.E.A. and Army Education and, in their persons, expressed the comradeship I always hoped to find in the Labour Movement. In the 1945 Election Laski's Marxist reputation was exploited by Lord Beaverbrook to brand him as Labour's bogey-man. The anti-Laski campaign was a 1945 version of Beaverbrook's attack on Morrison in the London County Council election of 1937. Labour leaders were then labelled 'hooligans' by this leading cut-throat of the Tory Press gang. The people of London reacted by voting Labour into power for the first time with a majority that sustained them for nearly thirty years. Laski could have repudiated Beaverbrook's slander that he believed in violence as a weapon of change and he could have counter-attacked Beaverbrook on the basis of his pre-war record. Instead, he resorted to the Courts, although he regarded them as a projection of Capitalist society in which he was, therefore, bound to lose. It was expected that Laski would announce at a meeting in Dudley his decision whether to sue or not. The dingy old Netherton Arts Centre was crammed from floor to ceiling. About a hundred pressmen were in the audience. Tension ran high. Behind the scenes, I begged Laski not to sue but to denounce Beaverbrook for what he was. Laski was adamant. Confident in the quality of his own thinking, he nevertheless denied its logic. He lost, and complained, not without reason, about the conduct and summing up of the Judge. I could only express my sympathy by organizing a whip-round among Labour M.P.s and sending Laski a donation towards the costs of his ill-fated action. He returned to Dudley to speak at the 1950 General Election so ill that I felt contrite about having invited him. He died a month later.

Sometime afterwards the Jewish Socialist Society decided to launch an appeal for a Laski Memorial and I was invited to speak in memory of a radically-minded, compassionate and good man. While speaking I received a message to meet Arnold Goodman at the back of Waterloo Station. I had promised to do a chore for him in connection with the defence of two young men charged with stealing from a bacon factory. The men claimed mistaken identity and the late Victor Gollancz instructed Goodman to defend them. The question was whether the police could have kept under observation two figures who, in the darkness, crawled along some half-demolished buildings and then descended to the street, where they were arrested. I agreed to examine the spot when weather conditions and moonlight were similar to those on the night of the arrest. The night of the Laski meeting was such a night—hence the message to meet Goodman. I went to Waterloo Station, equipped with binoculars with which to watch the two law clerks clamber over the ruins and drop into the street. While comparing notes with Goodman we were surrounded by policemen and looked like spending the night in jug. A citizen no less public-spirited than ourselves had seen our reconnaissance and telephoned the police. Seconds later another car arrived with a Commissioner from Scotland Yard who apologized for interfering with our preparation for the defence. I have never since doubted the efficiency of police communications! And I have enjoyed exchanging with colleagues stories of the strange experiences that befall M.P.s as guardians of the public interest. I gave evidence at the London Sessions and Gollancz's interest in the men's defence was justified; they were acquitted.

An inspiriting result for me of the 1951 General Election was the return to Parliament of Stephen Swingler who, after losing Stafford in 1950, was elected for Newcastle-under-Lyme, once the seat of the great and good Josiah Wedgwood. Swingler had come to North Staffordshire before the War with his young bride, Anne, who shared his social idealism, to live among the unemployed at Kidsgrove where men worked in stone quarries for ten shillings a week in order to get unemployment insurance stamps on their cards and thus qualify for benefit. He brought rich gifts of intellect and friendship to his work with the W.E.A. and, later, to the campaign for Army education. He served with the Royal Armoured Corps, until he was elected in 1945. When he lost his seat in 1950 he gave up the flat we shared with Harold Davies, who was joined by his recently married daughter. I left, having found a place in Pimlico which I developed as a library and work-base, and so it has remained ever since.

Our first campaign on Swingler's return sought to secure for Britain a more equitable sharing of the defence burden with our North Atlantic Treaty partners and the Commonwealth. Parliamentary questions established the facts. Young Britons served two years compulsory service. In other N.A.T.O. countries, with the exception of Canada and Iceland, the period varied between twelve and fourteen months. Besides ourselves, the only member of the Commonwealth which had adopted compulsory military service was Australia, and then only for short periods on a part-time basis.

On the Whitsun Recess Adjournment debate I argued that the defence burden was so inequitable that we could neither sustain our rearmament programme nor maintain conscription at the level thought essential. The noteworthy feature of the debate, to which Nigel Birch (now Lord Rhyl) replied, was that the subject attracted the attendance, apart from Swingler, Shinwell and the Minister, of only three or four other Members, two of whom were concerned with the next subject on the Order Paper!

This indifference to defence was a heart-breaking aspect of the truth that Labour had found no enthusiasm for opposition, the essence of which is to deny the Government *time* to promote its policies and legislation. The process often begins with a question which may be succeeded by a supplementary question or questions and can open up issues demanding disclosure and debate, thus disrupting the Government's time-table. Only one hour in each Parliamentary day is given to Question Time. Its attraction to the active M.P. is that, so long as his question keeps within the wide limits of Ministerial responsibility, he can put it without consulting the Government, the Opposition Front Bench or what are called 'the usual channels'; it is a guarantee of the M.P.s personal independence. Its value in a democracy is that it imposes upon every Minister accountability for the effects the actions of his Department have on the individual citizen. The question and the supplementary do not destroy bureaucracy; indeed, much of the expansion of bureaucracy arises from Parliamentary and public demand for precise information about the activities of Government. Above all, Question Time provides a daily opportunity for exposure, the essential safeguard against maladministration and even corruption.

Inside the Parliamentary Labour Party it was hell's own job to interest anybody in the opportunities for opposition presented by serious study of the Order Paper. The Shadow Cabinet under Attlee was incapable of directing a sustained campaign. It met once a week to hear the Chief Whip read out the arrangements he had made with the Tory Chief Whip for the conduct of next week's business, came to decisions, presented them to the Party meeting each Thursday night—then all of us were expected to lie low again. Election to the Shadow Cabinet was on the basis of a popularity poll. Among its members independent judgment was at a discount. Knowledge of Parliamentary tactics was not regarded as a virtue, and willingness to spend long hours in the House opposing the Government was deplored. I formed the view that the Party should abandon the method of selecting the Shadow Cabinet by election. M.P.s should elect the Leader and Deputy Leader and leave the Leader free to select his own Shadow Cabinet, as he would select his Cabinet on becoming Prime Minister. Such an approach might have given us a coherent battling team instead of the crowd of safety-first merchants with whom we were landed between 1951 and 1964.

What the Shadow Cabinet was unable or unwilling to direct, Geoffrey Bing and I decided to do. Bing, who possesses a first-class legal mind and untiring energy, was the ablest political tactician I have known. He was appointed a Junior Whip in 1945 by accident. Attlee's instructions to Whiteley, the Chief Whip, included the name of Joe Binns, well known in Metropolitan politics, to be a Government Whip—an obvious choice which might have turned out well. Luckily for Bing, Whiteley misread Attlee's scrawl. I often chuckled over the possibility that the appointment of a political nonentity, Lord Inman, as Lord Privy Seal, might have resulted from another Attlee squiggle. At the Party meeting following that surprising appointment, Stanley Evans asked Attlee to call upon Lord Inman to stand up so that members of the Party would know what he looked like!

Bing and I initiated our own guerrilla war on the Tories. The ploy I enjoyed most was not our most important effort; it is memorable because it invoked the wrath of our own Whips. In November 1953, Sir Hugh Linstead, a highly respected M.P. and Secretary of the Pharmaceutical Society of Great Britain, put down an Address praying that a Statutory Instrument concerned with glass imports be annulled.

Jim Simmons, M.P. for Brierley Hill, centre of the hand-made glass trade, and I, interested in Stourbridge's glass industry, added our names to the Prayer. The guess, upon which we based our tactics, was that after the Parliamentary Secretary to the Board of Trade had replied Linstead would ask leave to withdraw the Motion. We also anticipated, correctly, that many Tory Members would have gone home after the main division and before the Linstead debate. We arranged that R. H. S. Crossman would invite some Labour M.P.s to a 'secret' meeting at his home from which they could reach the House quickly, and that other colleagues would don coats and hats to leave the House by one door, returning by another. If things went our way, the Labour Whips would put on the Tellers and credit for victory would belong to the Party. The Government spokesman made sympathetic noises although he did not accept the Prayer, Sir Hugh asked leave to withdraw and the jaws of the trap closed. We shouted 'No'. The question was put. Then our Whips, with victory in their grasp, declared that they could not possibly associate themselves with anything so disreputable as defeating Tories on a snap division! Simmons and I acted as Tellers for the Ayes. I was overjoyed when the Clerk handed me the paper showing we had beaten the Tories by four votes. Morrison, who did not share the Whips' reluctance to be unkind to Tories, asked the Government to state their intentions in view of their defeat and repeated the question to the Prime Minister next day. Churchill tried to laugh off his embarrassment by referring to members of the 'Bevanite faction' emerging suddenly from dark cellars and other deep hiding places. At the next Party meeting Morrison walked the length of the room to congratulate me. He was the only ex-Minister who realized that we could have given the Tories the kind of treatment they meted out to us in 1950 and 1951—and with knobs on.

Almost a year before I had pulled off a similar and more important coup. In the early hours of November 26, 1952, at the end of the first of the two-day debate on the Second Reading of the Bill to de-nationalize steel, a quick check convinced me that the Tory Whips had lost their quorum of forty. I took Hugh Dalton on a ramble round the House, telling Labour colleagues to keep out of the Chamber; then I returned to call Mr Speaker's attention to the fact that a quorum was not in being. The bells were rung; the Tories, not expecting a division, had allowed their followers to go home; and the House stood adjourned without question put. Morrison relates what happened in his authoritative book on *Government and Parliament*:

This incident caused considerable parliamentary excitement and trouble. The Leader of the House and the Government Chief Whip, both of whom would be accountable to the Prime Minister

in the matter, were of the opinion that Colonel Wigg had pursued unfair tactics and claimed that their side had never done
such a thing when the Labour Government was in office. The
Labour answer was that as Government Business was being taken
it was clearly the responsibility of the Government Whips to
see that they had at least the necessary quorum present; that it
was for them to 'keep a House'; and that far from getting cross
with the Opposition they should really have got cross with
themselves for having failed in their duty. The Labour
Members concerned hoped that the progress of the Iron and
Steel Bill would be set back. The upshot was that after the
raising of lengthy and, as I thought, substantial points of order
with Mr Speaker, the Government gave way for the moment,
but in the end got its revenge by compressing two days Business
into a single sitting which resulted in the House deliberating
till 9 o'clock in the morning and then having to re-commence at
11 a.m. This in turn led to a Labour Motion of Censure on the
Government for failing to conduct the Business of the House of
Commons properly, which was moved but not carried in the
following week. So the Government first saved its day and then
lost it.*

It is a particularly satisfying experience to be able to use Opposition tactics for constructive ends. My experience at the War Office of
the operation of the Army Act inspired the hope of every active
M.P.: to initiate reforming legislation and assist its passage to the
Statute Book. The Act had not been examined since 1878 when a
Select Committee reported that 'the whole thing ... cried out for an
alert and effective opposition.' Bing and I provided effective opposition by holding up the passage of the annual Army and Air Force
Act by a 'procedural filibuster'. With other Labour M.P.s we put
down amendments to the Government's proposals on the twenty-two-
year's engagement. Altogether we devised over one hundred amendments which, later, Antony Head, Secretary of State for War, described as looking 'like a novel by Ethel M. Dell'. We put the Government over a barrel. Either it could suffer a dangerous hold-up of
supplies (i.e. finance) to the military machine or it could help me to
realise my dream that a vital aspect of national defence would be
elevated above Party politics and be made the subject of inquiry

* Herbert Morrison, *Government and Parliament,* (O.U.P. 1954).

by an all-Party Select Committee. I was summoned by Attlee to a conference with Eden behind The Speaker's chair and made my position clear to both Leaders. The Select Committee was appointed on May 22, 1952. I prepared a memorandum, accepted by my colleagues, setting out the basis of procedural reform: Parliament should maintain control by passing the Army and Air Force Act on a Substantive Resolution of both Houses; at the end of the fifth year a new Bill would replace the existing Bill; the House would have a general debate each year on the Estimates, and another debate on the Substantive Resolutions, thus avoiding the inconvenience of constant amendments to the Act while ensuring that the Act itself was kept up-to-date.

The Committee, born in controversy, as I told the House in 1954 when the Report was presented, contributed enormously to my education as a House of Commons man. Its Chairman, the late Lord Spens, rode out all angry outbursts, including mine, with the skill of a wise, kind man. I pay glad tribute to the spirit he brought to our deliberations. When the door closed on the Committee Room it closed also on Party controversy. The aim was to demonstrate that a legislative body, even one making no claim to expert knowledge, could put complicated technical matters right. A Departmental Committee sat in the War Office with a highly competent senior Army officer liaising with our Select Committee, which always remained in control. We produced a Report which, in effect, formulated a code for the soldier. This experience convinced me that, on intricate problems of magnitude, there is a powerful case for using the Select Committee procedure to establish basic facts before presenting them to Parliament for debate. My initiative on Army reform had been reinforced also by a desire that what I had done would not be done to any future Government operating on a small majority.

Antony Head teased me about what he called my 'Buchmanite confession' and, in leg-pulling mood, described the Report as being 'sired by Filibuster out of a mare called Necessity'. The Bill based on the Report was introduced on February 17, 1955. On July 12, the Secretary of State wrote to me, 'I have had a copy of the Army Act bound up and I hope you will accept it as a small souvenir of the work which you did on behalf of the Army. The whole Army will benefit from the Select Committee's excellent work and I would like to tell you, on behalf of the Army, how much it is appreciated.'

Colonel Wigg   Brigadier Head.

The inscription on the fly leaf read, 'To thank you for your good Act. With much gratitude, Antony Head.'

I regard my part in the reform of the Army Act as the most satisfying service of my political career. It justified the 'Wiggery-Pokery' of which I have always been proud despite the criticisms of alleged experts on Parliamentary procedure and of many writers in the Press; and I pay sincere tribute to my colleagues in all our adventures and to my wisest mentor, the late Sir Frederic William Metcalfe. On resigning his post as Clerk of the House of Commons Sir Frederic wrote to me: 'I am very sad to have left the beloved place. I wanted to say goodbye to you more than to almost anyone in the House . . . it has been a peculiar pleasure to know you during these last four years and, I add in all humility, I have admired your increasing Parliamentary ability and skilful work immensely.' Sir Frederic hailed 'the Wiggs, the Leslie Hales and the Geoffrey Bings as the successors, or superiors, of Pringle and Hogge'—W. M. R. Pringle, M.P. for Springburn, Glasgow, and J. M. Hogge, M.P. for Edinburgh Central, the last of the great Liberal Parliamentarians in the early 'twenties—and described our activities as 'the most successful obstruction since the heyday of Parnell'.

Another intervention in the early days of the Tory Government gave me some satisfaction and one disappointment. During the lifetime of the Labour Government, Ministers quite properly used chauffeur-driven cars to go about their business. Jealousy and snobbery induced Tory M.P.s to spy on these cars and, come 1952, a Tory posed an obviously 'inspired' question—or in plain English, a question the Government wanted to answer for propaganda purposes—on the Government car service. Out of seven hundred and twelve cars in use in London, Churchill announced, sixty-one had been withdrawn from service before the end of March, and a further seventy-five had been given up by April. The supplementary question, as expected, congratulated the Government on its economies and hinted that it was ludicrous for Ministers to expect such assistance in doing their jobs. Further questions about the allowances being paid to Ministers in lieu and the waste of time involved in the new system were brushed aside. Churchill had never even considered these matters. I intervened to ask whether, during the 1945 General Election, the Prime Minister had used, for Party purposes, a special train paid for by the War Office. Receiving only an aristocratic snort in reply, I gave notice that I would raise the matter on the Adjournment. The opportunity, alas, did not arise. I would have enjoyed reciting a *Daily Mirror* 'Live Letter' in which a reader complained not only that Churchill had travelled to Leeds in a special train at a time of grave fuel shortage but that he had left the train awaiting his pleasure pouring dirty smoke over the washing in the back gardens of little homes near the railway siding.

From the opening of the new Parliament in November 1951 onwards I hammered the Prime Minister whose handling of defence matters seemed to me to be a bad joke. Churchill lacked a sense of continuous effort. He was all start and stunt. In 1949 Churchill asked Attlee for access to the information available to the Government on defence promising, in return, to write a paper setting out the views of the Conservative party. He did not keep that promise. In February 1951, during the Korean crisis, Shinwell offered to give Churchill all available information. The offer was refused. Churchill preferred, as always, to be free to comment without knowledge of the facts and without responsibility. He hated the discipline of fact-facing.

Another aspect of the Tory Government's policy was Churchill's decision to be his own Minister of Defence. This had humorous overtones but the consequences were disastrous. He had combined the jobs during the war, sometimes with dire results as in the sinking by Japanese aircraft of the *Prince of Wales* and *Repulse* in 1941. That incident tolled the knell of the Admiralty; it was a factor, ten years later, in Australia's and New Zealand's decision to join the United States in a security treaty covering the Pacific without even consulting Whitehall. Now Churchill resumed the mantle of Director of Operations, playing with real people as in childhood he had played with toy soldiers. He misinterpreted the role of Minister of Defence. The Minister's job now was to act as overlord of the three Service Departments. Puffed up with self-importance Churchill announced that he would ask the House for a Secret Session. The idea had two purposes. He could develop his statement that on becoming Prime Minister 'he felt militarily naked' with little fear of public challenge since there would be no official record of the debate. He could also keep his private record, as he did during the war, and publish it later when it suited him. This senseless ploy never got off the ground. Soon, the job of Minister of Defence was handed over to a distinguished soldier, Field Marshal Lord Alexander. He, lacking political finesse, resigned in 1954. The disarray into which Churchill plunged Britain's defence resulted in a Department of State in urgent need of continuity having had eight different bosses in eight years—Churchill, Alexander, Macmillan, Selwyn Lloyd, Monckton, Head, Sandys and Watkinson—all of them completely ineffectual with the exceptions of Monckton and Head. These facts were noted and commented upon critically in American military literature.

Most startling of all Churchill's innovations, in the age of the atom bomb and with United Nations forces under pressure in Korea, was to re-create the Home Guard. Immediately on taking office he announced the formation of a 125,000-strong force to present the quills of a hedgehog rather than the paunch of a rabbit to the theoretical threat of Russian parachute troops who, presumably, would be recognized by the snow on their boots. On November 22, 1955, I enquired about the overall strength of the Home Guard. It consisted of 10,112 male officers and 25,016 male other ranks. Churchill's 'Dad's Army' had one officer for every two soldiers! A month later the Home Guard, still regarded as essential to our defence organization, was placed on a reserve basis. In June 1957, the War Secretary announced that Home Guard activities would cease as from July 31. Thus public-spirited citizens were held up to ridicule and public money wasted to perpetuate the myth that Churchill understood, or indeed was interested in, the breakdown of defence problems.

Early in 1952 I fell ill again. The cause of my headaches was traced to a blow about which I remembered nothing. No remedial operation was possible until my general health improved. An examination of Army records revealed an incident which made my nose nearly as distinctive a feature of my face as my elongated ears. During the War I had travelled by truck from Salisbury to Oxford. The car crashed into a farmhouse wall. I got a clout on the head. The A.T.S. driver, weeping, explained she had forgotten to replace the wheel-nuts, and flagged down an American lorry which took me to hospital at Newbury under an enormous load of boots.

I was operated on at the Middlesex Hospital in July 1952, and Shinwell, insisting on my having a holiday, arranged a trip for me to Canada on a cargo ship. I had two marvellous weeks at sea, reached Montreal fully fit and, after three exciting weeks in Canada, returned home to find the Government's mishandling of the Mau Mau problem in Kenya marking the beginning of the political end of the Commonwealth in Africa. A few weeks later the Government admitted that the Colonial Forces could not be expanded to take the place once filled by the Indian Army. Also significant was the fact that the Tory White Paper accompanying the Defence Estimates in March 1952, was the first issued since the War in which nothing substantial was said about Commonwealth defence.

My association with Army Education, and Tory belief that its success had been a major factor in Labour's 1945 victory, made me a target at this time for Tory jibes. For example, I crossed swords with Prime Minister Churchill when he told a story that, during the War, he ordered Lord Montgomery by telegram to preserve German weapons against the possibility of their future use against the Russians. Here, indeed, was a hot potato! At a critical point in the controversy Lord Montgomery said he could recall the telegram. Ultimately, Churchill admitted no such telegram had ever been sent. I put down questions, and was handled roughly. I made no complaint about that. A different issue arose, however, when Churchill tried to escape from his difficulties by referring to me as an 'Army

Schoolmaster'. I had never been an Army Schoolmaster. I enlisted on a Regular engagement, and where I was sent I went. Nobody asked me where I should go, or under what conditions I should serve. On rejoining the Army in 1940 I volunteered for the Pioneer Corps and was posted to the Army Educational Corps. To a man of Churchill's mentality the Pioneer Corps was for those born in a social strata far beneath his ken. He had opted for the 4th Hussars. From what I can gather he stayed with his Regiment, enjoyed long leaves, did what he liked and went where he liked. Subsequent to Churchill's jibe, I made a personal statement to the House explaining that I was never an Army Schoolmaster, although I would have been proud to have been one. Churchill was allowed by Mr Speaker, quite contrary to the Rules of Order, to comment on my statement. The Speaker's ruling was challenged. In the controversy that followed I squared the account. I cite Hansard for December 21, 1954:

Mr Wigg:	May I make it quite clear, Sir, that I much prefer the Prime Minister's insults to his apologies, because I know that his insults are sincere.
Mr Speaker:	I cannot allow this to go on.

A happier note was sounded when Hardie Ratcliffe, Secretary of the Musicians' Union, and his assistant, Ted Anstey, sought my aid in ameliorating the irritation caused to professional musicians by competition from Army bands. Before World War I, during debates on Army Estimates, the Union hired barges, moored them on the Thames, and serenaded the Commons as a form of protest. Occasionally they joined military bands in street marches turning music into a strident blast of noise. The solution proved to be simple: care and co-operation in observing War Office policy, which required that Commanding Officers should not allow the acceptance of orchestral and dance band engagements so frequently as to interfere with military efficiency; they should not seek to displace civilian bands with long-standing engagements; and they should always re-member that many players in civilian bands are ex-soldiers. We achieved amity by arranging for the observance of these sensible arrangements. The Musicians' Union, electing me an honorary mem-ber, required a membership form to be completed. To the question about what instrument I played I replied, 'Harp—in the future, I hope'. Hardie Ratcliffe welcomed me with a quotation from the pre-*New English Bible* version of the 98th Psalm:

> 'Praise the Lord upon the harp,
> Sound on the harp with a psalm of thanksgiving.'

Disclosure being Parliament's business, I exposed the fact that, in 1953, the Ministry of Supply were canvassing for sales of armaments to Egypt and that, in 1956, guns in tanks were on sale overseas without the breech rings being cut. This latter revelation blew up into a major scandal. Valentine tanks being exported as cheap scrap needed only breech blocks to make them effective weapons of war. I charged an *entrepreneur*, operating under an alias, with offering old Valentines to his compatriots in Israel and, on being rebuffed, trying to palm them off on Colonel Nasser. As the result of a leak to the Americans that 'the Limeys were selling Lease–Lend material behind the Iron Curtain' the American Government made representations to Whitehall and the arms merchant, who wanted £500,000 for stuff costing him £90,000, was left stranded. My charge against the Government was this: Britain was releasing sterling balances to Egypt for arms purchases and supplying Centurion tanks to Jordan and Iraq at a time of growing tension in the Middle East. In the course of this one-man 'demo' I expressed my view that 'the great menace overshadowing the Middle East now is political chaos, and we have made a contribution to it'. I condemned the handling of the Cyprus problem as one aspect of the policy of politicians hellbent on making the hydrogen bomb and seeking a base from which to deliver it. 'The country,' I told the House, 'has not the economic strength to deliver the bomb even if we were able to build it ... we are, I believe, incapable of building a Strategic Air Force.'

Outside Parliament, a constant pleasure was my friendship with Arnold Goodman, who combines immense legal knowledge and experience with great wisdom and human concern for those who need his help. I owed much to the late Albert Griffiths, a 'Black-country' man, and a product of Dudley Grammar School who, by his initiative and industry, built up a successful business. The kindest of men, in 1952 he gave me a job with his firm which added to my income and enabled me to get the smoke of industry in my nostrils— an invaluable experience for any M.P. Another great friend was Arthur Hodgson, Editor of *The New Citizen*, our local Labour paper, while it lasted. Arthur and Mrs Hodgson provided a home from home for me and inspiring companionship during my General Election campaigns.

Meantime, a heavy cloud darkened Parliamentary thought and action, and threatened the future, even the survival, of the Labour Party.

Labour in opposition had become so pre-occupied with internal divisions that it could not find the sense of unity that must precede its return to power. Its disharmony was aggravated by the knowledge that it must soon elect a new leader. The normally cleansing clash of debate between Right and Left within the Parliamentary Labour Party became a mongrel dog fight. I recalled often the comment of the American Professor Adam B. Ulam in his study of British socialist thought from Hobbes and Locke to Laski and Lindsay: 'In the democratic system as it has unfolded in Great Britain—i.e. a system in which a competently run Party, capable of maintaining its own cohesion will have to take its turn in government—no responsible Party can afford to become or remain doctrinaire. Political power creates its own atmosphere and its own interests.'* That statement defines the legitimate limits of dissent. *Keep Left*, however, had become a raucous fragment successful mainly in provoking wrath on the Right. From 1950 onwards the Bevanites packed the Constituency Section of the Labour Party National Executive with their own nominees, all supporting Bevan's claims to leadership. The battle spread to Party journals. The famous old Scottish Socialist weekly *Forward*, in which Tom Johnston once advocated the policy of coalition between Labour and Industry to curb the power of Finance, was revived as a Right-wing organ against Bevan's *Tribune*. Labour tycoons like Lord Cohen put up the cash. The Transport and General Workers' Union and the National Union of General and Municipal Workers paid for a 'guaranteed circulation'. The late Lord Francis-Williams accepted the editorship. The venture was a feeble flop, a mere symptom that Labour was repeating the frightening blunder from which, after 1945, Butler had rescued the Tories. It was forgetting the national interest in pursuit of internal personal issues.

Attlee had lost capacity for control. He remained Leader only in

* Philosophical Foundations of English Socialism, (Harvard-Cambridge 1951).

the hope of riding out the storms around him and helping the Party
to recover its cohesion. Evidence of this came when Foreign Secretary
Eden made a statement about South East Asia defence to which
Attlee did not object. Bevan's dissent took the form of a vulgar
attack on Attlee followed shortly afterwards by his resignation from
the Shadow Cabinet and an effort to carry the mass membership of
the Labour Party against Labour-Tory consensus on German re-
armament. The late Arthur Deakin demanded Bevan's expulsion
from the Party. Attlee ignored Bevan's insulting conduct and Deakin's
call for blood. He had indicated Gaitskell as his successor. In a
debate on German re-armament, Gaitskell fluffed badly and affronted
pacifist opinion throughout the Labour Movement. He just did not
understand that, historically, Labour pacifism was largely an expression of idealistic hope for working class international solidarity.
In February 1955, Bevan rallied a large-scale abstention on the
Opposition amendment to the Defence White Paper announcing that
Britain would make the hydrogen bomb. In consequence he lost the
Party Whip. These events, coupled with Churchill's resignation,
made May a merry month for Eden. He called a General Election.
Labour went into the electoral battle without a considered policy or
plan of campaign. Attlee played issues as they arose, by ear. Morgan
Phillips, ill at this critical time, worked heroically but received little
help from the Party leadership in managing the campaign. The
Tories and National Liberals won 345 seats, a comfortable majority.
Attlee resigned seven months later.

I was interested in the 1954 election for the Shadow Cabinet,
having accepted nomination. I got forty-three votes, dead-heating
with four others including Emrys Hughes and George Isaacs, the last
of the thirty-five candidates being Woodrow Wyatt, who collected
twelve votes. Harold Wilson, with 120 votes, was the highest unsuccessful candidate. Thus, when Bevan resigned, the vacant place
was offered to Wilson. I greatly admired Wilson's work at Fuel and
Power during the War where, with Dr Joan Mitchell, he created an
efficient Statistical Department. As Parliamentary Secretary at the
Ministry of Works he assisted me, in 1946, to expose in the *Sunday
Mercury* the 'rats' of the Midlands who were black-marketing labour
and materials which ought to have been devoted to building houses.
I did not approve all his policies at the Board of Trade. Nevertheless, his reputation as an energetic, efficient Minister was well-
earned; but there was a flaw. He tended to wait on the march of

events before taking the decisions which his own research and acute intelligence had already revealed to him as being the right ones. Bevan's claque became loud-mouthed in pressurizing Wilson to stay outside the Shadow Cabinet. One threat was that, if Wilson took Bevan's place, his erstwhile comrades would organize to defeat him at the next election to the Constituency Party Section of the National Executive. Wilson decided to put Party unity above all other considerations. He joined the Shadow Cabinet while making clear his agreement with Bevan on many policy issues. That step towards gaining the confidence of the Parliamentary Labour Party and the Labour Movement was his first long stride towards No. 10 Downing Street.

When the Parliamentary Labour Party, on December 14, 1955, elected its new Leader, the fact that Bevan offered to withdraw and let Morrison succeed Attlee if Gaitskell would also withdraw had no influence on my vote. I had had my fill of the Gaitskell–Bevan brawl. Morrison had defects as a leader, some of them serious. Yet he had administrative gifts as good as Bevan's and a down to earth commonsense beyond Gaitskell's ken. Above all, his attitude to the job—get on with it—and his basic loyalty to the Movement were qualities which at the time the Party in the House and in the country needed. The voting was Gaitskell 157; Bevan seventy; Morrison forty. Morrison, with great natural dignity, refused Gaitskell's offer of the Deputy Leadership and, a shattered man, shuffled slowly out of the room. I followed, grasping his arm and leading him gently to the House of Commons bar. I put a glass of whisky in his hand, gave him a cigar and stood silent while he sipped and puffed. He shook my hand, said 'I needed that, George, thank you,' and left the House to which he had given so much of himself and in which his most cherished ambitions now lay buried.

The Suez crisis of 1956 plunged the whole country into despair and division. A library of books has been written exposing and explaining the motives and actions of those involved, but the basic facts are not in dispute. President Gamal Abdel Nasser needed the new Aswan Dam to develop the meagre economic resources of his country; the 'dam of freedom, dignity and grandeur' had become a national dream. The United States and the United Kingdom, in association with the World Bank, had agreed in principle to finance the project. On July 19, John Foster Dulles announced that American financial assistance was 'not feasible in present circumstances', these circumstances being that Eisenhower, facing an election, might lose the massive money support of American Jews by aiding Nasser. Eden at once toed the American line. Seven days later Nasser, having been denied international co-operation in building the dam, repudiated international agreement and convention by nationalizing the Canal and became the hero of the Arab World.

Any anthology of Parliamentary flippancy in moments of crisis would include Hugh Fraser's supplementary question after Eden had repeated Dulles's repudiation of their joint promise to Nasser: 'I am sure the Prime Minister knows that the decision of Her Majesty's Government not to proceed with this project has been welcomed throughout the country for hydrological, economic and technical reasons, but will he now consider, in view of the fact that the Aswan folly is out of the way, the idea of a Nile Valley Authority ... ?' Folly indeed! The Aswan Dam and Nasser's name are imperishable in Arab history. The folly was that a youthful political Canute should think the Eden Government had either the will or the power even to contemplate a Nile Valley Authority project. Almost as foolish—and more disastrous—was Gaitskell's reaction, despite advice and warnings, to the whole issue. He compared Nasser with Mussolini. He was as ignorant as Eden about Middle East affairs and about the mind of Nasser and the mood of the Arab peoples. Indeed, the only sensible Labour statement on record was issued on August 15 by the Executive of the Australian Federal Parliamentary Labour Party. Replying to Mr (now Sir) Robert Menzies's sneering reference to the United Nations at the London Conference convened by Eden it pointed out that 'the situation between Egypt and the Suez Canal Company (registered in Egypt) is purely local and contractual and in no way prohibits Egypt from nationalizing the shares of the Company, subject to compensation', which Nasser undertook to pay. That view, I presumed, was formulated by the late H. V. Evatt, one of the most distinguished international lawyers of the day.

Nasser had taken part in his first important international conference at Bandung in 1955, where African and Asian Powers had adopted the policy of Non-Alignment. He received the news of the thumbs-down to the Aswan Dam project at Brioni where, in company with Tito and Nehru, he had taken his place as a World Leader of Neutralism. He wanted Britain out of Egypt. He did not want Soviet Russia in Egypt. He wrote a clear exposition of his Arab

Nationalism.* The man on whom he modelled his style of leadership did not speak Russian but Turkish—Kemal Ataturk. Years afterwards, when I visited Nasser in his home at Shubra, near Cairo, I heard that H. C. Armstrong's study of *The Grey Wolf* was Nasser's bed-side book. Nasser himself told me that, when considering the possible military consequences of his action, a major factor was the run-down state of the British Army and its equipment. He was well aware of what Parliament was not permitted to learn—we had not a single squadron of swept-wing fighters in the Middle East and new drafts had raised the strength of the 2nd Battalion Grenadier Guards to only just over 550! He thought a military *putsch* unlikely but, if it did come, it would be launched from Malta or Cyprus. The weakness of his appreciation, about which he was quite frank, was the collusion between the Israelis and the French which surprised him; Israel's aim was to retard Arab progress and France believed Nasser's aid to Algeria was contributing to her military defeat in North Africa. He thought Eden was too honourable to wobble into an aggressive co-partnership with Israel and France.

My gloom increased when I received a message from Antony Head's Private Secretary inviting me to come to his office. I excused myself, being at the Middlesex Hospital where my daughter, Audrey, was expecting her first child. A second, more pressing message, how-ever, took me to Head's house in Cowley Street to talk over my line in the debate that would follow the announcement that Her Majesty had called out the Army Reserve. This was an administrative matter involving the well-being of the Army and I wanted to help although I disliked the reasons which had given rise to the necessity. The power to recall Section A of the Army Reserve without a proclama-tion arose from an Act passed by the Labour Government to meet the kind of emergency now confronting the Minister. It would have been unpatriotic folly to deny the need for the recall of Section A. I promised to be careful when commenting but I expressed the hope that we were not biting off more than we could chew.

I decided to go to the Middle East and see things for myself. I arrived in Alexandria on Saturday, October 28. A tense British Consul enquired if we had seen any submarines on the voyage from Haifa. Mustapha Barracks, where I had enjoyed many a night's 'kip'

* Gamal Abdel Nasser, *Egypt's Liberation: Philosophy of the Revolu-tion,* (Cairo 1955 and Public Affairs Press, Washington, 1955).

when attending Alexandria race meetings, were cordoned off. Egyptian sentries guarded every petrol station; Egyptian mobs made a speciality of arson. There was, however, a complete absence of any sign of military preparation. All was calm.

I encountered no hostility when I talked to people in the streets and elsewhere. The obvious fact that I was English provoked no resentment. Everybody was enthusiastically pro-Nasser, bitterly anti-French and suspicious of the Russians' eagerness to get into the act. I was on my way to Naples on October 31 when Almaza, Inchass, Abu Sueir and Kabrit were bombed. Anxious to get back to the House, called to meet on Saturday, November 3, I was lucky to find a plane taking merchant seamen from Naples to Blackbushe. I asked the Minister of Defence, Antony Head, on the basis of the information I had collected, what equipment had been used in the Suez operation which had been supplied through Mutual Security Aid and whether permission had been obtained from the United States Government for its use. I asked also if the R.A.F. had bombed the Almaza Hospital at Heliopolis and what warning had been given to the civilian population, including the Greek, Italian and French communities living there. The replies were evasive. The first warning was at 1600 hours, the first attack at 1615 hours. The Almaza Hospital, on the edge of an airfield, was thought to have been converted into a military school. As regards the mis-use of United States equipment, Head said it was operationally impossible to segregate items of equipment. The American view, as stated by their Defence Department on November 15, was that the British and French Governments had violated the 1950 condition about the use of arms under the Mutual Defence Assistance Agreement.

I was called during the debate on the Queen's Speech on November 8. As a friend of Jewry, I felt moved to express my view that the people of Israel had made a terrible mistake, and had destroyed the basis on which Israel could become viable. I recalled that, as a young Sergeant, I found myself one Easter-time in Jerusalem and went to the First Station of the Cross. At the place where Pilate sat was written the words, 'Father, forgive them; they know not what they do'. That, I told the House, 'applies to the Jewish people. For in sorrow must I say that I regret that after two thousand years of wandering, of the ghetto, the concentration camp and the gas chamber, the Jewish people have learned nothing.'

Six days later I upset a Tory motion on the Adjournment, the historical significance of which remained obscure until the spring of 1968. At 6.50 p.m., on November 14, the motion having been made and the question proposed that this House do now Adjourn, Mr (now Sir) Peter Rawlinson rose to say that he shared what he believed to be a widespread impression that the B.B.C. had not maintained standards of impartiality during the past three weeks over the crisis in the Middle East. Especially in external services, which broadcast extracts reflecting opinion in Britain about Suez, Rawlinson complained, more emphasis had been accorded *The Times* and the *Manchester Guardian* than the *Daily Express* and the *Daily Mirror*. Charles Pannell drew an admission that Rawlinson had not himself heard every broadcast to which he objected; he appeared to be speaking from a prepared brief. His demand was that 'the overseas broadcast should speak in the name of the Government of the day' and that the foreign policy of the Government 'should be the only thing that should be sent out in the name of this country'. The Tory proposal, clearly, was for dictatorial control of the B.B.C.

The motion 'That this House do now Adjourn' is moved on most days of the Parliamentary year at 10 p.m. If moved at that hour it is followed by a debate which lasts for thirty minutes. The House then adjourns without question put at 10.30 p.m. If the business of the House folds up before 10 p.m. the Adjournment lasts from the cessation of business till 10.30 p.m. The Tory plan covered an arrangement whereby Tory speaker after Tory speaker would criticize the B.B.C. Overseas Broadcasts to which a Minister would then have made a sympathetic reply and a basic British freedom would quickly and quietly have been placed in jeopardy. I decided that the Tory plan must misfire. I caught Mr Speaker's eye at 8.08 p.m. and moved quickly to an attack on the Conservative Central Office: 'What happened was that they looked around the benches and saw a young man who had a good record in dock briefs, in getting a man off with fourteen days instead of twenty-eight—the Hon. Member for Epsom [Mr Rawlinson]. They supplied him with a brief, and hoped he would come to the House between 10.00 and 10.15 p.m. and speak for fifteen minutes and that the Minister would speak for another fifteen minutes in reply, with the result that the screw would then be put on the B.B.C. which would make it a little safer for the Tory Party. Unfortunately, the business has not worked out that way. I have now got two and a quarter hours in which to outline my case and I propose to do it.'

It was a lively occasion. I knew, what no Tory opposite seemed to understand, that on an adjournment motion I could speak on any subject under the sun so long as I did not ask the House to pass legislation. Mr (now Sir) Gerald Nabarro almost at once made the first of several slips into his pit of procedural ignorance. He intervened on a point of order to suggest that my remarks were irrelevant to the subject of the debate which he understood was about the partiality or otherwise of the B.B.C. Mr Deputy Speaker answered: 'The Honourable Member for Kidderminster is mistaken. The question before the House is "That this House do now adjourn".' There were many interruptions, some by helpful colleagues to give me a chance to regain my breath. The late Sir Cyril Osborne moved me to bitter tears by pleading that he and his friends had gone without their dinner, presumably in order to gag free expression of opinion! The proceedings reached a point of hilarity when the Tories unsuccessfully sought to count out the House and withdraw from the Parliamentary engagement they themselves had started.

I had little praise for the B.B.C. Its Top Brass, in the main, had been appointed by Tory governments and my Party had been a frequent victim of their political bias. I recalled my recent speech when I exposed—I believe for the first time—Great Britain's foreknowledge of the French-Israeli collusion in the attack on Egypt; the fact, now admitted, which made humbug of Eden's plea that Britain and France were engaged on a peace-keeping operation. The information I had gathered indicated that the Israeli attack on Egypt had been launched from Eilat (Akaba) where the 10th Hussars and a Company of the Middlesex Regiment were stationed. Thus the main lines of the Israeli offensive were covered by British troops, the Egyptian Air Forces were destroyed before the British and French started their offensive, and it was quite impossible for our Ministry of Defence to be unaware of the position. This vital truth, as far as I knew, had not been reported by the B.B.C. nor by any British newspaper. It had, I suggested, been censored.

Turning to the Suez operation, I recalled that at the World War II landing at Anzio, we had used fifty-six tank-landing ships. On August Bank Holiday, 1956, the British Government which had spent £6,000 million of our money—nine per cent of our National Income—on armaments, set out to invade Egypt from Malta and Cyprus with two tank-landing ships. This information also was withheld from British viewers, listeners and readers. I gave the reason, ignored by all media of communication, for American indignation over our action at Suez. We were in breach of the Mutual Defence Assistance Agreement under which arms provided by America for mutual purposes could not be used without the prior consent of America. In order to crush Nasser we had literally diverted to our own use five hundred and fifteen Hunters and one hundred Seahawks for which the Americans had paid.

Ten o'clock, when the Motion for the adjournment of the House lapsed without question put, came too soon for me. The attempt to increase the powers of censorship and control over democracy's right to be informed had failed. At Christmas I received an anonymous card from a member of the B.B.C., inscribed: 'In gratitude for your magnificent and never to be forgotten show on November 14, 1956.'

In March 1968, Harman Grisewood, Chief Assistant to the Director-General of the B.B.C., revealed in his autobiography that, towards the end of October 1956, Anthony Eden instructed the Lord Chancellor to prepare an Instrument to 'take over the B.B.C. altogether and subject it wholly to the will of the Government'. As events moved towards the engagement in Egypt, 'Eden wanted to make an eve of war broadcast and he wanted it to be national in character. The mantle of Churchill should now enwrap him, and he would appear on the screen as a war leader supported by the nation, the father of the people, the hero of the hour.'* The Board of Governors followed the lead of courageous members of the B.B.C. Executive Staff and refused to place dictatorial power in the hands of Eden. Did somebody inspire Rawlinson, Nabarro and Osborne to give Eden's move the apparent support of Parliament? Or did these three decide spontaneously to try to suspend freedom at home while Eden sought to 'knock Nasser off his perch' and murder freedom in Egypt?

A few days later I discovered how President Eisenhower had learned the truth about British, French and Israeli plans; the Americans broke our codes. I handed this confidential information, including the location of the American units involved, to our Authorities and, on November 29, put down a question to the Prime Minister asking what steps were being taken to re-establish the integrity of our ciphers and codes. I have italicised the key words in the reply given by Mr Butler. As I expected, he said it would be contrary to

* Harman Grisewood, *One Thing at a Time* (Hutchinson 1968).

183

public interest to give information about cipher policy and procedures, adding, '*we have no evidence at present to confirm the information given by the Honourable Member* of any insecurity in confidential code or cipher systems in use by Her Majesty's Government;' and that 'whenever there is even suspicion that such a system may have been compromised, immediate remedial measures are taken'. I followed with a supplementary giving the Lord Privy Seal a second opportunity to deny the truth of my statement. He made no denial. His final words were: 'All I can say is that I have examined the statement made by the Honourable Member, and if he would care to see me and give me further information, I should be only too glad to consider it.'

My personal view on the question of British involvement in collusion was expressed in *The Times* on November 27, following Selwyn Lloyd's denial at the United Nations that 'the United Kingdom had instigated the Israeli attack or had had any kind of agreement with Israel'. 'I accepted this statement,' I wrote, 'for I believe that those who charge the Government with collusion are trying to prove too much. Surely the basic issue is simple? Did the Government or, more precisely, the Prime Minister, Foreign Secretary, and the Minister of Defence, know in advance that an attack by Israel was to be made and were they aware of its limited scope?' I suggested that a Select Committee of the House of Commons could establish the facts; a finding that the Government had been telling the truth would do much to restore British prestige in the world. The complementary but separate charge that Britain and France had collaborated in using the Israeli campaign as a pretext for launching operations against Egypt was becoming blacker as the facts accumulated to establish beyond doubt that France not only helped to plan and equip Israel's attack but took an active part in its execution. 'While British action,' I concluded, 'if based upon prior knowledge of French and Israeli plans, reflects upon the integrity and good faith of the Government, it does not amount to collusion.'

The Eden story stuttered to a sad end on December 20. I was arguing the case for a Select Committee on Suez or, alternatively, that the House should remain in session over Christmas, when Black Rod summoned the Commons to the House of Lords. On our return Eden rose, a nervous, tired man, mumbling and almost incoherent. Suddenly he threw his pencil down on the Table before him, raised his voice to declaim, 'I would be compelled . . . if I had the same very disagreeable decisions to take again, to repeat them,' and moved out of the Chamber to which he was never to return.

During a speech in my constituency I proposed a collection to aid people rendered homeless and hungry by armed action in the Middle East. This collection by Dudley folk suggested a wider appeal for which my friend, Arthur Walters, J.P., of Dudley, became Treasurer. Newspaper references resulted in money trickling in from all over the country—small postal orders from old age pensioners, collections from Trade Union and Labour Party branches and individual cheques—and in a few days the fund rose to £117 12s. 6d. Miss Janet Lacey, Director of the Inter-Church Aid and Refugee Service, undertook to receive monies from Walters and to see that disbursement was made to and for the purposes approved by her Organisation. Miss Lacey's one condition, since her office was handling relief for Hungary, was that donations should be acknowledged by Walters and myself. I agreed to bear all expenses and my secretary, Miss Dorothy Golding, volunteered to do the clerical work in London. The fund yielded £2,025 9s. 7d.; a fine expression of the generous heart of the British people. To my shocked surprise my Tory opponent sought to make this enterprise an issue of the 1959 election. In Stourbridge a woman screamed, 'Where are the receipts for the money you collected for your friend Nasser?' I ignored this but the Tory candidate acted differently. He decided to pose the woman's question for her. I gave him every opportunity to withdraw the obvious innuendo by offering him or his Agent access to all the accounts and correspondence. On the day I asked my solicitors to issue a writ I received a letter from the Tory candidate saying he did not wish to examine the receipts as 'this was never in question' and, he wrote, 'I fully accept your statement of fact as to the final destination of the money and that answers my question'. There being neither retraction nor apology the case went to the High Court where, in July 1960, my opponent finally apologized and agreed to pay costs and substantial damages.

Another aftermath of Suez was the plight of four hundred and seventy-two British subjects working in the Base and interned during the débâcle. They formed themselves into the Suez Employees Association under the chairmanship of Lieutenant-Colonel N. A. Fisher, O.B.E., and sought my help in obtaining compensation for the losses they had suffered. I headed a deputation to the Under-Secretary of State for War and later had an interview with the Prime

Minister who, on June 2, 1959, made valuable concessions to the Association.

The Suez episode in perspective was disastrous to the future of peace in the Middle East and to the prospects of the British Commonwealth of Nations. During the long years of Tory rule 'formal Commonwealth consultation at the United Nations ceased to have meaning ... because of avoidance of controversial issues' like South Africa's policy of apartheid; 'a similar disinclination has deprived the Prime Ministers' meetings of the authority they might have had.'* Eden's statement to Parliament on October 30 that 'we have kept in close consultation with the Commonwealth Governments' was denied in his own November 3 broadcast when he said: 'our friends inside the Commonwealth, and outside, could not in the very nature of things be consulted in time.' The British writ no longer ran in India, Africa or Asia; its validity in Canada, Australia and New Zealand had become doubtful. Nasser turned perforce to Russia and the influence of Russian-style Communism supplanted that of the Western Democracies in Arab affairs. Russia, too, exploited the crisis to crack down brutally on the growth of democratic tendencies in Hungary. Ben Gurion, to the dismay of many Jews and the disgust of Eisenhower, announced that the new area occupied by Israel would never be restored to its rightful owners; aggrandizement on the Hitler model, as every Arab now believes in his blood, became the objective of Jewish policy. Meantime, Egyptians made a mockery of all the idiot propaganda that they could not run the Canal efficiently; they expanded its services with a competence far exceeding that of the previous consortium of owners. The fact, unforeseen at the time, that developments in technology and transport would reduce the economic, strategic and political importance of the Canal, does nothing to destroy this truth: a new balance of power had made the Middle East as dangerous and explosive a cauldron for our children as Germany was for us and for the fathers of our generation. Over all looms the threat of an aggressive China with an ever-increasing interest, like the Soviet Union, in the Middle East. We have gone. They are there.

* John W. Holmes (President, the Canadian Institute of International Affairs), *The Times*, January 7, 1964.

Chapter Nine: Russian Visit

The humiliations of Suez and Labour's built-in self-destructive tendencies were not the only political obsessions of the 1950s. As the great Powers competed in the search for a balance of nuclear terror, problems of State security acquired new portentous dimensions. Espionage and counter-espionage in a world of developing technology put both national economy and national security at increasing risk. Infiltration, too, acquired a meaning beyond the capture of secrets of defence and trade. Russia perfected it as a political weapon of Cold War. All over the Western World Communist Parties, the majority of whose members responded to the idealism of a cause, renewed and intensified their activities as agencies for enervating non-Communist societies and promoting the violent overthrow of the 'enemies' of the Union of Soviet Socialist Republics. Communist cells resumed their attacks on Trade Unions at national and international level. T. A. Jackson, most cheerful of the early British ideologists, once chortled, 'We shall take the Labour Party by the hand in order to grasp it by the throat.' Thanks to the basic integrity of the British Labour Movement that hope never materialized. By 1941, however, a Communist cell had taken the hand of the British Foreign Office and, soon, was reaching eagerly for its throat.

These issues burst dramatically on the British public in May 1951, when Guy Burgess and Donald Maclean, two Foreign Office officials, defected to Russia after being tipped-off by another official (the so-called third man), Harold ('Kim') Philby, that they had come under suspicion. Philby's warning to his collaborators did not spring from pure comradely concern. He had just emerged from a gruelling interrogation at the hands of Mr William Skardon of M.I.5. He feared Burgess and Maclean would crack under similar examination and implicate him. The trio of traitors had been undergraduates together at Cambridge. Burgess was a homosexual. Maclean had homosexual tendencies. All three were drunks, products of one of the more arrogant permissive societies of our times. Philby was the ace practitioner in the politics of treason and corruption.

Herbert Morrison succeeded Ernest Bevin as Foreign Secretary just before the Burgess–Maclean defection. Four years later he still persisted in the view that Foreign Office *esprit de corps* was in part responsible for the affair. *Esprit de corps*, apparently, had kept Morrison ignorant of information implicating Maclean, which had been given to the Foreign Office by Stalin's former agent, Walter Krivitsky, in 1940; it had also kept him ignorant of the Volkov revelations, made through the British Embassy in Turkey, implicating Philby and handed over to, of all people, Philby for 'treatment'. That took the form of Philby warning Moscow that London was in possession of details of the Soviet spy system, suppressing this vital information and conniving at the liquidation of Volkov, presumably by murder.

Foreign Office *esprit de corps* is, I believe, a device to preserve an artificial exclusiveness which frequently functions without effective ministerial oversight or control. An 'expert' Foreign Secretary is easy money; there is no mug like a fly mug! Macmillan's *apologia* for the set-up in the debate of November 7, 1955, did nothing to shake my beliefs. In that debate Morrison said he had regarded Maclean as a minor official with little knowledge of what was going on. Nonetheless, he had sanctioned his interrogation on May 25, 1951, the day on which Maclean and Burgess disappeared. It was a Friday, when the Foreign Office fell into its customary Friday to Monday torpor. In due course the gleeful Russians circulated the damaging story that the two traitors had had an uninterrupted trip to Moscow—not an unlikely story, given Foreign Office inertia; not an unlikely cover story for the operations of a Soviet Agent in Britain, the fourth man. Was there such a man? If that obvious question was ever asked, clues to the answer had gone cold long before the Foreign Office got on the job. Action was not even taken to prevent the defectors from drawing money from their British bank accounts, even after they reached Moscow!

Burgess, although usually drunk, was not a 'wet' like Maclean. Lively and extrovert, he was a popular figure in London clubland and enjoyed the patronage of prominent politicians. As Personal Assistant to Hector McNeil, Minister of State at the Foreign Office, he was informed about important State secrets. He had been reprimanded in 1949 for disclosing secret matters. Our Ambassador in

Washington had required his removal because of his disgraceful personal conduct and carelessness in handling diplomatic papers. Perhaps McNeil, like Lord Francis-Williams, was deceived by the fact that Burgess 'seemed more drunken and irresponsible than any spy could afford to be'.

Philby was asked to resign his post following the 'discovery', in July 1951, that he had had Communist associations during and after his University career. He emerged from his shadowy activities in 1956 to act as Middle East correspondent of the *Observer* and the *Economist,* cover jobs for his British-cum-Moscow-controlled role. The Foreign Office gave the Editors of both these journals clearance as to Philby's character. He defected to his spiritual home in January 1963.

Part of Macmillan's defence of the Foreign Office was to gloss over the Burgess record by commenting: 'He had been indiscreet but, then, indiscretion is not generally the characteristic of a secret agent.' Macmillan said of Philby: 'No evidence has been found to show that he was responsible for warning Burgess or Maclean. While in government service he carried out his duties ably and conscientiously. I have no reason to conclude that Mr Philby has at any time betrayed the interests of this country, or to identify him with the so-called third man if, indeed, there was one.' Has any other traitor in history ever had so rare a cloak thrown over his treason? The question I constantly ask myself is, since the Foreign Office denied the existence of the third man and were wrong, was there and is there a fourth or fifth or, perhaps, a sixth man?

One member of the Labour hierarchy, the late Maurice Webb, Minister of Food, did not hide his suspicions of Burgess. Webb had worked with Burgess in the B.B.C., knew him to be as dedicated to Communism as to alcohol and deplored his influence on McNeil. He expressed his fears to me in 1950, hoping, no doubt, that I would report back to Shinwell. My attitude then, as always in such matters, was that Webb should tabulate the facts he possessed and send them to the responsible Minister. Only in this way could he place himself in a position to use Parliamentary procedure effectively to force action. I did not believe then and I do not believe now that, if Webb had so acted, Bevin would have hesitated to deal with Burgess.

In an *Empire News* interview on October 16, 1955, the late Norman Dodds, M.P. announced that he had written to Macmillan asking him to 'set the law in action to decide on the third man's guilt' and threatening to name Philby if the Foreign Secretary refused. A few days later, accompanied by John Hunt Crowley, an able reporter from the *Empire News*, Dodds sought my help in drafting Parliamentary questions that would lead him to make the disclosure. My advice was that he should not raise the matter in the House but should reveal facts of substance in his possession to the Foreign Secretary and then, if necessary, pursue the matter in Parliament. Crowley objected strongly; he believed that if Dodds so acted officialdom would find ways and means of covering up. However, I shook Dodds sufficiently for him to go cold on the idea of revealing what he knew before informing the Foreign Secretary. Next day, my old friend Marcus Lipton, M.P. approached me on the same subject. I urged him to inform the Foreign Secretary that Burgess, on being recalled for interrogation, had made a telephone call to America from a flat in Bond Street, London, costing seven pounds, leaving the bill to be paid by a friend. A telephone message of that duration might be still verifiable and yield clues to the traitor's associates in America. On Tuesday, October 25, rather inadvertently, Lipton referred twice in the House to the 'dubious third man activities' of Philby. Already, on October 23, the New York *Sunday News* and, next day the *Daily News* which had syndication arrangements with the *Empire News*, had blown the Philby story wide open. The American Press and public were better informed about the state of British security than Macmillan proved himself to be in the important debate of November 7. Lipton was under pressure to withdraw his aspersions on Philby which I begged him to resist, being by now convinced that he was almost certainly right. The incident removed a stigma from the name of a traitor and cast over the reputation of a patriotic, courageous M.P. a cloud which remained on the record of Parliament during the remaining eight years of Philby's operations.

In February 1956, Burgess and Maclean called a Press Conference in Moscow, denied that they had ever been Soviet Agents and refused to answer questions. The Foreign Office presumed that one purpose of the Conference was to forestall awkward questions being put to Khrushchev and Bulganin during their visit to Great Britain. Awkward questions arose all right. Who decided that somebody must have a look, while she lay in Portsmouth Harbour, at the bottom of the Russian cruiser *Ordzhonikidze* which brought the guests to our shores? Lionel Crabb, a frogman with a fine record of service and a George Medal to his credit, was chosen for the job. Then middle-aged, Crabb fluffed it and was drowned. In the hue and cry the Special Branch removed the page of the register at the hotel where Crabb slept on the eve of his fatal dive, and our enterprising news-papers put the fat in the fire. Britain's reputation for integrity and competence took a knock. Foreign Office *esprit de corps* could not ride out Prime Minister Eden's rage and the clamour for reform. The mysterious 'C', co-ordinating Head of the Secret Service, was due to retire. He was replaced by Sir Dick White whose indigna-tion at finding that Philby was still on the 'strength' led that traitor to seek the job of representing newspapers in Beirut to which the Foreign Office did not object.

The long story of governmental folly turned full circle on July 1, 1963. Edward Heath, then Lord Privy Seal, gave the Commons an account, in appropriately tortuous language, of the Philby affair. Lipton posed the key question: 'Does the statement mean that Mr Philby was in fact the "third man" they were talking about when Burgess and Maclean disappeared?' Heath answered, 'Yes'. At Lipton's request I acted at once to clear his name, negotiating with the Chief Whip of the Labour Party and the late Iain Macleod, Leader of the House, the proposal and unanimous passage on July 17, 1963, of this resolution: 'That this House desires formally to record that the assumptions which prompted the honourable Member for Brixton to make a personal statement on 10th November, 1955, regarding Mr Harold Philby were wrong and that his allegation of 25th October, 1955, has been justified by subsequent events.'

To the end of the decade much time was spent on security pro-cedures. A Conference of Privy Councillors on Security, set up in November 1955, reported, in March 1956, that the Foreign Service, Defence and the Atomic Energy Organization had become increas-ingly sensitive areas and required more stringent security precautions than elsewhere. It made recommendations recognizing that defects of character, such as drunkenness and loose living, could make a man unreliable and expose him to blackmail or influence by foreign agents. It reasoned that 'whereas once the main risk to be guarded against was espionage by Foreign Powers carried out by professional agents, today the chief risks are presented by Communists and by other persons who for one reason or another are subject to Communist influence'.

My knowledge of Alan Nunn May, sentenced in 1946 for passing atomic information, was acquired after 1957 on visits to Ghana. It is said of scientists that they can be bigots in their own field and babies outside it. As applied to May, part two of that description appeared to be accurate. I am prepared to accept that, under the influence of Maclean, an associate at Cambridge, May gave Soviet agents access to information about his atomic research believing he was advancing the cause of international Socialism. It may be that Klaus Fuchs and Bruno Pontecorvo, too, had been deluded into believing that Soviet Communism was an expression, not of organized tyranny, but of individual human freedom. It was, nevertheless, amazing that the Privy Councillors' Conference should reach the conclusion that Soviet espionage had ceased to operate through the massive Moscow-directed corps of tough, superbly trained professional spies and was in the hands of the almost comically incompetent political Communist Parties of the West.

The Conference recommended the continuance of the Tribunal of Three Advisers created in 1948 to combat Fascist influence in the Civil Service. That Tribunal's main task now was to consider the cases of civil servants suspected of past and present Communist association. There arose the problem of employees of private companies known to have had Communist sympathies and, therefore, regarded as politically unreliable, having dealings with government departments about orders for military material. There were debates on security reports to Commonwealth Governments, security activities at Universities and the prerogative power of intercepting telephone communications. All to little avail. The early 'sixties were to reveal that kid-glove security, like kid-glove diplomacy, has no place in the modern world.

In September 1954, I was among those chosen, in response to a Soviet Government invitation, to be a member of a Parliamentary Delegation, representing all Parties in Lords and Commons, to visit the Soviet Union. Before departing, we received briefings on current prices in Moscow, wages and workers' overhead expenses, social benefits and food and farming statistics. When invited to state personal preferences for subjects of interest, I chose the Soviet Army. Some background notes were made available, but I was given little hope that my thirst for military knowledge would be satisfied. Still, Uncle Joe was dead, his henchman Beria had been executed in December 1953, and Soviet scientists having exploded an atom bomb in 1949 and the H-bomb in 1953 Russian political postures suggested a slight thaw in the Cold War.

We landed in Moscow on September 30, were greeted by Mr Tarasov, Vice President of the U.S.S.R., and piled into big black Zims for the journey to the city. Aerial views of flat, featureless country, relieved by occasional pockets of timber, soon gave way to vistas of broad, straight roads almost traffic-less by London standards. Suddenly there appeared a building so tall that its peak was swathed in cloud. It was Moscow University. At its base there loomed great ultra-modern skyscrapers alongside the shacks and hovels of Russia's yesteryear. New broad streets cut through mean, aged properties as in any bustling modern Western Capital. Traffic became heavy and fast, snarling into frequent blocks. Like his Western counterpart the Soviet citizen was driving at ever-increasing speeds to points of ever-increasing congestion; and he was fully capable of out-honking his fellow motorists in London, New York and Paris. My heart was in my mouth as pedestrians dodged from every pavement into the middle of the road, stood between two safety lines to recover breath, then dashed like mad for the opposite pavement. The car population of Zims, black limousines and smaller cars like the Opel was as numerous as the heavier commercial vehicles. Crossing a fine new bridge over the Moscow river we glimpsed the Kremlin on the left, shot into Red Square, passed the Lenin Mausoleum and the Historical Museum, and so to our hotel, the brand new Sovietskaya. I thought it a remarkable example of Victoriana. The marble staircases were heavily carpeted. The superbly appointed suite, shared with my colleague the late Stanley Evans, was lined with blue silk tapestry. Lighter blue silk covered the chairs. Everything for comfort and convenience was at hand or within call. The pipe-opener to our first meal was caviare and crab, vodka and wine, sucking pig and salad, smoked salmon and salad, mineral waters and more wine. Then followed soup, chicken dressed in vegetables and rich sauces, ice cream and fruit, champagne and brandy and coffee.

This gargantuan feast preceded a drive to the Kremlin where, in a room lit by arc lights and lined by cameramen, Mr V. T. Latsis, Chairman of the Council of Nationalities and Prime Minister of Latvia, and Mr A. R. Valkov, Chairman of the Council of the Union of the U.S.S.R., bid us welcome to Russia. We were then taken to the Bolshoi theatre, with its beautiful auditorium, museum of relics of great artists, producers and authors, and many ante-rooms for

conviviality and conversation, to see a new opera, *The Decembrists*
The play is based on the rising of the gentry and aristocracy against
Tsar Nicholas I in December 1825, a precursor of the Bolshevik
revolutionary movement. That was the first of several visits to the
Bolshoi. Our last was to a magnificent production in our honour of
Romeo and Juliet with Ulanova dancing Juliet and Czydano dancing
Romeo—an imagination-stirring and ever-memorable experience.

Our first official duty on October 1 was to pay our compliments
to Mr N. I. Bobrovnikov, Deputy President of the Executive Committee of Moscow Town Soviet. He presented a clear picture of
'The Apparatus', or administrative organization, the process by which
500 Deputies rubber-stamped the decisions of the twenty-five-strong
Executive Committee—which took its orders from the Party—then
reported the decisions back to 1,500 members or town councillors for
application in their local areas. In company with an interpreter and
Conservative colleagues Mr (now Lord) Erroll and Mr Mott-
Radclyffe I walked to the British Embassy for lunch. We wandered
as we pleased. Erroll photographed people and places without interference. *Pravda* and *Izvestia* having reported our arrival just
prominently enough to indicate that the Party bosses regarded our
visit as important, people in the streets looked at us with courteous
curiosity and were delighted when we hailed and questioned them.
In a large provision store I saw shelves bulging with food; butter
at varying prices, tinned salmon, lobster and crab, a wide range of
cheeses and cuts of meat. The bustle and excitement was rather like
Saturday morning shopping in any London supermarket. Customers
selected their purchases, paid the bill at the cash desk, then returned
to collect their goods at the counter. To my uncritical eye, the
women looked dowdy but warmly dressed and adequately shod.
They answered our questions readily and enquired if our shops were
as full as theirs and what English women looked like. The most
notable difference from conditions at home was that shops kept
open to meet the housewives' needs. This was one aspect of the
equality of Soviet women who worked shift systems in factories, on
building sites, and even as street cleaners, on the same conditions
and at the same wages as men. Some shops remained open until
8 p.m., others till 10 p.m. and midnight. At a crowded book store
there was an English section displaying prominently Charles Dickens
titles like *Hard Times, Dombey and Son* and *David Copperfield*.
I bought an English primer for children for about five shillings. Our

halt at the kiosk to stock up with picture postcards gave the Muscovites another chance to show their friendly interest.

After lunch we strolled to a meeting of the 1500-strong Moscow Soviet. I offered to lay a colleague ten to one that on arrival we would find a member of our delegation addressing the Assembly. Sure enough, there was the late Ness Edwards, the Welsh miners' leader, in full neo-Marxian flight. What the Russians made of him we couldn't guess. For me the outstanding personality was Marshal Budenny, a successful Cavalry leader during the Revolution and an Army Commander in 1941. He was now a kind-faced mild-mannered old patriarch, very grand in his much bemedalled uniform. Of our many engagements two on the following day were among the most important—to the Red Proletarian Machine Tool Factory and Moscow University.

The factory was a self-contained community modelled on those constructed by great industrialists throughout Europe. Houses were built on the factory site at rents related to pay. There were medical clinics, crèches for children, a summer camp and a stadium and club for sporting and cultural activities. The two-shift system—from 7.30 a.m. till 4.30 p.m. and from 4.30 p.m. till midnight—was operated by five thousand workers, two thousand of them women. A training department ran work-study courses on a voluntary basis and offered educational facilities fitting students to enter university. Well laid out workshops were equipped with American, German and British machine tools. The workers, encouraged to fraternize with us, asked about industrial conditions in England, why Germany was being re-armed, and why the Soviet Union was being hedged round by American military bases. A foreman who spoke English told me he thought his country had got through the worst of the post-war reconstruction period. There was still much waste from faulty workmanship, but the quality of production had been made a prime objective. Russia wanted only to be free from fear of an American atomic attack to go right ahead.

Moscow University was an eye-opener. Nothing had been spared to enable its eighteen thousand internal students to enjoy a full and happy life of learning. The vast assembly hall was furnished superbly, there was an indoor swimming pool and very adequate study-cum-bedroom accommodation for the seven thousand five hundred who lived in. The twelve faculties and two hundred and ten courses were manned by two thousand five hundred professors and teachers. Correspondence courses were provided for another five thousand students.

Next by train to Leningrad across a flat, featureless terrain. Many of the houses we passed were mere shacks, suggesting that Russia on the march was still not out of the log-cabin stage. But what a city! New buildings rising everywhere and, everywhere, living memories of the past: the Peter and Paul Fortress, the old Bourse, the Square of the Winter Palace, scene of the massacre of 1905, and the hulk of the cruiser *Aurora*, whose gunners in the October Revolution forced the surrender of Tsarist troops defending the Winter Palace. Tomorrow was represented by a wonderful Sports Stadium on the North bank of the Neva with seats for ninety thousand; yesterday lived gloriously and for ever in the Hermitage, containing one of the great art collections of the world. We were taken to the Anti-Religion Museum—'a scientific approach to the history of religions' our hosts described it—to see a reconstructed scene of a Spanish Inquisition Trial and a display of books on the Index. But I returned to the Hermitage. My eye had caught the sage green of Wedgwood Jasper ware. I was entranced by an inscription on the famous white Queen's ware which read: 'This Table and Dessert Service, consisting of 952 Pieces, and Ornamented, in Enamel, with 1244 real Views of Great-Britain, was made at Etruria in Staffordshire and at Chelsea in Middlesex in the year 1773 and 1774, at the Command of That Illustrious Patroness of the Arts, CATHERINE II, Empress of all the Russias, by *Wedgwood and Bentley*.' The Duke of Wellington, erudite, witty, the natural leader of our delegation, had served in our Embassy before the Great War. He recalled that, as long ago as 1912, a Dr Williamson had visited the Hermitage to gather material for a book on world-famous Wedgwood. Then, only two hundred pieces could be found. Now eight hundred pieces were known to exist. The possible explanation was that post-revolution zeal had unearthed pieces hidden in Tsarist vaults. At the Hermitage I found a photographer and the Curator, delighted in my interest, insisted upon presenting me with a complete set of photographs of the Wedgwood display. Back home, Wedgwood's own Museum, to which, in turn, I presented the photographs, identified some of the pieces of Jasper as Adams, a few others as Whieldon or Wedgwood-Whieldon. Mr John Wedgwood noted that there was now more Wedgwood ware on show in Leningrad than when he was there in 1931! Old pottery can make the whole world kin!

Back in Moscow one of our diversions was an Arsenal *v.* Moscow Dynamo football match which excited me mainly because the preliminaries included the playing by the Red Army Band of 'God Save the Queen'. After an even first-half Dynamo won with ease. That added a not-too-welcome variation to the usual questions we were asked in streets and factories: 'Why can't Arsenal play football?'

Besides Leningrad, with its lovely gardens and civic grace, I think my most moving experience was in Stalingrad. Of course we had to *see* the mighty tractor factory. What we *felt* was the murder of a city by the Nazi invaders and its glorious re-birth in the first two months of 1943 when Russia tore the guts out of the German Army and helped to ensure the success of the Anglo-American invasion of Europe. Russian soldiers dead numbered 46,700, the number of civilian dead was nearly as high, and there were also 50,000 civilian wounded. Soon after the Battle of Stalingrad— incidentally, the title of the greatest film I have ever seen—a party of Allied politicians, including Averell Harriman, visited the scene of desolation. Every house on every street had been defended. Great industrial enterprises, one hundred and sixty schools and eighty-six crèches were fought for and laid waste. In all, a million and a quarter square metres of living space, with all its public services, were destroyed. The visitors proposed that the ruined city should be abandoned and re-built elsewhere and, undoubtedly, Americans would have contributed generously to such a project. A proud people decided to re-build Stalingrad on its own ruins. Reconstruction of the city stretching for seventy kilometres along the West Bank of the Volga began by the removal of the dead bodies of 130,000 German soldiers.

Our crowded programme included visits to Tiflis and Georgia's model Collective Farms; Sochi, the Black Sea Rest Centre offering holiday incentives for good work and promising to become one of Russia's show pieces; and Kiev, home of the Nazi-inspired Ukrainian Independence Movement and, in 1954, thought to be an objective of American infiltration; then back to Moscow to meet Malenkov, Molotov and Marshal Voroshilov.

Malenkov, short and burly, his features calm in repose but extraordinarily alive in conversation and speech, was an impressive figure. Since Communists consider that the collapse of Capitalism is inevitable, he was asked, was Russia's policy of peaceful co-existence permanent or were the Soviets seeking to take Capitalism by the hand in the hope of grasping it by the throat? The reply was a counter-question: 'How is the peaceful policy of co-existence to be carried out?' The U.S.S.R. believed that Collective Security was the answer and condemned the creation of military *blocs*. The argument was stated with a conviction that assumed the Berlin blockade to be a myth, Korea a fairy tale, and that Russia had never said 'No' in the Security Council. He described the Cominform not as an instrument of defence, but as a bureau of information free from Soviet control.

Molotov, contrary to the reputation for flinty obstinacy which he had acquired, looked and spoke like a benevolent uncle regarding Malenkov as a gifted nephew. He told me that he shared Malenkov's desire for closer cultural ties with the West and, especially, for an increase of tourist exchange between Russia and Britain. I told him how impressed we had been by the quality of the English tuition at Moscow and Tiflis Universities although none of the teachers we met had ever been to England. He endorsed my suggestion that exchange visits should be promoted between teachers of English in Russia and teachers of Russian in England. Both men answered fully our questions on the quality of consumer goods, agriculture and kindred matters. The one sharp rejoinder followed a nitwit enquiry about the training of Communist agitators in Moscow, the name of Harry Pollitt being mentioned as a visitor whom people in Britain regarded as a traitor. Malenkov, like lightning, retorted that delegations of Labour, Conservative and Liberal politicians had visited his country —what about them?

Marshal Voroshilov was a typical 'old military gent' carrying himself with an air of authority. He invited our views and I, having consulted articles in the *Large Soviet Encyclopaedia* on the Great Fatherland War of the Soviet Union 1941–45 (Vol. VII) and Second Front (Vol. IX 1951), was willing to oblige. I declared my pride and emotion on walking ground honoured by the blood of the Red Army at Stalingrad and assured the Marshal that I had never heard anything but praise for the Red Army's part in World War II. Then I drew attention to statements in the *Encyclopaedia* that, in Britain in 1945, 'almost openly cadres were being prepared to crush the national-liberation movement in the countries of Central and South Europe' and 'the delay in opening the Second Front was not accidental; it was dictated by reactionary circles of Britain and the U.S.A. who were pursuing their self-seeking aims,' one of these aims being to enable Hitler to transfer strategic reserves from Western Europe to the Eastern Front against the Soviet Army. Great Britain, I protested, was the only country which entered the war voluntarily, and we stood alone for more than a year. Our integrity, courage and honour were affronted by such statements. The Marshal answered that he had never spoken slightingly of the British war effort and, indeed, had praised it to Mr Churchill. The point struck home, however. Gromyko intervened to make the embarrassing explanation that there must be some misunderstanding. Stanley Evans insisted on four reasons for suspicion about Russian intentions: the Berlin blockade, Czechoslovakia, Tito and Korea. Voroshilov evaded the questions with dexterity but with complete lack of conviction.

A day or two before our farewell conferences Sir Otto Prior Palmer, M.P., and I were permitted to visit the Red Banner School of the Red Army, Lenin's favourite Unit because, we understood, it had defended the Revolution in 1917. A two hours drive took us to a stockade surrounding the camp in a forest. Across the entrance fluttered a banner inscribed, 'We are standing for Peace. We are defending the cause of Peace.' Commandant General Lemnov led our tour of inspection. Under an arc light at the foot of the stairs stood a soldier holding a rifle, as rigid as an aluminium cast. Fine looking youths were training as officer-cadets. They served their first year as private soldiers, the second as N.C.O.s and the third as officers. The attractive dining-room had tables for four with carafes of a brown liquid on each spotless table cloth. Wine? Alas, no; it was cold tea. Although life was hard and frugal and discipline strict, morale was that of completely dedicated Communists. The curriculum covered six hours per day for six days per week and every evening was given over to study, mainly of Marxism. We saw nothing resembling a N.A.A.F.I. The Unit club, from which alcohol was barred, contained a museum, a good library and a cinema showing three times weekly, not slap and tickle, but films of Soviet achievement.

The Russian officer who accompanied us to and from the camp was an intelligent fellow who answered readily questions about pay, recruitment and call-up and, in turn, sought information about British military organization. What he could not understand was the position of the conscientious objector in Britain. Sir Otto and I spelled out the facts in every way we could devise: a young Briton with a genuine conscientious objection could claim and obtain exemption from service and his personal rights as a citizen in our democratic system would be protected fully even in time of war. Suddenly our guide exclaimed, 'You mean to say that there are men in your country who, when called upon to join the Armed Forces, may refuse to do so?' We explained again that a British citizen, on the basis of a genuinely held conscientious objection, could be exempted from military service. Our young Russian friend threw up his arms in amazement. 'I cannot understand,' he cried. 'If a man is required to serve, it is his duty to serve.' I have pondered over that conversation many times. It seems to reflect the difference in the philosophies of Democracy and Communism. Within the Communist *bloc* disciplined response to obligations imposed by the State is a way of life. Without such disciplined response may not the sense of duty die in democratic countries? That may well be the big question mark over the future of this world of ours.

I collected a vast volume of social, economic and industrial statistics on all phases of Soviet Communism. These, now out of date by nearly two decades, pointed to problems, especially in relation to international understanding, still clouding the future. This great and very articulate people suffered more in World War II than public opinion in the West ever suspected. Estimates put their dead at twenty millions. Enormous mass movements of the civilian population aggravated a housing problem bigger, pre-war, than any such problem known to the West. Transport was rendered almost non-existent. In great cities like Moscow at the end of the war there was not a tintack, a nail, a piece of soap or a skein of wool available for sale. Stalin's decision to reconstruct out of Russia's own depleted resources meant that her capital investment programme was driven through with little regard to short-term human needs. As in war, only the armed forces and young people enjoyed priorities in the social spending of surpluses available after capital investment. Now the mighty effort was yielding social and economic dividends. Citizens even felt their country could enter the nuclear age without hurt to living standards. The masses were better off than at any time in Russian history.

One of my ablest mentors in Moscow was U Maung Gyi, the Burmese Ambassador, whom I had met frequently while he represented his country in London. He was a fruitful source of information and interpretation. Russia's attitude he said, and the West's attitude to Russia, reminded him of the problems created by the Indian caste system. Regular rebuffs had induced a sense of inferiority which, since the time of Peter the Great, had fed upon itself. Russia did not understand the West. The West did not understand Russia. The ordinary man regarded the British as hopelessly bourgeois with a conception of freedom the Russian had never known, never understood and did not want to understand. Russia's investment programme had been given a priority it could never have secured through free institutions and the ballot box. Her history was one of being invaded rather than of invading; in one sense, he thought, the Cold War was an expression typical of Russian military caution. The Russian's real fear was of America yet, like Americans, Russians worshipped size and material values and believed that in materialistic terms progress was eternal.

Our homecoming caused more hilarity than almost any other experience during my political life. The late Dame Edith Pitt, a Conservative member of our delegation, was presented with a heavy aluminium kettle made by convicts in a prison she had visited. On the plane she asked if anybody would relieve her of the kettle. I volunteered partly out of gallantry but mainly because I am always prepared to act on the old soldier's principle of accepting something for nothing. At London Airport the kettle monopolized much of the publicity accorded to our return. It became the most photographed and the most paragraphed kettle in all history. Long afterwards, the Dame visited my constituency, singled me out for attack as an arrogant publicity-seeker and, although admitting she had asked if anybody wanted the kettle, moaned, 'George Wigg took it. His instinct for publicity is unfailing.' I still have the kettle. It is a prized possession—like the wooden porridge spoon an unknown correspondent sent to help me 'to continue to stir things up'.

Chapter Ten: Defence

We came back from Russia to an uneasy House of Commons. Both main parties were involved in leadership problems with Ministers and Shadow Ministers speculating about their fates and future. Prime Minister Churchill was on the way out. Eden was showing all the nervous anticipation of a favourite son uncertain when—indeed if— the self-centred old man would release the power he wanted to keep but was incapable of exerting. Eden had to wait until April 1955, for his belated legacy. Attlee, unlike Churchill, was in full possession of his faculties. His purpose was to remain Leader until the warring elements in the Labour Party acquired the appearance of a viable alternative government. Meantime, Labour was failing as an effective Opposition. I discussed this problem with my old friend Willie Whiteley, the Chief Whip. He had gone through fifteen tremendous years as a loyal servant to Attlee and the bonds between us permitted me to tell him that he should now step down. Whiteley agreed, and he and I nominated Herbert Bowden (now Lord Aylestone) as Chief Whip, a choice endorsed unanimously by the Party.

I became increasingly concerned about the organization and efficiency of the aircraft industry and the way in which aircraft supply problems were being handled. I had the advantage of the friendship and advice of Richard Worcester, one of Britain's really disinterested experts in aviation matters. If Worcester had been listened to the Rolls-Royce disaster would have been avoided and Britain would now have a healthy, thriving aircraft industry. The writing has been on the wall for years. The humiliation of 1971 is the direct result of the wasted 'fifties and 'sixties.

Memories of Moscow were revived when I accompanied Ellis Smith, M.P. for the constituency in which I live, to a Russian Embassy celebration of the October Revolution. Ellis Smith had been a popular junior Minister in 1945, but no political honour afforded him more pride than having been selected to play football at right-half for the Rhine Army after World War I. He heard that

Russian footballers were among the guests and he eagerly assumed they were in our immediate party. He called in as interpreter Mrs Zelda Coates, Russian-born wife of Pat Coates, Secretary of the Anglo-Soviet Parliamentary Committee, and proceeded to sing the praises of Sir Stanley Matthews, the wizard outside-right of Stoke City and England. Soon Ellis was dribbling an imaginary football up and down the room, wiggling his bottom *à la* Stanley, leaving opponents stranded on the floor and crashing the ball into an imaginary net. It was some time before Mrs Coates was able to hold Ellis up long enough to explain that the amazed Russians to whom he had been talking were not football players but poets.

When the Crabb case was debated in April 1956, the Prime Minister, declaring it would not be in the public interest to disclose the circumstances under which Crabb died, nevertheless made it clear that Crabb engaged in his exploit without the authority or knowledge of Her Majesty's Government and 'appropriate disciplinary action was being taken'. Gaitskell deployed his case without laying the Party and himself open to a charge of damaging our security interests. He argued that the basic principles of security are that a Secret Service, being necessary, must be secret; as a Service it must be efficient and, in a democracy, it must be subject to democratic control; it must not embarrass Britain's international position; and it must be reasonably successful.

I had discussed the problem with Gaitskell and during the debate we drove home the point that naval equipment had been used and, whether or not the First Lord of the Admiralty knew about it, he must accept responsibility for what had happened. Was the Prime Minister, on whom ultimate responsibility for the Secret Service lay, Gaitskell asked, to be the only Minister to exercise adequate control over that Service? Gaitskell's speech was a model of lucid restraint yet it threw a fierce light on the muddled relations between the Secret Service and the Security Service which stemmed, primarily, from the incompetence of successive Tory administrations. What had been lacking was a regular examination, essential to co-ordination and efficiency, of problems common to the three Services and their political masters.

Gaitskell invited me to speak from the Front Bench as understudy to Strachey on Army matters. Strachey was not an easy colleague. He was an intellectual, living in the realms of economic theory and abstract thought and regarding the simple multiplication problems of Army organization as beneath notice. He was just not interested in Army nuts and bolts. As a backroom boy he had great possibilities. On the Front Bench he was of little use; he lacked guts and judgment. As Secretary of State for War Strachey had supported the idea of a three years' service engagement for the Army, a proposal for getting quick results regardless of the future problems such a change would create. Like the Tory Secretary of State who succeeded him and eventually introduced the idea, he never understood that military manpower is counted in man years; whereas one hundred men for three years is equivalent to three hundred man years the same number of men for seven years is equivalent to seven hundred man years. Thus a three years' engagement was a mere gimmick making no effective contribution towards long-term man-power policy.

Under Eden's flabby guidance the country was slithering towards the drama of Suez and the tragedy of the end of Britain as a first-class power. One small aspect of the Suez aftermath was a Wiggery-Pokery effort to bring the Tory Whips to heel. Although even less efficient than Labour Whips in the conduct of Parliamentary business they applied a Draconian discipline to whipping their votes. A Tory Suez rebel, Patrick Maitland (now Lord Lauderdale), who opposed our withdrawal from the Canal, was reported in *The Times* of December 8, 1956, as complaining about 'extraordinary and unexampled pressures, some of them altogether underhand, to force the Tories into line'. I used this statement as the basis of a complaint of privilege in the doubtful hope that Maitland would support me. I quote Peter G. Richards: 'The attempt failed because only Maitland could initiate a complaint about the nature of the pressures to which he had been subjected. That the activities of the Whips might constitute a breach of privilege is a novel and stimulating doctrine; if ever it were accepted, the effect on the character of the House of Commons could not fail to be profound!'*

During these two years I had worked with colleagues on several joint committees of the Parliamentary Labour Party, the National Executive of the Labour Party and the Trades Union Congress to

---

* Peter G. Richards, *Honourable Members: A Study of the British Backbencher*, (Faber & Faber 1959).

study defence in relation to manpower for industry. The most important of our committees was a high-powered Tripartite Working Party to inquire into the National Service Acts. As Chairman, Shinwell stated that the Parliamentary Party sought a review of the manpower position and the effect of National Service on the economic and social life of the country. The general opinion was that abolition of National Service was impossible at that time. During our proceedings the 1955 Trades Union Congress passed unanimously and without discussion a resolution proposed by two unknown persons to reduce the period of National Service. The Labour Party Conference followed suit by adopting a resolution demanding a review with the aim of reducing the period of National Service. Thus some members of our Tripartite Working Party were already mandated upon the most vital aspects of the problem we had been formed to investigate. We were repeating the folly so often witnessed in Parliamentary debate in which M.P.s are expected to take policy decisions before they have established the facts. My membership of the Working Party confirmed me in the view that defence should be lifted out of the arena of Party and inter-Party controversy through the functioning of a Standing Select Committee of the House of Commons. This would enable basic defence facts to be ascertained and thus make possible debates informed by knowledge.

In June 1956 the Tripartite Committee presented its conclusions which, for brevity, I paraphrase and summarise:

Changes in the world situation require a re-examination of strategy and defence; but two decisions of immediate urgency were the future of National Service and the size of the defence budget.

Both decisions must be taken in conformity with our N.A.T.O. commitments and phased plans for carrying them out should be presented to and discussed with the N.A.T.O. Council.

The Government should decide now to stop the call-up and fix the end of 1958 as the target date. In the absence of such a decision there should be an immediate cut in the period of National Service.

Research and development in the sphere of defence should be shared among the N.A.T.O. countries and the results of research already carried out should be shared.

The Ministry of Defence, the Service Ministries and the Ministry of Supply should be reorganized with a view to ultimate unification of the Services.

There should be concentration on a few types of weapons and, in the aircraft industry in particular, greater concentration of productive resources, if necessary by reorganization.

The Government should make a global cut which would substantially reduce the defence budget.

I rejected the proposals as politically dangerous and, in defence terms, disastrous. On July 17, 1956, I informed Carol Johnson, Secretary of the Parliamentary Labour Party, that I desired to amend a Motion, to be moved next day at the Party meeting, giving general support to the proposals. I wished to re-affirm the line of policy adopted by the Party in the Defence debate in February. The Party then opposed a Government Motion approving the Statement on Defence, 1956. Our Amendment regretted 'that despite the expenditure of five thousand seven hundred million pounds in four years, the Statement on Defence, 1956 (Command Paper No. 9691), discloses grave weaknesses in our defences; makes no provision for an immediate cut in the period of National Service nor for any specific plan for its eventual abolition nor for an inquiry into defence manpower; and contains no adequate proposals for a more economical and effective allocation of resources between the Services.'

The T.U.C. General Council Report to Congress in 1956 included a passage along the lines of the conclusions of the Tripartite Committee. Sir Thomas (now Lord) Williamson explained that more than one view had been expressed, but a Motion for a speedy and progressive reduction in the period of National Service was carried. So emerged the pattern of the strange march of events: two unknown members at the 1955 Congress forced the issue against National Service; the General Council of the T.U.C. were too indolent or frightened to contest their arguments; the National Executive of the Labour Party burked the issue, as did the popularly elected Shadow Cabinet. Thus the defence policy of the nation's alternative government was decided by two unknown members of the T.U.C. The unknown two also had a profound influence on the Government's policy, for the Tories have always been afraid of the conscription issue.

George Brown took the Party line in a debate on July 31, 1956, trying to get round the flank of the Tories, and reached the position of demanding the abolition of conscription as a political vote winner. I stated my case and, having resigned my role as a Front Bench spokesman, abstained from voting. Although Brown was conciliatory to pacifist opinion, he propounded a case that eventually evoked bitter controversy within the Labour Party until it was reunited on defence by Harold Wilson in January 1964.

As Prime Minister rescuing the Tory Party from the shambles of Suez, Harold Macmillan was a resounding success. The Tory bosses preferred him to Butler for, although, like Butler, possessed of a social conscience, he had no time for 'Butskellism', the name given to the vague form of 'mixed economy' which Butler advocated and Gaitskell, to the dismay of many Labour M.P.s, endorsed. On this kind of issue Macmillan's neo-Marxism, when he wrote *The Middle Way* in 1938, made him a hard-liner on the Right, just as Bevan's Marxist training produced a hard-liner on the Left. He was friendly, even charming, in his relations with M.P.s of all Parties. He enjoyed, too, his own superb command of language. At the Dispatch Box he unconsciously responded to his own witticisms and well-turned phrases with a joyous little kick of his right foot—a mannerism I used to watch for. I imagine he really enjoyed turning the Cabinet Room into a slaughter house, butchering traditional Tory monuments like Lord Chancellor Kilmuir, and playing the game of Family Favourites by promoting inconsequential nonentities. He played politics rough and he was a ruthless debater. He was, of course, lucky in the Opposition. Nobody on Labour's Front Bench could stand up to his teasing raillery and savage mockery.

Having united his Party, Macmillan proceeded to dismember the Commonwealth. Before becoming Prime Minister he had indulged in what he called 'a pipe dream' of financing social and economic reconstruction by knocking, in contemplation, seven hundred million pounds off the annual cost of defence; the kind of dream indulged in by a man who gives up smoking only to find that he eats more sweets and spends more money taking off weight. I formed the view that in spite of or as a result of his visit to Russia and his effort, made abortive by the crash of the American U.2 spy plane, to effect a rapprochement between Khrushchev and Eisenhower at the Paris Summit Meeting in 1960, the Prime Minister had failed to understand the significance of Soviet possession of the H-bomb. That event, together with the American reaction to Suez and Hungary, marked the great divide between fantasy and fact in foreign policy. Russia could not be confined within her own frontiers by force. She was a nuclear giant and her massive conventional strength was an additional guarantee of her security.

Meantime, the Prime Minister was planning to out-manoeuvre the Labour Party on the conscription issue while solving the vexing problem that Britain, having agreed in 1954 to maintain four divisions of troops with a supporting tactical Air Force element in Germany for fifty years, was ratting on that commitment and earning the contempt of our N.A.T.O. partners. The 1957 Defence White Paper announced the decision to develop an independent nuclear deterrent which would, so it was said, make possible a reduction in military manpower. This, it was asserted, would make it possible to end conscription by 1960. Macmillan's famous 'Winds of Change' speech in racialist South Africa was a reaction to the obvious fact that African nationalism posed questions to which colonialism had no answer. It was also a cover for the run-down of conventional forces in Africa, regardless of the fact that a continuance of the peace keeping, stabilizing role of the British Army in Africa would be essential to the survival of the new inexperienced régimes. Another straw in the winds of change was that the 1957 Defence White Paper which usually appeared in February for debate early in March, was not to be available before April.

Before the publication of the Defence White Paper I accepted an invitation to write a policy pre-view and a forecast of its cost for *Peace News*. This was a useful exercise, since the Government had leaked sunshine stories to the Press which had become so exaggerated that even the Minister of Defence, Duncan Sandys, found it necessary to sound a note of caution. Returning to Britain from a visit to General Eisenhower he said that 'some of these speculations on astronomical cuts in defence belonged more to the Geophysical Year than to the realms of reality'. In my article I repudiated the suggestion that the Government would end National Service immediately or that it would consider any scheme for selective service. It was more likely to continue the system of exempting coal miners, agricultural workers, merchant seamen, scientific research workers and similar categories while maintaining the myth that the call-up was universal. I made two forecasts. The three years short service engagement would go as a first step towards abolishing National Service. The 1956 White Paper objective of reducing the manpower ceiling of 700,000 National Service and Regular soldiers by 1958 would be replaced by a new target of 400,000 male adults. This figure of 400,000 I broke down as: Royal Navy 80,000 to 90,000; R.A.F. 110,000 to 120,000; Army 200,000. I estimated that the total expenditure Parliament would be asked to approve would be 1,450 million pounds. The actual figure published in the Defence White Paper was 1,483 million pounds.

In the event the three years engagement was abandoned. The ceiling for the three Services was set at 375,000 but this figure was not broken down until a year later. It was then revealed as: Royal Navy 88,000; R.A.F. 135,000; Army 165,000, a total of 388,000. In March, 1959, the Army's target was raised to 180,000, bringing the total for all the Services to 403,000. Not surprisingly the notional target of 165,000 for the Army was not published in the 1957 White Paper. It was not made known until 1958. In 1959 the Army's *real* target of 180,000 was revealed. It then became clear why Antony Head refused Macmillan's offer to remain Minister of Defence. A man of honour and integrity, Head refused to accept an Army manpower target of 165,000, for that figure was not related to the Army's requirements. It was the figure thought to be obtainable by voluntary recruiting for the Army. Such was the phoney basis upon which the defence policy of our country was planned.

The 1957 White Paper was the most disastrous document published during my Parliamentary life. It based our defence policy upon an an independent nuclear deterrent we did not possess, do not possess now and, I forecast, will not possess in the foreseeable future. The new dream, inspired by the idea that nuclear defence must be retaliatory, was to carry a nuclear warhead right to the heart of the Soviet Union by means of a liquid-fuelled rocket, Blue Streak, to be entrenched in underground emplacements. The new policy represented a choice between expenditure on nuclear deterrence, the need for which might never arise, and expenditure on the recruiting and maintenance of conventional forces so that our influence outside our shores could be expressed by the faithful discharge of our Commonwealth and international commitments.

By 1960 Blue Streak was cancelled—as I had forecast—after one hundred million pounds had been spent on it with bills for many more millions still to be met. The idiotic alternative was to buy Skybolt from America with Britain supplying her own nuclear warheads. Independence was to be purchased from the United States upon whom, already, we relied for developing defence measures like the Ballistic Early Warning System. The situation acquired all the characteristics of tragi-comedy in December 1962, when America cancelled Skybolt!

An interesting aspect of how politics were intertwined with defence was revealed when on February 10, 1959, the Minister of Defence criticized the Polaris missile submarine as both costly and detectable. Newspapers went to town on the story that Blue Streak was 'in' and Polaris was 'out'. Meantime a Departmental Committee, under Sir Richard Powell, was deciding that 'the best hope for the future lies in the mobile deterrent system that can find protection in elusiveness'. So it was Blue Streak with its allegedly underground emplacement that was out!

The cancellation of first Blue Streak and then Skybolt left a yawning gap in the Conservative Government's defence philosophy. This was filled with words by the Macmillan decision, so dear to the Tory heart, that British influence in world affairs must depend upon the possession of an independent nuclear deterrent. Turning to reality, there were only the remains of the V-bomber Force, for what that was worth, so the Tories pushed ahead with the Polaris programme. In April 1963, the Government concluded the Polaris Sales Programme which made Polaris missiles, minus warheads, available to Britain. The Americans build forty-one Polaris submaries armed with A-1, A-2 and A-3 missiles. The Russian deployment of their anti-ballistic missile complex, however, made it necessary for the Americans to step up the re-equipment of all their forty-one submarines with the A-3 type missile. These vessels, each carrying sixteen missiles, when the conversion was up-dated, were capable of firing a total of six hundred and fifty-six missiles. By 1967, the American Secretary of Defence, Robert MacNamara, was considering the conversion of the Polaris programme so that a large number of the forty-one submarines would be in a position to fire the Poseidon missile. MacNamara asserted that 'the cost of converting a submarine to Poseidon, of procuring new missiles, and of ten years of operation, is about half again as much as that of operating the Polaris submarines for ten years', adding that 'the effectiveness of the Poseidon submarine is several times greater'. He estimated the total cost of developing Poseidon and deploying the proposed force at 3.3 billion dollars. The Americans have now decided, because of the cost, to fit only thirty-one of the forty-one submarines with Poseidon.

Ten years ago when the nation's money was being gambled on the Blue Streak project, the value of the Polaris missile-firing submarine was being called into question. Although it fired its sixteen missiles while under water the question arose: How long would it remain undetectable and invulnerable?

All this changed and, indeed, is still changing. The Polaris submarine, of which we have four armed with the A-3 (planned, according to the Americans, to have a range of 2,500 nautical miles), is to remain equipped with a version of the A-3 specially designed to penetrate ballistic missile defences. In plain English, this implies that the Russians are almost certainly capable of destroying the original A-3 missile by the use of an anti-ballistic missile. The Americans have also demonstrated by their actions new doubts about the efficacy of A-3. This explains why they are going ahead with the much more expensive Poseidon which we cannot even pretend to afford. The fact is that the four Polaris submarines we do possess cannot maintain a continuous patrol. The necessities of refitting mean that for periods there will be no British Polaris at sea. The grim joke is that it does not matter. On October 1, 1963, it became known that the missiles of the four Polaris submarines are now targeted in accordance with the N.A.T.O. programme, although they could, in the national interest, be re-targeted to meet the needs of a British programme! So the four British Polaris submarines, built to maintain Tory Party morale, are targeted to suit N.A.T.O., that is American, interests. If, at some point, a conflict should develop between British and American policies we could re-target, and of course the world would be informed; otherwise, what pressures would be exerted on the Russians if they were not told that from a number of points they might be attacked by missiles fired from British submarines? Then what would the Russians do? The British action would give them the vital information that N.A.T.O. was in political disarray. If they thought there was a serious military threat, the likelihood is that Britain would be subjected to the counter-threat of being ordered to sail its four Polaris submarines under the white flag into Russian ports or to wherever Russia demanded. The idea that the possession of four submarines, which on the evidence of the established public facts are armed with weapons obviously less efficient than those the Americans wield, really constitutes any threat other than to ourselves is beyond me.

An additional fact is that the Labour Government, in 1964, inherited the burden of a programme for five Polaris submarines. As the fifth submarine had not been started we proceeded with the programme for the four, which it was cheaper to develop than to cancel. At the present time yet another Conservative Defence Minister is playing defence politics. He, according to the kites he flies, plans to spend, in association with France, money on maintaining our nuclear forces in being. *The Times* recently described the situation in these words: 'A small fleet of nuclear submarines, armed with Polaris missiles with multiple warheads, gives this country an ultimate capacity to defend itself such as it could seldom have had in its history.' This means that if ever the chips are down we shall have the capacity either to surrender publicly, in the most humiliating fashion possible, or to commit suicide! The threat to Russia, if real, will bring the suicide; if the threat is not real it is a sick joke. The Russians, a people with a highly-developed sense of humour, will see the joke. The British people will pay the bill.

The notorious 1957 White Paper was followed by another reduction of the Regiments of the Line to forty-nine which, with eight battalions of Guards and three Parachute Regiments, gave a total of sixty major units discharging the Infantry role. My own reaction was that amalgamation of Regiments should be linked with future recruiting and I deplored the fact that the world had seen innumerable British Regiments hardly able to move their own baggage. Churchill's reaction, according to an apocryphal story worthy of being true, was rather different. His old Regiment, the 4th Queen's Hussars, was to be amalgamated with the 8th King's Royal Hussars, and the War Office had the happy thought that Field Marshal Montgomery should be briefed to break the news to our war-time Prime Minister. Monty, so the story ran, introduced the subject with his well-known tact: 'My Royal Warwickshire Regiment is all right. Yours is to be amalgamated.' Sir Winston's reaction as Monty rattled on was to engage himself in lighting a big cigar and puffing it before enquiring: 'Pray, what has happened to the Regimental Bands?' Monty had no information. Sir Winston puffed some more then asked: 'Pray, what is going to happen to the Royal Horse Artillery?' Again Monty's brief was blank. There followed a long pause as Sir Winston withdrew the cigar from his mouth, thrust the wet end at Monty's face, and demanded: 'Pray, what is going to happen at my funeral if there are no Royal Horse Artillery and no Regimental Bands?'

Two fresh aspects of Labour's drift towards consensus with the Tories on defence soon emerged. Bevan had composed his differences with Gaitskell on domestic policy. He was now Shadow Foreign Secretary and had been converted to the view that, without the atom bomb, he would go 'naked into the Conference Chamber'. He feared the icy blast from which the bomb we did not possess would protect him. At a Party Meeting towards the end of 1957 he fought down a plea that we should oppose the policy the Government had endorsed at the Paris N.A.T.O. talks. In support of his insistence for a free hand he pontificated on military matters which had developed considerably since he had pulverised Churchill in the 1950 Parliament. In the course of our exchanges I commented, 'Do shut up Nye. When you behave as if you were God I can tolerate you, but when you assume the mantle of Napoleon I become very frightened indeed.' There was reality behind the crack. The most bellicose people I know are those members of the Labour Party who, late in life, dream they will be in command of Armies, Navies, Air Forces and, in Bevan's case, nuclear launching pads. The second turn in events—in March 1958—thrust me into the centre of still another flare-up revealing the sad state of political thinking about this key question: what would happen if the West, relying for defence upon the deterrent effect of nuclear weapons and the capacity to deliver them, had to face a conventional attack in overwhelming force? Strachey addressed himself to the question in the House of Commons. He took what he described as a fairly obvious example of what we ought to do and what we ought to let the Russians know we would do in the event of a Soviet attempt to throw our garrison out of West Berlin. If the Russians attacked with conventional forces we, of course, would not dream of dropping H-bombs on Moscow; the West would meet such a conventional attack on a limited scale with conventional forces. Emrys Hughes interjected: 'How?' 'We are there now,' said Strachey and on Hughes' insisting, 'How can we do it?' replied: 'We can do it. If the Russians attack the West Berlin garrison with two divisions, that garrison must defend itself.' Then, after arguing that our garrison was in considerable strength, he continued, 'The conventional forces that we have in Berlin might be overrun and, of course, this would mean that the Russians were raising their stakes and they could do that in two ways, either by sending in a number of divisions which we could not match, or by beginning to use tactical atomic weapons.' This was the Sandys White Paper doctrine in full fatal operation. Since we lacked conventional forces because of the failure of our manpower policy, the answer must be to use atomic weapons. It was also the Strachey version of the Brown theme—which he quoted—that if the Russians raised the stakes so must we, and with atomic weapons we did not possess!

I gave Strachey notice that, if I were called upon in the debate on the Air Estimates, I would refer to his speech. I was called. The plain implication of his policy, I pointed out, was that three British Infantry battalions with no supporting arms of any kind, plus one American Regiment, would take on two Russian divisions; that would not be war, I said, but murder. I denounced the statement, made without proper inquiry, that conventional forces were available in West Berlin in considerable strength and answered my own question: Who would be the first victims of the use of atomic weapons? The British troops who were there and the civilian population. To enlighten Strachey's ignorance I described the atomic weapons available for our defence of Berlin. They were the Valiant V bomber and the Canberra, not yet provided with a nuclear capacity, and Corporal, another of those still-to-be-deployed weapons which spokesmen from both Front Benches invoked in their imagination when driven into a corner.

Strachey notified me that he was reporting me to the Parliamentary Committee of the Labour Party. Gaitskell immediately summoned me from my home to announce that I was being charged with using Parliamentary privilege to make an attack which, if it were made outside the House on a colleague, would be actionable at law. On my commenting that there was only one thing I could do, Gaitskell said, 'I am glad to hear you say that. I presume you will attend the next Party Meeting and apologize.' 'Oh, no!' I answered. 'I shall go to Strachey's constituency, repeat my attack, and if he wants to sue me, he can.' I refused to accept Strachey's explanation that his argument about the use of British troops in Berlin and their support by tactical atomic weapons 'was made only by way of illustration'. Our talk moved on to less argumentative lines. I expressed my fear that our Party, having been bamboozled into accepting the 1957 and 1958 White Papers, was drifting into a divisive debate about non-existent atomic weapons. Personally, I accepted atomic strategy insofar as we live under the umbrella of American nuclear weapons, but for Britain to pursue an independent nuclear strategy would deflect public attention from the really important matter of providing adequate conventional defence besides being economically and politically ruinous. I urged Gaitskell, as a Privy Councillor, to seek a talk with the Prime Minister to ascertain the truth about our strength and to discover whether or not we had tactical atomic weapons.

Reflecting on Gaitskell's remarks I wrote him a letter reiterating that my words were in no way libellous—on this I had now received legal advice—and adding that the implications of Strachey's policy had never been put before the Parliamentary Labour Party, the Parliamentary Committee or the National Executive. Accepting the need for Party discipline, I proposed that the issues raised and their relation to the events of the past year should be considered by the Labour Party as a whole. For good measure I reminded Gaitskell of the March 6 statement of the Under Secretary of State for the Army that 'there are as yet no tactical nuclear weapons in the British Army in Germany'. My letter produced no reply. Whenever I sought to speak on defence at Parliamentary Labour Party meetings, I was not called. I gave up attending these meetings.

Another problem in 1957 arose from the prosecution of Dr John Bodkin Adams of Eastbourne on a charge of murder of which he was found innocent. This prosecution was preceded in August 1956 by a Scotland Yard probe into what newspapers described as 'mass poisonings at Eastbourne' and the regurgitation of an inquest story about a suicide in whose will Adams was a beneficiary. The popular Press—with the exception of the *Daily Express*, whose crime reporter, Percy Hoskins, refused to risk sacrificing an individual's freedom to newspaper greed for circulation—entered upon an orgy of sensation-mongering. Adams's life was made a hell on earth. There was no evidence on which to base a charge against him. He was made the subject of what *Tribune*, on August 31, described as 'trial by newspaper'. He issued libel writs against three newspapers which did not contest them; whatever the agreed damages, nothing could compensate any man for the ordeal Adams suffered nor restore easily the reputation of British justice based on the principle that a man is innocent until he is proven to be guilty. For me, this was also a problem of security; the security of the freedom of the individual from newspaper attack based on leaks whatever their source. A posse of Press photographers were present when Adams was arrested. Soon, against this background there arose another issue: the danger that publicity attaching to a hearing at the Magistrates Court—which cannot determine guilt or innocence but only whether or not there is a case to go for trial—might prejudice a jury in the higher court.

Adams appeared before the Eastbourne Magistrates on January 14, 1957. An application by his Counsel for the evidence to be heard in closed court was neither supported nor opposed by Prosecuting Counsel. It was rejected by the Magistrates although the Magistrates Court Act of 1952 gave them specific powers, which some legal luminaries believed they always possessed, to hear evidence in private where privacy was considered necessary in an accused man's interests. In the Central Criminal Court, which found Adams not guilty, Mr Justice Devlin (now Lord Devlin) warned the jury more than once that they must pay no attention to what they had read or heard about the case, the reason being—to quote the late Lord Birkett— that 'some matters of the gravest and most damaging kind, which had been referred to at the preliminary investigation and had been fully reported in the newspapers, were not now before the jury'.

On April 15 I asked the Attorney General, Sir Reginald Manningham-Buller (now Lord Dilhorne), whether he would institute an independent inquiry 'into the preparation, organization and con-duct of the Prosecution's case against Dr Adams'. He refused, despite widespread public unease, and I gave notice that I would raise the matter on the Adjournment. On that Motion on May 1, the Attorney General declared that if my information 'is worthy of credence at all, or if it is even a justifiable basis for the wild allegation he has thought fit to make, I am quite certain that my Rt. Hon. Friend, the Home Secretary, will be only too glad to investigate that in-formation'. In reply to another Member, the Attorney General said, 'The fact that there was a second indictment on the file was not well known, except to the Prosecution, the Court and the Defence.' I wrote to Home Secretary Butler on May 8 informing him that the Defence became aware that knowledge of the second indictment had leaked to the Press. I also had information to the effect that a police investigation had failed to induce three newspapers, which I named, to reveal their sources. I suggested an investigation by a High Court judge and announced that I had put down a question on the subject of the application of the Official Secrets Act to members of the Police Force. Butler replied on May 15. He had decided no useful purpose would be served by any further inquiries into the matters I had raised. Inconclusive? I, at least, do not regret my modest support for the brave stand of Michael Foot in *Tribune* and Percy Hoskins in the *Daily Express*. In the thirteen years since, no such scandalous treatment as Adams suffered has besmirched the reputation of British justice.

Among my constituency cases, success in amending the 1957 Finance Act gave me great personal satisfaction. The Simon Engineering Company had devised and produced telescopic contrivances used for erecting, inspecting and repairing overhead structures. Besides acquiring world rights outside the U.S.A. this Company were developing it for use by our Armed Forces. I wanted to remove a clause in the Act which meant that when this equipment was used on the roads it became liable to Vehicle Tax. Nobody rated my chances as good. I had to present the amendment in proper order, get it called by the Chairman of Ways and Means and, finally, induce the Government to accept it; three daunting processes. Somehow or other I got my clause through and, amid laughter, Enoch Powell, then Financial Secretary to the Treasury, commented: ' "the setting sun and music at the close is . . . sweetest last" '; my constituents had won.

In November of that same year I caused a considerable furore in Parliament and Press by getting the House of Commons into closed session. It was another example of Wiggery-Pokery—an instinctive reaction to that dear brain-child of mine of using Parliamentary procedure to hold up Government business which I thought was wrong. The Home Secretary, Butler, had refused to reply to points in a debate on the Committee Stage of a Bill regulating the use of cars in elections. I rose and said, 'I spy strangers'. Sir Charles MacAndrew, the Deputy Speaker, put my 'motion' that strangers withdraw. Labour Members cried 'Aye'. Sir Charles declared the motion carried. Butler objected that there had been a shout of 'No' from the Tory benches, to which Sir Charles replied that he had heard Ayes but no Noes. The Government Deputy Chief Whip declared he had said 'No', but Sir Charles ordered the Serjeant at Arms to clear the galleries. The House resumed and sat for two hours after Press and public had been expelled. Even more amusing than my unexpected exposure of Government incompetence were some Press comments. Under the heading 'Wigg the Wag', Cassandra in the *Daily Mirror* wrote: 'He is an odd bird; vigilant, unpredictable, shrewd and solitary. . . . He is the chillie pepper in the Parliamentary chutney. Very hot and inclined to burn the mouth. But George Wigg keeps the boys on their toes and when the House gets dull Wigg the Wag shakes 'em good and hard. Which is no bad thing.'

J. P. W. Mallalieu, in the *New Statesman*, made the most of the discomfiture of the Government but thought 'it was generally agreed that Wigg had inadvertently performed a singular disservice to his Party'. 'However,' he added, 'this will worry Wigg not at all; and, without pause for breath, he will no doubt resume the probing, harassing, lecturing, bullying of the Government which, almost single-handed and with immense skill he has carried on for the last seven years.' To emphasise that *Daily Mirror* readers paid their money and took their choice, that newspaper printed a leader suggesting that the episode would be regarded as 'derogating from the dignity of Parliament, which does not exist to be a vehicle for childish tricks' but forgot, of course, to mention that my action was derogating to the efficiency of the Tory leaders of the House and of the Tory Whips who had not paid Parliament the modest compliment of learning how to conduct their business.

Later, Shinwell and I visited East Germany. We found there an almost mystical yearning for German reunification tinged with fears about the continuance of Nazi influence within the Federal Republic which, in its turn, harboured apprehension of the strength of Soviet influence in the so-called Democratic Republic. Shinwell, as he subsequently told the House, gave me one moment of consternation. He insisted that I shoot against some of the magnificently trained young East German soldiers we inspected. Luckily I was in form.

The result of the General Election of October 1959 was a foregone conclusion. Gaitskell's 'mixed economy', including promises of reduced taxation, made no impact despite his obvious sincerity. Macmillan's electioneering skill simply overwhelmed him. The Tories won 365 seats, twenty-one more than in 1955; Labour won 258 seats, a loss of twenty-two; the Liberals retained six seats. The Gaitskell hierarchy reacted within a month by initiating at the Blackpool Conference of the Labour Party a campaign to water down and finally to remove from the Labour Party Constitution Clause Four which defines the broad objective of the Socialist Commonwealth and gives cohesion in general policy to all the democratic sections of the Left. It was a repetition, this time on the Right, of the tactics of Bevan in 1954 which nearly destroyed the Left. Labour entered the 'sixties disheartened and disunited. I came close to a decision that Labour politics had become a tragic nonsense from which I ought to resign.

Chapter Eleven: The Missing
V.C. and other Problems

The clash and excitement of great Party issues notwithstanding, nothing gives a Member of Parliament more satisfaction than to help put right a citizen's personal grievance. On New Year's Day 1960, my depressed spirits were uplifted by the news that a case in which I was concerned had been resolved—the case of the lost Victoria Cross.

After winning the V.C. in India in 1857, Captain Robert Shebbeare volunteered for service in the China Wars, was engaged in the attack on the Taku Forts, then contracted a disease from which he never recovered. He was embarked for home on the S.S. *Emu* and died at sea off Shanghai on September 16, 1860. In 1949, responding to a public appeal for exhibits, the Shebbeare family lent Robert's V.C. with his Indian Mutiny medal to the Indian Army Exhibition at the Royal Military Academy, Sandhurst. In September 1957, the family planned to hold a Centenary Party in honour of their gallant kinsman, and sought the return of the medals from the R.M.A., only to be told the V.C.. was missing. Had it been lost or stolen? Nobody knew. Eminent soldiers, including Field Marshal Auchinleck, interested themselves in restoring the precious heirloom to Mr Claude E. Shebbeare, acting for the family. The R.M.A. reported the setting up of a Court of Inquiry. Efforts to trace a former Curator who might have some information and police enquiries proved to be fruitless. Neither the R.M.A. nor the War Office made an offer to replace the medal or pay compensation for its loss. In March 1958, an old Army friend asked me to help. Satisfied that the V.C. had been loaned and not gifted to the R.M.A., I got busy.

I contacted the Secretary of State for War, Christopher Soames, who acknowledged his Department's awareness of 'this most regrettable state of affairs'. From then until the end of 1959, when the Shebbeare family received a replacement V.C. and what they agreed was reasonable compensation, I wrote forty letters, held numerous interviews inside and outside the House of Commons, and raised the question in debate; my activities stemmed from determination that the Army must right a wrong, however inconvenient it might be. Christopher Soames and his Parliamentary Secretary, Hugh Fraser, helped me.

A personal issue involving the entire nation arose in February 1961, when Mrs Thomazina Probert petitioned the Queen's Most Excellent Majesty in Council to report to the Home Secretary 'that there is ground for thinking that there may have been a miscarriage of justice in the conviction of Timothy Evans for the murder of Geraldine Evans'. The details of this human drama are well known; how Timothy Evans, Mrs Probert's son, paid the death penalty on March 9, 1950, for the murder of his child Geraldine, and how Reginald Christie, principal witness for the Prosecution at Evans's trial, was found guilty on March 26, 1953, of the murder of his wife at 10, Rillington Place, London, W.11, and confessed to killing several other persons including Geraldine and Mrs Evans.

Public demand for a review of the Evans case was answered in an unusual way. The then Home Secretary, Sir David Maxwell Fyfe, who believed that 'the chances of error in a murder case did not constitute a factor we must consider,' appointed a one-man Inquiry, Mr John Scott Henderson, Q.C., to report whether, 'in his opinion, there is any ground for thinking that there may have been any miscarriage of justice in the conviction of Evans for the murder of Geraldine Evans'. On July 13, Scott Henderson presented his Report summarising his findings as follows:

1 : The case for the prosecution against Evans as presented to the Jury at his trial was an overwhelming one.
2 : Having considered all the material now available relating to the deaths of Mrs Evans and Geraldine Evans, I am satisfied there can be no doubt that Evans was responsible for both.
3 : Christie's statements that he was responsible for the death of Mrs Evans were not only unreliable but were untrue.

Parliament received the Report next day and on July 29 my colleague, Geoffrey Bing, initiated a debate, having given the Home Secretary prior notice of the points he would raise. Bing's analysis and criticism of the form and findings of the Inquiry produced a rejoinder from Scott Henderson in a Supplementary Report and stimulated, especially among legal reformers and supporters of the abolition of hanging, a continuing public interest which Mrs Probert's petition brought to issue again in 1961.

As expected, the petition was rejected. Chuter Ede, Home Secretary when Evans was hanged, was in close consultation with the then Home Secretary, R. A. Butler. They had been war-time colleagues. Now they were comrades in the anxious search for an honourable solution. On March 10, Chuter wrote a private letter which Lord Butler has given me permission to produce in full:

'The further conversation we had yesterday evening about the case of the late Timothy Evans caused me great distress of mind. After you had disclosed to me that your mind was moving in the direction of saying that you would have to make a statement declaring that there was no precedent for removing, by any official action, the stigma from the name and memory of this man and that the law requires that his remains shall be interred within the prison in which he was executed, you asked me, as a former Home Secretary and as a friend to give you my comments. My personal reaction is given in the first sentence of this letter.

'Following our conversations on 14 February I wrote to you very fully on 15 February and I see no reason to modify any of the phrases I used in that letter. I would again draw your attention to the opinion on this case expressed by Lord Birkett in the *Observer* of 15 January, 1961. When it comes to precedents I doubt if there has ever been as strong a pronouncement by a high legal authority as Lord Birkett's pronouncement: "If the facts as they are now known had been known in 1950 no jury could possibly have said that the case against Evans had been proved beyond all reasonable doubt".

'I am quite certain that so emphatic a pronouncement as this has had a great influence on public opinion. I concede that you are faced with an unprecedented situation. I hope you will believe that in this you have my sympathy for I know how lonely the Home Secretary is when he has to make decisions in these cases, but may I remind you of the following passage from Milton's Tenure of Kings and Magistrates: "... not mortal man, or his imperious will, but Justice is the onely true sovran and supreme Majesty upon earth.... And if the Parlament ... doe what they doe without precedent, if it appeare thir duty, it argues the more wisdom, vertue and magnanimity, that they know themselves able to be a precedent to others. Who perhaps in future ages, if they prove not too degenerat, will look up with honour, and aspire towards these exemplary and matchless deeds of thir Ancestors, as to the highest top of thir civil glory and emulation . . .".

'If justice requires that a precedent shall be set it may be a heavy burden but it cannot be evaded.

'With regard to the statutory requirement that the remains must be interred within the prison, that can be dealt with by a short Bill allowing those of Timothy John Evans to be exhumed and buried in ground consecrated according to the tenets of his relatives. Although if a posthumous act of clemency had quashed the conviction presumably the law might not apply and a Bill might be avoided.

'As you know, owing to the devoted labour of Colonel George Wigg, M.P., the authorities of the Roman Catholic Church are willing to facilitate this. This has only been done after the most careful enquiries by the ecclesiatical authorities. I will not stress the inferences one can draw from this but they cannot be absent from your mind.

'This brings me to a point which I put before you as being of the utmost importance. An unprecedented act of clemency may remove officially from the name and memory of Evans the conviction which sent him to the scaffold but there are those still living who feel that they are involved in the condemnation. His mother and two sisters are obscure people who were humiliated by the knowledge that this man had been compelled to pay the dreadful penalty for murder of one to whom he owed natural love, affection and protection. Their religious beliefs make the retention of his remains in ground which to them is unconsecrated a matter of grave concern. I do not share these views, but I do know my own religious beliefs press on me the inescapable duty of securing complete recognition of other people's religious beliefs no matter how much they differ from my own. As the one who finally sent Evans to his doom I owe a duty to these three women to relieve them of the spiritual anguish in which they have lived since this man's execution . . .

'To the living on whom this terrible miscarriage of justice still causes acute agony of mind and soul it is still possible to grant such relief and if to do it precedents have to be set, in my opinion, they must be established in order that law and justice are reconciled.

223

'You spoke to me with frankness of your difficulties and I hope you will pardon the frankness with which I have replied.'

In Parliament on June 15, Home Secretary Butler, rejecting Chuter Ede's argument, pleaded lack of precedent. The British public, its memory and conscience kept alive by reforming writers and journalists and by Victor Morley Lawson, a solicitor who devoted many years of service to Timothy Evans's cause, refused to be appeased. A full scale legal inquiry was set up in 1965. When the Abolition of the Death Penalty Act, suspending the death penalty for five years, was passed by the Labour Government in 1965, the way was cleared at last for a free pardon and the re-burial of the remains of Timothy Evans in consecrated ground. Now a Minister, I had always shared Chuter Ede's concern that the body of Timothy Evans should be delivered to his relatives with reverence, and with care that its re-interment, in accordance with his mother's wishes, should not be attended with graceless publicity. This, with Home Office co-operation, we achieved in November, 1965. In October 1966, Home Secretary Roy Jenkins recommended to Her Majesty that a free pardon be granted. The dedicated labours of my friend Morley Lawson received the solemn reward they deserved—the thanks of Timothy Evans's mother and sisters.

A happy event on my return to full Parliamentary activity in 1960 was the Government's decision, forecast in the Queen's Speech, to modernize the law on Betting and Gaming. As a confirmed punter and racegoer and a member for some years of the Racecourse Betting Control Board, to which I had been appointed by Lord Blakenham when, as John Hare, he was Minister of Agriculture, I was interested in improving the organization and prospects of British racing and British horse breeding. I gave evidence to the Departmental Committee, under the chairmanship of Sir Leslie Peppiatt, appointed by the Home Secretary to consider whether a levy on bookmakers was desirable and, if so, how it could be applied. My experience on the Racecourse Betting Control Board had led me to two conclusions. One was that the principles defined by the Peppiatt Committee for a Levy Board were sound. The other was that the Jockey Club did not at that time provide the leadership required by horseracing, a great national pastime and an important national industry; the Jockey Club, steeped in tradition, had failed to adapt itself to modern needs and opportunities. In the event, the Peppiatt Committee proposed a levy to yield £1,500,000 a year against the Jockey Club's estimate of £3 million. When, in 1967, I became Chairman of the Horserace Betting Levy Board I formed the view that the minimum figure required was £5 million.

The Horserace Betting Levy Board consisted of a Chairman and two members appointed by the Home Secretary, two nominees of the Jockey Club, one nominee of the National Hunt Committee, and the Chairmen of two bodies newly created under the Bill, the Bookmakers' Committee and the Horserace Totalisator Board. As originally drafted, the Bill precluded M.P.s from Membership of the Levy Board and the Horserace Totalisator Board. A number of Conservative M.P.s paid me the compliment of deciding they wanted me on the Horserace Totalisator Board, and they proposed an amendment to the Bill to make this possible. Their amendment was accepted and the Home Secretary, R. A. Butler, invited me to join the new Board. In 1964 Home Secretary Henry Brooke asked me to continue for a further three years. I resigned on becoming Paymaster General.

My work as a member of the Racecourse Betting Control Board, which I greatly enjoyed, did not prevent me from being increasingly aware of the Services' worry about the Government's defence policy, which had been mounting steadily with the slow realization of what the 1957 White Paper meant in practice. The Sandys theme of an independent British nuclear deterrent sprang from the failure of the Tory Government to find and apply an effective manpower policy. It was the subject of a lecture by Lieutenant-General Sir John Cowley, delivered at the Royal United Services Institution on November 4, 1959, and published in the Institution's *Journal* in February, 1960, which registered the intensity of Army dissatisfaction. Cowley, at that time Master General of the Ordnance, cleared his speech before delivery with the Secretary of State for War. He deplored the neglect of conventional forces and composed a verse on deterrent weapons which ran:

'I also have a plan to spend a thousand million pounds,
To buy some guided missiles and to hide them in the ground,
And then to clearly paint on each "these things must not be used",
No wonder our citizens are getting so confused.'

The Times, on November 12, 1959, considered it undesirable that senior officers should hold forth in public too readily, but pointed out that in recent years there had been 'no way for the public to know whether or not crucial defence decisions were being taken against the advice of the Government's professional military advisers. Strategy has had to be accepted in a vacuum. Public opinion has been denied its proper part because there has been no access to the views of the senior officers of the three Services.' The Government's reaction was that, thereafter, clearance of speeches of serving officers by the Secretary of State for War would not be enough. Such speeches must be referred to the Minister of Defence.

The decision to cancel Blue Streak was announced on the day the House broke up for the 1960 Easter recess. George Brown welcomed the Government's belated decision for which, he said, the Opposition had been pressing for three years. I could not believe my ears. Only six weeks had elapsed since I had stood alone at a Parliamentary Labour Party meeting and had been roundly abused for describing Blue Streak as a very dead duck. One M.P. colleague, Lawson by name, had demanded that the Whip should be withdrawn from me. When M.P.s resumed business after Easter they found that the debate on the cancellation of Blue Streak would end at 7 p.m. and be confined to a procedural point. Shinwell and I challenged this arrangement and forced a full-scale debate. I failed to catch the Speaker's eye although I sat right through the debate. I had done as much detailed study of the Blue Streak project as anybody in the House including Ministers. I had opposed the Labour Party Front Bench in the House and at a Parliamentary Party meeting had cast the only vote against the nuclear deterrent idea based on Blue Streak. I was infuriated, but not dissatisfied.

By cancelling Blue Streak, the Government had switched their bet overnight to Skybolt and Polaris which, in 1959, one year earlier, the then Minister of Defence, Duncan Sandys, had knocked severely.

From the Labour Party point of view the important aspect of the Blue Streak fiasco was that, with Gaitskell absent on a visit to Israel, Brown and Wilson switched the Party line several degrees in the direction of reality. Brown invited me to help him shift the Party's defence policy on to a sounder basis. Shinwell and Crossman supported this proposition and, in a speech to his Belper constituents, Brown laid down the guide lines for unity and electoral victory. The old Trade Union-inspired doctrine, he said, must prevail; the Party must not split. Crucial issues of policy must be disentangled from personal prejudice and predilections. The Party should recognize one of the advantages an Opposition possesses over a Government; it can and must avoid adopting committed positions on details of policy. Labour should announce the general principles guiding its policy on defence while remembering that defence is an arm of foreign policy.

The new mood reflected itself at the next meeting of the Shadow Cabinet and the Parliamentary Labour Party. There were no scenes, no melodrama. Brown had created a temper-relaxing tone giving promise that the Party would be able to play a significant part in leading the nation to a realistic policy on defence. The one fly in the ointment was that, on his return from Israel, Gaitskell continued to speak and act as though the world had stood still in his absence from Westminster. His May Day message to the Movement made no reference to the shift in the defence situation. It merely reiterated Labour's pre-Blue Streak nuclear policy.

Despite Gaitskell's *faux pas*, which later events suggested may not have been unintentional, Brown continued in the spirit of his Belper speech trying to unify Party defence policy in co-operation with Wilson, Crossman and myself. Crossman and I jointly contributed a series of articles to the *New Statesman*. We deployed the case for a break with Government thinking on defence and pointed the way to Labour Party unity on the subject while accepting that we could respect, without endorsing, the attitudes of pacifists and unilateralists. We also prepared a paper for Brown summarising our proposals. Unfortunately, an accident put Brown out of commission at the critical time. Leaving the House one night he slipped on a step, struck his head on a wall, and was taken to Westminster Hospital with a suspected fracture of the skull. I took to him the Crossman–Wigg proposals which made military sense and could have held the Party together. The Parliamentary commentator of the *New Statesman* described them as the work of 'Four Wise Men' designed to prevent a repetition of the wantonly produced and disastrous conflict over Clause Four. My personal belief was that the overwhelming majority of the Parliamentary Labour Party had grasped the fact that an independent deterrent was impractical. I hoped the Party would expose to the nation how the cancellation of Blue Streak meant that the Macmillan–Sandys 1957 White Paper had run its course and, true to the tradition of faithful Opposition, Labour would now lambast the Government mercilessly for the biggest military fiasco since Suez.

Instead, the Labour Party plunged into a new crisis threatening its very existence. There came a proposal—said to have emanated from Gaitskell himself—that the Party should advocate a Joint Western European Deterrent, a proposal as unacceptable to non-pacifist unilateralists as it was to pacifists and to those of us who tried to think of defence in terms of reality and practical politics. The Campaign for Nuclear Disarmament acquired a fresh head of steam. Its most vocal elements included those who saw nothing wrong in Russia having nuclear weapons yet objected to the Strategic Air Command. Honest pacifists gained recruits from the deepening disillusion of Labour Party supporters. Some Right Wing M.P.s regarded Brown's efforts as a nuclear somersault aimed at undermining Gaitskell's leadership. The one shaft of sun-lit sanity in a dark sky was Gaitskell's call for political control of N.A.T.O.

I refused to give up hope that the forthcoming Labour Party Conference would find unity on a practical defence policy. As late as mid-July I was still meeting Brown's request for views and advice and, in the Parliamentary debate of July 20, I expressed pleasure that the Labour Movement should rise openly above the reservations of individuals and unite to make our country's foreign and defence policies effective. I approached Sidney Silverman, Frank Cousins, and many others who had doubts about the Party line and—perhaps because I was over-optimistic—held fast to my faith that the Gaitskell group would accept a compromise. I was disappointed.

Soon after the T.U.C. Conference in September had rejected the Joint Western European Deterrent, having a speaking engagement at Stevenage and anxious to avoid widening the breach within the Party, I had a long talk with Gaitskell. I found him eager to build bridges and felt able to ask, 'Hugh, why did you take the line you did last March on defence when you still had the Clause Four row on your hands? You must have known that Blue Streak was a dead duck, and that Sandys would have cancelled it a year earlier but for his obstinacy and determination not to embarrass the Tories at the General Election. Why didn't you then condemn the Government's policy? Had you done so, there would have been no new splits in the Party and you would have had a sound basis for attack when the

Government announced the cancellation of Blue Streak which, by March, was clearly inevitable.'

'My dear George,' Gaitskell replied, 'of course I agree with you. I would have done what you suggest but George Brown was opposed and, as he was Defence spokesman, I could not over-rule him.' I thought this was a bit hot and, when the House reassembled, I told Brown what Gaitskell had said. Brown's only comment took the form of a question: 'Did he really say that to you?'

The more I think over what appears to be a direct conflict of evidence, the more convinced I am that both men acted honestly and spoke in good faith. The truth is that neither ever really mastered the basic elements of defence policy. Within the Gaitskell circle were men who supported the idea of an independent nuclear deterrent from a naïve longing, shared with many Tories, to drop something big on somebody small as an expression of power and because they thought the Russians were still a push-over. Brown, as Shadow Minister of Defence, had picked up and endorsed too many of the ideas of the Service Chiefs until the complete collapse of the policy of the 1957 White Paper converted him to a more realistic view. Both Gaitskell and Brown were conned into accepting the fatal, foolish proposition that the source of British influence in the world was no longer our political genius and our capacity to pursue a policy of international co-operation but was to be found in the power of nuclear terror.

By September the issue was bogged down in the mud of internal controversy. On the eve of the Labour Party Conference Brown sought to submit to a meeting of the International Sub-Committee of the National Executive a memorandum aimed at reconciling T.U.C. policy—which Frank Cousins had been delegated to expound—with Labour Party policy on defence. Gaitskell would not permit Brown to be heard. He was employing the method which had failed so miserably when he sought to amend Clause Four, the method of bulldozing the Party into agreement with his personal view. I attended the Scarborough Conference hoping to put the facts, as I saw them, before the delegates and urge the case for compromise. Mr Chairman Brinham told me bluntly, 'You won't speak and you will be wasting your time if you stand up and try to be called.' This was the fifth successive Labour Party Conference at which I tried to speak and I was never called once. Minority views got better protection from Mr Speaker. Gaitskell moved the Executive's resolution in his famous 'fight, fight and fight again' speech. For the second time in twelve months he split the Labour Party down the middle—tragically and unnecessarily.

The one satisfactory outcome of the Party's self-immolating crisis was Wilson's challenge on October 20, 1960, to Gaitskell's leadership of the Parliamentary Labour Party. Anthony Greenwood had resigned from the Shadow Cabinet; a preliminary move, some thought, to a bid for the leadership for which, apart from a fine family tradition, he was in no way fitted. Wilson's announcement that he had decided, reluctantly, to accept nomination for the Chairmanship because 'the issue is not defence; it is the unity and survival of the Party', produced at once a real alternative to the 'scrap Clause Four' and the 'fight and fight again' attitude which was tearing the Party in the constituencies to shreds and destroying the public image of Labour as an alternative Government. Crossman, then Chairman of the Labour Party, came out for Wilson. 'My prime concern', he said, 'is not defence, but the kind of leadership the Labour Party needs if it is to become once again a fighting Opposition and is to regain the confidence of the electorate. . . . During the General Election I saw Hugh Gaitskell at close quarters and I appreciated better than most the qualities he showed. But since the Election, also at very close quarters, I have seen the last twelve months wasted on the Clause Four dispute which has cost us a large part of our electorate's support. If Gaitskell gets his way, once again we shall consume the next year on a much more violent and unnecessary controversy about defence. This could mean the end of the Labour Party.' Brown, who might also have challenged for the Chairmanship, slipped sadly away from his brave posture on defence. His strenuous campaign for unity revealed that his influence on and in the Transport and General Workers' Union was very limited and this had dampened his characteristic ebullience. At a Parliamentary Labour Party meeting, organized to promote Gaitskell's candidature, Brown turned on Wilson and denounced further efforts at compromise on defence. 'I know,' he exclaimed, 'I have tried and not succeeded.'

My own position was clear. I told my Dudley comrades that once defence policy became the child of political expediency nobody could win. I expressed confidence that, if Wilson became Leader, he would convene a meeting between the T.U.C., the National Executive and the Parliamentary Labour Party with the object of rescinding the contradictions in the Scarborough defence decision which had arisen, not from conflicts about defence, but from distrust about what Hugh Gaitskell and some of his Right Wing friends would do if they had the power. Gaitskell's strength lay in the unanimous support of the Shadow Cabinet for his H-bomb policy. Thus the Parliamentary Labour Party adopted one policy and the Annual Conference of the Party another. The battle was joined between the will of the rank and file and the detailed doctrinal dogmatism imposed by a Party Leadership which was quite alien to the Labour Movement and its traditions.

Wilson did not win. The Whips, among others, were active on Gaitskell's behalf. I advised Wilson against conducting any personal campaign. What he had to represent was the existence within the Parliamentary Labour Party of considerable support for the ideals uplifting and sustaining the rank and file of the Movement in the country; the theme of unity which, alone, could ensure political survival. He did just that. He attracted eighty-one votes against 166 for Gaitskell. Those eighty-one votes were the basis on which I calculated his chances when he sought election as Leader of the Party in 1963.

Defence was my major interest and concern. On the day before the Trooping the Colour in 1960, M.P.s were invited to attend the School of Infantry annual demonstration at Warminster. One M.P. attended—Wigg. Next day, however, there was a considerable muster of M.P.s to see the Trooping the Colour. This took my mind back to the start and development of the Aldershot Tattoo which I first saw as a lad in 1913. It grew and grew into a public event so massive that Staff Officers and troops stationed at Aldershot between the two wars did little else but prepare for and take part in the spectacle. The crowds loved it, as I loved it when I was a boy. As an example of detailed military planning it was admirable but, that apart, it was no more than an exciting hallucination conveying to the public a picturesque conception of defence with little or no resemblance to reality. The present day Trooping the Colour is as pictureque as the Aldershot Tattoo but it, too, is a military fairy tale. Not believing in fairy stories I wrote the following letter to *The Times*:

The approach of the House of Commons to our current defence needs is best illustrated by the large attendance of members of Parliament at the Trooping the Colour yesterday—a performance that is always a magnificent spectacle but has little military significance. On the previous day, however, the invitation to M.P.s to attend the annual demonstration of infantry equipment and fire power at the School of Infantry, Warminster, produced only one M.P., who had the chance to notice the enthusiasm and efficiency of the human element and the poverty and obsolescence of their equipment.

He is still wondering whether this is not, at least in part, a reflection of cause and effect. Perhaps if M.P.s and the public were less dazzled by spectacle and were more interested in the realities of defence we should not have an army that must be, in relation to its commitments, one of the worst equipped in the world.

The truth is that Service displays, whether they be the Trooping the Colour or the Royal Tournament, are part of the world of entertainment, and my sole consolation was that no Army organizer of the Trooping the Colour had ever been so bureaucracy-ridden as the Air Force officer, about whom I told the Commons, who issued a circular inviting the staff to buy tickets for an R.A.F. concert and to tell all their friends about it, and stamped the circular SECRET.

The year 1961 opened sensationally with the arrest, on January 7, of Gordon Arnold Lonsdale, Peter John Kroger and his wife Helen Joyce Kroger, Henry Frederick Houghton and Ethel Elizabeth Gee on a charge of conspiring to obtain Naval secrets. All five were convicted at the Old Bailey on March 22. Lonsdale was sentenced to imprisonment for twenty-five years; the Krogers to twenty years each; and Houghton and Gee to fifteen years each. An important lesson of the trial was its exposure of the futility of the findings and recommendations of the Privy Councillors' Conference of 1956. Lonsdale, a Russian who spent several years developing a Canadian identity, was 'exchanged' in 1964 for Greville Wynn. Lonsdale was maintained by the Russians as a student and business man in this country over a period of five years. Observing him at the trial my personal impression was of a supremely competent professional. Kroger, a member of the International Brigade in the Spanish Civil War, had become an American citizen and an associate of a notorious Soviet spy, Rudolf Abel, then serving a thirty year term of imprisonment in America; Kroger and his wife, who was of Polish origin, were highly paid operators of intricate transmitting and receiving equipment, found in their home at Ruislip, Middlesex. Houghton was a retired Naval Petty Officer. He had been transferred from the British Naval Attaché's Department in Warsaw as an unsatisfactory clerk to the Admiralty Under-Water Weapons Establishment and, since 1957, the Port Auxiliary Repair Unit at Portland. His friend, Miss Gee, was a clerk at the Admiralty Under-Water Weapons Establishment. The unreliable Houghton and Miss Gee had obtained access to secret pamphlets and other documents. The man did not appear to have an affiliation to anything but the bottle; the woman thought she might vote Liberal. So much for the Privy Councillors' view—still, I told the Commons, the guiding principle of our Security Service—that Soviet espionage had ceased to be professional and was dependent on political affiliation to Communist Parties.

Next day, Prime Minister Macmillan made a statement reminiscent of his speech on the Philby-Burgess-Maclean issue in November 1955—clever and indecisive. Of course, security experts had started reviewing security arrangements on the day the spies were arrested, and the First Lord of the Admiralty would now set up an Inquiry to be presided over by an independent person of high standing to determine where responsibility lay and then to consider the disciplinary aspects of the whole matter. He blah-blahed about whether negative or positive vetting should be applied, and to what groups of people. He speculated whether we must make 'further sacrifices in what is really unpleasant—the watching of people and so forth' and dodged my straight questions: 'Will not the Rt. Hon. Gentleman agree that . . . he must not run away from his personal responsibility for espionage services? Will he therefore look forthwith at the Security and Intelligence Services as a whole?' Macmillan tried another delaying gambit. 'I am informed', he said 'that although there is a notice of appeal which, of course, may take some time, it should not really impede—at least not seriously—what we want to look into.' I squashed that evasive move on a point of order. I had given notice to raise the case on the Consolidated Fund Bill later that evening and had been told by the Registrar of Appeals of the Central Criminal Court at noon that no notice of appeal had been given. I then arranged to telephone again at 4.30 p.m.

I opened the debate at 11 p.m., having ascertained that no notice of appeal had been given. I congratulated the Police and the Security Service on catching two spies who had evaded the American network. I addressed myself mainly to the responsibility of the Prime Minister, who was then on his way to the Bahamas for his meeting with the President of the United States. I said we did not need an inquiry; the Prime Minister had the duty and the power to take and apply decisions himself. What had been wrong at Portland was that Houghton and Gee found they could remove documents on Friday, take them to London to be photographed or shown to Lonsdale, and then return them on Monday morning, in the sure knowledge that there would be no check during the week-end. I sought an assurance that the security of all branches of the Armed Forces would be reviewed with a consciousness of the enormous new developments in intelligence techniques. I pleaded that Members of Parliament, in a non-Party spirit, should aid Ministers in their task by vigorous and competent scrutiny of the Estimates which, as now presented, included things that were never included before the war. When these matters were discussed, in my experience, there were seldom more than half a dozen Members in the chamber.

The effect of my pleas and arguments is a matter of conjecture. The facts are that the Romer Committee of Inquiry—so called after the name of its Chairman, Sir Charles (now Lord) Romer—was appointed by the Government, and not by the First Lord of the Admiralty, and was given wider terms of reference than those first proposed by the Prime Minister. It was instructed to 'survey the field which has come into question as a result of the recent conviction of certain individuals on a charge of conspiracy at the Central Criminal Court' and to report direct to the Prime Minister. Meantime, security procedures in the public service as a whole were being examined by a Committee headed by Lord Radcliffe to which, Macmillan told Parliament on June 13, the full Romer Report would be referred, a summary of some findings of the Romer Committee having been circulated in Hansard of that same date. The 'revelations' numbered three. First, in 1954 a junior official who was Houghton's immediate superior received an allegation that Houghton was taking secret papers out of the Establishment. This official told his informant to see the Security Officer or the police. In 1956 no proper enquiries were made into suggestions that Houghton was a security risk. Second, there was a general lack of 'security mindedness' in the Under-Water Weapons Establishment, for which responsibility must rest with the Captain of the Establishment. Third, the Security Service was efficient. It did not overlook any ' "lead" which might have resulted in earlier identification of

Lonsdale and the Krogers as spies while they were in this country' and, indeed, 'professional skill of a high order was shown in establishing the necessary evidence against them once such a "lead" had been received'.

With typical British reticence nobody asked why the Russians mounted a brilliantly planned, long sustained and costly enterprise in return for secret information of little value to them. What they did achieve was a damaging blow at the confidence of our N.A.T.O. partners in the integrity of our security procedures. They scored a political success in the Cold War. And how we abetted their victory! Information about Lonsdale's arrest was leaked and heaven knows how many members of the Soviet spy gang took the tip and got out of England. Then the name of a member of the Romer Committee was leaked to the Press—'obviously', I told the House on March 29, 'either from a Minister or a Civil Servant'. The whole miserable business emphasised once again my views that security, like defence, must be elevated above the level of party controversy; that M.P.s must be more alert in discussing such matters so that deficiencies and weaknesses can be put right before they are revealed by events to our national detriment; and that a Standing Committee of the House, backed up by experts, should be fully armed to investigate the facts without delay and recommend action.

The traumatic wound of unchecked incompetence continued to fester. George Blake, a Foreign office official, was arrested on April 18 and, at the Old Bailey on May 3, was sentenced to forty-two years imprisonment. He confessed that for nearly ten years every official document to which he had access was passed to a Soviet contact. Having been caught by our Security Service he escaped our Civil Security in October 1966, when he was 'sprung' from Wormwood Scrubs! Like defectors Burgess and Maclean he reached the haven of Moscow where he shares with Philby the shame of being a Hero of the Soviet Union.

Next came the arrest on September 12, 1962, and the conviction on October 22, of an Admiralty clerk, William John Christopher Vassall, who went to prison for eighteen years. Vassall was employed in the office of the Naval Attaché in Moscow. He appears to have been a rather simple fellow, Conservative in politics, victimised by the old fashioned trick, by which, according to Upton Sinclair's novels, American bosses many years ago used to suborn active trade union leaders. He had been induced by a locally-employed Russian on the Embassy staff to attend a party and indulge in compromising sexual actions. His party piece was photographed and he was then blackmailed into betraying his trust. Back in England, although a modest clerical officer earning under £700 a year, he had access to secret documents. He took these to his flat, photographed them, then handed the undeveloped film over to a Counsellor of the Soviet Embassy before returning the documents to their files. The Royal Navy's honoured tradition of sleepless vigilance did not yet extend to its shore-based Establishments.

Vassall's conviction sent Macmillan into a fantastic flap. He announced a Committee of Inquiry of three Civil Servants—Sir Charles Cunningham, Permanent Secretary at the Home Office, Sir Harold Kent, Treasury Solicitor, and Sir Burke Trend, Second Secretary at the Treasury—to determine what breaches of security arrangements there may have been which enabled Vassall to supply the Soviet Union with secret information over a period of six years. Specifically, the Committee was to seek to determine 'whether there was any neglect of duty by persons directly or indirectly responsible for Vassall's employment and conduct, and in particular for his being treated as suitable for employment on secret work; and to draw attention to any weakness in existing security arrangements which may come to their notice in the course of the Inquiry, having regard to the full recommendations of the Radcliffe Report'. The intention was to conduct an internal inquiry, reporting directly and, as it appeared, privately, to Macmillan himself.

This proposition—an admission that, despite Lord Radcliffe's detailed Report, Government policy on security was still in disarray—never got off the ground. Gaitskell, with whom my personal relations had improved, pressed for an independent inquiry in a mocking speech. He noted that the seven Cabinet Ministers and fifteen other Ministers sacked by Macmillan in July must now be asking themselves if they had done as badly as the First Lord of the Admiralty and the Under Secretary of State for Scotland, formerly Civil Lord of the Admiralty, whose Department twice within recent memory had been involved with security matters warranting investigation. Later in the debate George Brown announced, 'We cannot leave the Vassall case where it is. There are letters in existence, copies of which I, and, no doubt, others have seen, the originals of which are in the hands of what are called the "authorities", which indicate a degree of Ministerial responsibility which goes far beyond the ordinary business of a Minister in charge, being responsible for everything which goes on in his Department.' These letters were exchanged between Vassall and the Civil Lord and became the subject of comment in some sections of the Press. Their real import was that Vassall, who as assistant to the Civil Lord's Private Secretary acted occasionally as a messenger between the Department and the Civil Lord, was seeking to convert an ordinary official contact into a friendship which a kind-hearted, rather inexperienced, junior Minister of unimpeachable integrity had not rejected as firmly as he would have done had security been alert. Macmillion whipped himself into a lather of indignation and, a few days later, moved in the House to set up an inquiry under the Tribunals of Inquiry (Evidence) Act, 1921. This Tribunal, with Lord Radcliffe as Chairman and Mr Justice Barry and Sir Milner Holland as members, would have power to take evidence on oath and thus render witnesses who perjured themselves liable to prosecution. The Prime Minister did more than personalize the issue. He turned it into a political campaign.

The Motion to set up the Tribunal reached the Order Paper on November 14, the day of the debate. I submitted to Mr Speaker that this fact limited the right and opportunity of the House to move amendments. When I was called in the debate I criticized the whole procedure involved in the Tribunals of Inquiry (Evidence) Act which had an unhappy record. The Act and its methods of procedure were devised in 1921 when the Coalition Government came under criticism because of the way the Ministry of Munitions had been run. Its use had resulted too frequently in damage to innocent persons. I argued that the Prime Minister's attitude to the questions put to him—he regarded them as 'accusations or smears'—had made the problem a Party issue which security ought not to be. Given this form of procedure I suggested that the legal costs of persons called upon to defend their reputations should be paid by the State if such person were found to be innocent. The real need, however, was for a full scale inquiry, at least ten years overdue, into the security service as a whole. The model should be along the lines of a Service Court of Inquiry behind closed doors; there the facts should be uncovered and, if it were found necessary to formulate charges, any person involved would not be pursued on allegations arising from speculation and rumour.

My arguments did not impress the Prime Minister. He, upon

whose shoulders rested full responsibility for security, did not seem to realize that he was even more on trial than any of his Ministers. My arguments, however, did impress the Leader of the Opposition. Hugh Gaitskell agreed the Labour Party should seek legal advice and, happily, chose Arnold Goodman, now Lord Goodman. When the Tribunal opened Gerald Gardiner, Q.C., later Lord Chancellor in the Labour Government, instructed by Goodman, Derrick & Company, made application that legal representation be accorded throughout the proceedings to Gaitskell in his capacity as Leader of the Opposition.

Counsel's first point was that the Tribunal was not a body to which the doctrine of judicial precedence applied. Discretion was given to any particular Tribunal appointed under the Act, and no Tribunal was bound in law by any decision which any previous Tribunal had made as to who appeared or did not appear to them to be interested parties. Paying tribute to the skill and integrity of the Attorney General, Sir John Hobson, Gardiner argued, nevertheless, that to many people in the country which since the war had been divided almost equally between supporters of the two main political parties, whatever the Party in power or in opposition, 'justice will not appear to have been done if, where the conduct of Ministers is in question, the proceedings appear to be conducted by another Member of their own Government'. In the last precedent case, in 1959, the Tribunal was assisted by independent Counsel and not by a Law Officer of the Crown; there was no need whatever for the Attorney General to appear otherwise than as a representative of the Government. The procedure was still in a fluid state. It was not part of the historic function of the Attorney General to take part in these Inquiries.

Gaitskell's interest was described under two headings. There had been an Inquiry following the defection of Burgess and Maclean and, soon after that defection, two spies had been found to be at work in one particular Government Department. Thus the present Inquiry should be as thorough and searching as possible but care must be taken to ensure no harm be done to innocent persons. Gaitskell, said his Counsel, was concerned to see adopted a procedure which would minimize such risks as far as possible. Thus he asked the Tribunal to consider whether they ought not to be assisted by independent Counsel rather than by a Member of the Government whose Ministers' conduct was being enquired into; and to consider also whether anyone applying for legal representation should not be granted it.

Gerald Gardiner established two other points which I regarded as vital. The Report of every previous Tribunal had been presented to Parliament; in this instance, the Prime Minister had announced he would decide what parts of the Report would be presented to Parliament. It had been usual for the establishment of the Tribunal to be preceded by a brief, factual, non-controversial statement. 'That,' said Gardiner, with a masterly touch of meiosis, 'can hardly be said to have been a distinguishing factor in this particular case.'

Lord Radcliffe and his colleagues, having thought the application over, rejected it. Gaitskell was not to be represented. The application, nevertheless, had two satisfactory results and a third of considerable public consequence. Counsel was appointed to look after the interests of persons called to give evidence and unable to obtain legal representation. In reply to my question the Home Secretary announced that in cases where the Tribunal allowed legal representation, provided the person involved was found not to be blameworthy, the Government would consider claims for contributions from public funds in respect of the expenditure involved. Furthermore, with the Labour Party outside the scope of the Inquiry, the full consequences of the Prime Minister's action in making security an issue of Party politics would be borne by him alone. In the Report itself perhaps the most interesting revelation was that the Tribunal sat *in camera* on sixteen days and six half days and in public on seven days and seven half days. Its only public impact was that it was interpreted as putting the Press on trial. Two journalists who refused to disclose the sources of their information were sentenced to imprisonment.

In the high summer of 1962 I sustained a blow almost as cruel as an intimate domestic tragedy. Mob violence, described in some quarters as 'Race Riots', broke out in my beloved Dudley. A Saturday night fight between a white man and a coloured man was thought to have set alight the train of trouble. Local police were alert and a group who went hunting for coloured men was handled competently. Another fight on Monday night, in which a knife was used and a white man taken to hospital, triggered off an obviously preconceived plan to incite disorder. Immediately the pubs closed, a mob of one hundred and fifty young people, armed with sticks, staves, chair legs, coshes and bottles, surged into North Street, in the words of the Deputy Chief Constable, 'like a pack of ravening wolves after their prey'. Dudley's small police force bore the brunt of brutal attack until reinforcements arrived from Wolverhampton, Brierley Hill and West Bromwich. The next night went into our local annals as 'Black Tuesday'. The Chief Constable, Mr C. W. Johnson, a policeman of great experience who, with his men, had always been fully integrated with the life of a law-abiding town, called in reinforcements of men and dogs.

I went to my constituency and at once identified myself publicly with the Chief Constable's action. He faced a rough situation. He played it rough but fair. He was right to do so. In his Annual Report Her Majesty's Inspector of Constabulary commented that 'the prompt infliction of salutary punishment by the Magistrates was a vital factor in quelling the disturbances.' I endorsed that view. The Wolverhampton *Express and Star* reported me under the heading 'THE SAD FACE OF GEORGE WIGG' as saying, 'I am saddened by what has happened in Dudley for this is a community that has a great tradition of public service. I have every confidence in the Chief Constable and of forces under his command to handle the situation. This is a matter for the police and the Courts.' I visited the homes of accused men to help them get legal aid, and the families of men sentenced to prison to help them get assistance, and I asked nobody what 'side' he or she was on. I reported my views on the situation to the Home Office and, in relation to one case, made a plea to the Director of Public Prosecutions for clemency.

The problem as I saw it was a symptom of the general social unrest of our times. All the rioters were under the age of twenty-five. Most gave their occupations as scrap metal merchants or labourers. Their mixed motives were that immigrants lived crowded together like animals and scrounged on National Assistance, that coloured men were stealing white women, and so on. I pleaded that the Mayor, Church leaders, educationalists and police should ask themselves why a tiny minority of young people with leisure and money should resort to hooliganism. Their victims happened to be West Indians. They could as easily have been Jews, Eskimos, an opposing football team or any other definable minority. How little reason lay behind the trouble was revealed in my investigation of the facts. In August 1961, Dudley's registered unemployed numbered four hundred and four, seventy-two of them Commonwealth immigrants. In July 1962, there were eight hundred and five unemployed, of whom two hundred and two were immigrants. There was not one case on record of a coloured person drawing National Assistance for week after week over a long period.

A source of bitter discontent was the failure of local and national authorities to deal with the housing problem. Housing conditions, generally, were shocking. The Industrial Revolution had left a once lovely countryside gnarled and snarled by a rapacious capitalism. The sale of property to coloured people all over the Midlands was piling up fortunes for landlords now protesting to high heaven about the colour problem. Typical of many of my constituents was the old friend who said, 'Look George, the Missus and I have put our all into our house and we have almost cleared the mortgage. Now, three doors away a coloured family have moved in and knocked five hundred pounds off the value.' I inspected a place in Stourbridge where Pakistanis were occupying a house on the shift system; as one lot went to work another lot occupied the beds. A young couple showed me a house with a ladder running straight up to the bedroom from outside; the shift system was operating with such intensity that the lodgers entered through the upstairs window rather than the door. What could I answer to the question, 'How would you like it?' I could do my best to understand and sympathize. I could consult the Town Clerks and the Medical Officers of Health, all as eager as I was to help, but how? A related problem was the large number of unskilled men being sucked into the Midlands motor industry, the humdrum jobs being allocated to coloured workers, to whom also went similar jobs in the local foundry industry. At the same time, the community depended almost entirely on coloured labour for public services like hospitals and transport. What was being enacted before our eyes in microcosm was the massive tragedy now unfolding in North America.

Harsh though the conditions were I experienced no political backlash during the remainder of my representation of Dudley. Many of my friends disagreed with me, but for all of us these were problems to be faced together. In the neighbouring constituency of Smethwick Patrick Gordon Walker was beset by similar difficulties. A meeting in his constituency to which I had been invited to speak was cancelled because, I learned later, my presence might stir up memories of the Dudley Riots. My impression was that his local Labour Party was failing to face the problems, so Gordon Walker lost his safe seat to a Tory. I heard nothing from Enoch Powell in nearby Wolverhampton. He wrote in the *Daily Telegraph* on February 16, 1967, that immigration was the principal and, at times, the only political issue in his constituency during the years from 1954 onwards. Yet it was not until fourteen years after his Maiden Speech on March 16, 1950, in which he advocated a Colonial Army of Europeans and non-Europeans to defend the Commonwealth, that I found any report of a reference by him to control of immigration, the need for which I had been advocating for years. Some of Powell's statements of fact to justify his speeches about the coloured population were exposed as being no more valid than those offered by the rioting skinheads of Dudley. Powell, of course, was not alone in this silence during the Dudley riots. There was no comment, as far as I am aware, from any prominent political figure despite the widespread publicity given to the incident. Only the Bishop of Lichfield and the local clergy spoke out manfully and well.

In the light of my experience then I would add a postscript. During the General Election of 1970 Anthony Wedgwood Benn, speaking on television, drew comparison between Powell's speeches on the racial situation in this country and the Nazi expression of race hatred. I thought the speech an act of folly. Powell is neither a Nazi nor a Fascist. I once described him as 'the cleverest fool in politics'. I had in mind his intellectual 'superiority' and the intensity with which he assumes that a single facet of a problem represents the whole, an attitude and approach quite alien to British traditions. Such a man can never understand that when one of my former constituents refers to a 'black bastard' the words are as likely to be spoken in friendship as in abuse. The human aspect of the coloured problem in our country will be settled by our traditional social solidarity, the real basis upon which we judge our fellows, not by the colour of their skin but by their worth as individual citizens.

Late in 1962 I was involved in issues arising from the British troop landings in Kuwait on July 1, 1961. Our troops had been sent on the plea of the Ruler of Kuwait to repel an alleged threat of invasion by Iraq. The Prime Minister's statement on July 3, 1961, explained that the emergency had been reported to the Security Council of the United Nations and he received the blessing of Her Majesty's Opposition. The landing—soon to be described as a 'model' operation—was hailed as having laid the grisly ghost of the Suez débâcle, thereby restoring British prestige in the Middle East.

My knowledge of the area and understanding of the importance of water supplies prompted me to ask the Minister of Defence on

July 7 about the number of men requiring medical treatment and admitted to hospital, the dietary arrangements made to prevent heat hyperpyrexia, and which specialists in this sphere were serving with our Forces. The Minister promised a statement during the following week. Next day I put two more questions: Whether the statement made on July 5 by Brigadier D. S. T. Horsford, Commanding 24th Infantry Brigade in Kuwait, that he believed an Iraqi attack would take place, was made with the Minister's knowledge; and whether the statement of Air Marshal Sir Charles Elworthy, Commander-in-Chief British Forces, Middle East, in Kuwait on July 6, that Iraq was unlikely to make a move was also made with his authority. The Minister replied, 'No. I would not expect to be consulted about the day-to-day assessment of a rapidly changing situation by the Commanders on the spot.'

On July 11 the Minister of Defence made his statement. He said that heat was the main problem, the number of cases of heat exhaustion being on average only twelve a day—'well under one per cent of the total force'—needing hospital treatment. Medical facilities available were very comprehensive; where those in Kuwait were not adequate, provision existed for evacuation either to Bahrein, Aden or H.M.S. *Bulwark*. There had been only one fatal casualty. Beer and soft drinks were available in large quantities, thanks to the generosity of the Ruler of Kuwait, and there were plentiful supplies of fresh water and salt tablets. He was circulating further details in the *Official Report*. This unusual procedure had been agreed with the Opposition, the joint intention being to avoid questions and discussion.

I invited the Minister to say whether the War Office had consulted Professor Woodruff, the Army's Consultant on Tropical Medicine, Dr Cuthbertson, Consultant on Physiology and Nutrition, and Professor Maegraith, who had done research on the spot into extreme heat conditions in the Kuwait area. The reply was that all the reasonable needs of the troops were being met, the operation had been carried out with expedition and efficiency, and most of the problems had been thought about in advance. The two thousand word account in the *Official Report* added little to the Minister's previous answer. No difficulties had been experienced in providing a palatable and adequate diet. Salt tablets were being supplied, good drinking water to meet heavy requirements was available and troops had been briefed on the elementary techniques of avoiding heat exhaustion. Experts in hyperpyrexial diseases and senior consultants in Hygiene and Medicine were available at all times, both in the Near East and United Kingdom, to fly out to the Persian Gulf if necessary. As my personal inquest into Operation 'Vantage' was to prove, the *Official Report* was a load of official 'bull'.

Meantime, in the columns of the *New Statesman* on July 14, 1961, I addressed myself to the politics of the situation. Iraq's traditional claim to Kuwait, repeated by the Iraqi leader, General Kassem, on June 25, had been urged time and time again by his predecessor, Nuri Said, an old friend of Macmillan. If, now, Kassem were threatening armed invasion he would hardly have given us time to mobilise; as things were, the despatch of a battalion would have been enough to warn him off. Instead we had sent a force larger than a token of our interest, and one without the right military balance to repel an all-out attack. The suspicion was that Macmillan was motivated by something other than threat of invasion; where Nuri Said had talked of war, Kassem talked about water. 'Kuwait remains barren and dry,' he had said. 'We have frequently sought to pipe sweet water to them, but imperialism prevented these sheiks from allowing this because imperialism wanted to sell them special machinery for the distillation of sea water. . . . Kuwait is now an indivisible part of the Iraqi Republic. The first project to which the Iraqi Republic will give prior consideration and which it will implement is the extension of sweet water and the establishment of schools and hospitals.' Inevitably, I argued, the Ruler of Kuwait's own declaration of Independence on June 19 would evoke again Iraq's demand that Kuwait was hers. That demand was based on the alleged illegality of the original sale of Kuwait, then a tiny bit of the Ottoman Empire, to Britain in 1899 for fifteen thousand rupees—about one thousand pounds. Macmillan must have known all this. His motive for military action could have been fear that Kassem would nationalize the Iraqi oil-fields. Faced with a mounting economic problem in Britain he could not afford another Abadan.

Macmillan had told the Commons that 'on June 29 and 30, evidence had accumulated from a number of sources that reinforcements, especially reinforcements of armour, were making towards Basra'. This evidence was the basis of the Ruler's request on the morning on June 30, for British assistance under the exchange of Notes on June 19. 'We had,' said the Prime Minister, 'no option but to act in the circumstances as they were on Friday.' Friday, June 30, was thus the vital date; any move before that date must obviously reflect on Macmillan's candour.

My article, which I have summarized and paraphrased, proceeded to state the facts about the dates of 'Vantage', code name for the Kuwait operation. H.M.S. *Bulwark*, with 42 Royal Marine Commando, based normally at Singapore, was at Karachi, the nearest friendly port to Kuwait. She had sailed for Kuwait on June 29. By another happy accident, a Squadron of the 3rd Carabiniers with Centurion tanks reached Kuwait on Saturday, July 1. As a rule this unit was stationed at Aden and, the Centurions being too heavy to be lifted by air, they must have been transported by sea, presumably aboard the tank landing ship H.M.S. *Striker*. Certainly, if these tanks were at their usual station at Aden, they must have moved several days before the vital date—June 30—in order to reach Kuwait on July 1. Was this luck again, or accident, or design? The build-up of the Kuwait force, apart from the 3rd Carabiniers and the 42 Royal Marine Commando, was based on troops flown from the United Kingdom, Cyprus and Kenya into Bahrein, then ferried over to Kuwait. This quite considerable movement of armour and supplies—decided upon, according to the Prime Minister, on June 30—had mustered in Kuwait the very next day! The British public were being told how the wisdom of Government policy and the speed of its implementation had impressed the entire world. 'The truth', I remarked, 'is that the Kuwait operation was a certain success—but only so long as there was no opposition to it. In the event it has come off, but at the cost of demonstrating—and the Russians and the Americans know this even if the British public does not—the lamentable weakness of our inadequate forces.' I went on to describe the imbalance of our out-dated equipment; for example, the absence of an adequate long-range freighter plane was due to Duncan Sandys's misconceived defence policy with its foolish emphasis on an independent nuclear deterrent.

My conclusions numbered two: the important military lesson of Kuwait was that, as in Cuba, the possession of atomic weapons was irrelevant; our need was for a defence policy based on adequate modern equipment designed for the conventional role. Although the Government had blundered, neither the policy nor its implementation had been debated or seriously questioned in the House of Commons.

The fact that the Government was shirking debate and had been aided in so doing by the Labour Front Bench, provoked many back-bench questions. There were questions, for example, about the Ruler's sterling balances, said to be three or four hundred million pounds, which the British Government was eager to retain in London. The cost of the military operation was, I elicited, around a million pounds. The Government had nothing to say about how much of the total cost had been recovered from the Ruler. Shinwell put the penetrating query on July 25: 'As it is now clear from the statements made by the Minister of Defence and by the Secretary of State for War and the Secretary of State for Air that the number of our forces is very limited indeed, what is the purpose of retaining them in that area when it is quite impossible for them to deal with any act of aggression?' To this knife-thrust the Prime Minister replied: 'The Rt. Hon. Gentleman rather over-simplifies that question. I would rather leave it where it is.'

Newspapers too were beginning to do a job of disclosure. The *Sunday Pictorial*, on July 16, carried a man-on-the-spot story that we were 'preparing to keep some 2,000 men, dug in, in this furnace-hot hole in the sand facing an enemy who isn't there,' adding that since there were never any British troops in the area when it was a British protected Sheikdom, Kuwaitis did not want our troops soldiering on semi-permanently now that Kuwait was independent. The correspondent's account verified the inadequacy and imbalance of equipment I had noted in the *New Statesman* two days earlier. 'At one stage the Royal Engineers', he wrote, 'were laying dummy mine-fields with old tins in the hope of fooling Iraqis who weren't there!' The *Sunday Telegraph*, which had hailed the landing with enthusiasm, reported on July 23 that it would take 'at least another two years before R.A.F. Transport Command is strong enough to meet any fierce flare-up of aggression on a larger scale than Kuwait.'

With the Opposition Front Bench co-operating in the Government's conspiracy of silence, I mounted an attack in the House of Commons on August 1. I drew attention to the words used by the Prime Minister on July 3, to which I have already referred, when he said that 'evidence accumulated from a number of sources that reinforcements, especially reinforcements of armour, were moving towards Basra.' The Minister of Defence's view, on July 11, was not so definite. He justified the operation 'in the light of indications that Iraqi forces in the Basra area were being reinforced with tanks.' The official document issued by the Kuwait delegation to the United

Nations, which I had obtained, was to this effect: 'In the last week of June reports were received from many sources of preparations being made to move units and a tank regiment from Baghdad to Shaiba, an area near to Basra, and Basra is only a few miles from the border of Kuwait.' Baghdad, I informed the House, is over five hundred miles from Shaiba. Moreover, the distinguished newspaper correspondent, Ian Colvin, had been to Basra and, on July 22, reported to the *Daily Telegraph* that 'for twenty miles at least behind the border there is nowhere that armoured or motorised troops could be hidden or housed. Roads and all approaches to the front are bare and open. Among the Britons in Basra I have not found one who has seen tank transporters in the past month.' Obviously, there had been either hard lies or incompetent intelligence from Kuwait.

I revealed that H.M.S. *Bulwark* had sailed on the Thursday before the event and, if it had not missed the tide, would have arrived even earlier; the facts were recorded by Lloyds. An examination of maps of Arabia suggested that our lumbering Beverley freighters overflew Iran and Saudi Arabia. As there had been no diplomatic relations between Saudi Arabia and Britain since Suez, my question about over-flying Saudi territory was passed to the Foreign Office. It produced no result. We lifted seven thousand troops and seven hundred tons of stores. The American Operation 'Big Slam' earlier in the year lifted eleven thousand tons of stores and was condemned as a failure. The truth was we could not lift stores to Kuwait or anywhere else over a similar distance for we did not possess a long-distance freighter-plane. On the problem of heat hyperpyrexia I had consulted Professor John Yudkin, the distinguished Professor of Nutrition at the University of London, and he advised me that nowadays nobody should suffer the effects of heat because there were well-established methods of dealing with the problem. 'The War Office', I alleged, 'had not consulted their own Consultants for the simple reason that "A" and "Q" planning throughout the Armed Forces does not measure up to General Staff thinking.'

Studying Royal Army Service Corps experience in the Western Desert in World War II, I had learned that 'As a transport load, water easily gave more worries and anxiety than any other, not excluding petrol. A simple calculation will show that to deliver even one gallon a man a day requires for a Division, say eighteen thousand strong, about twenty-seven additional three-ton vehicles. But as the three-ton vehicle was seldom loaded to that amount in the desert, the equivalent of more than a platoon was required for each echelon. This was something that had never been taken into account when planning transport establishment.' The same source recorded that 'The occasions when petrol was scarce may all be attributed to the four-gallon flimsy can, from which losses in transit were so great as sometimes to imperil operations . . . the four-gallon can showed poor resistance to Middle East climatic conditions . . . and many of the cans leaked if stored in the open for any length of time'. The problem presented by these flimsies—under the worst conditions the loss of petrol reached 'thirty per cent or even more'—was solved when, in 1941, quantities of the German twenty-litre steel welded cans were captured in the Western Desert. The 'jerrycan' was superior to any type of petrol container known in the United Kingdom before the war. A sample was sent at once to the War Office. Eventually it was produced on a world-wide scale for the Allied Armies, but only after all operations in the Middle East were over. That was in the early 'forties.

Twenty years later, once again, too little of the documented evidence on water and heat problems had been considered in launching Operation 'Vantage'. This was made plain in a *Survey of Factors Affecting the Health and Efficiency of Troops on Operation 'Vantage'*, by Lieutenant-Colonel J. M. Adam, R.A.M.C., reviewed in *The Times* on July 23, 1962. The most surprising fact was that the Army Medical Expert first heard of the Operation on the B.B.C. news early on July 1—D-Day. A Senior Principal Scientific Officer did not leave for Kuwait until July 12 and Colonel (then Major) Adam was scheduled to leave on July 13. The comment of *The Times* Defence Correspondent is apposite: 'If there had been any fighting in Kuwait at the time of the crisis last summer there would have been heavy casualties from heat exhaustion among British troops, especially those sent direct from the U.K. . . . in units which were already in Aden or the Persian Gulf when the operation began, casualties from the heat were negligible; in those from Cyprus or Kenya the casualty rate from this cause was higher but still not serious; but in the units which moved from England as many as ten per cent were out of action from heat disorders in the first five days, although they were not engaged in active operations.'

The Minister of Defence's statement to me and his statement circulated in Hansard—'that only about one per cent of the total force each day had been in need of hospital treatment through heat illness'—made after the Force Commander said 'quite a lot' of his men were suffering from heat exhaustion caused *The Times* to write, 'It now appears that this was an average figure which failed to make clear that many of the men were treated in their units and in medical establishments other than hospitals, and that the heat casualty rate was much higher in the early days of the operation.'

Medical case histories of thirty-two men treated in unit lines indicated that eighteen became ill in the first week; eleven men could not remember advice on danger signs and fourteen claimed that they did not receive any instructions. Twenty-six had had an inadequate food intake for at least two days before they became ill. Many problems arose over the supply of water. Buses conveying one Regiment to their position took two and a half hours to cover seventeen miles with all the men out and pushing in places; the buses 'bogged down' and boiled dry in the sand; at least two had cracked blocks and two more had burnt-out clutches. One half of each man's personal water ration went into the radiators. A 6,000 gallon bowser of water arrived eight hours late and delivered only one sixth of its load. A sixty-ton articulated lorry with stores of three Companies and jerrycans did not reach its destination until D plus seven. And those jerrycans! The 11th Hussars rejected one third of their issue as unfit to contain drinking water. Not only were Army salt tablets unsatisfactory; it was not understood that the salt should be taken in fluid, and nausea, vomiting and stomach upsets were common as a result. Because the food was unpalatable many units were buying food and drink out of their own resources. The plain truth was that, in relation to the health and comfort of the troops, Operation 'Vantage' had been planned, if planned at all, without foresight and without the expert knowledge available to the authorities.

I decided to raise the subject on the Adjournment Motion on Friday, November 23, 1962. Since I would ask for a Select Committee on Kuwait I notified the former Minister of Defence, Harold Watkinson, that I intended challenging the accuracy of some of his answers in July, 1961; my case would be that the Department had given him a brief which events had shown to be inaccurate. I had visited the War Office frequently in the course of my inquiries and I gave notice to the Secretary of State for War, John Profumo, of the matters I proposed to discuss. Having shown him this courtesy I expected no quarter; simply that the exchanges, however hard hitting, would be directed towards informing the House about the facts and reassuring the public that the lesson learned would safe-guard the welfare of British soldiers in the future.

Profumo did not respond either to our agreement or to my hope that he would address himself to the real issues. When he spoke he moved immediately on to the Kuwait problem and in the course of his reply he quoted from two Sunday newspapers and, having implied, whether inadvertently or not, that these articles had originated with me, then denied this was his intention. He knew his implication was utterly untrue. His reference to the articles indicated an attitude to grave problems which I can only describe as irresponsible. He also cited letters from two Commanding Officers suggesting—as though anybody would expect otherwise—that everything in the garden had been lovely.

I raised the question of the two letters on November 26, pointing out that they came from officers serving in the Gulf at Sharja and Aden and that, these units having been acclimatised before Operation 'Vantage' started, they naturally suffered less than others from heat exhaustion. I went on to quote the authority of Erskine May, which governs the proceedings of the House, that the Minister must lay the whole of the correspondence before the House. I argued also that having quoted these letters the Minister was in duty bound by the rules of the House to produce all analogous matters, including the Survey by the Army Operations Research Group. I filled in details about the newspaper articles which, the Minister had claimed, had been widely ascribed to me. The articles appeared on September 2. I visited the War Office on September 4 with Profumo's full know-ledge and made it plain to the Under Secretary that I was in no way responsible for the articles. Everything I wanted to say about Kuwait was in Hansard. On the Tuesday before the debate of November 23, I told the House, I visited the War Office at the Minister's request and, in the Under Secretary's room and with his Private Secretary present, gave him details of the points I would raise. On the eve of the debate Profumo telephoned me at home and we went over it all again. He made no point then about the letters, or about the newspaper articles, which he had exploited to dodge the real issues. Once he had quoted the letters—one from the 11th Hussars, the only unit that came out of the report well—he was under an obligation in honour to place before the House for its information the Survey carried out by the Army Operational Re-search Unit.

In the course of the exchanges Profumo agreed to lay both letters in their entirety before the House. I felt, however, he was playing politics with a matter of the gravest national importance. His excuse for quoting these letters only in part was that I, quite rightly he agreed, had made a big case, had spoken for one and a half hours, and had monopolized the debate, the suggestion being that I had left him too little time for his reply. To that I answered, 'On Friday afternoon there were no fewer than four Front Bench speakers in succession, so there was ample time for the Minister to speak . . . he knows that the time he rose to speak was the time that he had arranged.' The duel ended on November 29 when I put down a Written Question enquiring whether the Minister had reconsidered the advisibility of publishing any further documents concerning the Kuwait operation other than the two letters he had promised to lay before the House. Profumo answered, 'I have now laid these two letters before the House. I certainly accept the Hon. Member's assurance that the newspaper articles which gave rise to them were not published with his authority. I am satisfied that, as a result of last Friday's debate, the questions raised about the Kuwait operation have been put in their proper perspective and that no further action in this respect is required.' The Minister was still wriggling.

The appropriate postscript appeared in *The Lancet* on December 8 under the heading 'Vantage Wigg'. Pointing out that the Secretary of State for War had not yet published in full the details of heat illness among British troops during Operation 'Vantage', it commented, 'An impression is left that unpalatable facts have been shelved. Yet here, as in the United States, most of the research into human problems of thermal regulation in hot surroundings has been sponsored by the Government and the Services; and it therefore seems strange that the Army should be above criticism in the management of men exposed to unaccustomed heat'. There followed a well annotated argument on the subject and this conclusion: 'As Mr Wigg said, there is nothing new in all this; it has happened before. It happens every year in the Mecca pilgrimage, and for that matter among the people of Kuwait and other towns exposed seasonally to severe heat. The fact is that environmental heat is a phenomenon as natural and as hazardous as cold, flood or tempest. It is to be hoped that the lessons which have been set once again have been understood and that the principles of prevention of the heat disorders will be applied with more success when next required; and the Army Health Specialists are as well qualified as any others to give the necessary advice.'

The issues of Kuwait, the Dudley riots, the re-burial of Timothy Evans, and the case of the lost V.C., are all part of the life and work of an ordinary back-bench M.P. For me, as for many of my colleagues of all Parties, such issues meant work and time expended over and beyond the normal which the constituency and Party interests impose, quite properly, upon a Member of Parliament. The job is, and should be, full-time all the time.

My reactions to big political issues were always intense. With the Labour Party wobbling into weakening disunity and my health indifferent, this was the period when I came close to giving up politics. Kuwait was one issue that decided me to soldier on. Not less important was the influence of Sir Frederic Metcalfe, former Clerk of the House of Commons. I had confided to him that I was depressed and despised myself for lack of results and I harshly criticized Parliament as an institution. Sir Frederic rebuked me sharply. He wrote that my criticism of Parliament was quite invalid unless I had honestly tried to make the institution work. In one letter, during the Kuwait debates, he said I did all the things he admired most: 'You made up your mind on the lines of attack or on the things you wanted to get done; then you settled down to hours of preliminary work to get the facts sorted out and prepare your case. And then you would move into action.' I admitted to him that what had really happened to me was that I had been tempted to give up trying. Now, in the spirit of A. D. Lindsay's *General Will and Common Mind*, I once again felt that 'when men and Movements respond to challenge they renew their strength'.

Soon all personal problems were forgotten and controversy was muted by the death, on January 18, 1963, of Hugh Gaitskell. He had been ill for several weeks, and had come out of hospital for Christmas, then been re-admitted only, alas, to die. I had admired Gaitskell since our pre-war association in the Workers' Educational Association. I differed from him then in his conception of Socialism and even more when, later, he propounded views on defence which were linked with the power struggles within the Labour Party. What I never doubted was his sense of commitment to the Labour Movement and of service to his fellow men. His qualities were integrity and great clarity of mind. His real weakness revealed itself in his struggle to consolidate his leadership after being chosen as Attlee's successor. He owed his victory largely to Trade Union influence which sought an opponent of calibre against Bevan, yet he did not understand the Trade Union Movement and its unifying sense of solidarity. That sense of solidarity had saved the Labour Movement against MacDonaldism, a virus of the Right, and in Gaitskell's election as Leader had asserted itself against Bevanism, a virus of the Left. Gaitskell despised many Trade Union Leaders, some of them openly, and sought his inspiration in policies defined in the drawing rooms of Labour's wealthy and so-called intellectual patrons. He was a first-class administrator as I had learned at the Ministry of Fuel and Power. I felt his loss the more keenly because I thought he was showing signs of understanding that people on the Left of the Party were also among the true inheritors of Labour tradition and the Movement's most selfless adherents.

Within days of the death of its Leader the Movement suffered another blow in the passing of Morgan Phillips, Secretary of the Labour Party. Inevitably, varying views were held about his abilities as an organizer. What was beyond doubt was that his heart and soul were in the Party, that he sustained it as a Movement and was wise enough to get able people around him to make Transport House tick. These were precious gifts in the organizer of a National Movement of ordinary folk who can win only when they fight a soldier's battle. The loss of Morgan Phillips's gifts, when added to the low state of Party morale and the weakness of its organization at both national and local levels, resulted in something about which I think all informed observers will agree—the Labour Party at the 1970 General Election was in worse shape than ever before in the Party's history.

Chapter Twelve: Finding a Leader

I would have voted for Wilson in the Labour Leadership election in February 1963, whether or not I had been closely associated with his candidature. His courageous decision to take Bevan's place in the Shadow Cabinet preserved the unity of the Party in 1954. His challenge to Gaitskell's leadership reaffirmed the broad basis of Labour Party interests and closed what might have become an electorally disastrous breach in Party cohesion in 1960. This, too, was his purpose when, in 1962, he stood against Deputy Leader Brown who decided to follow Gaitskell slavishly in policies as divisive as dynamite. Wilson attracted 103 votes against Brown's winning total of 133. These figures were significant. Wilson had gained twenty-two votes on his poll of eighty-one when he had opposed Gaitskell. Brown's votes suggested that some Gaitskellites did not regard him highly since the Whips were as active for Brown as they had been for Gaitskell.

Looking back, I think Brown's campaign on a right-of-centre ticket might well have nailed him when the leadership succession arose. The vigorously promoted idea that Brown's majority of thirty assured him victory in a major contest existed only in the minds of some feather-brained Lobby Correspondents. Two other candidates were presumed to be prepared to be drafted for duty—Gordon Walker and Callaghan, both of them in political terms then light-weights and make-weights. I remember Callaghan describing to me, way back in the 'forties, his own recipe for political success: wait till the Trade Unions decide their line and follow them.

There was nothing complementary in the characters and careers of the chief contenders. Brown was born in the Labour Movement and no man is better able to maintain a dialogue with Labour's rank and file. He is extravert, full of bonhomie and slap and tickle. He generates enthusiasm and communicates it easily both to individuals and mass audiences. His one lack compared, say, with Herbert Morrison, is a characteristic I can describe only as the 'puritan' touch. He has great generosity of spirit, rare courage, untiring

energy and, when his interest is captured, a quite brilliant capacity
for mastering the details of any proposition or argument. Even the
strange inconsistency which leads him occasionally into pronounce-
ments and courses of action completely foreign to the thought and
tradition of the Labour Movement is readily forgiven. Wilson, on
the other hand, is introvert, ambitious and, although kindly and
considerate of others, self-centred. He seldom reveals how keen about
the success of Huddersfield Football Club and Yorkshire cricket he
really is and how fully he identifies himself with the cares and
concerns of ordinary people. Many of his colleagues think Wilson
wants watching, an attitude deriving from his tendency to urge other
people to action rather than take the lead in action himself. His
true character speaks in the intense, single-minded efforts that took
the scholarship boy to Oxford, won him a brilliant First and earned
him office leading to the most envied position in Parliament and
public life without benefit of back-bench experience. Indeed, I have
no doubt that if Wilson had engaged in the rough-and-tumble and
comradeship of the back benches his acknowledged academic abilities
would have been translated into more effective leadership of the
nation.

With two such contrasting personalities in the field those newspapers engaged in a never-ending search for the triumph of triviality
enjoyed a bonanza. I had, however, no fear that Press tittle-tattle
would influence the result. The real issue at stake was something
dear to the hearts of the majority of Labour M.P.s, however varied
their motives and however strong their personal feelings. It had
nothing to do with the old Gaitskell–Bevan, Gaitskell–Wilson
clashes; these were closed chapters. The common purpose was to
establish and preserve unity. A wise choice was vital; the new Party
Leader would occupy No. 10 Downing Street.

Wilson confided in me when he joined the Shadow Cabinet in
1954, when he opposed Gaitskell in 1960, and again when he fought
Brown in 1962. I was, therefore, not surprised that he sought my
advice and assistance in the election for the Leadership of the Party
in 1963.

At the start there was an amusing incident in Wilson's room at
the House. I found him completely immersed in preparing a speech
for a Boy Scouts meeting or, perhaps, writing an article for a Scout
magazine—a desirable enough objective but, as it seemed to me, a
bit off-beam in relation to the business in hand. It may well have

been an example of Wilson's ease in switching from one subject to another without loss of concentration, but it evoked my comment, 'You want to make up your mind whether you want to become Leader of the Labour Party and Prime Minister or Chief Scout.'

This was the first occasion on which I took notice of Mrs Marcia Williams, for some years Wilson's secretary. I expected that henceforth our relations would be something more than a nodding acquaintance. My impression was of a competent, hard-working shorthand-typist. Since she possessed a University degree she was obviously well qualified to act as secretary to a busy politician who was about to become Leader of his Party and, in the near future, Prime Minister. Neither then nor later could I be numbered among those who considered Mrs Williams possessed abilities calling for special comment. My hope was that we could co-operate in serving Wilson efficiently at the House of Commons and, the sooner the better, in No. 10 Downing Street.

The basis of all my consultations with Wilson was that the Party wanted '1 and 2 or 2 and 1'—Wilson as Leader with Brown as Deputy, or Brown as Leader with Wilson as Deputy. Any third candidature would be irrelevant and destructive of Brown's chances. I dismissed completely the possibility of a fourth candidate; the vote for such a one would be derisory. We decided that there should be no campaign in the sense of a canvass. Our aim was not to 'whip' votes but to seek disclosure of voting intentions as a guide to action and, when appropriate, to make Wilson himself available for interview by colleagues who wanted to talk things over. I attached only one condition to my offer to help Wilson and I mention it only because of suggestions that R. H. S. Crossman played the role of 'king maker'. Crossman, I insisted, must be excluded from any knowledge of our plans and activities because he could not be relied upon to keep his mouth shut.

The colleagues who helped me were Mrs Judith Hart, Harold Davies and the late Ben Parkin. We listed those we thought doubtful and who, therefore, might welcome a talk with Wilson. The others we grouped under the names of colleagues—I apologize here and now for using their names as political seaweed—to indicate the interests and associations Members shared with each other and which might influence the casting of their votes. The group names were Mrs Hart, George Thomas, Harold Davies and Stephen Swingler, Walter Monslow, Jack Mendelson, Dick Plummer, Tom Swain, Laurie

Pavitt and Ben Parkin. If, to take the obvious example, we placed a name under the heading 'Mrs Judith Hart' that Member was certain to have a Scottish accent and a bias left of centre. Wilson, naturally, kept his own lists of supporters. No whisper went beyond the walls of my flat. The election lists were filled out by me on the basis of the information we gathered and were never allowed out of my possession. We collected quite quickly accurate knowledge of the movement of opinion and some information that was surprising and amusing. One gentleman, for example, his eye on a seat in a future Labour Cabinet, wrote to Wilson and to Brown, swearing undying loyalty to both. This 'Mr Janus' was given a place in the first Wilson Government!

My old friend Chuter Ede had little time for Brown, whom our lack of noisy campaigning was now unnerving, but even less time for Wilson. I tried hard but Chuter Ede would not be won over. Ness Edwards was a very vocal supporter of Brown and, being a betting man, was offering to back his favourite. In the tea-room one afternoon I found him offering odds against Wilson. 'I want to back Wilson,' I said. 'What will you lay?' Ness hesitated, and I bid again, 'How much? Fifty pounds?' He replied, 'Two pounds'. I closed the deal with a comment: 'Is that all? You can't hold your views very strongly, but I'll take it.' Word went round the tea-room and beyond that George Wigg was willing to back Wilson for fifty pounds. By the end of the evening the figure had gone to a hundred pounds and, a day or two later, to my great delight, it reached five hundred pounds. Meantime, the Press were recounting stories of electoral pacts between Wilson and Brown of which I knew nothing and about which I did not believe a word.

The Campaign for Democratic Socialism, first formed to save Gaitskell from the crass follies of his pro-bomb and anti-Clause Four policies, re-entered the field. It found itself unable to unite behind Brown, vigorously though it opposed Wilson. Jack Diamond, operating from his flat, took a hand in the game. My representative reported that, at the end of a meeting in Diamond's home, they were no nearer agreement than at the beginning in their search for a third candidate and, being able politicians, they realized how foolish failure would make them look. They clutched at a straw poll. It showed Wilson slightly ahead of Brown. These were the circumstances in which Callaghan received his eagerly-awaited order to be drafted.

My respect for Denis Howell, Brown's campaign manager, was considerable, but I counted our cause lucky in Brown's flag-bearers. One was Dingle Foot, an ex-Liberal with neither status nor the prospect of status in the Labour Movement, from whom I won a few quid as I found him willing to back his opinion. I am glad to report that, unlike some, he paid up promptly. The other was Desmond Donnelly, a comic-opera figure always bound to disappear eventually in a cloud of personal vanity. Perhaps they raised the temperature too high for Brown; the oft-repeated whisper attributed to Donnelly—'To keep the spirit of Gaitskell alive, vote for Brown' —might well have driven a less volatile person than Brown round the bend. Perhaps the effort to do a deal with Callaghan bored him. Whatever happened, Brown blew his top. He announced, so the story ran, that on being elected he would accept Wilson as Deputy Leader only if, at a Party meeting, Wilson declared his full acceptance of Brown and all he stood for. That condition was offensive to Party opinion. It ensured that No. 1 in my '1–2; 2–1' theory would be Wilson. Indeed, from then on, my concern was not that Wilson might fail but that he might sweep both Brown and Callaghan off the board at the first count. That kind of shock might have so devastated Brown that he would immediately have taken his bat home and left the Party split down the middle. The result of the first poll, declared on February 7, was: Wilson 115, Brown eighty-eight and Callaghan forty-eight. Wilson needed only a handful more votes for victory.

The problem then was to identify quickly by whom votes were cast for all three candidates and who were non-voters. Our information produced two answers, both indicating that Wilson would poll over one hundred and forty votes. The real guesswork was—who would join the bandwagon now rolling on to victory? My favoured list put Wilson's vote as high as one hundred and forty-nine. As we went to the Committee Room on February 14, to hear the result, Wilson asked me for the umpteenth time, 'How many, George?' I told him, 'You are over a hundred and forty for sure.' 'I don't think you can be right,' he commented, to which my obvious reply was, 'Bet you a pound'. 'Yes,' said Wilson. I collected. The result was: Harold Wilson 144; George Brown 103. In 1964, when Wilson selected his first Cabinet, I counted among its members eight who had voted for Callaghan seven for Brown and six for Wilson. From the moment of his election as Leader of the Opposition until the day he ceased to be Prime Minister in 1970, Wilson seemingly forgot the existence of his enemies within his own Party. Indeed, the more violent and loud-mouthed an opponent had been, the better was his chance of being included in the Wilson administration. That was a characteristic I never quite understood. Forgive, yes—forget, not bloody likely! Many times I told Wilson he was a modern counterpart of Richard III, who advanced his enemies, forgot his friends, and 'got done' for his trouble.

On the great night we went to Ben Parkin's flat in Winchester Street to celebrate. There it was that Wilson raised his glass to the memory of Nye Bevan, 'the architect of victory'. This delighted the militants, all of whom were Bevanites, and buried recollection of the truth. For the first step towards Leadership and Premiership was Wilson's defiance of the worst that Bevan had threatened in 1954, when Wilson took his place in the Shadow Cabinet. Next morning Wilson explained to *Daily Herald* readers that the real mood and spirit animating him for nearly ten years was 'to maintain the present inspiring unity the Party is showing. To keep up the attack in Parliament and the country. And to do everything possible to release the energies of Party members and Party workers everywhere to ensure that Labour policies make the maximum impact. The Leader is elected by the *whole* Parliamentary Labour Party,' he said 'and his loyalty must be to the *whole* Party in the House and in the country.' That statement was in accord with Wilson's attitude on defence and on the Clause Four controversy about which, in a speech to the Parliamentary Press Gallery in February 1960, he had commented: 'Let us unite on policy, not divide on theology.'

Pre-occupation with Labour's leadership did not stop me keeping an eye on Macmillan. He had returned from his Nassau meeting with President Kennedy, buoyant and happy. His Polaris deal symbolized the idea in relation to defence that the British nation had 'never had it so good'. The terms, he announced at London Airport on December 23, 1962, 'are very good' and he explained why:

'We pay nothing for development. We purchase the missile and put it into our British-built submarines—we have already built two nuclear submarines. We have a programme for building further nuclear-driven submarines.

'In the new submarines room will be made for the missile. These weapons will be British-owned, manned by British officers and men with their allegiance to the Crown.

'At the same time, while these forces will be nationally owned where national interest demands, and will be at the sole disposal of the British Government, yet normally they will be applied to the international defence of the Western Alliance.

'The President made me this offer. He was willing we should continue the Skybolt programme if we would pay one hundred million dollars for the development. Up to now we have paid nothing. We were to buy the completed missile. I did not feel, in view of the uncertainties, in view of the time factor, that this would be the right deal for us to enter into.'

The Prime Minister concluded the romantic rodomontade with a gay assertion that under the Polaris agreement Britain received the benefit of about eight hundred million dollars worth of expenditure in research to which we had contributed nothing, and we acquired a completed, proved and successful weapon, the cost of which would be spread in the defence budget over a number of years. It was the Prime Minister, in Dickensian mood, bringing tidings of great expectations.

I noted the leading article in the next day's *New York Times*. It suggested that the British had contracted for 'a considerably more expensive nuclear deterrent and one which would be much delayed,' adding that though the communiqué did not specifically say so Washington may have agreed to underwrite many of the Polaris costs. Three days later, the *Sunday Telegraph*'s Defence Correspondent understood that the Government had protested (already) to the Americans against paying the additional costs, 'but the United States had been adamant'. Subsequent newspaper comment was directed to denying that the Premier and President had got down to financial details. Finally, on January 29, 1963 the *Guardian* Washington Correspondent reported:

'The trouble seems to be that Mr Macmillan and Mr Kennedy did not at Nassau go fully into such details as finance, so, when the experts began their talks on the application of the agreement, it came as something of a surprise to the British team that the United States, according to Mr McNamara, the Secretary of Defence, has laid down that "America would not subsidise any of the costs of the United States Polaris missile system which Britain now plans to use in British-built submarines".

'At the same time the United States administration has apparently been pointing out to Britain and other Allies in the North Atlantic Treaty Organisation that they would also be asked to share in the cost of the medium-range ballistic missile which the Administration had been urging on the Allies. The new ruling would also apply to the development of any new conventional arms which the NATO Allies wanted to buy.'

My reading of the situation was that Macmillan was making a last desperate throw to stride the world stage as the representative of a nation which ten years of Tory government had reduced to second-rate status. In September, 1962, the Commonwealth Prime Ministers' Conference had been less than lukewarm about British entry to the European Economic Community on which the Conservative Party was hell-bent as a solution for our fast declining economic and political influence. In the week before Christmas Macmillan had visited President de Gaulle at Rambouillet in the hope of thawing out the General's opposition to our application to join the Common Market; he faced a frozen mitt. Now he was exploiting our 'special relationship' with America by exaggerating, perhaps because he had failed to understand, the benefits of the bargain struck with President Kennedy at Nassau. It was a time for greatness, for adopting in co-operation with our still powerful Commonwealth a new role that might have given us leadership of the non-nuclear nations and a moral influence in world affairs of which the nations were in desperate need. Our Prime Minister chose to interpret strength in military rather than moral terms.

The debate in the Commons on January 30 on the Statement on Nuclear Defence Systems, following the Nassau meeting and the rejection of our application for membership of the E.E.C., was a farce. It was not concerned with defence. Nuclear weapons, apart from anti-ballistic missiles, are not weapons of defence; they are weapons of attack. Macmillan recited the long story from the Attlee Government's atom bomb enterprise to the Skybolt project—which his henchman, Duncan Sandys, in 1959 had praised in preference to Polaris—in the vain hope of giving reality to the will-o'-the-wisp of an independent British nuclear deterrent. Now, without a blush, the British public were invited to believe that there was no difference between Polaris and Skybolt. Failure to master even the simple facts was revealed in Macmillan's Polaris statement. 'It is operational,' he declared, 'and the Americans already have about twenty submarines in service'. I put down a question on February 7 to ask the Prime Minister 'In concerting defence plans with the United States President at Nassau, what information he was given as to the number of Polaris submarines in service at the present time?' This was the reply:

> 'The Hon. gentleman very courteously sent me a message to say that his question referred to my statement in the Defence Debate on the 30th January that the Americans already have about twenty Polaris submarines in service. I find on further enquiry that the latest figures are as follows: nine submarines are deployed, one has been commissioned but not yet deployed, seven more have been launched, twelve more keels have been laid, six more construction contracts have been let and long lead items for six more have been authorised. I regret it if I inadvertently misled the House in the figure I gave.'

No doubt inadvertently Macmillan did not add that the corrected figures covered the entire American Polaris undertaking. Next came an admission by the Secretary of State for War that the Prime Minister's statement to the House about atomic tactical weapons was also wrong. I had asked the Minister if 'he will state the atomic tactical weapons in use in the British Army'. The answer was 'None'.

The tragedy was that pursuit of nuclear deterrence continued to bedevil our chances of creating a viable system of defence. Sir Alec Douglas-Home made possession of the deterrent a major theme of his 1964 General Election campaign. In 1970, as the new Foreign Secretary, he persisted in this expensive, exploded delusion, but gave it a new twist. He told Parliament on July 6, 1970, that the Russians had 'a submarine fleet of three hundred and fifty'. That summoned up the Tory blood just as Macmillan had done in 1951 when he announced that the Russians had 'between three hundred and four hundred submarines', and added, 'It is said by some authorities they are likely to have one thousand within three years!'

Chapter Thirteen: The Denning Report

On November 11, 1962, I attended Armistice Services at Stourbridge and Dudley, then went for lunch to the home of our Labour Party Agent, Councillor Tommy Friend, where I found there had been a 'phone call for me. I telephoned my home in Stoke, but my wife had neither called me nor received a message. Soon afterwards the call to Friend's house was repeated. A muffled voice said, 'Forget about the Vassall case. You want to look at Profumo.' Then the 'phone went dead. Driving back to London, the nagging question kept recurring: how did the unknown caller know where I was, and how did he get the number? The incident came to mind repeatedly as the whispered scandal involving a Minister and a Russian diplomat gathered weight and pace. The first authentic information about the business was sent to me, unasked, by the late John Lewis, a Parliamentary colleague from 1945 until 1951, and it steadily developed into an intensely worrying security problem.

Lewis had attended a pre-Christmas party where a Miss Christine Keeler talked excitedly about a recent shooting incident, the first of several events destined to endow her with what she appeared to crave—the reputation of being the most notorious woman in London. Miss Keeler, who said she had heard a Mr Stephen Ward refer to Lewis, asked if she could telephone him and, a few days later, sought his help. She then spoke about her friendship with John Profumo, Secretary of State for War, and with the Russian Naval Attaché, Captain Eugene Ivanov. Miss Keeler alleged that Ward had asked her to obtain from Profumo information about the supply of atomic weapons to the Germans although, according to Lewis's account, 'she had never told this to Profumo'. Lewis advised the lady to consult a solicitor.

I rejected at once the idea that Profumo personally was a security risk. I had found him politically untrustworthy but I never regarded him as a fool, and I could not be persuaded that an obviously ignorant girl would be used as a go-between. It seemed to me the man to keep an eye on was Ivanov. Lewis agreed that the matter must be handled exclusively on the issue of security. I urged him to talk to the police and, at a later stage, advised him to talk to Commander Townsend at Scotland Yard. Lewis did talk to the police but, being dissatisfied with the results, returned to me again and again.

I was faced now with one of the most difficult decisions of my political life. Never before had I raised an issue affecting a Minister without notifying that Minister of my intention in advance and, where appropriate, setting out the facts and arguments. The one occasion on which this principle of action had been exploited against me was by Profumo during the Kuwait debate. Should I now seek an interview with Profumo? Bearing in mind his conduct over Kuwait, could I trust him again? There was one alternative open to a Member of Parliament facing such circumstances and fearing, as I now feared, that security could be put at risk by Ivanov. That was to use Parliamentary privilege to expose the situation. This, Gaitskell had advised in our discussions about the Vassall case, is exactly what privilege is for.

I had not resolved my heart-and-mind searching when, on Sunday, March 10, I returned to London to attend a party at the home of Mrs Barbara Castle. Harold Wilson was there and we found a room in which to talk privately. I made the point that the situation was moving to a climax. The March 8 issue of *Westminster Confidential*, a small monthly news-letter, had summarized the stories which the girls—Miss Keeler had been joined by a Miss Mandy Rice Davies— were selling to newspapers. One of the points raised in the news-letter was, 'Who was using the call-girl to "milk" whom of information—the War Secretary or the Soviet Military Attaché?—ran in the minds of those primarily interested in security'. I told Wilson there were rumours that the story was about to 'break' in overseas newspapers and that two Sunday newspapers, expected to blow the gaff that morning, had not published a line of their boasted 'scoops', although one of them, the *Sunday Pictorial*, had bought from Miss Keeler a story based on a letter addressed 'Darling' and signed 'J'— a signature with which I was familiar. I pointed out that the names of prominent persons were being associated with Christine Keeler and Dr Stephen Ward, a society portrait artist and osteopath, and that Captain Ivanov had left England hurriedly on January 29. I drew attention to the fact that Miss Keeler who, on December 14, 1962, had been shot up by a West Indian, John Edgecombe, jealous of her preference for another West Indian, 'Lucky' Gordon, had gone abroad, although she was a vital witness in the trial, now pending, of Edgecombe.

The time had come, I urged Wilson, to press the Government to make a statement. The opportunity might arise on the Service Estimates during the coming week that the Government should be urged to hold an inquiry, in private if it wished, and then make a statement in the House. We agreed that should a demand for an inquiry emerge, we would ask for a Select Committee with terms of reference to include the nature of the Prime Minister's responsibility for security.

Wilson's attitude indicated that he wanted to play it cool. He invited me to pursue the subject 'on my own responsibility'. I decided not to raise the matter in the House of Commons unless circumstances forced my hand. Should that happen, I must find a form of words neither libellous nor unfair, whether spoken in Parliament or outside it, and I sought the advice of Arnold Goodman.

On the night of Thursday, March 21, stories about pending revelations in the Foreign Press came to a head. The matter was in everyone's unspoken thoughts. Earlier in the day the late Ben Parkin had been pulled up by the bewildered Chairman of a Standing Committee when, speaking on the subject of London sewage, he had commented, 'There is the case of the missing model. We understand that a model can quite easily be obtained for the convenience of a Minister of the Crown'—the reference being to a model provided by the Ministry of Transport to illustrate proposals for London traffic. It was also reported that Mrs Castle intended during the debate on the imprisoned journalists later that night, to raise the matter in the context of the 'missing witness'. So I decided to act. I rose at 11 p.m. to take part in the debate about the two journalists, Reginald Foster and Brendan Mulholland, who had been committed to prison for refusing to disclose their sources of information to the Radcliffe Tribunal on the Vassall case. This was the nub of my speech:

The Press can exercise freedom over its criticism of the Executive, the Opposition and Hon. Members—but it should have regard for the public good. . . . The Tribunal had a job to do. They were not there in order to bring the mailed fist of totalitarianism into it but to do a job that the House of Commons had by unanimous resolution authorized them to do. If Hon. Members now grumble about the result, I ask them where they were on 14 November when we were raising our voices against this particular form of tribunal.

So far, so good. Here was a set of rumours that gained and gained in strength, consumed men's reputations—might, in fact, have destroyed them—and which here infringed on the security of the State.

But are we quite sure that the same thing is not happening again? There is not an Hon. Member in the House, nor a journalist in the Press Gallery, nor do I believe there is a person in the Public Gallery who, in the last few days, has not heard rumour upon rumour involving a member of the Government Front Bench.

The Press has got as near as it could—it has shown itself willing to wound but afraid to strike. This all comes about because of the Vassall Tribunal. In actual fact, these great Press Lords, these men who control great instruments of public opinion and of power, do not have the guts to discharge the duty that they are now claiming for themselves.

That being the case, I rightly use the Privilege of the House of Commons—that is what it is given me for—to ask the Home Secretary who is the senior member of the Government on the Treasury Bench now, to go to the Dispatch Box—he knows that the rumour to which I refer relates to Miss Christine Keeler and Miss Davies and a shooting by a West Indian—and, on behalf of the Government, categorically deny the truth of these rumours.

On the other hand, if there is anything in them, I urge him to ask the Prime Minister to do what was not done in the Vassall case—set up a Select Committee so that these things can be dissipated, and the honour of the Minister concerned freed from the imputation and innuendos that are being spread at the present time.

It is not good for a democratic State that rumours of this kind should spread and be inflated, and go on. Everyone knows what I am referring to, but up to now nobody has brought the matter into the open. I believe that the Vassall Tribunal need never have been set up had the nettle been firmly grasped much earlier on. We have lost some time and I plead with the Home

Secretary to use that Dispatch Box to clear up all the mystery and speculation over this particular case.

R. H. S. Crossman endorsed my plea for a Select Committee and remarked that 'by this evening a Paris newspaper may have published in full the rumours which have run round this House and the country and are touched upon day by day in the Press'.

The debate rambled on for forty minutes before Mrs Castle spoke as she intended, but in a manner I thought maladroit and unfortunate. Citing a statement reported to have been made by the Clerk of the Central Criminal Court, Mr Leslie Boyd, that 'if any member of the public did know where Miss Keeler was it is his or her duty to inform the police,' she asked: 'If accusations are made that there are people in high places who do know and who are not informing the police, is it not a matter of public interest?' In my view, then and now, nothing could have been more helpful to the rattled Government than to drag the red herring of Miss Keeler's disappearance across the trail.

Just after 12.30 a.m. the Home Secretary, Henry Brooke, rose to wind up for the Government. Mrs Castle's intervention enabled him to wrap us up together in this reply: 'I do not propose to comment on the rumours which have been raised under the cloak of privilege and safe from any action at law. The Hon. Member for Dudley and the Hon. Member for Blackburn should seek other means of making these insinuations if they are prepared to substantiate them.' I had made no statement which, if repeated outside the House, was actionable at law. I had quite deliberately narrowed the issue to make impossible the opportunity opened up by Mrs Castle for the Home Secretary to turn a security question into an attack on the Labour Opposition and myself. Harold Wilson rose to speak a few minutes before 1 a.m. He had not been present throughout the debate but had been informed of what had taken place. He dealt caustically, although not severely enough in my opinion, with the Home Secretary.

Tension in the House, high though it was, could not match the atmosphere of crisis behind the scenes. The Government had to answer my questions—and Mrs Castle's charges—and, the next day being Friday, to answer them before the week-end or run the risk of adverse comment by the Press, now much less muzzled than hitherto. The Attorney General, the late Sir John Hobson, and the

Solicitor General, Sir Peter Rawlinson, consulted the Chief Whip, Martin Redmayne. In the early hours of the morning they wakened the sleeping Prime Minister to suggest that the form of reply should be a personal statement by John Profumo. The Prime Minister agreed. So they dragged Profumo out of bed and back to Westminster. There, the group were joined by the late Iain Macleod, Leader of the House, William Deedes, Minister-without-Portfolio, and Profumo's solicitor. The absence of the Home Secretary, Henry Brooke, who had gone home to bed, provoked criticism. Although the Metropolitan Police, for whom he answered in Parliament, had not yet given him the information they had obtained a month earlier from Miss Keeler about her association with Profumo and Ivanov, a simple request by the Home Secretary for further information would have revealed the truth to him. Then the sequence of events might have been very different.

The five Ministers engaged in nocturnal discussions with Profumo were not seeking to extort the truth from him. They believed that was contained in his many emphatic denials. These denials cleared him as a security risk and tended to justify the view that he could have no motive in being a party to Miss Keeler's disappearance. Only later did the suggestion arise that the Chief Whip and the Law Officers, who had interviewed Profumo several times, may not have asked the right question; the real point, Lord Denning considered, might have been '*not* whether Profumo had committed adultery, but whether his conduct (proved or admitted) was such as to lead ordinary people *reasonably to believe* that he had'. Ministers knew nothing of statements made to the police by Miss Keeler on January 6, and by Ward on February 5. The Ministerial task force of five, in the early hours of Friday, March 22, believed their only job was to prepare a personal statement to be delivered by Profumo when Parliament met that day. The comings and goings incidental to the drafting of the statement continued until 3.30 a.m. It was presented to the Prime Minister at 9.30 a.m. He decided to attend the House as a sign of confidence in Profumo who, at 11.08 a.m., read the following statement:

> I understand that my name has been connected with rumours about the disappearance of Miss Christine Keeler.
>
> I would like to take this opportunity of making a personal statement about these matters.

I last saw Miss Keeler in December 1961, and I have not seen her since. I have no idea where she is now. Any suggestion that I was in any way connected with or responsible for her absence from the trial at the Old Bailey is wholly and completely untrue.

My wife and I first met Miss Keeler at a house party in July 1961 at Cliveden. Among a number of people there was Dr Stephen Ward, whom we already knew slightly and a Mr Ivanov, who was an attaché at the Russian Embassy.

The only other occasion that my wife and I met Mr Ivanov was for a moment at the official reception for Major Gagarin at the Soviet Embassy.

My wife and I had a standing invitation to visit Dr Ward.

Between July and December 1961, I met Miss Keeler on about half a dozen occasions at Dr Ward's flat, when I called to see him and his friends. Miss Keeler and I were on friendly terms. There was no impropriety whatsoever in my acquaintanceship with Miss Keeler.

Mr Speaker, I have made this personal statement because of what was said in the House last evening by the three Hon. Members, and which, of course, was protected by privilege. I shall not hesitate to issue writs for libel and slander if scandalous allegations are made or repeated outside the House.

It was an ingenious statement with only one specific denial that 'there was no impropriety whatsoever in my acquaintanceship with Miss Keeler'—and that was a barefaced lie. The statement disclosed the fact that the influence of a Russian diplomat and spy was prevalent in some of the scruffier sections of upper-class society. The statement, necessarily, would have been far different if Mrs Castle had not raised the irrelevant gossip about Miss Keeler's disappearance. That afternoon Profumo savoured his triumph. He and his wife joined the Queen Mother at Sandown Park Races. The only satisfaction I had was the comment in *The Times* leading article next morning that my action was 'a proper use of privilege'.

On Tuesday, March 26, around 5 p.m. I was handed a telephone message by a House of Commons official, asking me to ring Stephen Ward at a Paddington number. That same morning I had received an excerpt from the judgment delivered on December 3, 1954, in a contested divorce action in which John Lewis was the successful applicant and Ward a witness on the other side. The eminent judge described Ward as 'a far from attractive witness ... one on whose word not the slightest reliance could be placed as regards any point on which he was called'. I rang Ward from the one telephone to which an earpiece was attached to the ordinary receiver so that Wilfred Sendall, the distinguished political journalist who was with me when I received Ward's message, could take a note of the conversation. Ward, it appeared, had been agitated by my comment in a television programme the previous evening that the real issue involved was security. He rambled on about persons and places. I cut him short with an intimation that I was not interested in private lives, but if he wanted to talk about security I would meet him in the Central Lobby at 6 p.m. Sendall witnessed his arrival.

Immediately after Ward left the House at 9 p.m. I told Harold Wilson that my visitor claimed to have written both to him and to the Prime Minister towards the end of the Cuban crisis. The letter was immediately extracted from the files and Wilson at once recalled a phrase about an approach made by Ward on behalf of Ivanov to the Foreign Office: 'I was the intermediary', Ward had written. Next day, Wilson handed Ward's letter to the Prime Minister and expressed his now acute anxiety about the implication that Ward was a contact between Ivanov and people of influence in this country. I recorded my conversation with Ward which I showed to Wilson, who asked me to prepare an appreciation for his information. I completed this task on March 29. Wilson also asked the Chief Whip, Bert Bowden, to seek Sir Frank Soskice's advice. When Wilson returned home from his visit to the late President John Kennedy the same old questions rose again: was there a *prima facie* case for an Inquiry and, if so, what form should it take and how should the Opposition seek to obtain it? Soskice (now Lord Stow Hill) thought there was a clear case for further action based on my appreciation. With Bowden agreeing, the document was handed to the Government Chief Whip together with a covering letter, dated April 9, from Wilson addressed to the Prime Minister.

The following is a summary prepared from the document sent to the Prime Minister, especial care having been taken to record Ward's statements with absolute accuracy.

On our way to the Harcourt Room, Ward chatted about his familiarity with the House of Commons, to which he had often brought Ivanov, and about his contacts with Members and Conservative Ministers. He was anxious I should know the truth about Ivanov and the circumstances in which he had met him. Then the sight of an ex-Minister seemed to unnerve him. 'He must not see me with you,' he exclaimed. 'I must leave at once. I ought not to have come here, I know too many people. I must leave at once.' I took him to a private interview room and we started our talk afresh.

Ward said he first met Ivanov some time in 1961 at a Garrick Club lunch where, with a journalist specializing in Soviet affairs, they were guests of a Fleet Street editor. Ward found Ivanov a charming man. He taught him to play bridge and, soon, was seeing him two or three times a fortnight. They had fun with girls, although nothing improper ever took place, and they played bridge. They had visited only one night club, The Satyr, together, and then only for ten minutes. Ward said Ivanov never spoke critically about the British people. His one desire, which Ward shared, was to foster Anglo-Soviet friendship. Ward said he last saw Ivanov shortly before Christmas.

The Security Service, Ward asserted, knew all about his association with Ivanov. Representatives of the Security Service had enquired about his various meetings and Ward had promised to keep them informed and had kept that promise. He cited two occasions on which he thought friendship with Ivanov had been of value to Britain. At the time of the Berlin crisis in 1962 he, acting for Ivanov, had informed Sir Harold Caccia and other Foreign Office officials that the Soviet Union would adopt a conciliatory policy in return for Western guarantees about the integrity of the Oder–Neisse Line. I pressed him hard at this point, enquiring if he personally saw Sir Harold or other Foreign Office officials. He was not prepared to say; many important people, including Conservative M.P.s, were involved in the business.

His second venture in Ivanov-directed diplomacy—again as a go-between—occurred during the Cuban crisis. This time, according to Ward, he was the link between Ivanov as peacemaker and the British Government, represented by the Foreign Secretary, Lord Home, and the Prime Minister. Ivanov told Ward the Russians would respond to a British initiative calling a conference in London by halting the delivery of arms and stopping all shipments of war equipment to Cuba. I pressed even harder on this subject for the obvious reason that I did not believe that Ward, personally, had been in touch with the Foreign Secretary and the Prime Minister.

Ward became cagey again. He was not prepared to say because too many important people were involved.

Having, as he thought, achieved his purpose of clearing himself as a security risk, Ward talked freely about his relations with Profumo whom he and Christine Keeler had met at Cliveden. A photograph of Profumo and the girl swimming there, he alleged, had been stolen recently from his flat. Profumo had visited Ward's flat at least six times. The Security Service knew all about these visits for Ward kept them informed.

Ward went on to say that about three weeks before the trial of Edgecombe opened Christine Keeler and Paul Mann had become aware of the cash value of letters Profumo had written to the girl— brief notes signed 'J', expressing regret for not meeting or making further assignations. Ward could have them for five thousand pounds. Otherwise they would go to the highest bidder. Mann was already seeking contact, Ward said, with the Manchester office of the *Sunday Pictorial*. Ward said that in a disinterested endeavour to protect Profumo, he arranged a meeting with him at the Dorchester Hotel where, according to his story, Profumo's reaction was that he could not remember the girl. Ward advised him to assist his memory by consulting the Security Service. They would be able to help for they had the data, including dates, which he, Ward, had supplied to them.

Ward next turned to his own relations with the Press. Christine Keeler had received two advances on account amounting to two hundred and fifty pounds from the *Sunday Pictorial*. In addition she had been installed in a flat at Park West by that newspaper. Learning that publication was imminent, Ward approached the *Sunday Pictorial*, challenged Miss Keeler's veracity, and made a deal resulting in the publication of his own story and the suppression of Miss Keeler's version. For that deal, he alleged, he received only a contribution towards his legal costs. An enraged Paul Mann then took the Christine Keeler story to the *News of the World*. Ward claimed he also intervened with that newspaper by providing material for an article which appeared simultaneously with his *Sunday Pictorial* story. Ward also referred to the activities of a person named Barratt or Bell who, citing Ward as his source, had sold stories to the *Express* newspapers and to the *People*.

Ward's narrative now moved on to the life of Christine Keeler and her friend Mandy Rice Davies in the Park West flat. 'Lucky' Gordon, the Negro slashed by Edgecombe, joined her there. So did his wife and family. Miss Keeler's relations with coloured men had always been a matter of deep concern to Ward. She had lived in lodgings with Edgecombe at Ealing. While there she bought a gun from a criminal Negro involved in what Ward called the 'Queen's Park hold-up', and this was the gun with which Edgecombe had fired shots into Ward's flat. After leaving Ealing with her landlord's son, Miss Keeler lived with both Edgecombe and 'Lucky' Gordon thus arousing the jealousies which provoked the knife slashings and the shootings directed by these men against Miss Keeler and against each other. All four actors in the drama—Miss Keeler, Miss Davies, and the two West Indians—were reefer smokers; all, Ward said sadly, were utterly unstable and unpredictable.

I questioned Ward closely about what exactly Christine Keeler and her new friend, Paul Mann, were offering for sale. Ward was positive that Mann had taken the photograph of Profumo and the girl, and he suspected that Mann also held the Profumo letters. He was certain Mann had not approached Profumo, but he was convinced Profumo had spoken to Miss Keeler by telephone. He was equally convinced Profumo had not compromised State security in any way and no security risk had arisen through Profumo's contact with Ivanov and Christine Keeler or through the girl's contact with Ivanov. He asserted that his practice as an osteopath was being ruined, the Press were pursuing him on all sorts of charges, and he had got nothing out of his efforts to protect Profumo's reputation. Yet Paul Mann and Christine Keeler had obtained considerable sums of money which rightfully should have been his. On top of all this he was worried by my television statement that security was the sole consideration. He had come to convince me that, on this aspect of the case, he was in the clear.

My appreciation set out the main points of Ward's story—with the proviso that nothing he said should be relied upon without corroboration. He had been untruthful, particularly on the subject of his last meeting with Ivanov. If his statement—that the meeting had taken place before Christmas—had been true, Ivanov would certainly have left this country long before January 29.

The essential facts, in my opinion, were these: Profumo was not, at any time, a security risk. The Security Service knew all about his meetings with Ivanov and Miss Keeler and about Ward's friendship with Ivanov. Ivanov's friendship with Ward enabled him to move freely in Ward's own wide and ever growing circle of acquaintances.

The Christine Keeler–Mandy Rice Davies relationships with West Indians, having exploded into violence, had attracted publicity without which the Ivanov–Ward contact would have continued undisturbed with unforeseeable consequences.

I added a note of doubt on the possibility of a relationship between Ward and the Communist Party. He was certainly quite ignorant of Marxian theory. If he were a member of the Communist Party his loyalty was based either on emotion or on hope of financial gain. I thought his friendship with Ivanov had developed exactly as Ivanov had wished. It was more than likely that Ward had received a payment but he left me with the distinct impression that he was genuinely convinced that Anglo-Soviet friendship should be encouraged.

On April 11, Profumo, who had already launched a successful action against *Paris Match* in respect of a picture which had been removed from copies sent to this country, was awarded agreed damages and costs against the distributors of *Tempo Illustrato*. This journal had printed the baseless rumour that he had been involved in Miss Keeler's absence from the Edgecombe trial, together with 'suggestions that Profumo had been, or might have been, in some improper relationship with Miss Keeler'. The agreed damages of fifty pounds were donated by the plaintiff to an Army charity.

Probably with these successful legal actions in mind the Prime Minister, on April 17, wrote this somewhat off-putting acknowledgment to Harold Wilson: 'My Chief Whip has given to me the letter and enclosure from you dated April 9 and dealing with George Wigg's conversation with a Mr Stephen Ward. I will ask the appropriate authority to have an examination made of this information and will get in touch with you later on, if this seems necessary.' No further communication was received. On May 13, Wilson wrote again, asking what action was going to be taken. The Prime Minister answered, 'There seems to be nothing in the papers you sent which requires me to take further action.' Later he was to make in Parliament a plea amounting to 'I did not know'. The real question, which he did not answer, was why he did not *want* to know.

Public interest in this sordid serial revived when Miss Keeler returned to London from her visit to Spain with Mann, attended the Old Bailey on April 1 to apologize for her failure to appear at the trial of Edgecombe and, on leaving the court, had to be protected by the police from assault by 'Lucky' Gordon. Seven days later while visiting a friend in Devonshire Street, Marylebone, she was attacked again by 'Lucky' Gordon who, on May 3, was committed for trial from Marlborough Street Magistrates Court charged with maliciously and intentionally causing grievous bodily harm. (His ultimate sentence was quashed on appeal.) Then Ward, now under police investigation, re-entered the scene. He telephoned the Prime Minister's Private Secretary requesting a personal interview. The Prime Minister decided his Secretary should see Ward in the company of a representative of the Security Service. Ward demanded that the police investigation be stopped, a demand to which the Government had no power to accede. Ward then asserted he was in a position to embarrass the Government. He said the Profumo statement was untrue and had misled the House of Commons. It was Ward's word against Profumo's and Profumo persisted in his story. On May 19—five days after the Prime Minister had notified Wilson that there seemed to be nothing in my document requiring further action—Ward wrote to the Home Secretary and to his local M.P., Sir W. Wakefield, repeating his demand for an end to police investigation and his charge that Profumo had not told the truth. He also issued this statement to the newspapers:

> I have placed before the Home Secretary certain facts of the relationship between Miss Keeler and Mr Profumo since it is obvious now that my efforts to conceal these facts in the interests of Mr Profumo and the Government have made it appear that I myself have something to hide—which I have not. The result has been that I have been persecuted in a variety of ways, causing damage not only to myself but to my friends and patients—a state of affairs which I propose to tolerate no longer.

Obviously Ward was now seeking to divert attention from himself to Profumo.

On Friday, May 24, Wilson, having received from Ward a letter couched in similar terms to those sent to the Home Secretary and the Prime Minister, sought an appointment with the Prime Minister. The appointment was fixed for Monday, May 27. On the previous Friday Ben Parkin had put down a question to the Home Secretary, asking, 'What conclusions he had reached about information supplied to him by Dr Stephen Ward and what action he proposes to take following recent Metropolitan Police enquiries to prevent the increase of expensive call-girl organizations?' Wilson reminded the Prime

Minister of the ruthless vigour with which Attlee had acted in the Belcher case—which had destroyed the reputation of a decent man who was not even remotely involved in security matters. But the Prime Minister was in his most casual mood and when Wilson left him he was still unconvinced of the necessity for action. The sequel was unexpected. The recording of the Wilson–Macmillan conversation was sent to the Security Service as a routine matter. It reached them on May 28. From their files there emerged a reasonably well-authenticated statement made by Miss Keeler on January 26 that she had been asked to question Profumo on secret matters. That statement reached the Prime Minister one hundred and twenty-three days after it went on the Security Service file, and how far it influenced him only he can tell. On May 30, he wrote to Harold Wilson to say, 'I have been thinking about our talk on Monday. I am sure in my own mind that the security aspect of the Ward case has been fully and efficiently watched, but I think it is important that you should be in no doubt about it,' and went on to state he had decided that Lord Chancellor Dilhorne should conduct an Inquiry. In Parliament that same day, the eve of the Whitsun recess, Wilson passed a scribbled note to the Prime Minister suggesting that the Lord Chancellor's Inquiry should be announced publicly since so many people knew about Ward's allegations. The Prime Minister maintained a stolid silence. The note was acknowledged formally by his Secretary later in the evening. The Prime Minister went off on holiday. The significant incidents observed by some M.P.s were two whispered conferences in the shadow of Mr Speaker's chair between Profumo and the Prime Minister and between Profumo and his Chief Whip.

The Opposition's immediate job, about which Wilson agreed with me fully, was to make sure that the Inquiry now being started by Dilhorne should concentrate upon security matters. Parkin agreed to withdraw his question on expensive call-girl organizations. The decision was then taken to prepare and put down a new question in the name of Chuter Ede, a member esteemed in all parts of the House. The question was drafted and it was handed in for Chuter at the Table Office. I went off to enjoy a too-infrequent pleasure, that of driving Chuter and his sister to Epsom, on this occasion to see the Coronation Cup. Suddenly the entire racecourse loudspeaker system brayed out a message: 'Would Colonel Wigg go to the weighing room.' The message I received was that the question needed to be redrafted. Chuter Ede and I got busy and amended it to read: 'To ask the Secretary of State for the Home Department what information he has received from Dr Stephen Ward in connection with enquiries carried out by the Metropolitan Police and what action he proposes to take.' Since the House was going into recess I decided to drive back to the House of Commons and check the final version prior to its appearance on the Order Paper.

Next day, May 31, Lord Dilhorne informed Profumo that he would see him on Thursday, June 6, then telegraphed him to say the appointment would be on June 5. Profumo, in Venice with his wife, returned on Whit Monday. On Tuesday morning, in the absence of the Prime Minister in Scotland, he interviewed the Private Secretary and the Chief Whip and confessed that over a period of four months he had lied persistently to his colleagues, to his wife, to the Law Officers of the Crown and, ultimately, to the House of Commons. On Wednesday, June 5, Political Correspondents were summoned to the Conservative Central Office to hear Mr Selwyn Lloyd report on the re-organization of the Conservative Party. At 6 p.m. that same day they received copies of Profumo's letter to the Prime Minister, sent from his London home and dated June 4. It read:

You will recollect that on March 22 following certain allegations made in Parliament, I made a personal statement.

At that time rumour had charged me with assisting in the disappearance of a witness and of being involved in some possible breach of security.

So serious were these charges that I allowed myself to think that my personal association with that witness, which had also been the subject of rumour, was, by comparison, of minor importance only.

In my statement I said that there had been no impropriety in this association. To my very deep regret I have to admit that this was not true, and that I misled you and my colleagues and the House.

I ask you to understand that I did this to protect, as I thought, my wife and family, who were equally misled, as were my professional advisers.

I have come to realize that, by this deception, I have been guilty of a great misdemeanour, and despite the fact that there is no truth whatever in the other charges, I cannot remain a Member of your Administration, nor of the House of Commons. I cannot tell you of my deep remorse for the embarrassment I have caused to you, to my colleagues in the Government, to my constituents and to the Party which I have served for the past twenty-five years.

The Prime Minister, from the house where he was staying in the Highlands of Scotland, replied to 'Dear Profumo' on June 5 in these terms:

The contents of your letter of June 4 have been communicated to me, and I have read them with great regret. This is a great tragedy for you, for your family and your friends.

Nevertheless, I am sure you will understand that in the circumstances, I have no alternative but to advise the Queen to accept your resignation.

A diary of events during the next few days has all the ingredients of high drama and low farce. On Saturday, June 8, Ward was arrested, taken to Marylebone Police Station, and charged 'that he, being a man, did on diverse dates between January 1, 1961 and June 8, 1963, knowingly live wholly or in part on the earnings of prostitution at 17, Wimpole Mews, London, W., contrary to Section 30 of the Sexual Offences Act 1956,' and he was detained in custody over the week-end. His trial opened at the Old Bailey on July 22; he died from an overdose of a sleeping drug before the Judge had finished summing up in a case the conduct of which, in the view of some commentators, did little credit to British justice. On the evening of June 8, the Prime Minister, at a roast ox and beer party at Strathallan Castle, near Gleneagles, told an expectant audience: 'Tragically, there hangs over the whole affair like a dark cloud the shadow ... of a political speech. ... They may call me a twister, but I do not do the Twist.' On Sunday, June 9, Miss Keeler had become the protégée of the *News of the World* to the great benefit of its circulation. The *Sunday Pictorial*, now the *Sunday Mirror*, printed as a scoop the already notorious 'Darling' letter, the original of which it had restored to Profumo. On Monday, June 10, the Prime Minister attended the installation of the Chancellor of Sussex University and, still in roast ox and beer mood, quipped 'Aren't politics fun!' On Tuesday, with *The Times* thundering 'IT *IS* A MORAL ISSUE', the Inner Cabinet met at Admiralty House, which was then the Prime Minister's residence, to receive the first copy of the Lord Chancellor's report and prepare for Wednesday's Cabinet meeting. The first editions of Thursday's morning newspapers were divided in their accounts. The *Daily Telegraph* and *Daily Mail* declared the Cabinet to be united behind the Prime Minister. *The Times* and the *Daily Express* forecast resignations. All the later editions of all newspapers announced dissension with Enoch Powell, a leading critic of the Prime Minister's handling of the situation. Another Cabinet meeting was held that Thursday, and Lord Hailsham appeared on a B.B.C. television programme, presumably to calm Tory nerves and soothe public fears. He achieved the exact opposite. When his interviewer, Robert MacKenzie, quoted *The Times* His Lordship yelled passionately, '*The Times* is an anti-Conservative newspaper led by an anti-Conservative editor ... A great Party is not to be brought down because of a scandal by a woman of easy virtue and a proved liar.' The view of less irresponsible elements in the Tory Party was being expressed by Selwyn Lloyd in a speech to Party members. 'The country,' he told them, 'is asking for courageous and competent leadership not based on expediency but on obedience to high moral standards and irreproachable behaviour in high places.'

Parliament reassembled on June 17 and Wilson, home from a visit to Moscow, opened the debate with a clinical analysis of the Profumo story. The Prime Minister's defence contained some amazing admissions. It revealed that Sir Norman Brooke, Secretary of the Cabinet, had warned Profumo in 1961 but Sir Norman's written record, said the Prime Minister, made 'no reference to his having informed me'. Three separate statements by Miss Keeler that she had been asked by Ward to obtain military information from Profumo had likewise never reached the Prime Minister—an admission that evoked the jibe, 'Nobody ever tells me anything!' That summed up the Prime Minister's case; a case without conviction presented without punch or panache. The Tory rebel speech of the day was delivered by Nigel Birch (now Lord Rhyl) one of the ablest brains in Parliament and a master of language and diction. Birch paid tribute to the Prime Minister as a man of honour then delivered the disembowelling sword thrust: 'What is to happen now? I cannot myself see at all that we can go on acting as if nothing had happened.

We cannot just have business as usual. I myself feel that the time will come very soon when my Rt. Hon. Friend ought to make way for a much younger colleague. I feel that ought to happen. I certainly will not quote at him the savage words of Cromwell, but perhaps some of the words of Browning might be appropriate in his poem on 'The Lost Leader' in which he wrote:

> '. . . let him never come back to us!
> There would be doubt, hesitation and pain.
> Forced praise on our part—the glimmer of twilight
> Never glad confident morning again.'

'Never glad confident morning again'—so I hope the change will not be too long delayed. Ahead of us we have a Division. We have the statement of my Rt. Hon. and Noble Friend, Lord Hailsham, in a personal assurance on television that a Whip is not a summons to vote but a summons to attend. I call the Whips to witness that I at any rate have attended.'

I followed Birch. In the course of my speech I told the House that information had come to me that another Minister might be involved. I went immediately to that Minister's P.P.S., ascertained that the sum total of the story was that the Minister had loaned his car as a friendly gesture to Profumo, and at once took steps to enable my informant to stop the spread of the canard. I had also reported to Scotland Yard information brought to me that Ward had deposited documents and photographs in the office of a newspaper preparing to print his life story. I had tried to be straight in my own dealings and I acquitted the Prime Minister of any act of dishonour. His defence, however, had been 'a record of incompetence that requires he should resign, and the whole of his Administration with him'.

The vote taken at the end of the debate revealed groups within the Tory Party willing to wound but afraid to strike at their Leader. Tory abstentionists numbered twenty-seven, 'not quite enough to force me out' the Prime Minister was reported to have said. The influential 1922 Committee, however, were known to have informed the Chief Whip that, although they would vote for the Prime Minister, their support must not be interpreted as a sign of confidence in his Leadership.

The year 1963 had been one of unrelieved disaster for the now doomed Prime Minister. He entered it bearing an unexpected rebuff from General de Gaulle over the Common Market which he wanted to enter in the hope of finding a solution to the ingrained inefficiency of British Capitalism and the consequential indiscipline of British Trade Unionists. The unemployed in January numbered eight-hundred and fifteen thousand. In that same month he had reported to the House of Commons an agreement with President Kennedy on Polaris which I helped to expose as nonsense. The target for economic growth—four per cent per annum for the five years 1961–66—had not been reached; the National Economic Development Council proposed in February a new target of five per cent growth to make good the shortfall caused by economic stagnation in 1961–62. March by-elections in safe Labour seats saw the Tories being pushed into third and fourth place behind the Liberals. The creation of a new Ministry of Defence in that same month merely aggravated the muddle into which defence policy had fallen. The Radcliffe Tribunal on the Vassall case had alienated the Press and its Report exposed the Prime Minister as being indifferent, even inefficient, in his handling of vital issues of security; the Profumo case revealed that that charge still had some meaning. In the Borough Elections in May, over 1,700 Labour Councillors, a record number, were returned. Overall, the disastrous policies of 1962, typified in the Beeching Report, persisted. The Tories had divided Great Britain into a technologically growing and prosperous Midlands and South East, and a decaying, bitterly neglected North and West. Class war had assumed a geographical aspect. The Prime Minister, the modern Disraeli, had abandoned the Disraeli dream of One Nation.

What now? The Prime Minister sought escape from some of his problems by appointing Lord Denning, Master of the Rolls, to undertake an Inquiry with these terms of reference:

> To examine, in the light of the circumstances leading to the resignation of the former Secretary of State for War, Mr J. D. Profumo, the operation of the Security Service and the adequacy of their co-operation with the Police in matters of security, to investigate any information or material which may come to his attention in this connection and to consider any evidence there may be for believing that national security has been or may be in danger and to report thereon.

The Labour Party opposed this form of Inquiry. We wanted a

Select Committee, on the lines I had suggested times without number, to investigate security in all its aspects and—as Harold Wilson had urged in debate and in letters to the Prime Minister—to ensure that the Inquiry should be directed to the relationships between the Security Service and the Government and members of the Government *inter se*. Wilson disappointed me by not forcing the debate to a division, but he was hampered by a weak and ill-informed Shadow Cabinet.

I received a letter delivered by hand from Lord Denning which began, 'As I expect you know, I have been entrusted by the Prime Minister with the task of enquiring into reports which are circulating which affect the honour and integrity of public life in this country.' How the terms of reference for the Inquiry could possibly be interpreted in this way completely baffled me. I tried politely to emphasize the absurdity of this interpretation to Lord Denning by saying, 'If you are going to enquire into the honour and integrity of public life you are not going to report in July.' I thought, privately, that he would be on the job for the rest of his natural life! I gave all the information I possessed to him and revealed my sources, but I refused to answer questions which had no relevance to security. When Lord Denning questioned me about the currently notorious Argyll case, I replied that I was not interested in divorce cases and knew nothing about them, and to His Lordship's question, 'But don't you think I ought to investigate an aspect of their divorce?' I answered, 'I have no views on the matter. It is entirely for you to decide.' I refused to express an opinion about aspects of the alleged behaviour of two Ministers; that was no concern of mine. Before seeing Lord Denning I had shown Harold Wilson the letter in which Lord Denning set out his interpretation of the terms of reference. After the meeting I told Wilson of my anxiety about the nature of the evidence Lord Denning apparently expected to receive. I also consulted Arnold Goodman and we drafted a letter for Wilson to send to the Prime Minister. This was the letter.

'Dear Prime Minister,

'Thank you for your letter of the 28th June.

'As Lord Denning has embarked on his investigation, I should not ordinarily have pursued this correspondence but would have been satisfied to have awaited a report before considering whether any further action was called for.

'However, because of certain information I have received from George Wigg, I am perplexed and deeply concerned about the seeming course which the Denning investigation is taking.

'I enclose a copy of a letter received by Wigg which I have no reason to suppose differs in character from those sent to other prospective witnesses. You will see from paragraph 1 that Lord Denning regards himself as under a duty to investigate the rumours circulating which affect the honour and integrity of public life in this country (irrespective of their having any security aspect—an investigation if I may so of quite impossible if not ludicrous dimensions.)

'That Lord Denning is taking this interpretation of his terms of reference quite seriously, emerges from the fact that, after Wigg had given him all the information he possessed about recent events relating to the Profumo scandal, Lord Denning asked him whether he did not agree that it was his (Lord Denning's) duty to investigate every rumour from whatsoever source that might be brought to his attention. Lord Denning then proceeded to instance two particularly scurrilous rumours and to enquire whether in respect of either of these Wigg had any information. In connection with one of them Lord Denning went so far as to mention the name of a senior Minister of the Crown as being the subject of the rumour. Needless to say George Wigg emphasised that his interest in the matter had been in its security aspects and that he knew nothing of either of these rumours and cared less.

'RIDER 'A'

'The apparent justification of the course adopted by Lord Denning would seem to be that any misbehaviour by a public man gives rise to a security risk on account of the vulnerability that then ensues. The extent to which he is prepared to carry this doctrine is made clear by the fact that one of the two rumours mentioned related to a Scottish divorce case totally devoid of any security aspect. In my opinion an investigation of this kind, untrammelled by any limitations, would, in the hands of a less scrupulous tribunal, become a long step towards McCarthyism in this country.

'If, in fact, Lord Denning is pursuing a secret enquiry along the lines suggested to Wigg this, in my opinion, is without precedent in British history and constitutes a far greater affront to the dignity of Public Life than any rumours which may be circulating. For, if this be the case, it only requires a private denunciation to set in motion a solemn investigation of anyone in public life without, as

Wigg understood it, even the preliminary necessity of any sort of case to answer.

'On the floor of the House on the 21st June and in my letter to you of the 25th June I raised with you my belief—which I still firmly retain—that the formal terms of reference were too narrow and in particular that they did not in my opinion make it clear that enquiry could be directed to the relationships between the security services and the Government and of Members of the Government *inter se*. However, as you will be aware, H.M. Opposition has throughout regarded as the pre-eminent consideration the security aspects of the matter and we have set our faces against any kind of roving inquisition into private morality since we regard this neither as necessary nor as the appropriate function of the House of Commons or any Tribunal appointed by it.

'The wide discrepancy between the formal terms of reference and what Lord Denning is apparently doing seems to me in the general interest to call for urgent action on your part and I would venture to suggest on the following lines:

'1: To clarify and amplify Lord Denning's terms of reference so as to make it clear that the enquiry is concerned with the national security and matters affecting the administration of justice. It should, I think, be made public that the Government is not prepared to dignify any piece of malicious tittle-tattle into a subject for solemn judicial investigation.

'2: The Tribunal should now be invested with proper powers. What the Opposition wanted and still wants is a tribunal with precise and well defined functions armed with the authority to elicit the truth and allay public anxiety. What at the moment we have got is precisely the opposite. The need for powers was only yesterday emphasized by the report that a witness whom Lord Denning desired to interview promptly departed for a holiday abroad. Episodes of this kind demonstrate the folly of setting up a tribunal without cloaking it with proper authority and the danger that it may be brought in contempt notwithstanding the eminence and distinction of the judge conducting it.

'3: Some form of tribunal should be agreed between us to deal with the question of Profumo's statement in the House. It is, if I may say so, nothing more than a debating point to suggest that this matter has been disposed of by the vote of the House at the termination of the debate. The crucial aspect of the matter from the security viewpoint is that, because of the convention that personal statements remain unchallenged, any enemy agents who may have secured or have tried to secure information from Mr Profumo through Miss Keeler, would have derived a high measure of safety under the cloak of Mr Profumo's uncontradicted denial. It is this aspect of the matter that requires investigation from the public viewpoint—and the sooner the better.

'Finally may I say how strongly I deplore the statement by Ministers that the whole country is alive with gossip and slander. The Profumo case unhappily aroused immense public interest and rumours and speculations, as with every previous public scandal, are bound to be rampant. But unless artificially fostered by the type of statement to which I refer, the whole thing will die a natural and a speedy death. The public image of this country has suffered serious tarnishing by recent events. It would be more than unfortunate if this should be augmented by circumstances surrounding Lord Denning's inquiry or by any suspicion of an attempt to turn it to political advantage.

                    Yours sincerely'

Although the Report, issued from Her Majesty's Stationery Office to immense queues of customers in the early morning of Thursday, September 26, was almost valueless except on three important counts, I respected Lord Denning for not pursuing what, I had gathered, as originally being his interpretation of the purpose of the Inquiry entrusted to him. My comment in the *Sunday Telegraph* of September 29 is still valid. 'The honour and integrity of public life are decided by the general advance of a civilization,' I wrote, 'and if Lord Denning had named names and pried into personal secrets it might have proved to be an alarming precedent. We might have been on a slope that leads to the Police State.'

The first of the three points I regarded as important was one that not a single person in ten thousand of Lord Denning's vast readership would even notice. It referred to the 'limitations of the Inquiry and Report', and read: 'It has been much debated what is the best way to deal with matters such as those referred to me. The appointment of a tribunal under the Tribunal of Inquiries Act, 1921, is an elaborate and costly machine, equipped with all the engines of the law—counsel, solicitors, witnesses on oath, absolute privilege, openness to the public (so far as possible) and committal for contempt—but it suffers from the invincible drawback, in doing justice, that there is no prosecution, no charge and no defence.' I wish I could have put the argument as succinctly and devastatingly when I opposed the form of Inquiry which the Prime Minister set up to deal with the Vassall case. Lord Denning, I am convinced, ensured that, in future, the Tribunal of Inquiries Act, 1921, would be used only in very exceptional circumstances such as those which arose in the Aberfan disaster.

Thus I forgive Lord Denning's mild condemnation of my own favourite proposal for the appointment of a Select Committee, 'said to suffer from the drawback (to some eyes) that the inquisitors are too many and may be influenced in their, often divergent, views by political considerations, so that there may be too much dissent to carry authority'. That view, as expressed, did not accord with my personal experience as a member of the Select Committee on the Army Act and, I am sure, it would be rejected by any M.P. who has served, for example, on the Committee on Public Expenditure which deals frequently with what are called 'sensitive' matters. So Lord Denning decided to be his own 'detective, inquisitor, advocate and judge' as though a judge should be expected to do anything but judge. Happily, he was faithful to legal tradition. He recognized 'the inescapable difficulties inherent in this form of inquiry' and acted on this principle: 'While the public interest demands that the facts should be ascertained as completely as possible, there is a yet higher public interest to be considered, namely, the interest of justice to the individual which over-rides all other. At any rate, speaking as a Judge I put justice first.'

Lord Denning made his second important point with crystal clarity. 'It has been suggested to me', he wrote 'that Ivanov filled a new role in Russian technique. It was to divide the United Kingdom from the United States by these devious means. If Ministers or prominent people can be placed in compromising situations, or made the subject of damaging rumour, or the Security Service can be made to appear incompetent, it may weaken the confidence of the United States in our integrity and reliability. So a man like Captain Ivanov may take every opportunity of getting to know Ministers or prominent people, not so much to obtain information from them (though this would be a useful by-product) but so as to work towards destroying confidence. If this were the object of Captain Ivanov with Stephen

Ward as his tool, he succeeded only too well.'

This, exactly, was the case I had made in every Parliamentary discussion on security during the previous decade.

The third point was sensationally revealing. In 1952, Sir David Maxwell Fyfe, then Home Secretary, instructed the Director General of the Security Service that 'you will be responsible to the Home Secretary personally'. Poor Henry Brooke! As Home Secretary he knew so little about his responsibilities and about the Profumo affair in March that he had to seek information from his own Security Service which had been on the job for a long time. And, alas, for the Prime Minister! He answered all questions on the Security Service in the House, obviously ignorant of Maxwell Fyfe's ruling, and neither he nor any other Minister knew the full facts about the Profumo–Keeler–Ward triangle until May 29.

The Denning Report pronounced the Security Service efficient in all its aspects. Its eye had been on Profumo and Ivanov and Ward since 1961. The menacing muddle, as I interpreted the findings, arose from the fact that the Service looked to the Home Office for its pay and rations and to the Prime Minister as its Operational Head and the two Ministers responsible either did not know or had never sought to define their respective roles in the system.

Lord Denning made one grave error despite the immense care he took to protect 'the interests of justice to the individual'. He summarized the speeches made by R. H. S. Crossman, Mrs Castle and myself on March 21 and commented, 'These remarks were of much significance. They clearly imputed that Mr Profumo had been responsible for the disappearance of Christine Keeler.' Neither Crossman nor I had made any such imputation; I, indeed, had repudiated it on several occasions. The late Iain Macleod then went on B.B.C. television and, although as Leader of the House he ought to have known better and almost certainly did know better, repeated the inaccuracy and suggested that all three Members should withdraw what two of them had never said. Crossman and I wrote to Macleod. We ultimately forced him to move that Profumo, in lying to the House on March 22, was guilty of a grave contempt and that, in reference to Crossman and myself, his words were tendentious. George Brown described the words as 'unfortunate'. Had I taken part in the discussion I would have called them 'unfair'. How different and manly was Macmillan's reference to this matter. 'I altogether accept what the Hon. Member for Dudley has said about his motive. I am sure we all agree that he was actuated solely from the security point of view.' At the end of the debate on December 16 Harold Macmillan walked out of the House of Commons for the last time, arm-in-arm with Harold Wilson.

With Stephen
Swingler at the
Millman Street flat,
1945
(*Syndication International*)

Arriving at the War
Office with Emanuel
Shinwell, October
10, 1947
(*Sport and General*)

On an aeroplane journey, 1950—listening to the Cesarewitch result

A visit by British M.P.s to General Eisenhower's SHAPE Head-
quarters, December 12, 1951
L to R: R. H. S. Crossman, A. D. Dodds-Parker, 'Ike', S. N. Evans,
George Wigg, J. Baird

The aftermath of the Profumo affair had as searing a reaction on the Conservative Party as did the rumpus about Clause Four and defence on the Labour Party. The selection of Lord Home as Conservative Leader and his succession to Harold Macmillan as Prime Minister was regarded by other aspirants with such bitterness that the Party agreed in future to follow Labour's more democratic procedure of election by secret ballot. Lord Home, soon to undergo a red-for-blue blood transfusion and re-appear under the title of Sir Alec Douglas-Home, was charged with one of the most difficult jobs ever imposed on a political leader, that of holding together a powerful party when it was in danger of falling into public derision and contempt. As a very interested onlooker, I think Sir Alec did that job admirably. He succeeded because he is simple and straight.

Meantime, I had to defend myself against those Tories who questioned my motives in the Profumo affair. An article in the *Daily Mail* on June 18, suggested I had been actuated by a desire to seek revenge upon Profumo because he had out-smarted me in the Kuwait debate. I did not and could not ignore the imputation although I regarded its publication merely as a reflection on the intelligence of the writer and his editor. The *Daily Mail* made a full withdrawal and apology in the Queen's Bench Division of the High Court of Justice, and that was the end of that.

A more painful issue arose on June 23. The *Sunday Citizen*, owned by the Co-operative Movement and formerly, under its old name *Reynolds News*, a paper of influence in the Labour Movement, published an article entitled 'Howl of Hate for Puritans!' written by Angus Maude, an experienced journalist.

'The Labour Party', Maude wrote, 'is feeling pretty pleased with itself. One of its M.P.s (who, the newspapers tell us, has long cherished a personal grudge against Profumo) unearthed a juicy scandal by snooping that would have done credit to a divorce detective, and the Party has cashed in on it.

'It has managed to smear the Prime Minister and the whole Conservative Administration, while retaining a smug appearance of morality.'

That might tickle the ears of groundlings in Stratford-on-Avon, Profumo's old seat, of which Maude became the Tory occupant, but I resented the ignorant slur and I issued a writ for libel. In its succeeding issue the *Sunday Citizen* published this retraction: 'In our feature "You are the Judge" ... Mr Angus Maude's contribution may have been thought to suggest that Mr Wigg, in the part he played in the Profumo affair, was acting out of personal spite. Nothing could be further from the truth. We and Mr Maude would like to take the earliest opportunity to contradict any such suggestion. We unreservedly accept Mr Wigg's assurances that he has been solely moved by a sense of public duty and we wish to offer our sincere apologies.'

I gave no such assurances to the *Sunday Citizen* for the obvious reason that, on my public record, there was no need for me to do so. The newspaper had to pay damages, but that was not the end of *that*.

The *Sunday Express*, whose editor, Mr John Junor, had sent me a letter congratulating me on my handling of the Profumo affair, printed an impudent comment in its 'Crossbencher' column which, following a threat of legal action, was retracted on January 26, 1964, by the publication of the following:

'In the *Sunday Express* last week' (the retraction ran) 'Crossbencher criticized Mr George Wigg, M.P. for having accepted substantial damages from the *Sunday Citizen* and Mr Angus Maude, M.P. for what was described as an article in which Mr Maude "gave his own somewhat jaundiced view of Mr Wigg's role in the Profumo affair". In fact, Mr Wigg was accused of raising the matter out of "a long standing personal grudge against Profumo" and of "having unearthed a juicy scandal by snooping that would have done credit to a divorce detective."

'In the circumstances the *Sunday Express* recognizes that these false allegations could not be allowed to pass by a self-respecting person without proper redress, and sincerely apologizes to Mr Wigg for any suggestion that the proceedings he brought were misguided.

'It is also desired to make it clear that any reference to other actions by Mr Wigg involve no reflection on their merit.'

Dudley was never out of mind, whatever my other preoccupations.

Towards the end of 1962, the shadow of financial difficulties fell over the respected family firm of John Barnsley & Sons, Ltd., of Netherton, engineers and ironfounders. Within a few hours of a meeting to consider a moratorium, the London representative of one of the largest creditors had threatened legal proceedings which would have killed off a business with a hundred and fifty years of history behind it. Very late at night I received an urgent 'phone call from Mr Jim Barnsley and, immediately, set out on a midnight search for this particular creditor. I was lucky enough to contact him; even luckier to find in him a man of generous spirit who grasped quickly, and sympathized with, the human aspects of the problem.

Ten years earlier the company's overseas markets for lifting tackle had begun to dry up. Confident in the rare skills of their labour force which had been operating worn-out plant, the directors decided to stay in the lifting business, producing large cranes instead of pulley blocks. They made progress, but not fast enough to provide the resources necessary to cover rising capital costs. Fortunately, they secured a unanimous vote for a year's moratorium. They reorganized the business. Mr C. B. J. Barnsley and his cousin, Mr J. R. Barnsley and Mr J. Guest, Technical Director, went out themselves in search of orders; and later Mr Leslie Oliver, an industrialist who had married into the Barnsley family, joined the company and helped to pull it out of the red in the financial year ending March 1964. *The Times* of May 1, 1967, reported that, by May 1965, every penny of debt had been cleared, new equipment had been bought and the old staff re-trained. It was a matter of personal satisfaction to me that my constituents had come through their difficulties and were producing one of the best single girder cranes in the United Kingdom.

Wilson was making rapid progress with the task of consolidating his position as Leader of the Party. Always a well-informed speaker, he emerged as the most formidable debater in the Commons. Outside the House, too, he took a more positive line on public issues than his predecessor had adopted, especially in relation to African affairs. A speech at an anti-Apartheid rally in Trafalgar Square in March was beamed all over Africa, special attention being given to his paraphrase of Lincoln's dictum that nations could not endure half slave, half free, and that the world would have to make up its mind about the abolition of the colour bar. This speech recalled to well-informed Africanists Wilson's plea to the United Nations Havana Conference (November 1947–March 1948) when, as delegate of the Labour

Government, he won the support of fifty-four nations for a Charter to fix 'commodity prices on the basis of equality, buffer stocks and controls to deal with shortages and surpluses without exploitation of either producer or consumer'. The Charter was, and is, one answer to the problem of economic development in countries which, because they pay high interest rates to finance export trade in their basic crops, are unable to pay a living wage to their own labour as well as retain a surplus for investment. The proposal, for which overseas aid and low interest rate loans have provided no effective substitute, was aborted by America's refusal to ratify the Havana Charter.

In the light of Wilson's reputation among Africa leaders, one reaction to the Trafalgar Square speech surprised us. Ghana Radio argued that his insistence on safeguards for the interests of the white minority was the old imperialism in modern guise against which President Kwame Nkrumah's new campaign for African unity and his brain-child, the Organisation of African Unity, was directed. Very probably these matters were in the mind of President Nkrumah when he sent me a pressing invitation to visit him. I knew and liked Nkrumah and had caused some raised eyebrows when, long before he became President, he visited the House of Commons dining-room as my guest. I landed in Accra, where I had served during the war, on Good Friday, 1963. Acceptance of Nkrumah's invitation gave me the pleasure of meeting my old sparring partner, Geoffrey Bing, then adviser to the President, and of reminiscing over our exploits in Parliamentary Opposition.

I was impressed and excited by the enterprise and bustle all around me. A thousand million pound Seven-Year Development Plan had been projected under the guidance of world-famous economists. It sought to achieve among people, of whom only a tiny minority had learned the basic industrial discipline of obeying the clock, an economic break-through such as that reached in highly-developed societies only after very many years of painful experience.

The Volta Dam was taking shape. The project, because of Nkrumah's care for human values, involved probably the greatest exercise in social engineering yet seen on this earth. The Dam project was intended to provide power for the expansion of basic industries like bauxite and agriculture but, unfortunately, it was impossible to use Ghana bauxite for the project and the Government reluctantly agreed that alumina must be imported. Ghana bauxite is still not being used in the smelter and until it is the full value of the Volta project will not be realized. But since, as well as developing bauxite mining and constructing a railway, an alumina smelter will have to be built the capital required will be enormous and so the aluminium industry in Ghana, as elsewhere in the world, remains in the doldrums. Secondary enterprises, apart from a few excellent British ventures, were almost non-existent in my time. The sight of costly computers was exciting; the fact that the more effective application of simple inexpensive techniques, like critical path analysis, were absent, aroused my doubts. For me, a recurring memory was a talk in 1944, about Ghana's post-war problems with a senior military officer responsible for internal security. According to him, post-war reconstruction meant armoured cars to maintain law and order while the returning ex-soldier settled down again within his tribe. Eventually all would be well for the senior military officer and his like, and life would go on again exactly as it had since the dawn of time. My reaction to that in 1944 was: what a hope! By 1963 I knew there was no room for that kind of thinking anywhere in Africa. Africa was awake.

The Ghana Institute of Ideology, devoted to the teaching of Marxian doctrine, might have encouraged the type of experiment in extra-mural education to which Nigerians had responded so eagerly. Instead it spread, on radio and in the Press, jargon slogans which were no substitute for any kind of positive thinking. These slogans were anathema to Nkrumah. He rejected emphatically the Marxian theory of class war in his aims for a better life for Africans. 'In the traditional African society,' he wrote 'no sectional interest could be regarded as supreme; nor did legislative and executive power aid the interest of any particular group. The welfare of the people was supreme.' That was the Ghana I thought I knew and understood. It possessed an effective, simple form of democracy with a built-in social security guaranteeing every man a share in the pot. All men were brothers within a matriarchal society. However, de-tribalization and the drift to the big towns were breaking down this traditional sociological structure and community life was disintegrating.

Probably as an aid in his struggle for power Nkrumah had accepted a constitution drawn up in Whitehall, suitable perhaps to British conditions but alien to African needs and circumstances. I think he was ill-advised, too, in adopting the role of Osageyfo, although I thought I understood his purpose. That purpose was to bring cohesion and control into the Convention People's Party. Many C.P.P. area leaders had assumed the authority of Chiefs without the sustaining and restraining influence of the Councils of Elders, who advised the Chief, made his rulings binding upon all, and removed him from office and authority if he misbehaved. The autocratic rule of British Governors in Colonial days had debased the original function of the Chiefs. They became the agents, not of their people, but of the Imperial power. Osageyfo assumed, subject to the discipline of Parliament, the autocracy of the Governor. He failed, however, to impose an effective discipline upon local Party leaders whose corrupt conduct poisoned the natural grass roots of African society.

Nevertheless, this man did great things for Ghana. For every child of school age in Britain there are, in proportion to the population, two in Ghana and, in addition, a backlog of illiteracy among people avid for education. Nkrumah tackled this giant problem by building schools, providing for the health and nutrition of children and beginning the long haul towards training the skills to make viable the wide scope of the Volta Dam Project, which has etched his name imperishably in the history of his country. He reorganized the port of Tema in a way that, given competent administrative direction, would have achieved important economies and arrested corrupt practices in marketing. He expanded university education, encouraged the study of science, and created a health service. He launched and directed a campaign against mass illiteracy and inspired Ghana's mighty regiment of matrons to lift up the quality of the nation's home life. He instigated new, exciting schemes of community self-development—a traditional idea in Africa. These included voluntary building of community centres, cleaning village and town streets, erecting public lavatories, and the cleansing of rivers of the filth that made them vectors for the malaria-spreading mosquito. He gave Africa a consciousness and a conception of unity. The big proviso in my hope for, and my belief in, a new Ghana arose from the truth that men must learn to walk before they run. Freedom is an appetite that grows on what it feeds on—experience.

I still respect Kwame Nkrumah, a man of physical and intellectual courage, a man of integrity, now exiled in Conakry where, in May 1959, he created a Union with Guinea and planted, with Sekou Touré, the seed of ideas which were to grow into the principle of African Unity. He remains on my short list of personal heroes. His name will live in African history—to quote Sekou Touré—as 'the elder brother of African Unity'.

I was happy to find that the Ghanaian Army had retained British traditions, traditions carried on by a fine body of instructors seconded from Canada. Politics were not the Ghanaian Army's business; the peace and order of the State were their concern. This thesis, which Nkrumah had made the subject of one of his lectures entitled 'Politics are not for Soldiers', lost its meaning on a fateful day early in February, 1966, when Nkrumah and his entire Cabinet left Accra on a visit to Peking and Moscow. No political head remained in Accra to control events and so General Kotoka, then a Colonel, later killed in the coup, seized power and made possible the rise of the dictatorship called the National Liberation Council. After Kotoka's death, Major Afrifa took over. He is a pleasant, well-meaning young man with plenty of drive but little political understanding. Why Nkrumah acted as he did remains a question mark in the unwritten story of one of the fascinating characters of the new Africa.

I had pleasant memories of horse-racing in Ghana. As a Colonel, visiting Achimota early in 1945, I joined three Brigadiers on a visit to Accra Races. We made a series of collective bets, all of which lost while my comrades were away drinking tea with the Governor. Left to my own devices, I bought 'blind' a ticket on the daily double. The first leg, a long shot, won; the second leg, well named *Eighth Army*, also won and I collected one hundred and sixty pounds, much to the chagrin of my tea-drinking friends. On my visit, nineteen years later, I found the totalisator had been mechanised to save labour in a country with thousands of unemployed! But, alas, when I was there the mechanical monster had blown a fuse and the machines issuing tickets did not work. There was racing but no betting. The Chairman of the Ghana Horseracing Board of Control was the late Mr Nartey Nyumutei. His main objective in life was to secure for the Accra Turf Club recognition by our Jockey Club. I took up his cause and remember gratefully that the Jockey Club agreed to his request before Nyumutei, a man of personal charm and probity, died in a motor accident.

Back in London, Ben Parkin, a near neighbour, called on several occasions to discuss scandals he had unearthed about housing conditions in his constituency. Parkin's health had been undermined in his long campaign against Peter Rachman who, by exploiting flaws in the Companies Act and the notorious 1957 Rent Act, terrorised tenants and, in the process, became a millionaire. Parkin prepared a dossier which I regard as one of the most moving social documents of our time. Of course, little was revealed that the Government did not already know. The B.B.C.s *Panorama* and the *Sunday Times*, among others, had done what any responsible Government would have accepted as an action-inspiring hatchet job on a thug who operated as in a Henry Fielding novel of London life two hundred years ago. The charge against the Government was that they deliberately disregarded the truth and, in so doing, sacrificed the health and happiness of ordinary citizens to maintain the market economy in housing.

Harold Wilson, in the Commons on July 22, delivered a speech about these scandals which stirred the conscience of the nation. He stated facts that aroused decent people to a fury of indignation: how a defective drain could be kept going to stink out tenants despite their alleged security of tenure; how tenants who had paid rent were told that, ownership having passed into the hands of Rachman, they must pay again, and were beaten up if they refused; how rent collectors, accompanied by Alsatian dogs and the 'Heavy Glove Gang' were employed to bash tenants and throw their belongings into the street at two hundred and fifty pounds a job. Wilson made a reasonable offer to Housing Minister, Sir Keith Joseph. The Opposition would provide full facilities for the speedy passage of a Bill 'to give powers to take over all the rented property in these zones of dubious ownership, wherever extortion and exploitation is the order of the day and wherever statutory notices are ignored'. It would, of course, be necessary to deal with the respectable banks and insurance companies financing the operations of some rack-renters, but it would not be necessary to pay compensation—Rachman, only one of many racketeers in the business, had never paid any income tax under Tory Government!

Sir Keith Joseph's reply defied satire as well as sanity. These scandals did not flow from the Tory Rent Act of 1957. They were the consequences of the Labour Government's policy of rent control! I would be surprised if, even now, Joseph understands that the 1957 Rent Act was an important factor in the pollution of our environment, which has become, perhaps, the most pervasive and intractable of Britain's human problems.

I found myself gradually becoming ever more actively engaged with Wilson in studying the political strategy to be pursued in the run-up to the General Election. Too many considerations, however, seemed to me to be conditioned by Wilson's reaction to the opinion polls. In my opinion their techniques in devising questions and in analysing answers were still far from reliable. I was not prepared to believe that the conclusions they drew, however honestly, were completely objective; and, of course, the interpretations presented in the Press were often highly subjective. What really mattered was not the results of a Gallup, hiccup, or any other form of poll, but the state of Labour Party opinion. Our rank and file would give gladly all it possessed to produce our maximum vote if we had the right leadership at the right time reinforced by a Parliamentary Labour Party united on policy; views that were to be justified to Labour's cost in the General Election of 1970. With Wilson providing effective leadership, the main problem, as always, was that of unity within the Parliamentary Labour Party.

In March 1961 five Labour M.P.s—Michael Foot, who had succeeded Nye Bevan in the representation of Ebbw Vale, Sydney Silverman, Emrys Hughes, S. O. Davies and William Baxter—had the Whip withdrawn for voting against the Service Estimates. I hold the firm view that there must be limits to dissent in any responsible Party aspiring to power in a political democracy. Nonetheless, Foot, Silverman and Hughes were custodians of the mood and spirit of many active Labour Party members. Their continued exclusion rankled in the minds of some eighty M.P.s, from Chuter Ede on the Right to Swingler on the Left, who were 'the heart of corn' in Parliament and the country. I had worked for the re-admission of the five through the last years of the Gaitskell era and before the vote for the Party leadership. I failed then. I failed again. The attitude of the hard-liners on both sides re-echoed the Independent Labour Party-Fabian Society controversies of sixty years before when George Bernard Shaw asked about an old campaigner who had failed to win a winnable seat in Glasgow: 'What was he there for— to win a seat for Labour, or . . . to give a striking exhibition of that detestation of expediency and compromise . . . which makes his character stand out so statuesquely against the drab background of mere success at the polls?'

Macmillan's last short-lived triumph—the signing of a Test Ban Treaty with Russia and America—was also the last act of positive government in 1963. Conservative activity awaited the return to the Commons of the Prime Minister, Sir Alec Douglas-Home, as Member for Kinross and East Perthshire. On December 10, Sir Gerald Nabarro—who, I always thought, might have risen high in the Tory ranks if he had been a snob and not a man proud of his

humble birth who owed everything to his own gifts of personality—
put down a question asking to what extent public opinion polls conducted between nomination day and polling day had influenced
recent voting at Luton and Kinross. I followed Nabarro's question
by asking Sir Alec, 'Will the Prime Minister also take into account
the amount of pints which he bought the electors during the course
of the campaign?' This sent the adrenalin rushing to the very tip
of Nabarro's massive moustache. He asked if it was in order to allege
that Sir Alec had bought pints for the electors, thereby imputing a
breach of electoral law, and whether Mr Speaker would require the
withdrawal of 'that opprobious suggestion'. The Speaker replied
that he had not heard me.

Entering the House around 2 p.m. next day I found a note from
Nabarro informing me that he intended to raise the matter again.
The Press Gallery was crowded. The kid from Kidderminster had
alerted Fleet Street about his forthcoming knock-out of my very
humble self. Nabarro read out the words I had spoken and continued:

> The purpose of my point of order is to enquire whether it is
> within the rules of order of this House for any Hon. Member to
> impute to another an electoral impropriety involving corrupt
> practice and a contravention of the Representation of the People
> Act, 1949. Mr Speaker, you did not hear the words yesterday,
> but they have now been printed. Though you did not hear them,
> I wrote to you this morning and asked you if you would read
> them, and I hope now that you will be able to rule that they
> are out of order and should be withdrawn.

Mr Speaker replied:

> I regret that it was not possible from this Chair at that
> moment to hear the words used with sufficient precision to rule.
> I know that there have been times when my predecessors have
> diplomatically not heard things. It was not an instance of that
> kind. It was physically impossible to hear the words. Had I
> heard them at the time it would have been my duty to direct
> that they should be withdrawn. At this moment of time I have
> no power so to direct.

I had just intervened when Mr Speaker said he had missed a
word; from the point of view of the Chair I was speaking from the
worst position, acoustically, in the House. I tried again and said:

I used the words referred to by the Hon. Member for Kidderminster. I have not denied it, but I did not say pints of what. It could have been pints of water, or pints of milk but, fortunately, in the *Daily Telegraph* on 30th October, there is a photograph of the Prime Minister drinking with two gentlemen, one of whom, Mr Copeland, said: 'The Prime Minister bought me a pint.' Mr Copeland is seen drinking a pint of beer and the Prime Minister is drinking whisky. The report quotes Mr Copeland as saying that he will vote for the Prime Minister.

I cited a *Daily Mirror* report of October 31, quoted from the *Daily Telegraph*, about a procession to the Amulree Hotel where Colonel and Mrs Haddow had assembled the local gamekeepers and shepherds, all of whom, although they had been given a drink, were too shy to ask the Prime Minister questions. Sir Alec, sensing this, made a brief speech instead and, said Mrs Haddow, 'That was just right. It was lovely,' to which Cassandra of the *Daily Mirror* added: 'It wasn't lovely, it was ruddy marvellous.' Then, after quoting a *Telegraph* interpretation of 'treating' as a corrupt practice under Section 100 of the Representation of the People Act, 1949, to a now hilarious House with most Members, including Sir Alec, laughing and heartily enjoying the discomfiture of Nabarro, I made this submission: 'there is no doubt whatever that the Prime Minister and his friends, in accordance with the feudal practices extant in Scotland, went about buying pints left, right and centre while they drank whisky themselves. I did not allege then, nor do I allege now, that this was a corrupt practice. This is just the way the Prime Minister behaves.

'May I now turn to the Hon. Member for Kidderminster?'

Mr Speaker gave me a gentle but emphatic turndown. I insisted that Nabarro had made a personal attack on me and, although giving me little notice, had alerted the Press. Mr Speaker reiterated his view that in the context in which my words of the previous day had been uttered he would have been bound to ask me to withdraw. He had no power to require their withdrawal now, and we could not continue the discussion. As a back-bencher believing that rules of order should be obeyed by everyone in the House, including the Speaker himself, I retorted, with respect, that if Mr Speaker had asked me yesterday or today to withdraw my remarks I would have refused and would have put down a motion of censure on him. Mr

Speaker replied, 'That would not have deterred me from doing what I thought to be my duty. What I concede to be my duty now is to put an end to this and to proceed.' That meant, in plain English, I had won.

Nabarro's exercise in Press relations had turned round and bitten him. The newspapers got an even better story than they had anticip-

ated. Emmwood, of the *Daily Mail*, who kindly gave me the original, produced a cartoon depicting me pouring a pint of beer over the disconsolate Nabarro. He left both the Chamber and the House and we never saw him again until he returned to the House as representative of another Worcestershire constituency. I was happy he came back. He is colourful as well as controversial, and is more able than many occupants of the Tory Front Bench.

The year 1964 opened on a hopeful note for Labour. In a defence debate on January 16, Wilson outlined a policy putting the subject into perspective both in relation to the country's capacity to assume an effective role abroad and to the financial problems that would face a Labour Government determined to improve living standards at home. Wilson made three points. He accepted the fact that we must continue to operate defence policy under the umbrella of the American Strategic Air Command. We must make our contribution to the defence of the West through N.A.T.O. in conventional terms. With Blue Streak cancelled we should abandon pursuit of an independent nuclear deterrent which did not strengthen the Alliance and which was, therefore, a waste of our economic strength. We should re-negotiate the Macmillan–Kennedy Nassau Agreement on Polaris.

That speech defined a proper place for defence on the agenda of a Labour Government. It eliminated a splitting element within the Labour Party. Indeed, just over a month later, when the Government announced its intention to buy a fifth Polaris, Denis Healey declared that Labour had no interest in Polaris as a contribution to an independent British deterrent. An immediate result of the Wilson speech was that it enabled me to re-open the question of restoring the Whip to Michael Foot and his fellow dissenters. This time I was successful and Foot wrote to thank me for my efforts, saying, 'I realize that you had good reason in the interests of the Party for what you did. But ... such acts of friendship should not pass without a word of gratitude.'

The affairs of the Government did not run so auspiciously. Sir Alec's first act as Prime Minister was the first of several major errors. He sent British troops back into Cyprus, on the invitation of Archbishop Makarios, to shore up the disintegrating peace between Greeks and Turks. He had to refer the problem in mid-February to the United Nations, where he should have sent it in the first place. On January 12, the Zanzibar Government was overthrown, one month after Independence. During January a battalion of the Tanganyika Rifles took control of Dar-es-Salaam and President Nyerere asked for the help of Royal Marine Commandos to mop them up. The Uganda Rifles mutinied at Jinja Barracks and President Milton Obote sent to Nairobi for British troops, while Jomo Kenyatta was calling for assistance to disarm mutineers at Lanet in Kenya. The British tradition of maintaining adequate conventional peace-keeping forces to co-operate with constitutional governments was proving its worth and highlighting the tragedy of its run-down in the Tory retreat from the ideals of Commonwealth.

The Prime Minister visited Washington on February 7, agreeing with President Johnson about American policy in Vietnam in return for American support for Britain in Malaysia. He then, on February 17, told *Panorama* viewers that 'the economy has never been so strong'. The trade figures issued the next day showed an export–import gap of £120 million—the biggest gap on record. When Wilson followed the Prime Minister to Washington, the *Evening Standard*, on March 3, reported that the Labour leader had proposed to hand over the Royal Navy to the United States! Wilson repudiated the astonishing canard on his arrival at London Airport next day, but the unfortunate Sir Alec, out of touch with the news, tried to revive the story in the House of Commons on March 5. Wilson tore a large strip off the bemused Prime Minister and forced an apology.

Meantime, another political scandal was besmirching the Tory image. Late in 1963, the Comptroller and Auditor-General reported that excessive profits of £2,700,000 had been made by the firm of Ferranti on the Bloodhound ground-to-air missile contract. Julian Amery, Minister of Aviation, set up an Inquiry. The possibility that the Inquiry might not operate fast enough to report before the General Election disappeared when, in April 1964, the Public Accounts Committee put the Ferranti excess profit at £4,992,000. The Ministry of Aviation was far from blameless in a matter which began in 1959 with prices fixed at that year's level. Reviewing these prices in 1960 the Ministry estimated labour costs at £1,305,000 and then multiplied this figure by a factor of 5.5 'to reach a figure for overhead'. The actual figure of labour costs, when the work had been performed, turned out to be £574,000. Sir Richard Way admitted the estimating failure but blamed the firm for not admitting the facts. Mr Sebastian de Ferranti—not to be confused with his brother Mr

B. R. V. Z. de Ferranti, a Tory Junior Minister until October 1962 —argued that the figures were fixed in good faith and that under a fixed price contract manufacturers invariably took all the risks and so were entitled, in addition to normal profit, to any available surplus. Amery's Inquiry, under Sir John Lang, reported on July 28. Its conclusion was that Ferranti's profit amounted to £5,772,964 or eighty-two per cent on cost. Ferranti agreed to repay £4,250,000. Tory honour was satisfied. Public confidence in Tory competence reached a new low and was pinned there firmly by other revelations from Amery. Concorde costs were to have been between £75 million and £80 million; they now amounted to £140 million. B.O.A.C., forced by the Government to subsidise private enterprise by purchasing V.C.10s which, having engines at the rear, were uneconomic, dropped its South American routes. These routes were kindly donated by the Government to the privately owned British United Airlines which was left free to purchase any planes it wanted.

I planned to re-visit Egypt during the 1964 Easter recess. I was drawn back there by nostalgic memories—'he who drinks of the water of the Nile shall surely return'. Relations between Britain and Egypt were far from cordial. What friendship and understanding did exist was due to the work of Sir Harold Beeley, our Ambassador in Cairo, who did his best, despite many difficulties, to build a bridge between Egypt and Britain. Sir Harold had a difficult, if not impossible, task. Nasser had been gradually sucked into a full-scale intervention in the Yemen. The South Arabian Federation, instrument of British control of Aden, our 'Gibraltar of the Middle East', demanded British help in March 1964, to check Nasser-inspired activities in the Radfan Mountains. Nasser told me conditions in the South Arabian Federation were those of the Stone Age. This view was confirmed by Sir Kennedy Travaskis, subsequently High Commissioner to the South Arabian Federation, who wrote in his *Shades of Amber** that the hinterland was 'a microcosm of our former Indian Empire. Like British India, the Colony of Aden was British administered. The protectorate was a conglomerate of separate autonomous Arab "states" whose "rulers" were linked to Britain by treaties on the model of India's princes.' Sir Kennedy wrote of Britain's rule, 'Only so divided and so subservient a population could have tolerated such sluggish progress for so long and with such

* Sir Kennedy Travaskis, *Shades of Amber*, (Hutchinson 1968).

indifference.' The inhabitants of both Aden and the Federation had reached the point of being 'neither amenable nor submissive'. Sir Kennedy also endorsed Nasser's description of Britain's legacy in the Protectorate in these words: 'After nearly a hundred years of British influence and protection it remained as backward and chaotic as ever.'

Nasser told me that Britain organized the regular smuggling of arms across the undemarcated Yemeni border to supply tribesmen with weapons to fight the Egyptians. Arms were transported by camels and the only solution open to him was to shoot the camels from helicopters, thus halting the traffic without killing human beings. Nasser's version is supported in some degree by Sir Kennedy Travaskis's account of the Royal Air Force attack on the Fort of Harib on March 28, 1964. He says the attack was sparked off by an Egyptian helicopter which machine-gunned a Federal Guard Post and some grazing camels close to the frontier at Jabal Bulaik. The R.A.F. attack was made after warning leaflets had been dropped fifteen minutes before eight Hunter jet aircraft went in with rockets and cannon fire. A High Commission spokesman was certain there were no civilian casualties. Another estimate was that ten Yemeni soldiers were killed and an unspecified number wounded. It was a wanton act, a foolish expression of the British Prime Minister's long since outdated idea of showing the flag and teaching the 'wogs' a lesson. Yemen requested a meeting of the Security Council of United Nations on April 1, claiming that twenty-five people, mostly women and children, had been killed and a number wounded. On April 9, the Security Council passed by nine votes to nil a resolution, sponsored by Morocco and the Ivory Coast, which: (1) condemned reprisals as incompatible with the purposes and principles of the United Nations; (2) deplored the British military action at Harib; (3) deplored all attacks and incidents which had occurred in the area; (4) called upon Yemen and the United Kingdom to 'exercise the maximum restraint in order to avoid further incidents and to restore peace in the area'; and (5) requested the United Nations Secretary General to 'use his good offices to try to settle outstanding issues in agreement with the two parties'.

Britain, of course, did not vote. America refrained because its proposals for a more comprehensive condemnation of attacks and reprisals was not acceptable to the Security Council. The wanton use of British air power won only the contempt of civilized opinion

throughout the world and finally destroyed any standing that might
have enabled us to retain 'our last and, perhaps, our most important foothold in the Middle East'. Sir Kennedy Travaskis agreed
that the attack on Harib was our biggest mistake—he ought to know!

When I arrived in Cairo on Easter Monday night I found at my
hotel invitations to call on President Nasser and on the British
Ambassador, Sir Harold Beeley. I have recounted in a previous
chapter a personal impression I formed of Nasser and the purpose
inspiring his policy. I found him disturbed but not surprised by the
folly of Harib—that was what he had come to expect from Whitehall.
We discussed British politicians and soldiers involved in Middle
East affairs. Nasser expressed a special kind of disregard for Eden,
and that is putting it very mildly. He respected our soldiers and
paid tribute to Field Marshal Lord Harding; he said that he never
had any difficulty when dealing with our soldiers, but he always
looked for broken promises and a failure to meet obligations when
dealing with British politicians. The sudden death of Gamal Abdel
Nasser on September 28, 1970, gave me a sense of personal grief
and political shock. He had become a giant figure in our contem-
porary world, strangely lacking outstanding men. His passing
endangers the promise of Arab unity to which he devoted his life.
He was perhaps the last remaining restraint on the spread of Soviet
influence, which he was forced to accept reluctantly by the folly of
Suez and what followed. I can only hope and pray that Nasser's
influence lives on to prevent the Middle East from becoming a new
cockpit of world politics.

Nasser was not anti-British. He wanted better relations with Britain
and if successive British Governments had wanted the same thing
Anglo-Egyptian relations would, I believe, have flourished and
Britain's influence in the Middle East would have grown. When I
met our Ambassador, Sir Harold Beeley, he was eager to learn
Egyptian reactions to the Harib incident. He told me that contact
with informed Egyptian opinion was never easy but the Harib incident
had cut him off from those sources he was most anxious to cultivate.
The Harib attack was bound to worsen Anglo-Egyptian relations and
the decision had been taken without any communication whatsoever
between the Foreign Office in London and the British Embassy in
Cairo. He learned of the R.A.F. attack on Harib only after it had
happened. I told Sir Harold that no Egyptian with whom I had
talked in Cairo had failed to recall the Douglas-Home broadcast

from Canada on February 11, 1963 when, speaking as Foreign Secretary, he said, 'I rather wish they—the Americans—had allowed us to deal with the Egyptians as we wanted to do at Suez.' Fateful words of a foolish man. He, with Sir Anthony Eden had ended the era of Empire and Commonwealth with two bangs and one final whimper.

When I came home I arranged for Harold Wilson to meet Arnold Goodman and, together, we brought representatives of the Association of Cinematograph, T.V. and Allied Technicians (A.C.C.T.) together with the Independent T.V. companies and helped to settle a television strike that threatened to go on indefinitely.

Another pleasant diversion from the doldrums of Tory inertia in the House of Commons brought me into proud association with The Cairn erected at the top of Ben Nevis as a war memorial and believed to be the first such war memorial built after World War II. The original plaque had been removed, presumably stolen by vandals, and the Boy Scouts of Dudley, learning from their friends in Fort William that the American Boy Scout movement desired to add a memorial stone to The Cairn, decided to replace the missing plaque. The new tablet, of solid granite weighing one hundred and forty pounds, had been prepared in Dudley. The problem of my friend, Bert Bissell, M.B.E., then Dudley's Probation Officer, was to get these loads to the top of Ben Nevis for insertion in The Cairn in time for the ceremony. I sought the aid of the Royal Air Force. They generously used their technical skill to deliver the loads by helicopter, thus contributing to the creation of an enduring memorial to an unforgettable past.

Sir Alec announced on September 11, that he would lead the nation into a 'New Britain' after the next General Election, fixed for October 15. Three days later, the Labour *Daily Herald* appeared for the last time and its successor *The Sun*, widely publicized as the first daily newspaper born of the age we live in, rose wan and warmless as a winter moon. Despite the loss of any effective voice for Labour in the Press, all the signs indicated that a new man would take over in No. 10 Downing Street. Harold Wilson's relations with his colleagues even those with volatile George Brown, had become easier. Opinion Polls encouraged speculation of a majority of between seventy and eighty seats.

I set myself my usual task of undertaking as complete a personal canvass as possible of Dudley and Stourbridge. I enjoyed meeting my young Tory opponent, David Howell, an economist and journalist, for whom I prophesied a distinguished political career, although not as Member for Dudley. Seven days before polling I had the great good fortune to break my leg. While talking to two ladies I turned to greet a third, slipped to the ground and sustained a Potts fracture. The leg was put in plaster and I was sent out of hospital with instructions to take things easy for a couple of days. That 'gammy' leg made front page news in the Wolverhampton *Express and Star*. Several national newspapers printed pictures of me in my chair of pain. After hobbling around on crutches and sticks for a few days I returned to hospital for examination and found my injury providing material for the television cameras. There was pain and inconvenience, but I am certain that the best advice I can offer any Parliamentary candidate anywhere is 'break your neck and hope for the best'. The one proviso would be: do it four or five days before polling day; a week is a little too long. My majority was 10,270.

Sir Alec Douglas-Home, short on oratorical ability and even shorter on policy, contented himself with meeting the people. Harold Wilson addressed himself to the Labour Movement and through it to the nation at great public meetings. The result was dramatic. Labour polled 12,205,000 votes, 200,000 more than the Tories, although 10,000 fewer than in 1959, and captured 317 seats against 258 in 1959. The Tory vote fell by nearly 1,750,000 and their representation dropped from 365 seats to 304. Our small majority was due to the massive rise in the Liberal poll from 1,638,571 in 1959 to just over 3,000,000 in 1964—a tribute to Joe Grimond's brilliant leadership—although the number of Liberal seats rose only from six to nine. The seats lost to Labour by the intervention of Liberal candidates—they numbered 365 against 216 in the previous election—made all the difference between a comfortable working majority and our tiny overall majority of four.

Chapter Fifteen: Paymaster-General

I arrived in London just after Harold Wilson had accepted the Queen's Commission to form a Government. I contacted him by telephone and arranged to accompany him to his Hampstead home later in the evening. We talked about the composition of the Government, and he asked me to become Paymaster-General and to work with him at No. 10 Downing Street. He wanted me to assist him in a personal capacity on a range of subjects connected with public and Parliamentary business, and to help him with security matters.

In forming his Government the new Prime Minister had been influenced by the need to take account of the Party's choice of members of the Shadow Cabinet. I thought he was too kind to some colleagues who, besides being anti-Wilson men, did not appear on past form to measure up to the posts he proposed to offer them. I would have gladly seen jobs going to men like Michael Foot and Ian Mikardo, and I thought a vigorous, hard-working Left-Winger like Jack Mendelson had earned a chance to show whether he could shoulder front-bench responsibility. Wilson certainly wanted Foot in his Government. He delegated to me the task of telling Foot he hoped to place him at a later date. The real trouble, I thought, was Wilson's fear that if he failed to dot the i's and cross the t's of Left Wing hopes and policies he might find himself faced with resignations at a very early stage of the Government's life.

Two of his choices were obvious in view of the Government's small majority: Bert Bowden had been a hard-working Chief Whip in Opposition and his selection as Leader of the House, supported by Ted Short as Chief Whip, gave the Government the authority the Parliamentary situation would demand.

The *Annual Register* described the Labour Government's inheritance as 'ghastly'. That was an exact description. The balance of payments deficit was worse than anticipated, and stagnation in the economy indicated that even under favourable world conditions the struggle to convert a balance of payments deficit into a substantial surplus would be a long, hard haul. And world conditions were ominous. President de Gaulle was piling up reserves of gold as a means of countering the spread of American influence—'neo-colonialism' was the word being used—through French industry. France was said to possess more gold than was buried in the vaults of Fort Knox. President Johnson was retaliating by curbing American investment in a world sorely needing development funds and increased liquidity. Confidence in the reserve currencies of dollars and sterling was being eroded. And because, under the Tories, Britain had earned a reputation as the 'sick man of Europe', the pound suffered most in the battle of the giants.

I accepted Wilson's view that we should not devalue. I saw force in the argument that if we had devalued immediately many of our problems would have been transferred, without warning, to the Americans. This would have angered President Johnson and endangered future Anglo-American co-operation. There also was the weighty fact that sudden devaluation could have estranged permanently those countries, some much poorer than ourselves, which, having deposited their reserves in London, would have lost a large slice of their sterling assets overnight. Certainly the decision not to devalue was a mistake viewed in retrospect and exclusively from the angle of our economic self-interest. Yet even now I am not sure that it would have been politically possible for the Labour Government to devalue immediately. Almost the only thing that can be said with certainty is that Wilson's solicitude about President Johnson's reactions was a misjudgment. I saw no sign that President Johnson ever regarded Wilson's policies with the respect they were supposed to have earned. We paid a high price, a very high price in economic terms, for nothing.

The decision not to devalue was followed by action eloquently expressing the compassion which Labour has always felt towards the old and needy. Despite doubts and a narrow Parliamentary majority an increase in social service benefits was announced. This did not increase the confidence with which the new Administration was regarded by foreign holders of sterling. The Government sought to hold the position by increasing the Bank Rate, only to be met with a run on sterling so serious that, soon, the prospect of forced devaluation had to be faced. Both inside and outside the Government pressures built up for one or other of two courses of action—to devalue or savagely, traumatically to deflate the economy across the board. But Wilson had a political ace to play, and within two months of taking office he played it. If his hand were forced he could call an immediate General Election which he would have won, and handsomely. I believe Lord Cromer, the Governor of the Bank of England, was left in no doubt about Wilson's determination to go to the country if he felt he had to. And so Cromer rallied the financial centres of the world and by mid-December, 1964, he had three thousand million dollars in standby credits for the defence of the pound.

The reactions of the Chancellor of the Exchequer to our troubles at that time bowled me over. Jim Callaghan's lips quivered, his hands shook he had no idea what had hit him. A gathering at Chequers during the November economic crisis lives in my memory. I remember vividly Callaghan mumbling, 'We can't go on. We shall have to devalue.' I decided that Callaghan was not the man to be Chancellor, and I am sure that Wilson and Brown reached the same conclusion. Callaghan was appointed as a result of Wilson's fatal tendency to appease rivals and because he was impressed by Callaghan's ability as an articulate extrovert to deliver, with nice rotundity of phrase, well-sounding speeches generally devoid of content. A few months later, when he got his 1965 Budget through, Callaghan was telling the country that 'not even the most doubting Thomas believes that the pound is likely to be devalued'. His economic and political *alter ego* was Lord Cromer. When he became Chancellor and constantly referred to 'Rowlie' I thought he was talking about a relative or a close friend; it was quite a while before I realized he was referring to the Governor of the Bank of England whom Harold Macmillan had chosen for the job in 1961. In contrast Brown was all for plunging into the task of working out a National Plan to effect a real relationship between prices and income, with industrial reorganization at its core. Through all his ups and downs Brown came closer than any member of Wilson's Administration to understanding the dream of some old Clydeside politicians—that democracy in Britain needs a coalition between Labour and Industry to control Finance. That fact explains why he won the confidence of many enlightened industrialists.

My faith in Wilson in those first troubled weeks of the Labour Government remained unshaken. He was equipped, I thought, to become one of the great Prime Ministers of history. His swift intelligence reinforces a powerful armoury of attributes. His calmness of spirit enables him to bear all the pressures of an onerous twenty-four-hour a day job. He had already proved his flair for political cut and thrust and his capacity as a speechmaker and tactician was well established. His personal habits are temperate and disciplined. He enjoys plain living, with the occasional luxury of a cigar and a drop of brandy. He is not interested in the high life. He observes rigidly his own routine for keeping fit – an occasional round of golf, a walk with the dog and, always that lively interest in the fortunes of Huddersfield Town football and Yorkshire cricket. He took into No. 10 the treasured values of work-a-day provincial England, values unknown to some of the rootless, social-climbing place-seekers with whom he surrounded himself. His hard provincial streak found early expression in his determination not to exercise the Prime Minister's powers of patronage for political services rendered.

Wilson was greatly blessed in the qualities of Mary Wilson. She rose gracefully and with natural dignity to every public occasion. She brought many fine assets to the Prime Minister and to her job at No. 10, including that of creating friendly relations among the wives of members of the Government, always and everywhere a vital element in the unity of men engaged in great endeavours.

Wilson had been fascinated by his visit to the late John Kennedy. He had been enthralled by the White House set-up. The President's exposition of consensus politics enchanted him. A progressive leader who had captured the middle ground in politics, so the argument ran, could make Capitalism work so efficiently that universal prosperity would end class struggle and usher in the golden age of a society based on a meritocracy and universality of opportunity. This concept inspired Wilson's dream of the 'hundred dynamic days'. His own ministerial experience had not taught him what Manny and I learned the hard way at the Ministry of Fuel and Power: swift decisive action demands foresight in anticipating events and ferocity of purpose in dealing with them.

The British governmental system, except in time of war, is ill adapted to formulating long-term policies. It is concerned essentially with matters demanding immediate attention because of pressure of events and the availability of Parliamentary time to introduce legislation to deal with them. In human affairs it is essential to have one man, or a small group of men, who, being sufficiently detached from day-to-day happenings, are able to concentrate on long-term strategy and planning. Neither the British governmental system, nor Wilson himself, was equipped for the task of planning future strategy or action. Moreover, with its frail Parliamentary majority the Government, whatever other problems faced it, could look only one Parliamentary week ahead. To effect a new style of political command, Wilson would have had to make radical changes in the system and, indeed, to have altered his own outlook and mental make-up. He spoke often enough about 'purposeful decisions' and 'the smack of firm government'. That, I was to learn, was Harold Wilson in the role of Walter Mitty, looking in the mirror at the man he would like to have been or thought he was. This political dream world as I saw it develop was, I thought, shared by Mrs Williams. Like every energetic secretary she became increasingly accustomed to taking day-to-day decisions on behalf of her employer. Now ensconced in No. 10 it seemed to me she failed to realise that action on behalf of the Prime Minister was very different from the business of working for the Leader of the Opposition. She now gradually came to take on responsibilities which I thought extended beyond those appropriate to a personal secretary and to behave towards myself, among others, as if she were a political force in her own right and a power to be reckoned with.

Another chilling fact was that, perhaps to a greater extent than any of his modern predecessors in office, Wilson was engaged in a perpetual balancing act to ensure that on foreseeable Cabinet issues he would not be left in a minority. Almost every senior Minister had voted against him in the election for the Party leadership. In accordance with custom, he mulled over the selection of his junior Ministers with Bowden, Short, Brown and Callaghan, to get the right balance of Party influence. Selection with a pin might have been preferable!

From the driving seat the Prime Minister can persuade and, if he is ruthless enough, sack Ministers. Yet although a Minister can be cajoled or cowed, especially if he is served by an able Permanent Secretary he can influence profoundly the implementation of policy despite Cabinet decisions. In his own Department, if he has guts, the Minister is lord of all he surveys. The Cabinet Secretary, sharing the Prime Minister's central role, has only limited power to drive policies through. He can persuade and educate the Civil Service, but he cannot issue orders over and above Cabinet decisions, and the interpretations of these decisions are subject to human vagaries and impulse. The system works. When Ministers and Permanent Secretaries are of high calibre, it works well. What it often fails to provide is the initiative and the studies essential for the formulation of long-term policies. A further weakness is that although the content of policies may be well defined, their implementation under the pressure of constantly changing events frequently lacks effective supervision. This means in practice that the Cabinet decides but Departments proceed as they think best—provided the disparity is not too noticeable.

In Opposition I thought I understood one of Harold Wilson's greatest needs. This was for a colleague who could take the products of his superbly questing mind, research them, and then formulate the results as material for future policies. Such activity, I considered, would provide the framework of proposals for the Shadow Cabinet and for the Government when we took office. As Prime Minister commanding a notably loyal and efficient staff, Wilson would still require this help; even a Prime Minister must know and understand the mood and spirit of his Party's reaction to policy. I laboured hard to serve Wilson in this capacity, and it was pleasant work in which we always co-operated easily. Indeed, we often chuckled to discover how smoothly our thoughts dovetailed without detailed discussion or argument. My single misgiving was that Wilson, supremo in the arts of Parliamentary debate and Opposition tactics, was instinctively disinclined to take long views, especially on economic issues. He is essentially a pragmatist; and pragmatism, if you are constantly below deck having a chat with the crew, is dangerous in rocky seas— the more so if you are disinclined to act before the crew have taken a decision.

On January 22, 1965, the Government sustained a body blow. The Foreign Secretary, Patrick Gordon Walker, lost the Leyton by-election. He had achieved the distinguished record of losing two safe Labour seats within three months! In October, 1964, the Labour majority at Leyton was 7,926; Gordon Walker converted it into a Conservative victory of 205. I was with the Prime Minister in his sitting-room when a re-count was announced on the radio. 'My God,' cried Wilson, 'we have lost the seat!' I knew that Gordon Walker was not a strong candidate; he was my neighbour at Smethwick and I had seen at first hand how he had handled the race issue, first by pretending it did not exist and when that line was played out by shying away from the problem. In Leyton he made history by becoming the first Parliamentary candidate to conduct an election campaign from the back of a van. 'His voice,' according to the *Annual Register*, 'echoed forlornly from the loud-speaker in the empty furniture-van from which he campaigned, and no-one in Leyton listened'. Bob Edwards, M.P., another political neighbour of mine and a first-class propagandist, offered to take his car and loud-speaker to Leyton to support Gordon Walker. He was told he was not wanted. Gordon Walker's tactics were to play the election down. Perhaps he thought that the mere fact that the Foreign Secretary, the Right Honourable Patrick Gordon Walker, was giving Leyton the privilege of voting for him was enough.

Following Leyton, Wilson and Brown decided I must look at the organizational problems of East Grinstead and Salisbury by-elections which were then pending. This was a daunting prospect. Both were safe Conservative seats. I had to recognize that responsibility for running by-elections lay with the National Agent, Miss Sara Barker, and her able staff at Transport House. Although they had not done well at Leyton they could not be expected to welcome interference from a member of the Government, and particularly one who might look at the prospects with a critical eye. However, I knew my Wilson and my Brown. The only thing to do was to get on with the job knowing that if anything went wrong I would be hung out to dry. I sought to persuade Miss Barker and her colleagues to pile all we had into Salisbury and to let East Grinstead 'go for a Burton'. Inquiries revealed that some local Parties were planning to send people to give support to the campaign. Where I could, I induced them to concentrate on Salisbury, while urging Members of Parliament to put their shoulders to the wheel. Charles Loughlin led many of his fellow M.P.s into action. Their arrival gave extra zest to a fine constituency Party. The tactics paid off. Labour's vote at Salisbury rose from 34.4 per cent at the General Election to 37.4 per cent, whereas at East Grinstead the Labour vote had been 19.8 per cent at the General Election and sank to 13.5 per cent at the by-election. The results proved that enthusiastic workers with a sense of purpose and good organization do produce political dividends. Salisbury, after the rout at Leyton, cheered up the hard-pressed Parliamentary Labour Party.

When I agreed to join the Wilson Government as Paymaster-General I realized I was cutting myself off from the House of Commons. I knew, also, that I would be assailed by the Tories and would not lack critics in my own Party. However, I was sixty-four and I had no political ambitions. Thus the fact that my general political position would be weakened did not worry me. Twenty years in the Commons under Manny Shinwell's tuition had taught me how to look after myself in a scrap and how to accept the ups and downs of political life. I comforted myself with the reflection that in our democracy a man can achieve much provided he seeks no credit for his work. I wanted a Labour Government, and a Labour Government that would succeed; my joy would be in its success. I knew Wilson well enough to understand the need for somebody near him who would speak fearlessly and would hold up a mirror from time to time. He did not want a crony. He wanted a colleague and trusted friend linking him with the outside world with which all Prime Ministers inevitably lose touch.

Looking back those first few months at No. 10 possessed a nightmarish quality. Wilson beset with great political problems and hampered by the narrowest of parliamentary majorities had much of his time taken up by political staff difficulties. Overwork, insufficient sleep and ever-increasing strain took their toll and the Wilson of 1967 was not the Wilson I knew in 1964. He displayed the methodology of a man never strong in his ability to take and implement decisions and who was beginning to weaken under the pressures around him. By 1967 there was no doubt that certain aspects of life in Downing Street had assumed a total unreality. This was in my view largely brought about by the fatigue of the Prime Minister, a condition which inevitably makes the facing of facts more difficult. Hence uncomfortable facts were pushed aside in favour of rose-tinted assumptions. In this attitude the Prime Minister was I thought encouraged by Mrs Williams. I am convinced that if Wilson had brought to the 1970 election the vigorous down-to-earth fact appreciating qualities that had won him the two previous elections, the Labour Party would still be in power at this moment of writing. This saddens me for I am certain Harold Wilson could have become what I always dreamed he would, the greatest Prime Minister of this century. But it was not to be. The increasing disquiet I felt at No. 10 was shared by many. It became all too clear that civil servants and ministerial colleagues had a formidable competitor for the Prime Minister's ear in Mrs Williams. Unfortunately her growing influence was not in my view always exercised with wisdom or discretion. It often disturbed the very competent private office in No. 10 and spread unease among men and women of great ability and complete loyalty. On the Prime Minister's political staff, several of whom had been transferred from Transport House, were some who also became unhappy and it became part of my job to dry their tears.

As I saw it, the influence exerted by Mrs Williams inside No. 10 was great and pervasive, for there was no doubt the Prime Minister rated her opinions as important and on many issues her reaction markedly influenced his thinking. Although I kept as far away from Mrs Williams as possible, clashes were inevitable. For example, I remember an encounter between Harold Wilson, Mrs Williams and myself. I wished to raise a matter of a confidential nature. I told Wilson I would not talk about it in front of Mrs Williams. Wilson courteously asked if she would mind leaving. She flounced out, obviously in a very bad temper. Mrs Williams had behaved in a similar manner on other occasions when I would not discuss confidential or delicate matters in her presence but I took little notice, for I thought she exaggerated the extent of her influence.

The office of Paymaster General was created in 1835 by the amalgamation of the separate posts of the Paymaster of the Forces, Treasurer of the Navy, Treasurer of the Ordnance, and Paymaster of Chelsea Hospital, there being added in 1848 the post of Paymaster of Civil Services. The office, in effect, is a non-clearing bank, receiving payment for the credit of Departments, including monies voted by Parliament, and paying on their behalf all sums chargeable to the respective Vote or Fund. The list of my predecessors shines with names like Walpole, William Pitt, Lord North, Burke, Canning, Richard Brinsley Sheridan, Lord Macaulay, the Duke of Marlborough, and my own favourite political nit-wit, living Parliamentarians excepted. He was Sir Thomas Winnington who, in the 1740s, objected to newspaper reporting of Parliamentary proceedings on the ground that such reports would make men inside the House responsible for their actions to voters outside the House! In modern times the post of Paymaster General had been occupied by Arthur Henderson as Labour Adviser to the Coalition in World War I, Earl Winterton, Lord Hankey and Lord Cherwell, who combined it with other appointments of a 'secret nature', Sir Walter Monckton and Reginald Maudling. On the whole, not bad company, and certainly Tories never pretended that the Office was a sinecure while a Tory occupied it.

My arrival at No. 10 was neither understood nor accepted by the Private Office. I had served a fair apprenticeship as Manny's P.P.S., first at the Ministry of Fuel and Power, where I learned a great deal from an able and wise Permanent Secretary, Sir Donald Ferguson; and later, at the War Office, where I had enjoyed the privilege of seeing how the Civil Service worked under the direction of Sir Eric Speed and Sir George Turner. On arrival at No. 10 I was given as an office a room with three doors. One door opened into a large room with a 'loo' in the corner. Two doors, opening outwards, had no keys. Having no Private Secretary, whenever I left my room I had to take sensitive papers to the Private Office for safe keeping or carry them in my pocket. This office problem eventually was resolved by my being allocated a pleasant room in No. 70 Whitehall.

I discussed the provision of a Private Secretary and asked for Noel Fish, who had served with me in the Army and was now in the Civil Service. His transfer to No. 10 as a Private Secretary would, I was told, create difficulties. I was experienced enough not to press the point; my sparrow could have had a very rough time among the canaries! So I deferred and accepted Reginald McKenna, formerly in the office of the present Chancellor of the Exchequer when Anthony Barber was Economic Secretary to the Treasury.

McKenna was a Higher Executive Officer. This was a sign that my position in No. 10 did not rank high in the eyes of the Civil Service. Soon I learned McKenna had not been granted a Private Secretary's allowance. That intrigued me. It was as significant as my early difficulties about accommodation and the absence of pictures on my walls! I asked that McKenna be granted a Private Secretary's allowance. This, I was told, was impossible for the most formidable of all reasons governing British public life: it had never happened before. No member of the Executive Class had ever been granted a Private Secretary's allowance. I suggested, in view of McKenna's excellent service and the care with which he had been chosen for me, that here was an opportunity to create a precedent. The next move in the game was a proposal to discuss the matter, to which I agreed readily. It was then suggested that, in the circumstances, it would be better if McKenna were replaced by another Private Secretary drawn from the Administrative Grade. I pleaded that McKenna and I had settled down together; his high intelligence and his desire to help me indicated that it would be unfair to move him. Difficulties about giving Private Secretary's allowances to the Executive Class were again outlined. I sympathized with all the apparently insurmountable obstacles and particularly with the argument that it had never happened before. Nevertheless, I insisted that it would be impossible for me to perform the tasks the Prime Minister might require of me in relation to other Departments if I visited them as the only Minister in Whitehall whose Private Secretary was the only Private Secretary without the appropriate allowance. That important fact was bound to become known. If I were to remain as Paymaster-General, McKenna must receive a Private Secretary's allowance. He got it.

When I ceased to be Paymaster-General, and McKenna returned to Departmental duties, he retained the Private Secretary's allowance which pleased me greatly. Many moons later I ran into a Permanent Secretary who congratulated me on securing the Private Secretary's allowance for a member of the Executive Class: something for which he had been striving for years! McKenna served me well during my three exciting years in No. 10.

On November 12, 1964, the Prime Minister in reply to questions, defined my duties to the House as follows:

> My Rt. Hon. Friend, the Paymaster-General, will carry out the duties which are assigned to him from time to time. It is a long established practice not to specify these in detail in the ordinary way, but the House will wish to know that my Rt. Hon. Friend will answer questions about the co-ordination of the Home Information Services. . . . the position has always been as it was stated by my Noble Friend Lord Attlee in 1948. I quote his words: 'In the appointment of a Minister either without Portfolio or with small Departmental duties it is not the custom to detail, except in certain cases, the particular duties assigned to that Minister'.

The simple point that, as Paymaster-General, I was responsible for answering questions about the co-ordination of the Home Information Services never penetrated the minds of Tory M.P.s who sought to embarrass me with questions about the Information Services of individual Departments. Each Minister, of course, retained responsibility for his Department. I was responsible only for answering questions about overall co-ordination. I enjoyed giving as much as I got to the aspiring 'mickey-takers', one of whom enquired if I thought my new post paid as good a dividend as the last one I held with the Racecourse Betting Control Board. I replied, 'If the Hon. and gallant Member's innuendo means that I profited personally from the R.B.C.B. he knows perfectly well that not only did I take no salary, but that I never even claimed expenses.' Another Tory asked what official invitations, as Chairman of the Governors, I had received to visit the Royal Hospital, Chelsea, during the previous six months. He followed up my answer of 'None, Sir' with what he regarded as a loaded supplementary: 'If the Paymaster-General ever went there again would he tell the pensioners there that he is against pensions for the very old and that he took steps to prevent discussion in the House of a Bill designed to give pensions to very old pensioners?' This was my answer:

> If I have the good fortune to go to The Royal Hospital, Chelsea, either as a visitor or a pensioner, for which I have the honour to be eligible, I shall at least have gone there more frequently than did my predecessors, of whom there have been six during the last ten years, for three of them never visited it at all and three visited it only five times. In my fifteen months of being Chairman of the Governors I have visited it five times.

I was speaking from memory of course, and I was inaccurate in speaking of six predecessors. There were only five, between whom only five visits were made.

My brief as Paymaster-General and Minister without Portfolio precluded—and how I hated it!—participation in Parliamentary debates. On March 25, 1965, the House considered the Consolidated Fund Bill which, in accordance with custom, provided Members with an opportunity of raising a variety of issues. The next day was a Friday, and as the long hours ticked away the Tory Opposition became frightened. They had planned, for that Friday, the Second Reading of a National Insurance Bill designed to pay pensions to old people who did not qualify under the existing Insurance Acts. The Opposition knew that if consideration of the Consolidated Fund Bill went on too long the House would be unable to meet on the Friday, and there would be no chance to consider the Private Member's Bill.

The Tories held the power for thirteen years, from 1951 to

1964, to introduce such a Bill, but they had not done so. Indeed, they had opposed a similar measure proposed from the Labour benches. Now, suddenly, they decided to extend their new-found compassion to the poor and needy and old in the hope of embarrassing the Government. Tory compassion had become a cheap vote winner, and the continuing consideration of the Consolidated Fund Bill would thwart them of a clever political victory.

I was paired, and had not intended to stay in the House. The Tory antics, however, amused me, and the longer the debate went on the more interested I became in their capacity to sustain their humbug. During the proceedings, Quintin Hogg protested against what he described as a filibuster, although the debate on the Consolidated Fund Bill was proceeding quite normally and, according to one Friday morning newspaper circulating long before Selwyn Lloyd rose at 9.42 a.m. to move the Adjournment, 'Mr Hogg gathered up his papers and swept out, chuckling'. So he had his sleep and had made headlines in the Press while the wicked Socialists were doing down poor people neglected by the Tories for over thirteen years!

When Selwyn Lloyd moved the motion to Adjourn the House I was the only Minister on the Front Bench. George Brown had left the House, and neither the leader of the House nor the Chief Whip was present. Thus the task of replying fell to me. Having no advice about the Government's policy I decided that the best defence was attack. It was obvious from the numbers of Tories who had returned to the House after a good night's sleep that the Opposition ploy was to bring the proceedings on the Consolidated Fund Bill to an end so that the Private Member's Bill, designed to embarrass the Government, could be considered.

I spelled out in detail the first duty of any Government, especially a Government with our minuscule majority: that duty is to control the agenda and time-table of parliamentary business. I had a good time delivering a speech that covered columns 1105 to 1121 of Hansard and was peppered with innumerable fatuous points of order and interruptions. When the division was called, being paired, I could not vote, but I had enjoyed my first and last Ministerial speech as much as any that preceded it. I ought in fairness to add that when Edward Heath's Government was elected in 1970 its first action was to introduce a Bill implementing the Private Member's Bill of 1964. Better nineteen years late than never!

The Wedgwood collection at the Hermitage, Leningrad

On the Moscow underground

At Kempton Park

Lord and Lady Wigg

The lessons on procedure I spelled out would not have come amiss to some Labour Ministers of long experience. Callaghan's first Budget did many useful things. It ended the scandal of 'expense-account' living, which cost the State more in lost tax revenue than would have financed the new Tory compassion for the aged poor several times over. It introduced Capital Gains Tax and a Corporation Tax provided an incentive to plough back profits into essential investments. The urgent need of the Government, however, was for the simplest kind of Budget compatible with national requirements and Government control of the Order Paper. The 1965 Budget was so complicated that the Labour Government nearly lost control of both the Budget and the time-table. The Opposition was given the opportunity to hold up the House to the point when the Chancellor was almost forced, through sheer physical exhaustion, to surrender. He should never have placed himself and the Government in such a position. A Budget so complex required a large majority to carry it through smoothly. Our political handful would have been better served by a simple Finance Act, and a parliamentarian who understood the workings of the House of Commons would have recognized that fact.

We cancelled the T.S.R. 2, not before time. The aircraft industry in 1964 absorbed twenty-five per cent of national expenditure on research and development while earning only two and a half per cent of our foreign exchange. We continued, however, to support Concorde, another expensive project which I suggest may never earn its keep. The Government too, under Healey's guidance, departed from the defence policy on which Wilson had united the Party in January 1964.

In 1965 there were, in fact, two White Papers: Healey's original White Paper and one upon which I insisted. Indeed I would have resigned if it had not been accepted. The original Healey White Paper avoided all criticism of the Tories' disastrous defence policy presented in 1957. Before his appointment as Minister, Healey had taken an ambivalent line on defence. His policy as Minister of Defence was a continuation of the 1957 White Paper policy with its reliance on the independent nuclear deterrent. When, in 1970, Lord Carrington took over he paid Healey a well-deserved tribute. Lord Carrington, of course, was critical of some aspects of the Healey policy, but there has been complete and disastrous continuity in defence policy from 1957 down to the present day. On occasion

Healey was driven towards a more realistic policy, and I did some of the driving. He wanted to cancel the P.1127, the V/STOL aircraft, subsequently called the Harrier. I helped to beat him on that one, and I note with satisfaction the élan with which he claims credit for its success. Similarly over the Reserve Forces and the Territorial Army—if he had not changed his mind I would have resigned. Thus, the Labour Government's defence policy was just a little more realistic than it might have been.

Two basic principles guided my interest in Security problems, both as M.P. and Minister. The first was expressed by Gaitskell in the Crabb debate of 1956: the operations of the Security Service as a whole must be secret, efficient, and exercised in a way that would never be embarrassing to international relations. Secondly, these operations, for which a Minister should be answerable, must be subject to democratic control. It required the Denning Report to establish another basic principle which I had preached in and out of season for years.

The head of the Security Service is responsible to the Home Secretary for the efficient and proper working of the Service; but he also has a right of direct access to the Prime Minister. The Denning Report made this clear and, in particular, brought out that the head of the Security Service might approach the Prime Minister himself on matters of supreme importance and delicacy. However, Harold Macmillan, as Prime Minister, certainly never understood this duty; nor did Henry Brooke, as Home Secretary, ever show any sign that he understood his job which, at Home Office level, secures the efficiency of the Security Service while protecting the freedom of the individual citizen.

The Security Service, the vital arm of security, cannot take direct action against a citizen. It must first establish its case and then hand over responsibility to the Police, who normally operate through the Special Branch. Thus, national security cannot be used as an excuse for political persecution. The Security Service must be the servant of democracy and the guardian of the national interest as well as the protector of individual freedom under the law. These overriding principles, establishing clear lines of command and action, are essential to enable the Security Service to carry out its job responsibly and effectively within the framework of a free society. From time to time I have read and heard references to the Security Service suggesting that it is an enemy of democracy and run by men seeking their own political ends. It is a grotesque description. During my three years with Harold Wilson I observed the Security Service at close quarters and came to respect the members of the Service for their high sense of duty, the quality of their thinking, and the keenness of their desire to act within the directives laid down by their political masters.

Ignorance of the simplest elements of security inspired gossip, among politicians and in the Press, that some of my Ministerial colleagues resented my so-called interference in security matters. Some, and they were not only Tories, described me as the 'Spymaster General'. This was an ill-informed canard. Each Minister is responsible for the security of his own Department. My task was to see a Minister and, with his approval, discuss security arrangements with those of his officials responsible for the Department's security. The Labour Government inherited from the previous Administration many examples of neglect and slackness, caused less from ignorance than from failure to take security seriously, so that quite elementary precautions were neglected. I found the professionals, departmental and specialists, absolutely first-rate. They found me, I hope, an appreciative listener and a willing learner, determined to draw attention to what was wrong and to help put matters right. I got on with the job being careful never to take on matters outside the realm of my own responsibility, which was to the Prime Minister. I had no executive powers, yet it was never necessary to invoke the Prime Minister's intervention for the solution of any problem. We produced the result we wanted. We steadily built up the status and quality of the Security Service. From 1964 until the moment of writing, there have been no major security breakdowns. The long debilitating progression from Philby onwards—which did so much to degrade our security reputation and diminish our influence in the international field—was over, I hoped for ever.

If I succeeded in doing anything it was by backing the professionals and raising their status. Readers of *SOE in France* by M. R. D. Foot, published by H.M. Stationery Office, will know how SOE's operations were hampered because, before the War, security had not been a subject of specialized study. In the Army, for example, security was part of the work of the Military Police, never regarded as a very attractive form of military service. It became, in short, an extension of police activities, and its operations were often of the crudest kind. It is not unkind to say that security in the Army when

Labour took office left enormous room for improvement, and its standards generally were the lowest of the three Services. In a very short time the standard of security in the Army, as in the other Services, improved immeasurably. What we did could have been achieved by any previous Government, but the task was left to us. We did our duty. I certainly agreed when strict action was proposed and taken in cases of breaches of security, but what could I say, apart from talking about resignation, when a Foreign Office official left important notes of a conversation of international importance on the counter of a Scottish Bank, and, in due course, was promoted? Perhaps it was thought impossible to discipline him in view of the fact that a prominent Minister had left classified information under his seat at a West End restaurant!

One of my ancillary jobs was that of ensuring that information was circulated in such a way as to enable Ministers in their public speeches and appearances to explain effectively the work of the Government. That was important because, to put it mildly, the Government lacked Press support. The only way it could get its case over to the public was through the machinery of the Labour Party. Thus it was desirable that Labour Party officers should be kept informed of Government policy outside the processes of Government machinery. Wilson was adamant that Party work should not be subsidized at the public expense. Persuading Ministers of their Party responsibilities was a task to be done outside my office and during my few leisure hours. The enthusiasm of the Party officers was undoubted. The idea promised them rich rewards by way of co-ordination of propaganda and policy, always difficult to obtain in a voluntary organization. For Ministers, it was a hard chore. Every public speaker likes to choose his own platform. However willing a Minister might be to plan ahead his dates and subjects, few public speakers are enthusiastic about providing digests of their speeches long enough in advance to allow the Party to make the most of their publicity value. Their co-operation involved me in endless pleading and sometimes bullying, but we got results. Our scheme quickly acquired shape. It won the appreciation of Party workers throughout the country and was of especial use at by-elections. By September 1965, my work had become sufficiently successful to be regarded with envy and suspicion, and Wilson decided that Crossman should take over from me as Chairman of our Co-ordinating Committee. The change was welcome; I needed a holiday and rest. There was also a substantial reason for giving the job to a senior member of the Government with a seat on the National Executive. With the prospect of a General Election in the not distant future, it was now essential that the Chairman of the Co-ordinating Committee should not only comprehend Government policy in the round but should be in communication with the Labour Party machine responsible for translating Government policy into language understood by the electorate. That job, obviously was not one for me. Crossman, a member of the National Executive, was better equipped. I was conscious, however, that the task demanded the understanding and flair for organizational matters which produce effective team work. From what I knew of Crossman these latter qualities were not the most easily discernible in his massive political armoury; they were the products not so much of intellect as of willingness to undertake the drudgery of constant application to detail. To do the job properly required a lot of work commanding little limelight.

I think my first real difference with Wilson on a question of policy arose over Southern Rhodesia, but the imponderables in that inherited, harassing situation made our differences marginal and I certainly did not press my opinion.

Wilson's public attitude on the principle of multi-racialism had won the support of the majority of the nation and, indeed, the sympathy and understanding of the civilized world. All felt that he was more likely than his predecessor in office to insist upon the guarantees of unimpeded progress towards majority rule as a condition of the Independence upon which Ian Smith and his Government of hard-line racialists had insisted from the first moment of their election in May 1965. Obviously, multi-racialism had become obligatory upon any British Government following South Africa's withdrawal from the Commonwealth in 1961. The hard core of the problem, however, remained. This was that, since 1923, political, police, and Military power had been controlled by a tiny white minority determined to make Southern Rhodesia, like South Africa, a vast prison for the black man. A solution, physically possible and morally right before World War II—a short, sharp military action— was now out of the question.

The situation, as I saw it, changed when Southern Rhodesia made a unilateral declaration of Independence in November 1965. Smith the racialist had become Smith the rebel. He could command political and, no doubt, police power. Could he command also the military power exercised by men who, without exception, owed loyalty only to the Queen; men trained in the British tradition that politics are not for soldiers? I thought this question should be posed by a demand for Smith's arrest. I still think, in the light of Smith's later troubles with his Army, that the question should have been posed. I respect the reasons why it was not formulated and pressed because I shared my colleagues' abhorrence of the use of force; but I abhor also capitulation to racially-inspired Fascist force, and I saw no future for Britain, either in Rhodesia or in Africa, if the British Army's traditional role down the centuries were to be abandoned. Naturally I supported sanctions. They are a weapon of defence, but their choice then as the only weapon was a soft option. Wilson, who throughout had cherished the idea that Smith would be less racialist than the more extreme members of his Government, defied history as well as reason when, at Lagos on January 11, 1966, he expressed the view that sanctions would be effective in a matter of weeks.

There came for me a hush in the political turmoil with the passing of my dear friend, Lord Chuter Ede. His death on Armistice Day, 1965, although not unexpected, was a hard personal blow. I respected him for his qualities of mind and character and came to share his affection for his native Epsom where, as a child, he went with his father to the Downs to sell bread to the gypsies. Chuter Ede rejoiced, with simple pride, in having been Charter Mayor of Epsom and Chairman of Surrey County Council, just as he rejoiced in service to his country as a Member of Parliament and Minister in war and peace. A few years later my memory of him was an inspiration when the generosity of Mr Stanley Wootton enabled me, as Chairman of the Horserace Betting Levy Board, to assist in securing for posterity the ownership of Epsom and Walton Downs, including Epsom racecourse, as a great public asset. Jim Chuter Ede and I became so identified in heart and mind that I felt bound to accept the proud and solemn honour offered me by his sister, Miss Ellen Ede, and the Mayor and Corporation of Epsom, to deliver the address at his funeral service.

Chuter Ede's Unitarianism implied distrust of priest and parson interposed between the individual and his Maker, but it gave depth and meaning to his religious life. He shared, however, my admiration for the Reverend Dick Sheppard in whose book *The Human Parson* I sought the theme that had inspired Chuter's life and work, and this theme I expressed in these words:

'James Chuter Ede was described by *The Times* as one of the most sensible politicians of his generation. That statement is true. A man does not serve the community as he did, both locally and nationally over so many years, without having his feet firmly planted on the ground.

'It is certainly true that he had the capacity to get to the heart of a problem. He never made quick, harsh judgments. He thought in terms of men and women and not in terms of statistics. He was at home with all sorts and conditions of men, women and children. He could make them laugh, for he had a joyous sense of humour.

'Perhaps his greatest gift was his capacity to understand. He could anticipate a need and often see a difficult situation before it occurred. He had an almost superhuman instinct for what ought to be done and how to do it. He preferred action to speech. He was ever on the watch for those who needed help. He was always gracious. He entered a humble dwelling with as much respect as he entered a lordly mansion. He could not patronize if he tried. He was always generous and yet strong in controversy. He was sometimes angry, for there was nothing sickly or sentimental about him. He knew how easy it is to sin, how difficult it is to live nobly.

'Yes, he was a sensible person, but the secret of Jim Chuter Ede, surely, is that he loved his fellow man. A man who lived as he did has gone right to the heart of things. He was no theologian but his faith in God was massive. My words this morning come from many discussions I had with him. Indeed, I have gone for inspiration to a wonderful sermon preached by Dick Sheppard forty years ago, a sermon the essentials of which Jim and I often discussed. I can say of Jim today he would have me urge you not to mourn but to thank God for the wonders He performs.

'It is an essential part of humanity that we sorrow and it is right that we pay our respectful sympathies to those he loved, but we shall not have read aright the lesson of Jim Chuter Ede's life unless at this moment we thank God for it and try to profit by the example he gave us. Of one thing we can be sure, that the message he leaves with us is that for him, as for us, today is not the end but the beginning.'

I have described the political background of events as I knew it. The public foreground was not much more reassuring. True, since the formation of the Labour Government in October, 1964, productivity had shown some improvement, but trade returns remained disappointing. In April, George Brown had announced his policy of three-and-a-half per cent annual increase in money incomes with additions for greater productivity, pending the full development of his National Plan. On June 3, Bank Rate was reduced to six per cent and although we were moving towards record export figures another run on sterling brought a fresh threat of devaluation. The big money boys in Britain were still willing to sell Britain short.

What emerged, despite all our troubles, was the personal popularity Wilson had won in the country. Certainly a contributing factor was the abject inadequacy, in public terms, of Tory leadership. Sir Alec Douglas-Home resigned as Opposition Leader in July and was succeeded by Edward Heath, then still an unknown quantity. The country realized and appreciated that Wilson could take on the entire Tory Front Bench any day on any issue and demolish it. Other factors were that the sophisticated British public had grasped the meaning of the 'thirteen wasted years' and, undoubtedly, supported the Prime Minister's Rhodesian policy. His policy on Vietnam, too, could be said to have been endorsed at the by-election at North Hull in January. A Left-Wing candidate, campaigning on the Vietnam issue, polled only 253 votes.

On the eve of the Tory Party Conference in October 1965, when Wilson made one of his many effective television appearances, the National Opinion Poll reported a lead of eleven points for Labour. There was growing public confidence that, given a real working majority, Wilson was the man to pilot the country out of a sea of trouble. Gordon Walker's dismal show at Leyton had reduced our majority to three. The death of Mr Speaker, Sir Harry Hylton Foster, on October 21, and his succession by a Labour nominee, Dr Horace King, brought the majority down to two. With a by-election pending at Falmouth and Camborne, following the death of its Labour representative, Fred Hayman, Wilson opted for a General Election on March 31. On March 4, the Gallup Poll gave Labour a lead of eleven points. Bookmakers were offering odds of four to one on.

Wilson conducted a magnificent campaign. He dominated the public platforms. He met electors at great meetings where, besides exposing the Tory record with devastating satire, he roused in the ranks of Labour much of the enthusiasm that had swept the country in 1945. Labour won 363 seats, a majority of ninety-six, and a clear mandate for far-reaching social change. Despite my not too happy

experiences of the previous eighteen months, my heart was uplifted
and I was glad to return to No. 10 with the Prime Minister, full of
fresh hope. Surely now the principle governing the choice of Ministers
would be capacity for the job; the line of command from No. 10,
the power-house of ideas, would become more clear and certain;
and all doubts arising from the extraneous influences exerted inside
No. 10 would be dispelled. Surely now, Harold Wilson, having
served his apprenticeship in the highest office of State, would fulfil
my own and the personal hopes of millions that he would transcend
in achievement the fine work of Clement Attlee.

Chapter Sixteen: Inside No. 10

Harold Wilson made twenty-five switches to form his new Cabinet of twenty-three Ministers. This reconstruction gave some promise of a more centralized and better co-ordinated direction of policy although, of course, it did not please everybody.

In the Queen's Speech the Government announced its willingness to enter the European Economic Community provided essential British and Commonwealth interests were safeguarded. Interest, however, centred on Budget Day. The Labour Government, with its now large Parliamentary majority, would then begin the herculean, and long overdue, task of reconstructing and modernizing Britain's economy.

The Budget's main feature was the introduction of Selective Employment Tax. This was a new money-raiser, also intended to secure a better distribution of labour between the service and production sides of industry. Another novel feature was a Betting Tax of two-and-a-half per cent based on turnover. During the Committee stage of the Finance Bill the Tories forecast that this tax would fail. It was a success and generously admitted to be so by the late Iain Macleod, one of the doubters. As a member of the Committee which reached the decision to impose the tax, I was sure it would do well. We had hammered out the principle thoroughly and left the details of application to a group of able Civil Servants.

Suddenly, the nation was plunged into the crisis of the seamen's strike—a strike involving issues much more complex than those of just another pay dispute. On May 16, when the strike began, the Prime Minister broadcast the Government's offer: an interim wage increase, a Court of Inquiry, and review and reform of the 1894 Merchant Shipping Act which imposed quite savage restrictions on seamen. This brought no response from the National Union of Seamen. Since strike notices did not take effect until a ship docked in a British port, the threat to the economy built up slowly over the forty-seven days of the strike's duration.

The N.U.S. demanded a wage increase of seventeen per cent against the three and a half per cent norm laid down by the Government. There were many foxing elements in the situation. The men had a case impossible to contest. The Union, however, both at home and abroad, had a reputation which denied it popularity. It had 'scabbed' in the General Strike of 1926. A Communist-inspired attempt, with the irrepressible Jack Dash as its instrument, to bring London dockers out in support of the seamen failed ignominiously. Foreign seamen refused to assist by boycotting cargoes for Britain. The N.U.S. met Ray Gunter, Minister of Labour, and George Woodcock, General Secretary of the Trades Union Congress, but took no notice of Gunter's offer or Woodcock's advice. The Interim Report of the Court of Inquiry, over which Lord Justice Pearson presided, proposed an interim wage increase and a two-stage introduction of the forty-hour week. This was rejected, literally, out of hand. The final report, providing a Charter which might have introduced a new era in what could be described as a sweated industry, was also rejected, almost without discussion. The Prime Minister's own unceasing efforts to end the strike in meetings with the Union and employers were unavailing.

I was neither involved in these negotiations nor called upon to express an opinion on policy matters. My assignment was to keep the Prime Minister informed about aspects of the developing situation, and I did just that.

I saw no conclusive evidence that the N.U.S. was dominated by the Communist Party although, for years past, it had been an obvious 'take-over' for them. Not one member of the Executive Committee was a declared Communist. The men of influence were Joseph Kenny of Liverpool and James Slater of South Shields, sincere Left-wingers who dominated the rather inert Executive long out of touch with the rank and file. Harold Wilson paid tribute in the House to the sincerity and competence of these two men. Their influence extended to all sections of the Union. Denied public and trade union support at home and abroad, they became associated with their sole supporters, the Communist Party. The Secretary of the N.U.S., eager to improve efficiency and stamp out malpractices, faced a situation which reduced him to a cypher.

The Communist Party was not without its own troubles. Its take-over of the Electrical Trades Union, and its conduct of the affairs of that Union, had been disastrous to its reputation. Since then, however, it had acquired an able technician in Bert Ramelson, National Industrial Organizer. Behind him stood the Communist Party's General Secretary, John Gollan, a canny Scot eager to improve his Party's fast-declining political prospects. Ramelson guided the strategy of the strike with considerable skill. But his handling of the strike situation could not disguise the failure to command international support. Even more devastating was the failure to extend the strike to other industries. This was a grave blow to Communist Party tactics. Extension of industrial disruption is basic to the Communist philosophy; a strike not spread is a strike doomed to failure.

The slow build-up of the strike offered two advantages to shrewd leadership. The home-coming seamen were going on strike supported by wages accumulated over weeks or months at sea. The steady increase in ships rendered idle—eight hundred and thirty-eight of them twenty-six days after the start of the strike—kept high the men's hopes of victory and obscured their failure to win public and trade union support. These were ideal circumstances in which to pursue the newly-devised Communist tactics of industrial and political guerrilla warfare. Ramelson was the author of this method of limited but effective Communist attack, operated by minorities, frequently outside the industry under attack. The tactics were so successful that a proposal to the Executive Committee of the N.U.S. that it should adjourn *sine die*, thus leaving the Union at the mercy of external influences, was defeated by only a narrow majority of votes. Had those tactics succeeded the British economy might have been pounded to its knees.

When the Prime Minister grasped the full significance of events he acted decisively and courageously. On June 20, he denounced the 'tightly-knit group of politically motivated men' holding the country to ransom. On June 22, the Government acquired Emergency Powers, and the Communist Party threw up the sponge. Wilson faced Parliament on June 28 to debate the Emergency Powers with his victory already won. To courage he added magnanimity. Probably for the first time in the history of Parliament, a Prime Minister stated the arguments of men on strike more persuasively than their own leaders. The N.U.S. cried 'quits' on July 2, by which time nine hundred ships were laid up in port. Wilson's conduct reached a high-water mark in his handling of this strike. Although deliberately misinterpreted, he acted like a man of stature, seeing his duty clearly and doing it without thought of self. Single-handed he smashed a strike which was nearing the point of no return; there could have been no alternative but surrender by one side or the other.

The moral and financial damage done to the N.U.S. by the strike was irreparable. Membership fell from 120,000 to 55,000. The Union is now an industrial weakling with, according to the *Economist* report of November 12, 1970, a deficit of fifteen hundred pounds on its weekly budget—a sickly warning to all trade unionists beguiled by Communist propaganda and suborned by strong-arm infiltrators.

As I have recorded, I was not involved in any way in negotiations or in policy-making during the strike. That fact, however, did not prevent me from becoming an object of abuse in some sections of the Press. In the *Daily Express* of June 21, Trevor Evans reported that 'the Government was tipped off on June 9 that if five members of the Executive were ditched there could be a settlement in half an hour'. That story, as the member of the N.U.S. who made the remark told me, was based on a casual encounter with Ray Gunter at the entrance to No. 10 Downing Street. Gunter had hailed his acquaintance by asking how things were going, to which my informant replied, 'We shall have to ditch four or five of the so-and-so's before we can get a settlement.' Somehow the story reached the Press and the comment was exploited by the militants as indicating what No. 10 was thinking. This was followed up by stories that organized efforts were made, particularly by me, to provide newspaper correspondents with evidence that Communists were responsible for the strike and the unnatural stubbornness of the seamen. These stories were, of course, quite untrue. Perhaps more serious were leaks emanating from the editorial conference of a responsible newspaper to the less responsible section of the week-end Press. I confess frankly that I had forgotten all about it until, later, I received letters from two journalists who had sought an interview with me at No. 10. One of the letters ended, 'I would understand if you decided not to talk to me again on virtually any terms, but it would make me unhappy. I have always enjoyed my interviews with you.'

The confusion and irresponsibility of Press comment over the strike issue was due, in part, to the fact that Parliamentary Lobby standards have fallen lamentably in recent years. At one time a conversation on 'Lobby terms' means that M.P.s and journalists could speak together in complete confidence. There are still Lobby correspondents, like Harry Boyne of the *Daily Telegraph*, Wilfred

Sendall of the *Daily Express* and Ian Waller of the *Sunday Telegraph*, whom I would trust with my life. The Lobby, however, has grown too large and competition between newspapers too fierce for the integrity of its standards to be maintained without reform. The urgent task is to reduce the number of those correspondents representing heaven knows who and what.

The immediate result of the seamen's strike was a fall in our trade figures and gold and dollar reserves. Central bankers at Basle renewed existing credits on condition that there would be no devaluation. The progress achieved by budgetary measures was being lost and we were sliding into the sterling crisis that blew up in July. Against the background of intense pressure on the exchange rate, despite a seven per cent increase in exports, we faced the fact that in 1965 the nation had drawn £1,800,000,000 more in money incomes, of which £1,500,000,000 was represented by wages and salaries, while production had increased to the value of only £600,000,000. We had to choose between a slow slide into bankruptcy, or a six months standstill on all incomes, with a further six months of severe restraint, plus measures to reduce demand on domestic resources by more than £500,000,000 in 1967 and to cut Government and private spending overseas by £150,000,000.

On July 16, while these measures were being worked out in detail, Wilson paid a return visit to Moscow—he had been there in February—to inspect the British Trade Fair as guest of Mr Kosygin. He hoped also to initiate a new peace move in Vietnam by activating the Anglo-Soviet co-Chairmanship of the Indo-Chinese peace-keeping machinery in order to reconvene the 1954 Geneva conference. As in February, so in July, *Izvestia* greeted the Prime Minister with sullen suspicion. There were newspaper rumours that he might be recalled to deal with problems at home, including a plot against his leadership. The atmosphere created by the Soviet Press made his mission a sleeveless errand, and newspaper rumours at home became a serial story burgeoning in October into the Great Plot That Never Was. I kept in close touch with Wilson while he was in Moscow assuring him that, despite all the idle chatter, there was no real dissension in the Cabinet.

Chancellor Callaghan wanted to avoid a situation in which we might be forced to deflate and, perhaps, devalue against a time schedule politically inconvenient to the Government. He agreed that the package deal should be announced on July 20 as arranged. Then, he hoped, Wilson would go to Washington and seek support to tide us over until the Spring when he would propose to float the pound.

I stressed the view I had been urging upon other colleagues, that if we chose this moment to retreat from our position in the Far East we were unlikely to command much sympathy in Washington. The purpose of defence economies, as I saw it, was to save foreign exchange and to husband our resources. Thus we should take two steps. First we should withdraw from B.A.O.R. say, one Brigade, and so force West Germany to assume a fair and realistic share of our defence costs there and at the same time convince the White House that we meant business. Second, while continuing our defence production programme we should slow down projects which we could not afford to develop at speed. Callaghan perked up on hearing these suggestions. They provided a possible theme for his talks with the Germans, due the following week, and they might contribute significantly towards easing the immediate situation.

Brown, although in accord with the proposed cuts, regarded them as a victory for Treasury policy which, he felt, was directed towards confining the scope of his Department of Economic Affairs and crippling his own labours to raise standards of industrial efficiency and productivity. He regretted bitterly that he had gone along with Wilson and Callaghan on devaluation. Like a latter-day Trotsky, he argued that as disaster piled upon disaster we should intensify the struggle. Thus he would have preferred to take the high line of devaluation related to a well-thought-out policy of economic reform and expansion. Nonetheless, his general attitude was that expressed by Michael Stewart and Denis Healey—complete loyalty to the Government although they were properly critical of the age-old system which permitted Treasury Ministers to take decisions affecting Departmental Ministers without effective consultation with them. Every Minister to whom I talked that week-end felt acutely that the Treasury were solving their own problems regardless of the difficulties being created for others.

Mrs Castle and Crossman, according to my information, were 'sound' but, as I informed the Prime Minister, I refrained from widening my contacts in order to limit the possibility of gossip. I met Wilson at the airport on the Tuesday, as arranged, and he at once began preparing for the Cabinet meeting next day.

That meeting added a new dimension to the crisis. Brown decided to resign. The Prime Minister gave me the task of dissuading him.

I stayed with Brown all afternoon and into the early hours of the evening, imposing on him my own addiction to strong tea and, because I like him as I think he likes me, arguing fiercely every inch of the way. I put my own view bluntly. I thought we should have devalued in 1964; because of the massive balance of payments deficit we had inherited, devaluation had become inevitable long before Labour took office. The Tories had shirked that decision for electoral reasons. I had neither the specialist training nor the knowledge to counter the decision taken at the time by my senior colleagues, including Brown himself. Having accepted their decision, however, I would be acting dishonestly if I now sought exemption from its consequence. I was in general agreement with Brown, but I told him that gossip-provoking publicity did not help and he could not hope, by threatening resignation, to stampede his colleagues into endorsing his point of view, despite the fact that over one hundred Labour M.P.s had sent a message appealing to him not to resign.

Ours was a confrontation with emotional overtones but without stress. We were friends, each trying to clarify the mind of the other. Brown left me for a talk with Wilson, promising to return to No. 10 for yet another session later. By this time Downing Street was filling up with journalists, television cameras and members of the general public sniffing the air of crisis. The Lord President of the Council, Bert Bowden, and the Chief Whip, John Silkin, joined Wilson, Brown and myself for the second informal session. It lasted over an hour. With Downing Street becoming ever more crowded, Brown turned to me and said, 'George, what shall I do now?' 'Get along that corridor on to the doorstep of No. 10 and tell the waiting crowd that you are going to stand your corner and stay in the Government,' was my reply. Brown, accompanied by Bowden and Silkin went on to the door-step and, like the big man he can be, announced he had decided his duty lay with his colleagues and he would continue to try to make a success of Labour's policy. At that moment I felt as close to him in spirit as I have ever been to any political colleague.

The economic measures announced next day by the Prime Minister, severe though they were, made sense only as a palliative and preliminary to the application of wide-ranging economic and social changes for which a revised prices and incomes policy, unaccompanied by other measures, was no viable alternative. In fact, they turned out to be destructive of the Department of Economic Affairs and a first step to Brown's transfer to the Foreign Office. Devaluation did come but not as part of any well thought out long-term policy.

Newspaper speculation about a plot against the Prime Minister did not die a natural death, probably because editors thought they had the Government on the run. Thickening was added to the political stew by the 'confidential' issue of the *Economist* of August 18, which published a story to the effect that Wilson had been planning a cabinet re-shuffle *after* the Parliamentary recess, and continued:

> Mr Callaghan began to repeat earlier noises indicating that *he* would like to move to the Foreign Office. Simultaneously, the rumour began to circulate at Westminster that if a Coalition Government had to be formed to cope with the nation's economic crisis and the Tories could not stomach Mr Wilson then Mr Callaghan would be 'available'.

> (That the notion of Mr Callaghan emerging as an Olympian national leader could be entertained even semi-seriously was in itself an index of the fevered mental health, possibly induced by sleeplessness, of Britain's legislators.)

> On August 10, Mr Wilson had it confirmed by the Whips that a sizeable revolt of his own back benchers against the wage freeze was imminent. The prospect of a long Summer recess during which the Labour Party would be bitterly and publicly derided loomed up before him. With 24 hours to go, he decided to act.

> By switching Mr Brown to the Foreign Office he killed three birds with one stone: he delighted his deputy; stymied his rival; and stole the headlines from the Labour abstainers on the vital Parliamentary Vote on the Prices and Incomes Bill. There was no time for the Prime Minister to work out the implications of Mr Brown's appointment; second thoughts at his holiday retreat in the Scilly Isles may be causing him some concern.

This tongue-in-cheek commentary ended with a forecast. 'The new Foreign Secretary has something of a reputation as a bull in a china shop,' it ran. 'But it is not so much the diplomatic coffee cups that Mr Wilson should be worrying about—although they will rattle from time to time—but rather the breakables in his own Cabinet.'

Another stir to the stew came in the October 6 issue of the Paris edition of the *New York Herald Tribune and Washington Post*. Reporting from the Labour Party Conference at Brighton an American Correspondent noted a dramatic 'Cabinet' meeting in Mr Wilson's hotel room, asked was there really a conspiracy against the Prime Minister in July, and quoted an 'informed observer' for what, in this context was untrue: 'Twice in July Wilson had very rough going in Cabinet sessions.'

On October 14, *The Times* recorded that 'American Correspondents in London had asked Mr Richard Crossman to explain what sort of man Mr Wilson was. In the course of his reply Mr Crossman left an impression that, during July, it was suspected that the City and the Treasury, worried about the sterling crisis, had begun to think that a Coalition Government might be necessary if the rot could not be stopped.' Meantime, the head of another American newspaper bureau in London had gone to the Tory Party Conference at Blackpool and blabbed to British journalists the gist of Crossman's off-the-record conversation piece! And hundreds of feet of British newspaper comment and speculation, most of it nonsense, followed.

Public Opinion Polls, after the crisis budget, showed a substantial rise in the Government's support and a strong preference for Harold Wilson as Prime Minister over the Tory leader, Edward Heath. Now, with the Great Plot That Never Was stuttering to its end, the Prime Minister summoned a meeting of Ministers at Chequers on Sunday, October 23. According to the *Guardian* of Monday, October 24, sixteen senior Ministers attended the meeting under the Prime Minister's chairmanship, and were 'understood to have discussed a detailed new study of the options open to Britain in its dealings with the Common Market'.

Official sources insisted afterwards that no firm conclusion had been reached or even sought at the meeting which was preceded by a meeting between the Prime Minister, Brown and Callaghan. The Prime Minister was under pressures generated by the appointment of Brown as Foreign Secretary. Having indulged in a bout of brinkmanship over the package deal, Brown had continued in office on the understanding that the Draconian measures announced on July 20 would be followed by effective action to stop the economic drift. He had wanted to devalue in July; Callaghan was prepared to consider letting the pound float, but only at a later stage. Each man for his own reasons had bought time, as had the Prime Minister, under the promise of effective new measures. The Prime Minister, therefore, having reached agreement with Callaghan and Brown that they should accept the package deal was now placed in the position of being forced to deliver the goods, and this in face of the fact that other Cabinet colleagues were restive. He solved the problem by revealing himself to Brown and Callaghan as a convert to the idea of the Common Market.

Wilson told me that his conversion resulted from an article in the *Economist* on October 22. I, too, had read the article. I have re-read it often since. I still doubt its influence on Wilson's 'conversion'. Wilson's swing from being a strong antagonist of the Common Market to becoming a protagonist ready to run risks to secure Britain's entry took its place among other historic phenomena exemplified by Paul's conversion on the road to Damascus. The one difference was that, judged by his subsequent actions, Paul's conversion was sincere. Wilson's conversion was not due to conviction. It flowed from the fact that he had to put Brown and Callaghan in baulk and hold the Cabinet together in the shadow of the July crisis. The Prime Minister had to produce a device that looked and sounded like business.

Another spur to Wilson's conversion was the need to face the House of Commons. This he did on November 10 when he announced his intention to tour the capitals of the Six in company with the Foreign Secretary and 'engage in a series of discussions with each of the Heads of the Governments of the Six'. I thought this decision was wrong, although I appreciated the reasons forcing Wilson into the corner in which he found himself at Chequers. The arch-pragmatist had solved the political crisis of the July package deal by promising to deliver the goods and to float the pound from strength. He could not do the first. He had no intention of doing the second. To tour Europe was his way out. I failed to convince him that, once the tour had taken place, he would have lost his ability either to stand up to British pressures to enter the Common Market or to resist pressures from the Six who wanted Britain in only on their terms. I expressed vigorously my view that we were once again drifting into an association with Europe in a general way and with France in particular without thinking out the long-term consequences. I was in favour of keeping all options open, including entry into the Common Market, but I was not prepared to forget the names of our friends in America and the Commonwealth in a gamble with Britain's future. For me the clinching argument was the historical view stated in the final paragraph of Sir Lewis Namier's *Vanished Supremacies*:

> In the end it was the entry into the war of the two great extra-European Powers, the Soviet Union, attacked by Germany, and the United States, attacked by Japan, which decided the issue. And when their armies met on 25 April, 1945 at Torgau, in the heart of Germany and the centre of the European Continent, the victory was won and the century of German preponderance in Europe had reached its term. So, too, had the supremacy of Europe in the world.*

The meaning of Namier's statement has not yet entered into the thinking and feeling of the British people. Thus we now find ourselves with a Tory Government determined to secure Britain's entry into the Common Market regardless of the price to be paid. Any terms the Six care to demand will ultimately be conceded, the Tory Government having now arrived at the point reached by Wilson on October 23, 1966. They have, I fear, closed all options. The current carrying the country into Europe is running too hard and too fast for the British people to generate the will and energy to swim against it. Now, whether we like it or not, Britain is just another island off the north-west corner of Europe. What neither Wilson nor Heath seem to realize is that time is not altered by stopping the clock. One day the British people will be faced with the real meaning of entry into the Common Market. There will be a revulsion and much more than the Common Market agreement will be broken in the public reaction. This may well lead to a re-casting of our defence and economic policies in such a way that the political parties as we now know them will be torn asunder.

Early in November, 1966, a question appeared on the House of Commons Order Paper asking the Paymaster General to publish a White Paper on the co-ordination of the Home Information Services. Answers to this and another question came forward for consideration on the morning of Friday, November 11, 1966. On that morning the *Daily Express* published a re-hash of a seven-week old news story with a headline announcing: 'Crossman to polish up Labour's Image'. As this announcement involved my being relieved of the responsibility for answering questions on the co-ordination of the Home Information Services, I telephoned Crossman's office and, on being told that

* Sir Lewis Namier, *Vanished Supremacies* (Hamish Hamilton, 1958).

he had not arrived, asked his Private Secretary whether he could give me any information since, in view of the publication of the *Express* story, my responsibility for answering the question was obviously involved. The Private Secretary had no information, but promised to enquire from Crossman. Within half an hour Crossman called me demanding to know how I dare telephone his Secretary and make allegations about a leak to the *Daily Express*. I answered that I had made neither allegations nor accusations about anything or anybody; I had sought information. Crossman refused to be mollified. He rattled on and continued to berate me, inducing the conclusion that he was relying on attack as the best means of defence. Eventually the conversation finished. Within seconds Crossman's Private Secretary was back on the telephone to say, 'Mr Wigg, I monitored your conversation, and I want you to know that never at any time did I tell Mr Crossman you had suggested that any member of his staff had talked to the *Daily Express*. I told him you had enquired on the telephone about the *Express* article because you had a question to answer on Monday, and before drafting the reply you wanted to talk to him about it.' That incident ended my long and friendly association with Crossman, a man of mighty wit and little wisdom.

On the Monday, being in an impossible position, I got a grilling from the Tories. The Prime Minister had relieved me of all responsibility for answering questions about the co-ordination of the Home Information Services. He had given Crossman the job, but had failed to inform the House of Commons about the changes. This led me to make a further protest to Wilson about our working relationship which, in fact, was friendly and pleasant when we were left alone. Wilson is the easiest man in the world to work for and with. He lets you get on with the job but, once outside pressures are exerted on him, his inability to make up his mind and take a stand, even when he knows he is right, renders personal relationships difficult.

The indefatigable Crossman next decided to discipline the Chairman of the Parliamentary Labour Party, Manny Shinwell! The ostensible reason was a desire to liberalize Party discipline. The real purpose, to my mind, was to win the support of the new intake of middle-class Labour M.P.s and put Crossman in a position to challenge for the leadership. Crossman's ally, who did not necessarily indulge his impossible ambition, was the new Chief Whip, John

Silkin. Brash and inexperienced, they were joined now in a noble venture. I quote the *New Statesman* of March 17, 1967. Crossman, it said, intended to adapt 'the party's traditional methods of discipline to the needs of an epoch which demands a greater freedom of debate and action inside their own ranks'. What Shinwell and Wigg 'have never grasped', the comment continued, 'is that changes which the Crossman-Silkin axis seeks to bring about are inevitable in the kind of parliamentary party now evolving'.

I have never taken much notice of comments seeking to put me in a false position. Several considerations, however, were in the forefront of my mind as the attack on Shinwell unfolded. We had turned into the New Year with the November export figures at an all-time high and with some hope of real progress if the Government acted vigorously and the Party remained united. Talk about liberalizing a Party which, notoriously, allowed M.P.s on occasion to act like anarchists, was just hot air. For two-and-a-half years during part of which our majority could be counted on the fingers of one hand, Shinwell had been the most binding influence in the Party, co-operating easily and smoothly with Bowden as Leader of the House and Short as Chief Whip, yet always looking at every proposition through the eyes of an intelligent back-bencher. Indeed, during that difficult period the Chief Whip had more trouble whipping up Ministers in the Division Lobby than in controlling the rank and file. Shinwell, too, had welcomed Crossman's appointment as Leader of the House in August 1965 and had offered him all possible help in establishing good relations.

The trouble with Shinwell started when Crossman attempted to intervene in the conduct of a Party meeting under Shinwell's chairmanship. Shinwell insisted he would either be Chairman or get out. I did my best to persuade him, in the interests of Party unity, not to resign but to try to make things work until Crossman and Silkin acquired some practical experience and formed an intelligent idea about their jobs. I pleaded that if Shinwell gave way to them the Party's capacity to discipline itself would be weakened and the skids would be under the Government. So it proved. The question—liberalization or discipline—blew up into a fiercely divisive issue and in 1970 as in 1951, 1955 and 1959, a divided Party headed for unnecessary electoral defeat.

On March 2, Prime Minister Wilson took a hand. Addressing the Parliamentary Labour Party he chastized recent abstainers on the

Defence White Paper. These included M.P.s who wanted us to oppose the use of American troops in Vietnam, to withdraw British troops from the Far East, and to send British troops into Southern Rhodesia. There were splinter groups concerned about prices and incomes policy and the Common Market, often expressing perfectly legitimate views in terms of what sometimes sounded like a vendetta against the Government. None of the abstaining M.P.s, declared Wilson, were there on their own merits. They were there as members of the Labour Party. A humorous reference to a dog being entitled to one bite was unkindly interpreted as an abrasive reference to M.P.s being licensed. *The Times*, next morning, described the speech as 'overall, a mocking, defiant, challenging speech', adding, 'Action to clear the air was obviously called for. That was the responsibility of Mr Silkin, the Chief Whip, and he has got full backing.' Then, mindful of its Tory loyalties, *The Times* followed up on March 4 with a stern warning to the Prime Minister that 'in addressing the Parliamentary Labour Party he is addressing his masters'. On television, on March 6, Michael Foot denounced the speech as 'deplorable', to the great delight of some sections of the Press. The late Sydney Silverman, who had not heard it, released for publication a letter describing the speech as 'the most dangerous attack on social democracy in my time', and received the grateful thanks of the *Daily Express*, which placed him 'among the political giants of our time'. It is marvellous how one grows in the estimation of the Tory Press if one says the things they want to hear.

The kernel of the problem, apart from its organizational aspects, lay in the 'conscience clause', which had always been well understood by the Parliamentary Labour Party. It applied only to members who were known to hold pronounced pacifist views and in matters concerning religion and temperance. The Crossman–Silkin axis sought simultaneously to increase the powers of the Chief Whip while extending freedom of conscience beyond those very wide boundaries.

I spent Sunday, March 5, at Shinwell's house. We hammered out a formula which, while keeping the conscience clause intact, proposed that any Member failing to support the Government in the division lobby would be reported by the Chief Whip to the Liaison Committee. That Committee could require the offender to explain his action and, if it considered his explanation unsatisfactory, could report him to the Parliamentary Labour Party. I read the draft formula to Silkin over the telephone. We accepted his suggested amendments, and I left Shinwell, happy in the belief that I had built a bridge between him and the Chief Whip. Wilson was informed. He, too, agreed the formula.

On March 7, Silkin sent Shinwell a document on organization and the way was cleared for a meeting convened for 5.30 p.m. on Wednesday, March 8, at which the Liaison Committee, with Crossman and Silkin present, would finalize an agreed document to be submitted to the Parliamentary Labour Party. On that Wednesday afternoon Shinwell was disturbed by a rumour that Silkin and Crossman had conferred and that in consequence Silkin was backing out of the agreement. To my telephone enquiry Silkin replied by inviting me to his office. I showed him our original draft of the formula and the draft with his amendments, being the one that all three of us, and the Prime Minister, had agreed on Sunday. He studied it for several minutes, frowned, and said, 'I do not agree'. I pointed out that he had agreed. He repeated his disagreement.

Further enquiries revealed that Crossman had issued a hand-out to the Press through Transport House of the public speech he was to deliver at Morden that evening, part of which read as follows:

> I know very well it is being suggested in some quarters that the Chief Whip and I are now under pressure to abandon the new liberalized disciplines which we introduced last November and which our colleagues approved by an overwhelming majority. There is not, however, a shred of truth in the story. As long as the Chief Whip and I are in charge there will be no question of putting the clock back.
>
> Of course there are members of the Labour Party (some of them in positions of influence) who have always been opposed to our new code of discipline . . .

This, by implication, was an attack on Shinwell and me and, since no new code of conduct had been evolved, a misleading statement. This, too, was after the Prime Minister and Silkin had approved the formula Shinwell was presenting to the Liaison Committee, and which Crossman, before leaving for Morden, had said was worth discussing!

The obvious question was *when* did Crossman issue his Press statement? I enquired at Transport House. The answer, confirmed on March 9 in writing, was that the typescript of the Morden speech was delivered for distribution to the Press at 5.20 p.m.—ten minutes before the meeting of the Liaison Committee was timed to begin. The letter from Transport House had a postscript which read: 'At the Small Committee last night Mr Crossman asked if the speech had been dealt with. I told him exactly what I had done and he said that Lobby correspondents would understand that he would not put out a speech of this nature without his showing it to the Prime Minister.' The draft of the speech may have reached No. 10 eventually, but the Prime Minister told me Crossman had not cleared it with him. Shinwell, understandably, boiled over. If I had thought for a split second that Wilson, having agreed my attempt to unite Shinwell and Silkin, and having agreed to the formula we had worked out, had cleared Crossman's speech, I would have resigned on the spot. When talking to him about the matter, I made it plain that I stood by Shinwell, and to the Prime Minister's comment, 'So you would rather be Parliamentary Private Secretary to Manny Shinwell than a member of the Wilson Government?' I replied, 'That may be meant as a jibe, but I accept it as a compliment and the answer is "Yes" '.

The outcome was twofold. Silkin's document on Parliamentary Labour Party organization, prepared with Crossman's compliance, was not even considered by the Liaison Committee and 'got lost'. Then I received a telephone call from Shinwell asking me to tell the Prime Minister that statements being attributed to him in the Press and purporting to put pressure on No. 10 were without foundation; his loyalty to, and regard for, Wilson remained unabated but he intended to resign in about a fortnight's time by quietly telling the Secretary he wished to relinquish the Chairmanship of the Parliamentary Labour Party.

On March 14, the Prime Minister summoned Crossman, Silkin, Shinwell and me to his room to hear his views. He argued that the speech of March 2 had been made necessary because dissent in one wing of the Party was being organized and was provoking similar action among Party loyalists to pay off old scores. A likely result was that the Party system would be made unworkable. His much publicized comment about a dog being entitled to one bite had wounded the feelings of many colleagues but the effect had been immediate and salutary. Some bruises remained, murmurs persisted, but the Party generally had settled down again. He hoped it could be united on the basis of a memorandum he had prepared, in which a stated first principle was that he, whether as Prime Minister or Leader of the Labour Party, ought not to have to concern himself with details of Party discipline, or the conduct of individual Members, or the day-to-day running of the Parliamentary Labour Party.

In view of Crossman's recent conduct a significant paragraph of this memorandum read:

> While the Liaison Committee is engaged in preparing the statement, none of the Officers concerned shall pre-judge the Committee's discussions by any published statement, or by any prejudicial briefing of the Press. Equally, once the decision has been taken all members of the Committee shall accept the principle of collective responsibility in commending it to the Party and thereafter. (Note: By 'officers' I mean the Ministerial and the elected members of the Liaison Committee.) No other Minister shall be involved in these discussions except on my direction.

I interpreted this paragraph as an instruction to Crossman to belt up, to consider the proposals in the Liaison Committee, and then take them to the Party meeting. Wilson was saying in effect that he did not want to be involved unless he had to be, which was a perfectly reasonable attitude. Shinwell, however, was not appeased. He could not believe that Crossman would have acted as he had done without the Prime Minister's knowledge, nor could be believe that the Chief Whip would follow Crossman around with such dog-like devotion unless at the sound of His Master's Voice.

Another section of the memorandum dismayed both Shinwell and me. Wilson argued that the problem lay not with the rank and file, but at the top. Thus, the time had come when he should define duties. He placed upon the Chief Whip responsibility for the discipline and general functioning of the Parliamentary Labour Party in consultation with the Leader of the House, the Chairman of the Parliamentary Party, the Liaison Committee and, if necessary, the Prime Minister, as he thought fit. 'No other person, be he Minister or Officer of the Parliamentary Labour Party has any authority to interfere with the Chief Whip in the performance of his duties. He should act in concert with the Lord President and, if possible, with the Chairman of the Parliamentary Labour Party and the Chairman of the Liaison Committee.' I thought this proposition, far from being a Charter of Freedom, gave licence to the Chief Whip to ride roughshod over the Liaison Committee and the Parliamentary Labour Party.

Shinwell studied the document carefully, then passed it back across the table to Wilson in a gesture of rejection which I knew meant his resignation from the post he had filled with competence and distinction. His words to me when he resigned were, 'When you meet Crossman, just ignore him. And don't you leave Harold Wilson's Government. At this moment Harold needs somebody he knows will stand by him through thick and thin.' A few weeks later, reminiscing about old times, Shinwell reflected upon our long friendship as being unusual in politics where many men are animated solely by strong personal ambition. And with a chuckle over the thought that some might wish to misinterpret our close association he said, 'And nobody could possibly believe that we are close friends if they heard us arguing, could they?' Recollecting some of the friendly adjectives we exchanged, I agreed!

While these internal Parliamentary Labour Party issues were unfolding, I was concerned with setting up a Committee of Privy Councillors to enquire into the 'D Notice matter'. On February 21, the *Daily Express* had published an article by Chapman Pincher under the heading 'Cable Vetting Sensation'. On that same day a question on The Press (D Notices) stood on the Order Paper in the name of Sir John Langford Holt. It was not addressed to the Prime Minister. It should have been answered by the Foreign Secretary, the Foreign Office being responsible for the subject dealt with in the Chapman Pincher article. Wilson, against the advice of his officials and certainly against mine, chose to answer the question himself. He told the House:

> Unfortunately, the confidence and trust which are the basis of the whole system have been called into question by the action of one newspaper in initiating this morning a sensationalized and inaccurate story purporting to describe a situation in which in fact the powers and practice have not changed for well over forty years; ... what I am concerned with today is a clear breach of two D Notices, despite the fact that the newspaper was repeatedly warned that it would be contravening the Notices. This, I think, creates a very difficult situation for the other newspapers which have honoured the arrangement throughout.

The action of the *Express* did indeed create a difficult situation. The *Daily Mail*, for example, had the scoop before the *Express* and had denied itself the privilege and pride of publication on the advice of the Secretary of the Services, Press and Broadcasting Committee. This Committee, representative of the interests of Defence, newspapers, news agencies, and broadcasting, administers the D Notice system to safeguard, on a voluntary basis, what can be broadly described as 'national security'. The Committee had worked reasonably well since the end of the war. Now, Wilson decided, a Committee of Privy Councillors, with Lord Radcliffe as Chairman, should be set up 'to examine the circumstances surrounding the publication' of the *Express* article 'in relation to the D Notice system; and to consider what improvements, if any, are required in that system in order to maintain it as a voluntary system based on mutual trust and confidence between the Government and Press in the interests alike of freedom of the Press and of the security of the State'.

I regarded the proposed procedure with some misgiving. Since the central interest was security, with which the Press is as deeply concerned as the Government, I suggested an inquiry by defence experts under the chairmanship of, say, Lord Head, to examine the problems in the light of modern conditions and in consultation with the Services, Press and Broadcasting Committee, leaving that Committee free, meanwhile, to deal with the immediate situation in its own way. I thought, with the results of the Vassall Inquiry in mind, that the Press generally might interpret the proposed inquiry as an attack on its freedom. I urged these views without avail. What the Radcliffe Inquiry, consisting of Lord Radcliffe, Selwyn Lloyd and Manny Shinwell, finally revealed was that the Foreign Office wanted to suppress the Pincher story, and that the D Notices invoked to support suppression lacked the necessary precision to secure that end. Although the Report was unanimous, the issue acquired heavily loaded overtones in Fleet Street. To judge by the postbag of No. 10, however, it put the public to sleep. The Prime Minister received twelve letters on the subject. I received one.

Lack of grip at the centre was making the Government increasingly accident-prone. One example was when the *Torrey Canyon* struck the Seven Stones Reef on March 18, and precious time was lost before effective action was taken. The commonsense view, subject to the advice of scientific experts, was that a tanker of that size could not be floated off the Reef. There was delay in calling upon the skill and experience of the Navy to contain the oil slick, and delay in applying the solution devised by Sir Solly Zuckerman: to split the deck by precision bombing and then to drop napalm, almost simultaneously, to set the oil alight. This hazardous operation was performed brilliantly by the R.A.F., but the public were left with the impression that the widespread and expensive problem of oil slick on our coasts was intensified because of lack of foresight and decision.

On April 10, the British public were again made aware of the long-simmering unrest in Aden. A United Nations Mission studying the situation there held a Press Conference presided over by the High Commissioner, Sir Richard Turnbull, at which a quite unimportant slanging match was blown up into an international incident, damaging to reasoned discussion and to British prestige. In an effort to silence a loquacious Afghan delegate, somebody asked, 'Is your country an important member of the United Nations?' To his reply, 'We pay our contributions,' someone retorted, 'But you don't pay as much as the United Kingdom,' and the counter-answer was, 'We don't cause as much bloodshed'. This exchange of schoolboy badinage was recounted irresponsibly in the Press Release and newspapers everywhere played up the theme that 'Britain has caused more bloodshed than any other nation on earth'. To repair the damage Lord Shackleton was instructed by telephone to fly to Aden. He went unbriefed and without powers, before he had even heard full news of the flare-up. It was another sad and sorry mishandling of Middle East affairs.

The end for Britain in Aden was in sight. Sir Richard Turnbull, said to favour a coalition in South Arabia which would have sufficient backing to become a new State independent of the United Arab Republic, was replaced as High Commissioner on May 10 by Sir Humphrey Trevelyan, who reportedly had some influence with Nasser. The *Daily Mirror* and the *Daily Telegraph*—the latter datelined the story from Aden—scooped this news, and the next day George Brown apologized for that leaky vessel, the Foreign Office, while declaring that he had nothing to do with the leak. On June 19, it was announced that Aden would become independent in January 1968. On September 5, Trevelyan recognized the Nationalist Forces as representative of the people. So we left Aden, and were thus bereft of a base on the most vital of our sea lines; bereft, too, of the influence that wise political action could have secured for us in one of the most sensitive areas in the world.

On April 2, 1965, I had been invited to visit Cairo by the Egyptian Government. In the absence, through illness, of Ambassador Hafez Ismail, I received the invitation at a lunch with Mohamed Anwar, the Chargé d'Affaires. My host stressed that the invitation was personal but, if I wished, it would be conveyed formally through diplomatic channels; surely an indication that the ice barrier between Cairo and London was melting. I replied, regretfully, that I would not be free for some time, and we went on to discuss Anglo-U.A.R. relations. I advised Mohamed Anwar that the quickest way of clearing the air would be for Egypt to stop supporting terrorist activities in Aden and to cease anti-British propaganda on the radio.

Naturally, I reported by letter to Michael Stewart at the Foreign Office. Stewart thought I had struck the right note in my talk with Mohamed Anwar and promised to let me know when the obstacles to a visit had been removed. They never were removed.

Field Marshal Viscount Montgomery of Alamein entered the Egyptian scene. He went to Egypt for the El Alamein celebrations. He had been treated as the conquering hero who had saved Egypt from the Nazis. He returned home convinced that Britain could still command a role in Egypt. He reported to the Foreign Office on May 16, 1967 and judging from a letter he sent to Lord Shackleton he did not appreciate very highly his reception there. He suggested to Shackleton he would like me to visit his home or arrange a meeting in London.

The opportunity arose on June 9, when I attended the Founder's Day Parade at the Royal Hospital Chelsea, with the Field Marshal as Reviewing Officer. The Governor, General Simpson, greeted me with a request that I should go to Montgomery's bedroom for a private talk. There Montgomery delighted and amused me with a vivid account of his adventures in Egypt. He had been made so welcome that he had felt no embarrassment—as if so forthright a personality ever would!—in speaking his mind to President Nasser and his senior officers. He had warned them bluntly that, if they attacked Israel, they would suffer defeat. The latest Russian equipment was no substitute for war's absolute imperatives: leadership, training and discipline. 'You probably have the leadership,' Montgomery told the President, 'but have you got the training and the discipline? The Israelis certainly have all three, and they are bound to win.' When his hosts recalled Suez, about which memory still ran deep and feeling high, and said they could never forget it, Lord Montgomery advised them that 'never' was a long, long time, and a very harsh word; he himself had used it on occasion and lived to regret it.

Monty's strongest impressions were that respect for this country still offered a basis for British influence in Egypt if we recognized two facts: Egypt would have no truck with the Foreign Office, and they regarded even Labour Ministers, with the exception of Lord Shackleton and myself, with suspicion. He also believed that he had a part to play. He would not be an emissary of the Government, but he was willing to go to Cairo on a mission of goodwill. There he could restore contacts, create a British presence and develop friendships that might yield results in the future. There would be no communication with the Government while he was in Egypt, but before and after the projected visit he would be happy at any time to meet the Prime Minister.

I reported fully to Harold Wilson. I could claim to know something of the mind and mood of Egyptians and I felt it was not impossible that the fact that we had not intervened on either side in the Six Day War might stimulate a reaction in our favour. I understood Nasser's contempt for British politicians, from Curzon to Eden, and his confidence in British soldiers. I felt that Lord Montgomery might well add another rose to his chaplet of great service to his country. I still wonder, sadly, how many more opportunities were lost by the Foreign Office through ignorance, indecision and inflexibility.

The Chief Whip decided to make the vote on the Common Market debate on May 10 a test of his new liberal discipline in practice. So I ignored the Whip; no coercion to vote in favour of the Common Market for me! A *New Statesman* comment by Paul Johnson on May 19, 1967 read: 'John Silkin, who now has more influence with the P.M. than Colonel Wigg, had assured Wilson that he could contain the Labour rebels, and the whips made unprecedented, but unsuccessful, efforts to make good his promise. As one M.P. put it to me, "there were tremendous threats and skulduggery".' The next morning was a Saturday, and before starting my usual daily stint at No. 10, I read a *Times* Diary story headed 'Coolness 'twixt Wigg and Wilson', inspired perhaps by Johnson's comment and a look at the voting list; 'mutual disenchantment has set in', wrote the diarist. 'Mr Wigg has not been seen lately at Downing Street, where he once had a firm footing . . . Mr Wigg is out of sympathy with some aspects of Government defence policy now being developed by Mr Denis Healey,' who '. . . completely possesses Mr Wilson's ear. . . . There are probably some personal factors at work, too. Mr

Shinwell has fallen out with Mr Crossman . . .'; the question 'Whether Mr Wigg shares Mr Shinwell's deep-rooted objections to the Common Market . . . is a question worth asking.' It was a neat little essay in the art of combining flashes of the obvious with ignorance of the facts.

On the eve of the Prime Minister's visit to the White House in June I was the recipient of views expressed by President Johnson to a British subject whose integrity and political judgment I value highly. The President, for obvious reasons, would have liked a British presence in Vietnam which was out of the question. What he did hope, however, was that there would be no hasty British withdrawal from the Pacific area. I informed the Prime Minister accordingly.

Judge my surprise when, on Friday, June 2, the front page 'splash' of the *Daily Mail*, written by its Political Editor, Walter Terry, carried these headlines: 'Clash over Vietnam Policy. Wilson and L.B.J.: is this the split?'

The story forecast 'fierce, maybe explosive disagreement' when Wilson and the President would meet that day for their first major confrontation in ten months. The Prime Minister would demand that there be no further escalation of the Vietnam war and that the United States should try again to bring about a peace conference, and he 'almost surely will be aggressive and highly critical during morning and afternoon sessions at the White House'. Another comment ran: 'President Johnson, with plenty of his own problems—on Vietnam especially—piling up, has become a Texan, fast on the draw with foreign visitors who dare to criticise the United States war in Vietnam.'

What Wilson intended to make 'insistently clear', according to the *Mail*, was this:

1 : The Americans need not think they can blackmail the British by warning that the United States will no longer shore up the £ in international markets. The short answer, be it right or not, will be that the United States is helping the £ because it also helps the dollar and it has nothing to do with Vietnam.

2 : In return for any peace gesture on Vietnam there is to be no basic change—despite American wishes—in the British policy to pull out forces east of Suez, particularly Malaysia, eventually.

No doubt to indicate the complete independence of its view and, perhaps, the 'independence' of the source of information which, I was certain, was confined to my contact and to very few persons inside No. 10, the *Mail* wrote: 'The sudden turn in British policy in Vietnam marks the end of a once-cosy arrangement between President Johnson and Mr Wilson. Maybe it was always something of a phoney exercise, designed by Mr Wilson to demonstrate his international prestige to voters at home.'

Was this just another example of irresponsible journalism? Or was it, as I feared, a well-informed disclosure of an irresponsible leak from No. 10?

Next morning, in a message datelined Washington, the *Mail* reported that the President was holding crisis talks and that Wilson's Vietnam warning had jolted the United States. What might have blown up into a diplomatic crisis, and must certainly have disturbed Anglo-American relationships seriously, was lost to public view in the launching of Israel's Six Day War against Egypt.

A few weeks later a Cabinet re-shuffle was on the agenda. On July 26, with Wilson absent, a Press conference was held to announce the appointment of Lord Hill as Director General of the B.B.C. That Press conference became notable for another reason. Not all newspapers were invited to send representatives, and during the evening some newspapers were told that Bowden would succeed Lord Hill at I.T.A., thus revealing that Cabinet changes were imminent.

On Monday, July 31, *The Times* thundered its displeasure at recent proceedings. 'P.H.S.' wrote in the The Diary:

In Westminster secrets tend to have short lives. So it has happened that at last the Tories have discovered that Mr Wilson is nursing a personally chosen inner lobby with special rations of guidance. An observant Tory, making his way from Mr Heath's room behind the Speaker's chair, was surprised the other day to chance upon a platoon of political editors and reporters slipping out of Mr Wilson's room with the air of men burdened with the responsibility of statesmanship on the highest plane.

He noted not only the men whom the Prime Minister had touched with grace but also some of the men and media who (for reasons he could only wildly surmise) had been excluded. Where, he asked, were the B.B.C., the Beaverbrook men, and

The Times? What could explain their exclusion, for all the world as though they were a tightly knit group of politically motivated men?

'P.H.S.' followed up with an open declaration of war. The members of the blackballed group were tightly knit now. They would accept as a challenge their exclusion from Wilson's inner lobby of presumably 'safe' men. They would report the briefing sessions as just another aspect of Westminster's closed politics; now untrammelled by obligations of non-attribution, they would use names and be as free as possible with quotations. I could only reflect, sardonically, that Wilson and his coterie had learned little about relationships with the Press.

At the end of August the Prime Minister at last announced his Cabinet changes. They reflected not, as I had hoped, the urgent need for clear direction and efficient conduct of Government but Wilson's incapacity to implement decisions dictated by his own intelligence. Crossman, Callaghan and Brown all stayed put. Gordon Walker who, for reasons beyond my understanding, had been brought back into the Cabinet in January as Minister-without-Portfolio, was moved to Education and Science. Crosland took over the Board of Trade from Douglas Jay, sacked presumably because of his much publicized opposition to the Common Market. Wilson himself assumed overall responsibility for the Ministry of Economic Affairs, where Michael Stewart remained as First Secretary. All this much ado about nothing was Wilson in his role of Walter Mitty applying the smack of firm government to our affairs. A month before the reconstruction, Chancellor Callaghan told the House that 'those who advocate devaluation are calling for reduction in the wage levels and the real wage standards of every member of the working class in this country'. Three months after the re-shuffle Wilson announced the decision to devalue, cushioning the blow with the fatuous comment that 'this does not mean that the pound in your pocket . . . has been devalued'.

By the Autumn of 1967 my stay at No. 10 was drawing to a close. I found relief from my growing concern at the disarray into which the Government's affairs were falling by working on an address on 'Democracy and the Press' to be delivered to the Annual Conference of the British Guild of Editors on September 8. The invitation came from the President, Clement Jones, Editor of the Wolverhampton

Express and Star, a newspaper whose enterprise and integrity I respected. The venue was Lindsay Hall, Keele University, a name rich in recollections of a friend and inspired teacher. On Lindsay's conception of democracy I base my views of the relationship between man and his Maker, man and society, and thus the relationship between the community and communications of every kind. These views flow from Lindsay's first principle of democracy as enunciated by Colonel Rainboro on behalf of The Levellers during the debates held at Putney in the autumn of 1647:

> Really I think the poorest he that is in England hath a life to live as the richest he. And therefore truly I think, Sir, it is clear that every man that is to live under a government ought first by his own consent to put himself under that government; and I do think that the poorest man in England is not at all bound in a strict sense to that government that he hath not had a voice to put himself under.*

Thus the 'poorest he' is not to be drilled, nor used, nor managed by other people. His life is his own. None can divest him of the right and the responsibility of living his own life in his own way. However different men may be in wealth or ability or learning, whether they be good or bad, living his life is a man's personal business. The individual's share in the Government of society implies access to all the information he needs to make up his own mind. A live democracy is a public meeting in perpetual session. The Press fulfils its democratic function as part of the process of creating public opinion by keeping the public well and honestly informed. Its contribution to the communal life of a healthy democracy is in sustaining an active partnership between government and governed on a continuing basis.

Three conclusions flow from this political faith. It rejects class division in any form whatever; class division implies the standardization of individual personality within rigid boundaries and, thus, the destruction of personality. It rejects also the uniformity implicit in egalitarian society; the glory of human society is in variety and difference, and variety and difference voiced through the Press and on platforms and in pulpits is the stuff of which democracy is made.

* As quoted from the Clarke Papers, Vol. I, page 301, Camden Society Publications, 1891–1901, by A. D. Lindsay in *The Essentials of Democracy*, (O.U.P. 1929).

Finally, my political faith affirms that only continuing and informed discussion can enable government to understand and care for individual personality—the basis of good government.

A democracy with its eyes on the stars must ensure equal opportunity to every man and woman to express his and her personality within the community and to be unequal, individual and happy. The most binding quality of a true democracy is that the poorest man and the richest, the meanest and the greatest can enrich society by living his life to the full. Politics have been the medium of the small part I have sought to play in realizing the ideal of releasing all the spiritual and material resources of our country to the glory of individual men and women, an ideal in which equality of responsibility becomes, to quote Lindsay, 'a religious and moral principle'. Lindsay called this Christianity, I call it Socialism. We are both right!

These views define for me the duty of communications whatever form they take. Communications, a product of community life, are the sounding boards and platforms of the modern nation state. Their efficiency and integrity are a condition of the health of democracy. When they fail in the task of educating the citizen, of enabling him to participate in the process of government, they put democracy itself at risk.

Few people would regard Lord Northcliffe, founder of the *Daily Mail*, our first mass-sale newspaper, as a social reformer. He did not so regard himself. He was in business to make money. Nevertheless, he initiated one of the most fundamental of social and political changes. His enterprise enabled the first generation of inheritors of compulsory elementary education to participate in the knowledge and excitement of the technological and industrial break-through of the early years of this century. He made mass communication a potent force in the development of British democracy. He forged a strong link in the chain which joins government with people going about the business of everyday life. Promoting the popular Press was as vital to democratic growth and progress as the pioneer work of the W.E.A. and the activities of the long line of political educators from Robert Owen and Keir Hardie and Lloyd George to the modern political prophets and teachers like James Maxton, Nye Bevan, Manny Shinwell and R. A. Butler. All belong in the great and good company of communicators who serve the cause of consent by persuasion.

From this idea there flows the thought that universal education, which Northcliffe exploited so brilliantly, may be expanded to provide equal educational opportunity for every citizen from childhood into and during manhood. I go back to Professor Tawney for the clinching argument. He demanded equal universal opportunity in education, as he explained in the May 1914 edition of the *Political Quarterly*, 'because society is one; because we cannot put our minds in commission because no class is good enough to do its thinking for another. . . . We want as much university education as we can get for workers who remain *workers* all their lives. The idea of social solidarity which is the contribution of the working classes to the social conscience of our age has its educational as well as its economic application . . . There is no inconsiderable number of men and women whose incentive to education is not material success but spiritual energy, and who seek it, not in order to become something else, but because they are what they are'.

During my adult life the Northcliffe tradition was perpetuated by Northcliffe's greatest disciple, Harry Guy Bartholomew. From my first meeting with 'Bart' I was fascinated by the achievement of the office boy who acquired influence over the direction of the *Daily Mirror* when the Northcliffe organization in despair at the paper's lack of success was thinking of cutting its throat. I became interested in the techniques he employed to lift the *Mirror* from near failure to brilliant success. I was on terms of friendship with 'Bart's' greatest journalistic discovery, Sir William Connor ('Cassandra'), who expressed the paper's reforming zeal in a daily column of sparkling wit, savage satire and superb simplicity of language. Here was a radical who made ideas come alive for *Daily Mirror* readers by expressing them in language they could understand. 'Cass' helped to make the *Mirror* of the immediate post-war era the largest-selling and most politically influential newspaper in the land. I held in esteem the Editor, Sylvester ('Bish') Bolam, whose one grave error of judgment earned him a three-month sentence for contempt of Court and brought a fine of ten thousand pounds upon his company. The issue concerned a murder case upon which many newspapers were commenting with such unusual freedom that the Police Commissioner, very properly, issued a warning from Scotland Yard. In circumstances which have never been explained, 'Bish' interpreted the warning as a challenge to editorial freedom and paid the price of brave folly. Bart, I understood, defied those directors insistent upon dismissal. In sympathy with a grand human being, Manny Shinwell and I visited 'Bish' in Brixton prison.

Bart salvaged the *Mirror* by making it a gay paper reflecting in text and pictures the interests and hopes of ordinary people. In search of real news about real people, he introduced into journalism able, individualistic reporters like Cassandra's buddy, the late David Walker, who became a distinguished war and Special correspondent. He gave scope to the abilities of sub-editors of original mind like Hugh Cudlipp. The *Mirror* communicated the colour and spice of life in plenty, all decked out in the typography of impact.

The decade of the 'thirties with its mass unemployment and drift into war stimulated the true journalist's urge to educate and inform in order to reform. So Bart came to understand and act upon a fact of revolutionary significance; that as late as 1939, and after nearly seventy years of compulsory education, only slightly over half the households in Great Britain took a daily newspaper and no newspaper provided the masses with a medium fully dedicated to their participation in the nation's affairs. The *Mirror* revived the campaigning spirit in which 'Tay Pay' O'Connor conducted *The Star* in its hey-day—'to put another lump of sugar in the charwoman's tea'—influenced newspapers everywhere and ousted the *Daily Express* from pride of place in the net sales charts.

The competition of commercial television in 1957 precipitated deplorable tendencies in nearly all newspapers. They became mere 'eye-catchers' for the advertising revenues necessary to survival. Thus I challenged in my address a trend endorsed by *The Times* on May 21, 1964, in a statement entitled 'Safeguard of Liberties' which read:

> The British Press is sustained by the independence that is guaranteed by diverse advertising revenues. They release newspapers from the moral Danegeld of the politically subsidised. Advertising (which is itself NEWS) is the foremost bulwark of the freedom of the Press. NEWSPAPERS, large and small, in democratic societies owe to advertising the liberty that safeguards liberties.

Advertisers, I argued, are concerned to make a commercial profit by concentrating their sales efforts on our few giant newspapers and on television. Of all the pressures threatening Press independence the most significant was the growing monopoly of its ownership. Indeed, it was possible to argue that the Press had exchanged the alleged tyranny of the political establishment for that of the commercial establishment, and that 'the moral Danegeld of the politically subsidized' had given way to the contemptuous pay-off from commercial advertisers; and this argument has acquired increasing potency since 1967.

The time spent working on this speech proved to be, in a very real sense, the fulfilment of my political life. As the shadows lengthen towards the end of an exciting journey, now seventy years long, I naturally think of the way ahead, especially when I look at my grandchildren. That way, I am persuaded, can be kept open only if we can find new methods of educating public opinion. The Press, the public meeting and radio have had their day. Television, the new instrument of enlightenment, tends to be trivial and superficial, a medium orientated to the organization of the commercial mass market rather than to the release of human personality. Thus the job of educating public opinion in our democracy must rest increasingly upon the political parties whose membership comprises men and women of like mind pursuing their lawful purposes in the fellowship of voluntary organizations. If mechanical means have failed, and if the influence of Press and television is diminishing and, as some say, is past, the question arises: Must we depend upon individual men and women in the race—to quote a Wellsian phrase—between Education and Catastrophe?

My answer is optimistic. My experience has been that the wisest judgments emerge from discussion between men and parties, whether their purpose is spiritual or material. Our salvation, I believe, will come from understanding that 'a democracy without aristocratic virtues, without a high sense of quality and distinction, and something corresponding to *noblesse oblige*, becomes, as Plato said long ago, and as we have sadly experienced, a tyranny, as an aristocracy which is not inspired by democratic ideals becomes selfish and arrogant.' Those words of Lindsay's are a signpost, but they are also a warning.

My address at Keele University aroused considerable controversy. This surprised me for I had attempted little more than to indicate how the Press might seek to serve our democratic society. True, I had emphasized my belief that the future of Britain economically, culturally and politically is with the Provinces and that the well-being of Britain requires the creation of a regional and provincial environment offering a counter-attraction to London. Had I sought to be controversial I might have taken the opportunity to express my feelings of disquiet about the growth of the 'inner lobby' at No. 10, with its special rations of influence exercised often unwisely and sometimes with very little thought or judgement. My worries on this score had caused me frequently to reflect on my own position.

I had experienced several years of intense mental and physical exertion in which there had been moments of satisfaction and great enjoyment as well as bitter frustration and intense anxiety. In a vague half formulated way I had begun to feel I would like to harness my energies to a single objective and so I pondered on a change, despite the sacrifices this would entail.

I had, of course, greatly enjoyed working with Harold Wilson. Although I have attempted no detailed study of his character the reader will have had an opportunity of seeing him, in the context of this book, as I saw him. His remarkable personal qualities aside it was in the main a joy to work with him because of his constant high spirits and courage and, above all, the affection and loyalty he transmitted to the few people in whom he really reposed his trust. Circumstances made the decision for me.

Earlier in the year, when Field Marshal Lord Harding announced his decision to retire from the Chairmanship of the Horserace Betting Levy Board, Home Secretary Roy Jenkins offered the post to Lord Head. I had fought many battles with Head when he was Secretary of State for War and I held in high regard his ability and integrity. He was well informed about racing matters and had ridden with distinction as an amateur before the War. I, and many others, would have rejoiced in his return to public life in service to my own favourite sport.

On Friday, November 10, 1967, Roy Jenkins informed me that Lord Head had declined the appointment and expressed the hope that I would accept the post. My closest friends considered that the job was tailor-made for me and should not be turned down. Harold Wilson told me the decision was for me to make. He was kind enough to express concern at the prospect of my departure but, all in all, the choice seemed pre-ordained. I accepted the job in the belief that I was exchanging a 'bed of nettles' for a 'bed of roses'. But that is a story for another day.

So you're off then?

Bibliography

Aspinall, Arthur *Politics and the Press c.1780–1850* Home & Van
 Thal 1949
Beaverbrook, Lord *Men and Power, 1917–1918* Hutchinson 1956
Beer, Samuel H. *Modern British Politics* Faber 1965
Blake, Robert *The Unknown Prime Minister: the Life and Times
 of Bonar Law* Eyre & Spottiswoode 1955
Bonham Carter, Lady Violet *Winston Churchill as I Knew Him*
 Eyre & Spottiswoode-Collins 1965
Brockway, Fenner *Inside the Left* George Allen & Unwin 1942
Broome, Vincent *Aneurin Bevan* Longmans 1953
Bullard, Sir Reeder (ed) *The Middle East* Oxford University Press
 1958
Butler, David and Jennie Freeman *British Political Facts 1900–1967*
 Macmillan 1968
Chandler G. and Hannah I. C. *Dudley: as it was and is today* B. T.
 Batsford 1949
Churchill, Winston S. *The Second World War* 6 vols. Cassell 1948–
 1954
Cole, G. D. H. *A History of the Labour Party from 1914* Routledge
 & Kegan Paul 1948
Cole, Margaret *Makers of the Labour Movement* Longmans 1948
Curzon, Marchioness *Reminiscences* Hutchinson 1955
Eayrs, James *The Commonwealth and Suez* Oxford University Press
 1964
Foot, Michael *Aneurin Bevan* Vol. 1 MacGibbon & Kee 1962
Grainger, J. H. *Character and Style in English Politics* Cambridge
 University Press 1969
James, Robert Rhodes *Churchill: A Study in Failure 1900–1939*
 Weidenfeld & Nicholson 1970
Kelf-Cohen, R. *Twenty Years of Nationalisation: the British Ex-
 perience* Macmillan 1969
Lacouture, Jean and Simone *Egypt in Transition* Methuen 1958

Marwick, Arthur *Britain in the Century of Total War* The Bodley Head 1968

McKenzie, R. T. *British Political Parties* Heinemann 1955

Moorhead, Alan *Gallipoli* Hamish Hamilton 1956

Mowat, Charles Loch *Britain Between the Wars* Methuen 1955

Normanbrook, Lord with John Colville, Sir John Martin, Sir Ian Jacob, Lord Bridges and Sir Leslie Rowan *Action this Day: Working with Churchill* Macmillan 1968

Pelling, Henry *America and the British Left: from Bright to Bevan* A. and C. Black 1956

Plumb, J. H. *The Growth of Political Stability in England 1675–1725* Macmillan 1967

Rowan, Richard Wilmer and Deindorfer, Robert G. *Secret Service: 3 Centuries of Espionage* William Kimber 1969

Sampson, Anthony *Anatomy of Britain* Hodder & Stoughton 1962

Seton-Watson, Hugh *The Pattern of Communist Revolution* Methuen 1953

Shinwell, Emanuel *The Labour Story* Macdonald 1963

Strong, Major-General Sir Kenneth *Intelligence at the Top* Cassell 1968

Taylor, A. J. P. *English History 1914–1945* Oxford University Press 1965
with Robert Rhodes James, J. H. Plumb, Basil Liddell Hart and Anthony Storr *Churchill: Four Faces and the Man* Allen Lane 1969

Wavell, General Sir Archibald *Allenby* Harrap 1940

Welensky, Sir Roy *Welensky's 4000 Days* Collins 1964

West, Rebecca *The Vassall Affair* The Sunday Telegraph 1963

Williams, David *Not in the Public Interest: The Problem of Security in Democracy* Hutchinson 1965

Index of Subjects and Places

248–9; on Profumo affair, 269, 279; on Suez, 181, 184, 204; on Wilson, 343, 351, 353–4
Times Educational Supplement, 96, 104
Torrey Canyon, wreck of, 348
Totalisator Board, 225
Toynbee Hall, 81
Trade Union Movement, 31, 80, 88, 106, 146, 187, 226, 229, 253, 281
Transport and General Workers' Union, 31, 174, 230
Trentham Park, 99–101
Tribunal of Three Advisers, 192
Tribunals of Inquiry Act, 237–9, 285–6
Tribune, 175, 215, 217
Trieste, 144–5
Triple Entente, end of, 40
Tripoli, 44, 144
Trooping the Colour, 231–2
T.S.R. 2, 321
Turkey, 39–50, 63–5
Tyrol, 49

Udine, 144
Ukrainian independence movement, 197
Unemployment, 93, 193, 240, 281
Unitarianism, 33–4, 43
United Arab Republic, 349–50
United Nations: Aden mission, 349; Cyprus problem referred to, 301; Korean War, 151–3; Yemen appeals to, 304
United States of America: British devaluation and, 309; Havana Charter unratified, 292; Japanese attack on, 340; nuclear weapons and defence policies, 209–11, 301; oil interests, 155–6; Pacific security treaty, 171; Russian efforts to divide from Britain, 286; and Suez, 177–8, 180, 183, 207; Test Ban Treaty signed, 297; U2 spy

plane crash, 207; Wilson's visit to White House, 352

Valiant V bomber, 214
Victoria Cross, lost, 220, 252
Vietnam policy, 302, 328, 334, 343, 352–3
Vine Hunt, The, 26–7, 36
Vladivostock, 40
VLAJKA, 147
Volta Dam, 292, 294

Wallis & Stevens iron foundry, 23
Wareham, Dorset, 25, 28
Warminster, School of Infantry, 231–2
War Overseas Pool, 108
'We Say No' campaign, 83
West Africa (weekly), 112
West African Review, 112
Westminster, Statute of (1931), 47
Westminster Confidential, 264
Wightwick Hall, 103
Woking, Army Pay Office, 38
Wolverhampton, 103, 241; *Express and Star*, 307, 354–5
Woolwich, Royal Herbert Hospital, 31, 50
Workers' Educational Association (W.E.A.), 14, 51, 79, 81–7, 90–2, 94, 117–18, 162–3, 252, 356
Wormwood Scrubs, 235

Yalu River, 152–3
Yarmouth, 33–4
Yemen, 158, 303–5
York, 87, 107, 114
York Trust, 95
Young Men's Christian Association, 34, 77, 92, 94
Young Turks, (Committee of Union and Progress), 43–5, 56
Yugoslavia, 145

Zanzibar, government of, overthrown (1964), 301